Language Arts in the Early Childhood Classroom

John Warren Stewig
University of Wisconsin, Milwaukee

Mary Jett-Simpson
University of Wisconsin, Milwaukee

W
Wadsworth Publishing Company

I(T)P™ An International Thomson Publishing Company

Belmont • Albany • Bonn • Boston • Cincinnati • Detroit • London • Madrid • Melbourne
Mexico City • New York • Paris • San Francisco • Singapore • Tokyo • Toronto • Washington

Education Editor: Sabra Horne
Editorial Assistant: Kate Peltier
Assistant Editor: Lisa Timbrell
Production Services Coordinator: Debby Kramer
Production: Cecile Joyner/The Cooper Company
Print Buyer: Karen Hunt
Permissions Editor: Jeanne Bosschart
Interior Designer: Janet Bollow
Copy Editor: Carol Reitz
Cover Designer: Cassandra Chu
Compositor: Graphic Composition, Inc.
Printer: Maple Vail Book Manufacturing Group/Vail-Ballou Press
Credits continue on page 324.

Printed in the United States of America
1 2 3 4 5 6 7 8 9 10—01 00 99 98 97 96 95

For more information, contact Wadsworth Publishing Company.

Wadsworth Publishing Company
10 Davis Drive
Belmont, California 94002, USA

International Thomson Editores
Campos Eliseos 385, Piso 7
Col. Polanco
11560 México D. F. México

International Thomson Publishing Europe
Berkshire House 168-173
High Holborn
London WC1V 7AA, England

International Thomson Publishing GmbH
Königswinterer Strasse 418
53227 Bonn, Germany

Thomas Nelson Australia
102 Dodds Street
South Melbourne 3205
Victoria, Australia

International Thomson Publishing Asia
221 Henderson Road
#05-10 Henderson Building
Singapore 0315

Nelson Canada
1120 Birchmount Road
Scarborough, Ontario
Canada M1K 5G4

International Thomson Publishing Japan
Hirakawacho Kyowa Building, 3F
2-2-1 Hirakawacho
Chiyoda-ku, Tokyo 102, Japan

Library of Congress Cataloging-in-Publication Data

Stewig, John W.
    Language arts in the early childhood classroom / John Warren Stewig, Mary Jett-Simpson.
        p.   cm.
    Includes bibliographical references and index.
    ISBN 0-534-25080-7
    1. Language arts (Preschool)   2.   Early childhood education.   3.   Chil-
dren—Books and reading.   4.   Curriculum planning.   I.   Jett-Simpson, Mary,
1938– .   II.   Title.
LB1140.5.L3S72   1995   94-33906
372.6—dc20

This book is printed on acid-free recycled paper.

❀

CONTENTS

Two

Understanding Literature As a Base for the Language/Reading Curriculum   50

Three

Understanding Listening As Part of an Integrated Program   86

Four

Understanding Oral Language As Part of an Integrated Program   128

Five

Understanding Reading As Part of an Integrated Program   174

Six

Understanding Writing As Part of an Integrated Program   231

Seven

Integrating the Separate Strands of a Program 288

Preface

The purpose of this book is to help you become a more effective teacher of young children. You may become a teacher of 3-year-olds in a day care center or a teacher of third-graders in a public school. In either case and in any other possible job roles and settings in which you may work, you'll spend much of your day helping children use language skillfully, to listen, speak, read, and write. Because language is so critical to success as an adult, we feel it is particularly critical that teachers attend to two tasks. *One,* we must be aware of the language skills children bring to an educative setting. *Two,* we must create contexts in which children can use language naturally to expand and extend what they can already do.

From the moment of birth, infants are immersed in language. Sounds surround children, and one of their first tasks is to begin to make meaning of the cacophony of sounds that assail their ears. When children come to school, whether to a day care setting or to a kindergarten in a public school, they've been active language users for several years. Not just receiving it through their ears, they've also been using language for expressive purposes. Talk is the medium of exchange between young children and the people in their worlds. Children are eager talkers, and their talk, if studied, demonstrates impressive competencies too often overlooked. Children have developed their competencies as they interact with language, trying to make meaning of their world. In addition to listening and talking, children have become aware of two other elements of their environment. Depending on circumstances, children are more or less conscious of the sea of written and printed symbols that surrounds them. When they come to us, they'll be aware that adults make these marks and that the marks, handwritten or printed, represent meanings. Too, children have begun to develop some awareness of the process of writing as they have, to some degree, watched adults encoding ideas. The chapters of this book will deal in sequence with each of these four functions in an attempt to help you think about each of them. We will, throughout, be emphasizing the importance of integrating these in school settings, however. In life, one never just listens. We listen and talk in response. We talk and assume others will listen. We read what others have written, and write so that others can read. We sometimes talk about what we've written, or read so others can listen to what we've written. Each of the four elements, considered here individually in order to emphasize their importance, is embedded in the others as we use them in life.

The opening chapter presents an overview of child language acquisition—*what* children can do at particular ages and *how* these abilities develop. Much of what we've learned about the processes children go through in acquiring language has implications for teachers. Knowing something about the language growth that occurs in the home—perhaps the most important language learning environment—allows us to more easily set up conditions in classrooms that will encourage language growth to continue. By drawing implications from the language acquisition research for teachers, the chapter lays a foundation for the practical experiences and activities we suggest later in the book.

Chapter 2, on the importance of children's literature, is based on the premise that children's own language is influenced by the wealth of rich adult-written language found in the best children's books. This is a time of burgeoning publishing in the book market, and teachers have a wider range of fine literature available than ever before. The chapter describes the uses of literature and the functions of a planned program of literature experiences. In addition, many practical activities are presented, with accompanying samples of children's responses. These are not included for you to follow prescriptively, but rather to show the many ways children's books can become integral, not peripheral, in the education of young children. There are too many fine books available now for any such short chapter to present a comprehensive survey of the books you should use. Rather, we hope that you will take these ideas and use them to provide a milieu in which children can expand their own language potential as they interact with what you read to them and—with older children—what they read to themselves.

Listening is the first channel of learning and remains, even for adults, the language art we use most. The majority of children can *hear* adequately. Teachers are aware of the need, however, to provide an organized sequence of experiences that can help children learn to *listen* more attentively. Without such conscious extending of children's ability to listen and expanding of their sensitivity to listening, few will become able to effectively learn as much as possible from their sound environment. In Chapter 3, as elsewhere in the book, we suggest a possible sequence of activities that need to be considered so you can apply the ideas inherent in the activities to your own group of children, adapting as necessary. Chapter 3 should make it possible for you to ensure that your students will be better, more careful listeners when they leave your classroom than when they arrived there.

Oral language remains, into adult life, the mode of communication most comfortable for many of us. Speaking seems as natural as breathing, yet there are certainly differences among speakers. Some are fluent in a variety of situations, speaking to different audiences (or listeners) with ease. Others put words together only with great difficulty. Chapter 4 on oral language suggests ways teachers of the young can organize environments and plan experiences that will develop oral fluency. Specific activities that are commonly part of many early childhood settings are described. Our hope is that you'll read these descriptions and then plan ways to adapt them to the particular group with which you're working.

Chapter 5, "Understanding Reading As Part of an Integrated Program," suggests that in every classroom children are developing print awareness as they move toward actual reading on their own. The setting might be a day care center in which 3-year-olds are just beginning to notice the variety of as yet undecipherable marks on paper with which the teacher has surrounded them. Or it might be a third-grade classroom where the teacher is helping children at many different developmental levels find and enjoy reading materials appropriate to their ability. In such a class we may well find children from *emergent* to *consolidator* readers. Chapter 5 helps teachers learn to cope with inducting youngsters into the world of print.

For many years, early childhood teachers felt that writing belonged in the upper grades, believing that handwriting (the encoding of ideas) and composing (the generating of ideas) were beyond their children. Research now shows clearly that many young children are indeed strongly motivated to write. Furthermore, children appear to progress through discrete stages in mastering the ability to write down their thoughts. This exciting research gives support to teachers who are providing time, space, and supplies for boys and girls to capture their ideas on paper. Much early writing may not be read easily, but it is important developmentally nonetheless. As children move through the primary school, they need ample opportunities to encode their thoughts in writing. Oral dictation of their ideas is also important to many children. The two processes can accompany each other during the early years. They are tied intimately into being a reader (as children remember their stories and retell them to an audience using their print as a memory aid) and into being a listener (as they attend to what other children have composed). Chapter 6 describes approaches to writing.

The last chapter includes an exemplary integrated unit, showing how these strands we've considered separately can be woven into a whole. We've not used the term *whole language* much throughout this book, even though it is currently very popular. Many people use the term, although in our experience, far fewer really understand the philosophical underpinnings experts feel must support genuine whole language teaching. Rather, we've described our approach as a literature-based, integrated approach. Much, if not all, of what we do in developing children's language can indeed be based on children's books. That's as it should be, we think, even though this means that the teacher must be aware of many hundreds of such books in order to choose those that are most appropriate for extending the language learning of a particular group of children. Perhaps few, if any, of the books we've recommended here will finally be useful to you in your own classroom. But what this text has tried to exemplify is the ways in which literature is indeed integral to everything we do in the classroom.

In addition, our approach is an integrated one, which simply means we don't set aside segmented time blocks ahead of time in which to teach particular discrete aspects of language. Rather we identify, or we help children to identify, a topic, perhaps like whales, or cities, or journeys. Then together we plan an array of listening, speaking, reading, and writing activities that will help children learn more about the focus of the unit. In the process, children become stronger listeners, speakers, readers, and writers.

Of all the elements in early childhood programs, language is probably the most pervasive and thus the most critical. The teacher's task is simple yet overwhelming: to retain the natural abilities children of any social class or ethnic group bring to school, and to develop these to their fullest potential. We hope that this book will help you in this vital task.

One

Understanding Language Development As a Base for an Integrated Program

The child acquires the adult system by creating its own structures and then changing these as the adult system becomes better known. . . . In other words, children's perception is not complete and consequently . . . is not just a mirror of the adult world.

Owens (1988)

A baby snuggles into the protective sanctuary of Mother's arms listening to the encouraging and loving sounds of her voice. Language learning is already well under way, yet few mothers and fathers realize that the child is energetically learning. From the moment of birth, announced by a bellow of protest, the infant is beginning one of the most complex learning tasks of being human—learning language.

In the beginning, the child lies in the crib and uses tongue and lips to make a variety of sounds, many of which are unintelligible to adults. The child is learning the entire time: listening to sounds, making sounds, combining them in new ingenious ways, making rudimentary attempts at communication—always experimenting. After this early experimentation, communication continues to develop as sounds become intelligible words and words, on a string of thought, gradually evolve into more and more complex sentence structures.

From their noisy beginnings, throughout the preschool years, and into the kindergarten year, children accomplish an amazing feat: they learn most of the basic language forms adults use. Until recently it was assumed that language development was complete when most complex syntactic structures had been attained. However, today we know that language development is a lifelong process that extends the learning so rapidly accomplished in the early years.

You may be wondering why we begin a book about language arts with a chapter on oral language development. We believe that all of the language arts have their origins in language development. Language is the foundation for the language arts. If you understand how children learn language, you will also understand a great deal about how children learn to express and understand language through listening, speaking, and reading and writing.

We will begin our discussion in this chapter with an overview of how language is learned, followed by some highlights of what is known about the development of language form, content, and use as characterized in Figure 1-1. Then we will talk about what characteristics of environments best support language development. The final section of this chapter will focus on implications for classrooms. It is impossible to capture all aspects of the rich field of language development in a single chapter. We hope that many of you will be so intrigued and fascinated with the topic that you will want to explore it further (Gleason, 1985; James, 1990; Lindfors, 1987; Owens, 1988).

How Language Is Learned

"Magic—it must be magic." During the last twenty-five years, researchers have amassed facts about the form, content, and use of language,

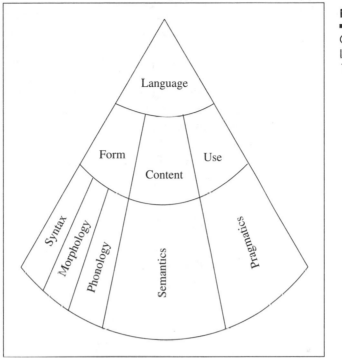

Figure 1-1

Components of
Language (Owens,
1988, p. 13)

but they are unable to agree on a theory of language acquisition that can explain them all. "The question of how children learn language has no definitive answer at this time. Several of the current hypotheses hold some promise for moving us closer to an answer. Meanwhile, we continue to observe and try to understand the fascinating and complex process known as language acquisition" (James, 1990, p. 187). Given the situation, is it any wonder that some noted researchers have used words like *magic* (Bloom, 1983) and *mysterious* (Gleitman & Wanner, 1982) to describe it.

Accepting that there are aspects of "magic and mystery" about language, we can make some observations about language learning that reflect agreement across most theories.

1. *Language learning appears to be the result of some combination of innate ability and environmental influence.* The debate among theory builders revolves around what portions of language development can be attributed to innate ability and environment. Some critical aspects of language must be innate because language is too invariant across languages and contexts not to have some innate component. On the other hand, children must be exposed to spoken or signed language to learn how to speak; those who are not do not learn (Bohannon & Warren-Leubecker, 1985).

2. *Imitation appears to be a learning strategy young children frequently use through age 2, but it decreases in effectiveness as language learning becomes more complex.* It seems to be particularly important at the one-word level of development in contexts where parents are pointing out and naming many objects in the environment. At first imitations of words approximate the adult forms: the child might say "ba" for "ball." Children also imitate parts of adult sentences that they partially understand, paying particular attention to endings such as in this example. Mother says, "Do you want to go out?" in response to her child who is standing in front of the door. The next day the child goes to the door and says, "Out." However, language learning is far too complex to be learned by imitation alone. Imitation cannot explain the creative linguistic forms children speak that are not part of their daily language environment, such as "I goed fast, Daddy" or "I amn't."

3. *Children are rule makers.* Children invent strategies to assist them in figuring out how language operates. They are like little scientists who collect their data from the environment by noting recurring patterns, similarities, and differences. From the data, they construct hypotheses or rules to test. Initial hypotheses are adjusted until they reflect the environmental data. Regardless of cultural origins, each child appears to engage in this kind of language-building activity. Much of this linguistic development parallels cognitive development to some extent, but there is not a one-to-one relationship. For example, as children develop their concepts of time, they are able to use them more effectively in their language (Owens, 1988, pp. 306–308).

4. *Language is learned in social settings.* In mainstream American culture, parents treat their children's conversations and first attempts at language as meaningful, relating to the children as full-fledged participants in conversations. Parents don't engage in direct language teaching. Rather, they name objects and events, respond to the child's gestures and initial commands, model, cue, prompt, expand, and extend their children's language constantly as they work toward establishing meaning. However, in some contexts, parental patterns are different. Heath (1983), in her ten-year study of a working-class African American community, found that as soon as boy babies were mobile and steady on their feet, they were allowed to join the outdoor community on the porches and other community centers. In this context, when they began to make sounds that could be construed as first words, these weren't acknowledged as language, just noise (Heath, 1983, pp. 75–76). The adults addressed very little talk to the children.

In another context, the Warm Springs Indian community in Oregon, adults were less likely to interpret babies' vocalizations or respond to them as if they were meaningful language than in mainstream culture. Instead, children were expected to do as they were told, therefore demonstrating their comprehension through actions, not words (Phillips, 1983, pp. 63–64).

> It is no longer possible to assert that particular interaction styles, contexts, and situations are universally the best for supporting children's language learning. Children develop language in many different social settings (Lindfors, 1987, p. 214).

5. *Children are meaning makers.* They expect language to make sense, and they set about to discover its sense. Language learning occurs in contexts where there are multiple cues to meaning provided for the child beyond language itself. Objects in the environment, facial expressions of speakers, manipulations of objects in the environment, and gestures are a few cues that contribute to meaning making

We are unable to describe precisely how learning language takes place, but we have rich descriptions of what children do with language that help us understand more and more about how it works. In the next section we will discuss some of the knowledge we have acquired about the components of language.

Components of Language

To study language, researchers have divided it into three components: **form, content,** and **use.**

As illustrated in Figure 1-1, form includes three systems: phonology, morphology, and syntax.

1. The *phonological system* is the study of the important speech sounds called phonemes, the rules for combining them to make words, and the "tune" of language: the stress (the loudness for syllables), pauses in words or sentences, and intonation patterns (the rise and fall of the voice) that accompany them.

2. The *morphological system* is the study of the smallest units of meaning in a language called morphemes.

3. The *syntactic system* is the study of the grammatical structure, the rules that govern word order in the language.

The forms defined are used to express idea **content** or meaning, which is called **semantics.** Semantic knowledge is how each language community represents its view of reality and how it divides that reality into categories and labels them with words. Reality varies from community to community. Eskimos, for example, have many words for snow, whereas English has only one. The study of semantics includes examination of rules for word meaning, relationships among words, and relationships within and between sentences. In addition, nonliteral meanings such as those expressed in metaphors ("He was white as a ghost"), proverbs ("Don't count your chickens before they are hatched"), idioms ("You're nuts"), jokes, and riddles are studied.

Children **use** language form and content to achieve communication goals, such as obtaining an object, getting information, or expressing feelings. The study of how children use language to express intentions and get things done in the world is called **pragmatics.**

It is important to remember that all language systems are developing simultaneously and do not operate in isolation. When the toddler says, "Cookie allgone," there is rudimentary form to the statement, it has meaning or content, and it is being used for a particular purpose, which may be communicating to Mom that it's time for another cookie.

These components of language all merge to make communication possible. An overview of some representative behaviors of the form, content, and use of language illustrates when and what characteristics of communication are emerging during the preschool and early school years. Table 1-1 on pages 8–9 shows the impressive feats children accomplish in learning language.

A summary table is, at best, an oversimplification because language learning is so complex. As you read any list of developmental patterns, keep in mind that the sequence of patterns is relatively constant but the rate of development may vary greatly. Some children may demonstrate a behavior before a listed age and others much later and still be within the range of normalcy. Weeks (1974), for example, studied a gifted child with an IQ of 139 over a four-year period and found that the child was significantly delayed in development in phonology, morphology, syntax, and semantics. These delays were not pathological, however, since the child was superior in ability in other ways and language did develop. Weeks cautioned teachers to be especially careful not to judge late-developing children as intellectually limited.

On the other hand, it is important to identify any children who appear to be delayed, to investigate further, and to determine an appropriate course of action. Michael, at 6 months, was not producing the expected baby sounds or reacting to sound, even loud banging next to his crib. After extensive testing and examination in four different settings, his mother found a doctor who took her concern seriously. When he examined Michael, he determined that Michael had impacted ears as a result of an allergy to milk, so he could barely hear anything. After an operation to remove the impacted material and a change of diet, Michael became a highly verbal youngster.

Before the Word—Prelinguistic Development

Even before the first word is uttered, many developments lay the foundations for the form, content, and use of language. Growth is occurring on all fronts. The path to the first word during the first year of life moves from reflexive crying, burping, coughing, and sneezing to cooing at 8 to 20 weeks. During the cooing stage, sounds are a soft vowel-like "oo." Crying becomes less frequent and more differentiated. To the joy of the family, the social smile and laughter also appear.

This is followed by a period of vocal play at 16–30 weeks, which flows into babbling at 25–50 weeks. Consonant-vowel combinations are repeated, such as "babababa" or "dadadada." With the advent of "dadadada," of course Dad is convinced that the first word has appeared. But it hasn't. The child seems to be experimenting with sound during this time. The experimentation evolves into more complex babbling at around 9–18 months, when there are a variety of consonant vowel syllables in an utterance. As the child babbles into a toy telephone or book, the intonation patterns resemble those of adult sentences. Although the babbled sounds of babies exposed to different languages are very similar, adults listening to a long string of babbles at this stage would be able to distinguish the language culture of the child (Boysson-Bardies, de Sagart & Durand, 1984; Sachs, 1985). With the physical growth of vocal structures as well as of the central nervous system, more varied sound production is possible.

Toward the end of the first year, before children begin to use speech, they show they are making attempts to communicate. Pointing to objects, handing objects to a parent, and making a consistent sound in the same situation are some of the most common behaviors observed by researchers.

Form

The Sound System—Phonology

The smallest unit of language is the phoneme, a group of sounds that are grouped together because of their similarity. As adults, we have learned not to pay attention to the subtle differences within a phoneme category. There is a difference between the /k/ sound in *car* and the /k/ sound in *key,* for example, although we would classify them as the same sound (James, 1990). (The linguistic symbol / / is used to show that a phoneme category is being represented.) Try it. Say each word slowly and concentrate on how you are positioning your tongue in your mouth. They aren't quite the same, are they?

Table 1-1

The Development of Communication in Early Childhood*

Newborn
Cries; makes noncrying speechlike sounds, usually when feeding

1–2 months
Responds to human voice, which has a quieting effect; cries for assistance; makes pleasure sounds
Distinguishes different (speech) sounds; makes more guttural or "throaty" cooing

3 months
Coos single syllable (consonant-vowel); turns head when hears a voice; responds vocally to speech of others; makes predominately vowel sounds

4 months
Babbles strings of consonants; varies pitch; imitates tones; smiles at person speaking to him/her

5 months
Vocalizes to toys; discriminates angry and friendly voices; experiments with sounds; imitates some sounds; responds to name; smiles and vocalizes to image in mirror

6 months
Varies volume, pitch, and rate; vocalizes pleasure and displeasure such as squeals of excitement and intonations of displeasure

7 months
Plays vocally; produces several sounds in one breath; listens to vocalizations of others

8 months
Listens selectively; recognizes some words; repeats emphasized syllable; imitates gestures and tonal quality of adult speech

9 months
Produces distinct intonational patterns; imitates coughs, hisses, tongue clicks; uses social gestures

10 months
Imitates adult speech sounds if sounds are in child's repertoire; obeys some commands

11 months
Imitates inflections, rhythms, facial expressions

12 months
Recognizes own name; follows simple motor instructions especially if accompanied by a visual cue ("Bye bye"); reacts to "no" intonation; speaks one or more words; practices words she/he knows and inflection

15 months
Points to clothes, persons, toys, and animals named; uses words in conversation; has four- to six-word vocabulary

*Adapted from Owens (1988, pp. 76, 77, 82, 83, 88, 89, 92, 93, 101, 324, 325).

Table 1-1   Continued

18 months

Begins to use two-word utterances; has approximately twenty-word vocabulary; identifies some body parts; refers to self by name; "sings" and hums spontaneously; plays question-answer with adult

21 months

Likes rhyming games; pulls person to show something; tries to "tell" experiences; understands some personal pronouns; uses *I* and *mine*

24 months

Has 200–300-word vocabulary; names most common everyday objects; uses short, incomplete sentences; uses some prepositions (*in, on*) and pronouns (*I, me, you*) but not always correctly; uses some regular verb endings (*-s, -ed, -ing*) and plural *-s* but not always correctly; engages in short dialogues of a few turns about a topic

3 years

Has 900–1,000-word vocabulary; creates three- to four-word sentences; uses "sentences" with subject and verb but simple sentence construction; plays with words and sounds; follows two-step commands; talks about the present; shows rudimentary beginnings of turn taking in conversation by acknowledging partner with "yeah" and "uh-huh"

4 years

Has 1,500–1,600-word vocabulary; asks many, many questions; uses increasingly more complex sentence forms; recounts stories and the recent past; understands most questions about the immediate environment; has some difficulty answering *how* and *why* questions; relies on word order for interpretation

5 years

Has vocabulary of 2,100–2,200 words; discusses feelings; comprehends before and after regardless of word order; follows three-step commands; has ninety percent grammar acquistion; produces short passives; uses mostly direct requests and some indirect requests

6 years

Has a speaking vocabulary of around 2,600 words and a comprehension vocabulary of 20,000 to 24,000 words; comprehends parallel embedding in sentences and imperative commands; has many well-formed complex sentences; uses all parts of speech to some degree; identifies syllables; acquires rule for plural as in *ropes, skis,* and *dishes*; uses adverbial conjuncts *now, then, so,* and *though*; responds to indirect hints; keeps a conversation going by elaborating on the topic

7 years

Comprehends *because*; follows adult ordering of adjectives; can use words *left/right* and *front/back*; is able to manipulate sound units to rhyme; recognizes unacceptable sound sequences; understands most relational terms; understands *here, there, this, that, I,* and *you* as referents in conversations

8 years

Uses full passives (eighty percent of children); is able to produce all English sounds; sustains concrete topics in conversation; begins considering others' intentions; little difficulty with comparative relationship; boasts, brags

It appears that children are born with an acute ability to distinguish sounds. Three-day-old infants can distinguish their own mothers' voices from those of other mothers (DeCasper & Fifer, 1980). Infants as young as 1 month can discriminate between speech sounds that differ in the initial consonant /b/ and /p/: "ba" and "pa." Infants can make the same discriminations if the sounds are from a different language, whereas adults given the same task confuse the sounds. For a period of time, children can distinguish any sounds with ease, but by 10–12 months this ability disappears. They have learned which phoneme categories are necessary in English, and they ignore the other possibilities (Werker & Tess, 1984).

For these young experts at hearing sound differences, learning to produce the sounds presents new challenges. It isn't just a matter of learning to produce a simple list of the acceptable English phonemes shown in Table 1-2 (Gleason, 1985, p. 62) because sounds in speech are related to each other in many rule-governed ways. Children actually learn sound sequences, not just sounds. For example, /ng/ is a common English phoneme, but no English word begins with the sound. Words can begin with /pl/ and /tr/ but cannot end with them; likewise, words can end with /lp/ or /rt/ but cannot begin with these sounds. So not only do children learn how to produce the right sounds but they also learn to put them in sequences that are allowable in English and to recognize variant phonemes as representative of the same phoneme.

TABLE 1-2

General American English Phonemes

Vowels		Semivowels		Fricatives		Nasals		Stops		Liquids	
/i/	bead	/j/	yet	/f/	fie	/m/	ram	/p/	pill	/r/	red
/ɪ/	bid	/w/	wet	/θ/	thigh	/n/	ran	/t/	till	/l/	led
/ej/	bait			/s/	sigh	/ŋ/	rang	/k/	kill		
/ɛ/	bet			/ʃ/	shy			/tʃ/	chill		
/æ/	bat			/v/	vat			/b/	bill		
/a/	tot			/ð/	that			/d/	dill		
/ɔ/	taught			/z/	Caesar			/g/	Gil(bert)		
/ow/	tote			/ʒ/	seizure			/dʒ/	Jill		
/ʌ/	putt										
/ʊ/	put										
/uw/	boot										
/aj/	bite										
/æw/	bout										
/ə/	about*										

*Unstressed syllables only; status as a phoneme arguable.

Reaching the point where children have control of most English phonemes, around age 6, is a progression characterized by a number of partly right and partly wrong pronunciations, a perfectly normal characteristic of language learning and learning in general. To produce a sound, children have to orchestrate the tongue, lips, mouth, and lower jaw position, air movement, and vocal cord vibration. It is interesting that each child has patterns of errors with common characteristics. For example, 2-year-old Amahl treated the beginning sounds in *toe, say,* and *chair* as the same, pronouncing them all as /t/ (Menn, 1985). The charming pronunciation errors that are part of "baby talk," "goggy" for "doggy," are not a result of lack of discrimination but represent rule-governed errors made on the way to getting productive control of the phonological system.

Generally speaking, children can pronounce beginning sounds in a word before they can pronounce the same sound in the middle or at the end of words. The last basic sounds usually acquired are /l/ and /r/. Consonant clusters like /pr/, /kl/, and /str/ are acquired after single consonants (Lindfors, 1987).

There may still be confusion about some of the phonemes for some kindergarten children. More difficult phonemes like the voiced and unvoiced /th/, as in *the* and *thing,* might show up in kindergarten language as /de/ and /fing/. The sound spelled as *s* in *treasure* is also developing at this age. The age of acquisition for some sounds may vary by as much as three years, and when dialect or a second language is added to the mix, the generation of phonemes is even more complicated. It is important for the teacher to recognize that "mistakes" in these contexts are a natural part of the learning process and to respond to the meaning generated in the child's speech utterance (Pflaum, 1986).

The other aspect of phonology, *paralanguage*—the stress, pauses, and intonation, is learned quite rapidly. Variations in these features of language can give a single word utterance completely different meanings. Consider some of the ways a child can say "mommy." Intoned one way it may mean "Help" or in other contexts "Where are you?" "I'm hurt," "This is my mommy," or "It's good to see you." Try it yourself. How many different ways can you say "mommy" that convey very different meanings?

The First Word

When children produce a phonemically stable combination of sounds in a particular situation for an indentifiable meaning, they are saying a word. If you were to stop now and write down ten to twenty words you think would be among the first fifty words children use, you would probably include words that name important people like Mommy, Daddy,

Granny; favorite foods like cookie, juice, milk; common animals like dog, cat, horse, pig; words that regulate actions like no, go, up, down, more; and social expressions like bye-bye and hi (Lindfors, 1987).

A particularly fascinating characteristic of this stage of development is *overextension:* when a single word is used to communicate multiple meanings. While children have such limited speaking (production) vocabularies, they will often make overextensions by using one word to apply to a number of objects that have one feature in common. For example, one child's name for dog was "wau-wau," which he used for all animals, a toy dog, and soft slippers. The common property was probably the texture of the objects (deVillers & deVillers, 1979).

Children at this stage use a single word very flexibly to mean many things. The example of the many meanings of "mommy" described earlier illustrates this. Context, intonation, and children's gestures that accompany the word are necessary sources of information to others in understanding what the child is communicating. "Cookie" uttered after the favorite chocolate chip cookie is snatched from the child's hand by the family dog is very different in meaning from "cookie" said after polishing off the last chocolate chip.

Even though children overextend the meaning of words in production, they don't usually overextend words in comprehension. Their comprehension ability exceeds their ability to produce words. They may call a horse "dog" but know that it is not a dog. In reading a simple picture book, for example, parents might find that when they ask their child to point to the horse, the child does so easily, but on a subsequent experience with the book, the child might spontaneously point to the horse picture and say "dog."

Children comprehend far more language than they can produce, and the rate of acquisition for comprehension seems to be faster. One researcher found that children understood fifty words before they could produce ten; they comprehended fifty words at about 13 months but didn't produce fifty words until around 19 months. Children, on the average, were found to increase their productions at a rate of nine to ten words a month and to increase their comprehension of words at about twenty-two words a month (Benedict, 1979).

The Word Formation System—Morphology

The gradual and lengthy development of morphemes begins when children start making two-word utterances at around 18 months and continues into the early school years. Words can be categorized as *free* or *bound morphemes. Free morphemes* are the smallest unit of a word that can stand alone and still carry meaning, such as base words like *dog, cat,* and *book.* These base words cannot be divided any further and still remain meaningful. If we make these words plural, *dogs, cats,* and *books,* a *bound morpheme* with a grammatical function has been added—the plural -s. Bound morphemes have meaning only when attached to free morphemes—in this case, adding the meaning of plurality. Some other examples of bound morphemes are prefixes (*un-, non-, in-, pre-*), suffixes (*-ly, -est, -er, -ness*), and inflections (*-s, -'s, -ing, -ed*).

The development of bound morphemes is interesting because their emergence so clearly demonstrates that children don't learn them by rote or imitation. In the process of working out the rule-governed system for morphemes, children make application mistakes. For example, they overgeneralize the use of the plural /-s/ form by creating words like *mans, foots,* and *teeths,* and the past tense by inventing words like *falled, goed,* and *broked.* These are not words they have heard modeled in their environments. The forms come from a developing internalization of the rules that govern the formation of morphemes (Brown, 1973). Regular forms for plurals and past tense further complicate the situation. Depending on the final sound for the base word, plurals can be pronounced /s/ as in *cats,* /z/ as in *days,* and /ez/ as in *kisses.* The regular past tense form can be pronounced /t/ as in *jumped* or *stopped,* /d/ as in *tried* or *banged,* and /ed/ as in *pounded* or *sounded.* There are a number of rules for the learner to sort out, and in the process, overgeneralizations are made with regular forms as well. Eventually, for most children, overgeneralizations are corrected as they internalize rules for irregular and regular plural and verb forms.

Berko's classic "wug" study, though done in 1958, is worth discussion here because it is an example of an interesting way to observe how children generalize their use of morphemes and it can easily be replicated. Berko read brief descriptions of novel pictures to children and asked them to fill in the missing words, as in the "wug" example in Figure 1-2. (For additional examples of the items used in the study, see the chapter appendix on page 45.)

Other nonsense words, along with representational picture cards, were created, showing the most common morphological features:

1. Plural and possessives of the noun
2. Third person singular of the verb
3. Progressive and past tenses for the verb
4. Comparative and superlative forms of the adjective

Berko reasoned that if children could supply appropriate endings for the nonsense words, then they had internalized the working system of those forms of English morphemes. The children, ranging in age from 4 to 7, treated the nonsense words as acceptable English words and attempted to supply morphemes to make them work in the sentences supplied. They were not always right as far as English is concerned, but they gave consistent and orderly answers. As was expected, older children did better than younger children. Children did best with those mor-

FIGURE 1-2

Two Example Items
from the "Wug" Test
(Berko, 1958)

This is a wug.

Now there is another one.
There are two of them.
There are two _____.

This is a man who knows how to rick.
He is ricking. He did the same thing
yesterday. What did he do yesterday?
Yesterday he _____.

phemes that were more regular and had the least variation. For example, the plural form *wugs* was correct for ninety-one percent of the children, and ninety percent of the children were able to supply the present progressive morpheme *-ing*.

THE SENTENCE SYSTEM—SYNTAX

Comprehension of syntax precedes production. Syntax is the term for the rules children use when they begin to put words together to make sentences, word order, and relationships between words and word classes. This is one of the most studied aspects of language. Studies of the development of syntax focus on both comprehension and production.

For some time, the conventional wisdom has been that comprehension always precedes production of language. This is true not only for the comprehension of words, as discussed earlier, but of syntax as well. For example, children comprehend the full range of passive constructions by the middle of the elementary years, but they don't spontaneously produce them until well into adolescence. The best current evidence we have is that the relationship between comprehension and production moves from comprehension of language structure in context, to production of language, to comprehension of language based on linguistic cues only where there is no physical context (James, 1990, p. 90).

Rich classroom environments offer settings where children can demonstrate language comprehension by carrying out actions in response to language: the housekeeping center, the clock corner, and the sand table, to mention a few. Through careful observation based on a strong knowledge of oral language development, teachers can soon accumulate a set of language observation notes that will yield a rich profile of their children's comprehension of language.

Production of the first sentence at around 2 years of age is an important milestone that indicates beginning attention to syntax. Descriptions of early syntactic development were established in the classic work of Brown (1973) and continue to be used in current research. His language development observations of three young children over a period of several years revealed that if age was used as the basis for categorizing the characteristics of syntactic growth, children's language varied greatly. However, if length of utterance (spoken sentence) was used, there was a high degree of similarity in the development as depicted in Table 1-3. To determine the average length of children's utterances, Brown and his colleagues took samples of fifty to one hundred utterances in natural settings, counted the number of morphemes in each, and then computed the average, calling the final score the mean length of utterance (MLU). He found that increases in MLU corresponded to increases in syntactic complexity up to 4.0 MLU. Beyond that point, the complexity of utterances related more to context. Table 1-3 summarizes his findings and

Table 1-3

Brown's Stages and Mean Length of Utterances (Brown, 1973)

Stage	MLU	Approximate Age (months)	Characteristics
I	1.0–1.0 (5)*	12–26	Semantic roles and relations in simple sentences. "Mommy go." "Doggy allgone."
II	2.0–2.5 (7)*	27–30	Modulation of meaning in simple sentences through the use of grammatical morphemes. "I going." "Block in box."
III	2.5–3.0 (9)*	31–34	Simple sentence development including negatives, questions, and imperatives. "No throw ball.""Daddy going?" "Tie shoes."
IV	3.0–3.75 (11)*	35–40	Embedding one simple sentence within another. "She want to go out."
V	3.75–4.5 (13)*	41–46	Joining of two or more simple sentences. "I hit the boy and the girl."

*Numbers in parentheses indicate the number of morphemes that are typically found in the longest utterance at that stage.

illustrates when some syntactic forms first appear. These findings have been subsequently confirmed by other researchers.

To fully understand young children's syntax, it is necessary to consider the meaning of sentences and the context in which children produce them. (This principle was firmly established through Brown's 1970 research and prevails today.) The same utterance can be produced in two different situations with two different meanings. The example he gave was of a child who picked up her mother's sock and said, "Mommy sock," where the relationship between Mommy and sock was possessive. In another context, mother was putting a sock on the child. The child said, "Mommy sock," meaning "Mommy is putting on my sock." The relationship between Mommy and sock was agent of action (mommy) and object of the action (sock). Because there was information about the context and meanings, it was possible to conclude that the child was representing two different syntactic relationships with the same utterance.

The information in Table 1-3 can serve as a useful guide for observing the general order and approximate age of the early development of syntax. Keep in mind that the developmental ages indicated reflect the average, not the full variability of children's ages of production. Many kindergarten and preschool students are discovering and experimenting with many variations of sentence forms in stages IV and V. Complex and compound sentence development, which begin in stages IV and V, continue well into the elementary school years, so primary-grade teachers will also find that their students are still acquiring standard forms. Clear deviations from these general patterns may indicate that a child could benefit from work with a speech teacher.

A fairly consistent pattern in language development is that children first construct a general principle or rule for producing an aspect of language and then gradually learn its variations or exceptions. This is true for all aspects of language but particularly for the acquisition of syntax. We can see gradual development of children's emerging control of sentences and some of its variations in Brown's (1973) description of the characteristics of early utterances in Table 1-3. "As children go along, ever gaining new information about how language is structured and used in their world, they continuously reorganize, restructure, reshape the language system they are constructing, to take new information into account" (Lindfors, 1987, p. 215).

Some Coping Strategies

During the process of gradual learning, children are confronted with all the variations of a general principle, including instances where the basic principle simply doesn't work. To deal with these confusing situations, children apply coping strategies, which are rules they develop to work out complex syntactic structures they don't yet fully comprehend. When we discussed morphology earlier, we saw that children applied a general principle, a coping strategy, for plurals: when it's plural, add an -*s*. When children use coping strategies, the resulting comprehension and production will be right sometimes, but with more complex forms the strategies won't work. These coping strategies are influenced by cues other than or in addition to those contained in the words and sentences. Consider, for example, the cues the child must detect when the simple subject-verb-object sentence is increased in complexity: (1) word order can change, (2) clauses can be placed in different places, (3) time relationships among sentence parts can vary, (4) several sentences can be combined in numerous ways, and (5) sentences can be transformed into questions, to mention a few. Children gradually gain control of some of these dimensions of sentence combining over a period of years (Lindfors, 1987). Coping strategies emerge in the context of the developmental patterns for some aspects of syntax.

Children seem to work with certain internalized rules in mind. Some of them are discussed here.

Equal Relationships   When children first combine sentences, they use the coping strategy of equal relationships. Their conjoinings are produced using *and* or *then* as in stage V: "I hit the boy and the girl." Later, as children mature and understand unequal relationships, they combine sentences of unequal status by using adverbials like *before, after,* and *because.* "After Susie ate the candy bar, she went out to play."

Combining sentences with *because* develops over a fairly long period of time beginning after stage V, although the word appears in stage III (Owens, 1988, p. 273). The first use of *because* for conjoining illustrates how the coping strategy is applied where it doesn't work. The child uses *because* like *and* and *then:* "I fell down 'cause I hurted myself" (Corrigan, 1975). The early *because* conjoinings overlap in time: "She played in the mud because she wanted to" or are two simultaneous events: "I like to play because it's fun." *Because* sentences that express cause/effect relationships are more difficult and develop later because not only is there a time relationship to identify, but the effect is usually stated first. This goes against one of the other coping strategies children apply—order of mention—where they expect that the first event mentioned in the sentence happened first: "Wayne changed his mind because he liked chocolate ice cream better." The use of *because* for combining sentences in the most complex cause/effect relationships isn't fully developed by most children until around 10 years of age (James, 1990, p. 137).

Keeping Clauses Intact   As children start to put clauses together, they prefer to keep them intact by first placing them after the main clause and then before the main clause: "The girl hugged the dog *that licked her hand.*" These are followed developmentally by sentences with interrupted main clauses where the clause modifies the subject: "The boy *who likes hot dogs* eats broccoli too." The insertion of the phrase interrupts the subject-verb-object relationship in the sentence and is illustrative of more advanced development. Both of these forms are usually in place at around 9 years of age (James, 1990, p. 139).

Order of Mention   Initially, children expect that the time order for the actions in a sentence corresponds to the order in which things are mentioned, so the first action mentioned should come first. This works some of the time, but English sentences are also constructed so that the first thing that happens comes last in a sentence. Consider the sentences in the following list. The starred sentences follow the principle of order of mention that children apply initially as a coping strategy in trying to figure out how sentences work. In the last three sentences, the action to be performed second is stated first. After you read the sentences, try predicting the difficulty for kindergarten and second-grade children by ordering them from easiest to most difficult.

*1. Move a red one and then a yellow one

*2. Move a yellow one before you move a green one.

*3. After you move a black one, move a red one.

  4. Move a green one, but first move a red one.

  5. Move a yellow one after you move a green one.

  6. Before you move a black one, move a yellow one.

When kindergarten children were asked to move different colored beads on an abacus according to these directions, many applied the principle of order of mention as their coping strategy and misinterpreted the directions in sentences 4, 5, and 6 by doing the task inaccurately (Hatch, 1971). These same children, when asked to repeat the sentences after they were stated by an adult, often turned them into conjoined sentences, such as for sentence 5, "Move a green one and (or, and then) a red one." Second-graders, who were also part of the study, performed better, but their error pattern was the same as the kindergartners'.

The "before/after" sentences were more difficult than the "and then/but first" sentences, so knowledge of the meanings of *before* and *after* added another layer of complexity. Hatch found that both order of mention and *before* and *after* meanings accounted for the order of difficulty, which was, from easiest to most difficult: 1, 4, 2, 3, 6, 5.

The Main Clause As the First Event   While children are in the process of comprehending time ordering and how it is represented in sentences, they are likely to use the main-clause-as-the-first-event as a coping strategy to interpret sentences. For example, "After she arrived at the party, Barbara put on the costume" would be interpreted to mean that Barbara put on the costume and then arrived at the party.

Assumption of Reality   The syntax children are trying to interpret may be so complex at times that they rely on what they know about the real world and ignore the syntactic complexity. Language is usually embedded in an event where there are many cues outside the language itself about what is going on. The cues children pick up from the context and from their background knowledge may be sufficient for accurately determining meaning when they don't understand the syntax at all. For example, it might appear that children understand a passive sentence like "The baby was fed by the mother," but they would be likely to reverse the order of action if the sentence was "The mother was fed by the baby" because in the real world it is mothers who usually feed babies (James, 1990, p. 100). In a decontextualized setting where only linguistic cues are available, children may be able to extract enough information from the sentence to demonstrate comprehension by simply paying attention to the subject and verb.

Minimal Distance Principle   This principle means that children recognize that in most English sentences the noun closest to the verb is the subject. However, there are exceptions to this general rule, illustrated by Carol Chomsky's (1972) seminal work with 5–10-year-old children. She gave children toys to demonstrate the meanings of sentences that contained the verbs *tell, ask,* and *promise.* When *tell* is used, it adheres to the minimal distance principle: "Bozo told Donald to stand on the book." The noun (Donald) is closest to the infinitive verb (to stand), so children will accurately demonstrate Donald standing on the book.

The verb *promise,* however, doesn't behave according to the principle. In the sentence "Bozo promised Donald to stand on the book," the grammatical structure is the same as in the *told* sentence, but the subject of the infinitive verb (to stand) is Bozo. The child who is applying the minimal distance principle is likely to show Donald standing on the book when it should be Bozo.

The verb *ask* sometimes follows the principle but other times it doesn't, as in the following sentences: "Bugs asked Daffy to feed Porky" and "Bugs asked Donald what to feed Porky." The application of the minimal distance principle for the last sentence would result in an inaccurate interpretation. Clearly, the *ask* constructions, which are more inconsistent, are the last ones to be learned at around age 10 (James, 1990, p. 140).

Coping Strategies in the Classroom

While children are gradually learning to comprehend and produce more complex syntactic structures, they are in school hearing the teacher's classroom language all day long. Children use a number of coping strategies and as a result will make some mistakes in production and comprehension. Imagine the impact on children's performance in following directions if they are applying the order-of-mention coping strategy when the teacher is giving directions in which that order is reversed. For example, the direction "Before you cut out your picture, color it" could result in cutting out pictures first. There is certain to be confusion unless the assumption of reality can compensate for it. Imagine other possibilities where children are using coping strategies to comprehend teacher language; there are many opportunities for mismatches. Teachers who are aware of these coping strategies and others not mentioned here (Lindfors, 1987, pp. 175–194) will be able to take them into account and adjust their language accordingly. They will also be aware of which language features to model in highly meaningful contexts to assist development. Teachers will recognize language development for what it is, and not make the mistake of classifying children who are making language mistakes as "dumb." The "mistakes" are giving the teacher messages about the coping strategies the children are using while trying to understand more complex aspects of language.

Even though the focus in this section has been on the acquisition of syntax, it is important to remember that in order to produce sentences, the child has to be able to coordinate all aspects of language: phonology, syntax, morphology, semantics, and pragmatics. It isn't only a matter of learning acceptable word order.

Content

The Meaning System—Semantics

Adding to, Revising, and Consolidating Vocabulary   Children have developed a prodigious vocabulary by the time they are 6 years old. As you can see from Table 1-1, they can produce around 2,600 words and comprehend around 24,000 words. These young learners are constantly adding new words to their vocabulary repertoire and revising and consolidating meanings. Revision of word meanings is manifested as the overextensions seen at the one-word stage of development disappear and are reshaped through use into specific individualistic definitions. Individual meanings are similar to Humpty Dumpty's view in Lewis Carroll's *Through the Looking Glass* (1988):

"When I use a word," Humpty Dumpty said in rather a scornful tone, "it means just what I choose it to mean—neither more nor less."

"The question is," said Alice, "whether you can make words mean so many different things."

"The question is," said Humpty Dumpty, "which is to be master—that's all."

Individual meanings evolve into socially shared meanings. As this happens, children gradually gain more abstract knowledge of a word's meaning independent of a particular context. They also consolidate meanings by bringing together all definitions that can fit under one word, including recognition that a word belongs to certain semantic classes like synonyms, antonyms, and homonyms. Over time, their ability to state definitions moves from single-word action definitions to expressions of complex relationships (Litowitz, 1977). The following definitions for *dog* (Owens, 1988) illustrate the shift from individual meaning to socially shared meaning and could span a time period from 3 to 11 years of age.

Dogs have yukky breath.

Dogs are always barking and breathing.

Dogs are things with four legs, tails and bad breath, and barking.

Dogs are animals that usually live in people's houses.

Relational Vocabulary   Vocabulary that specifies relationships among people, objects, and events is particularly important to teachers because of its high frequency in the language of classroom instruction and children's books. Although many relational terms are understood by age 5, at least in their simplest usage, many children are still acquiring production and comprehension control over them. Learning their meanings is compounded by the amount of adult usage, complexity of syntax, and semantic characteristics of other words in a sentence. You will recall, for example, that second-graders are still working to acquire mastery over the more complex syntactic forms that contain *before* and *after*. This creates a situation where there are many opportunities for children to be misunderstood as well as teachers and textbooks. The words in Table 1-4 represent some of the main relational categories and specific words that should receive careful attention.

Words that express dimensions such as position, time, size, weight, distance, height, speed, and amount are often dealt with in pairs, or opposites. Pairs like *tall/short* are adjectives that describe opposite ends of an object's dimension. For such pairs, it seems easier for children to learn what is called the positive end of the dimension, in this case *tall*, than the negative end, *short*. The negative end expresses an absence of "tallness." Following is the order of acquisition of some of these dimensional pairs. The first word in each pair is usually learned first (James, 1990):

big/little	wide/narrow
long/short	thick/thin
tall/short	deep/shallow
high/low	

A number of words describe the physical characteristics of objects and can also be used to refer to the psychological characteristics of people: *sparkling, hard, crooked, bright, sweet, sour* (James, 1990). First, children use these words to describe objects. At around ages 7–8 they begin to use the words to describe both objects and people, but they don't recognize the relationship between the physical and psychological meanings. By ages 9–10, many children are able to connect the meanings and use words accurately in both contexts, although others don't reach this point until around age 12.

Table 1-4

Relationship Concepts

POSITION CONCEPTS		TIME CONCEPTS	
up	down	early	late
in	out	night	day
beginning	end	winter	summer
high	low	spring	fall
before	after	morning	afternoon
near	far	next	
left	right	late—later—latest	
under	over	early—earlier—earliest	
above	below	**SPEED CONCEPTS**	
top	bottom		
beneath—through		fast	slow
between—among		quickly	slowly
SIZE AND WEIGHT CONCEPTS		fast—faster—fastest	
		slow—slower—slowest	
big	little	**NUMBER/AMOUNT CONCEPTS**	
tall	short		
heavy	light	all—some—empty—full	
thick	thin	whole—part—each—more	
narrow	wide	less—most—pair—few	
tall—taller—tallest		many—add—altogether	
short—shorter—shortest		first—second—third	
large—larger—largest		fourth—fifth, etc.	
big—bigger—biggest		**SHAPE CONCEPTS**	
OTHERS			
		round—square—circle	
and—or—only—if		curved—straight—triangle	
then—when—where			

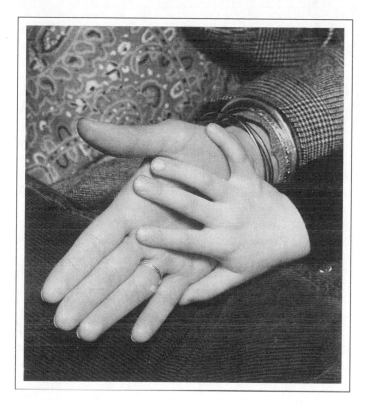

One of many concept books by Tana Hoban, this book helps children develop their semantic understanding of a variety of ideas.

From *Is It Larger? Is It Smaller?* by Tana Hoban, with photographs by the author (Greenwillow, 1985).

When discussing story characters' attributes, teachers usually want more than a physical description. Children may not have developed the language comprehension to be able to meet these expectations. In such settings, teachers could do "think-alouds"—when teachers model thinking by talking about it, making their thoughts public. For example, teachers could think aloud about why they think a character in a story is "cold" and "hard," to model how these words can be used to describe people as well as objects.

Wh- Questions

Understanding how meanings for *wh-* questions develop is helpful to teachers because questioning is central to instruction. Knowledge of *what, where,* and *who* develops early in children, appearing in the one-word stage. These question words refer to the names of objects, locations, actions, or a person, which are also the main referents for children's first content words. However, understanding *why, when,* and *how* requires knowledge of causality, manner, and time, which are more complex cognitive concepts and so develop later.

Understanding *wh-* questions isn't simply a matter of understanding the *wh-* words. The syntax of the question, the semantic features of the verbs in the question, and the context in which the question is asked also influence acquisition. For example, in the question "Who is kissing Mother?" the *wh-* word *who* replaces the subject and is syntactically easier than "Who is Mother kissing?" where *who* replaces the object. Semantically, no matter which *wh-* word is used with the verb *touch*, until children learn that *touch* can be used with the other *wh-* words, their coping strategy will be to respond as though the question was a *what, where,* or *why* question. For example, if a mother asked, "When did you touch Daddy's birthday cake?" the child would probably respond "Birthday cake." It is usually easier for children to answer a question in the contextual setting of the question. The exception to this is *where* questions. Children who were asked "Where is the girl eating?" when shown a picture of a girl eating an apple made more errors than those who were asked "What is the girl eating?" (Gleason, 1985).

Vocabulary—Multiple Meanings

The process of learning categories and vocabulary labels is made even more complex because a word can have multiple meanings in different contexts. Imagine the meanings and relationships children need to build for the word *run. Webster's II New Riverside University Dictionary* (1984) lists over 100 subtly to sharply different meanings, some of which may even be new to you. It is likely that the first meaning established would refer to someone in the family who goes on a morning exercise run, like Daddy. A rudimentary mental map for *run* might include this meaning, grammatical forms (*run, ran, running, runs*), and an opposite word association, *walk*. To rudimentary mental maps, children gradually add other meanings such as "a salmon *run*," "a *run* in Mom's stocking," "a home *run*," "*run* before the storm," and "*running* for president," to mention a few. Not only are there common dictionary meanings to be added to the meaning network, but because language constantly evolves, it is likely that *run* will be used in new ways that have not yet been catalogued in the dictionary. Children will also add relationships they have built between *run* and other words such as synonyms, antonyms, and homonyms. The full range of children's experiences with *run* will increase the complexity of their developing a semantic map for the word.

Teachers of young children will find that, because children's mental representations for all words used in the classroom are in different states, word meaning confusions will be almost a daily event. Understanding that children are reshaping their mental maps by adding, subtracting, and modifying information and restructuring helps teachers be alert for such events. To illustrate, a teacher was helping a child establish the sound/symbol relationship for /p/. The lesson language went something like this:

Teacher: What is in the picture?
Jason: A pig.
Teacher: Say it with me. /p/-/p/ pig.

Jason did as instructed.

Teacher: What sound do you hear at the beginning of /p/-/p/ pig?
Jason: Oink!

The teacher could have inaccurately concluded that Jason was being silly and may have done so if Jason had a reputation for "goofing off." However, on closer examination the teacher realized that Jason's meaning for *sound* related to noises things produce. Sound in reference to phonemes in words was not part of Jason's mental map for *sound*.

Use

The Functions of Language—Pragmatics

Language exists in the context of meaning and is used to communicate; it isn't simply structure and content. This is apparent in children's early attempts to communicate through gestures even before the first word. Parents assign meaning to children's early utterances. Children find out from adult responses what meaning is being given to what they are saying.

Halliday (1975) and several other researchers (Dore, 1978; Owens, 1988) established the framework for subsequent study of the early pragmatic functions of language. Halliday's categorization system is summarized in Table 1-5. The functions of language described appeared in his son's language during his first attempts at communication through age 2.

As children move into the preschool years and then into the primary grades, they are constantly refining initially established pragmatic functions into more and more socially acceptable communication forms. Several characteristics mark their emerging control.

Turn taking ability improves. The preschooler can maintain a conversation for several turns. In contrast, the primary-grade child is able to introduce a topic of conversation, sustain it through a number of turns, add new information, and close or switch the topic. In general, first-graders' responses to adult questions are brief, simple, and appropriate with little elaboration. But with peers, their responses are much more elaborate (Mishler, 1976).

Boys appear to be more successful in getting turns in school settings. They demand attention, are not admonished for calling out as much as girls are, and are given more wait time. Consequently, they are called on

Table 1-5

Halliday's Early Pragmatic Functions (Owens, 1988, p. 229)

Functions	Examples	Meaning
Instrumental	I want. I need.	Child attempts to satisfy needs or desires.
Regulatory	Do as I tell you.	Child attempts to control the behavior of others.
Interational	You and me.	Child establishes and defines social relationships and attempts to participate in social intercourse.
Personal	Here I come.	Child expresses individuality or gives personal opinions or feelings.
Imaginative	Let's pretend.	Child expresses fantasies or creates imaginary words.
Heuristic	Tell me why.	Child seeks information.
Informative	I've got something to tell you.	Child provides information.

to participate in classroom conversations more than girls are. Teachers' behavior could reflect a positive bias toward boys (Wellesley College Center for Research on Women, 1992).

Primary-grade children become more adept at dealing with conversation breakdowns by revising and repeating their original statements and adding information if necessary to be understood for at least three clarification requests. Preschool children, on the other hand, can respond to a first request for clarification but have difficulty after that.

Being able to take the perspective of conversation partners is an important milestone in developing pragmatic competence. Preschool children can make some adjustments to their listener's knowledge and information, but they have difficulty providing clear messages. Elementary-school children consistently improve in their ability to explain how to carry out activities by explaining a purpose and organizing the information in a sequence that the listener can follow. They also steadily improve in their ability to tell stories using the traditional folk tale story structure (Stein, 1979; Stein & Trabasso, 1982).

Owens (1988, p. 343) summarized the developing communication abilities of elementary-school children found by White (1975) as follows:

1. To gain and hold adult attention in a socially acceptable manner
2. To use others, when appropriate, as resources for assistance or information
3. To express affection, or hostility and anger, appropriately
4. To direct and follow peers
5. To compete with peers in storytelling and boasts
6. To express pride in themselves and their accomplishments
7. To role play

Classroom teachers who allow children to be oral language participants in the classroom will find many opportunities in day-to-day activity for children to increase their flexibility with language pragmatics.

Dialect Variation

An in-depth discussion of dialect variation isn't possible given space limitations, so this section will be confined to a summary of some key ideas based on Judith Lindfors's discussion (1987), which is an excellent resource for more careful study.

One kind of conversation that children can have is to talk with an adult about a book they've enjoyed together.

People from Australia, New Zealand, England, Wisconsin, Alabama, New York, and California all speak English, yet the words sound a little different. Many people in England follow "shed-jules" and wrap baking potatoes in "al-yew-min-i-um." Some words and word combinations are different. Some of us drink from a "water fountain" and others from a "bubbler." There are stylistic differences also: how fast to talk and how to use pitch, loudness, and tone of voice, to mention a few. Although we are likely to have preconceived attitudes toward people who use these dialects, for the most part these *geographical dialects* and speakers are eventually accepted.

Social dialects, which are the ways of speaking by particular social groups, have the same characteristics as geographical dialects except they are tied to status and prestige. "No dialect is inherently better or worse than any other" (Lindfors, 1987, p. 397). However, the differences in social dialects, such as "black English," that are spoken by groups with less power are typically thought to contain mistakes. They are regarded as substandard even though they are simply a language variation. The label "black English" itself is a misnomer because it suggests that it is the speech of all black people, which is not the case. In reality it refers *"to one particular version of communication some black Americans sometimes use (many features of which nonblack people also use)"* (Lindfors, 1987, p. 398).

What, then, is standard English? Lindfors (1987, p. 396) argues that all definitions are problematic because the term assumes that one dialect is inferior to another. Some common definitions of standard English include (1) "a dialect that doesn't call attention to itself"; (2) "the dialect Jane Pauley (or some national news broadcaster) speaks"; and (3) "the dialect I speak and write." Lindfors suggests instead that a *regional standard dialect* is a more accurate way to think about it. Recognizing that no two people speak exactly the same, we can define regional standard dialect as the dominant dialect spoken in a particular region.

One of the marvelous characteristics of language is that children gradually learn a range of dialects that they can choose to use appropriate to the occasion.

> My education and that of my Black associates were quite different from the education of our white schoolmates. In the classroom we all learned past participles, but in the streets and in our homes the Blacks learned to drop *s*'s from plurals and suffixes from past-tense verbs. We were alert to the gap separating the written word from the colloquial. We learned to slide out of one language and into another without being conscious of the effort. At school, in a given situation, we might respond with "that's not unusual." But in the street, meeting the same situation, we easily said, "It be's like that sometimes" (Angelou, 1970, p. 191).

Teachers are likely to have children in their classes who speak a variety of dialects, some of which are different from theirs and the regional standard dialect. It is important that they understand some of the phonological, syntactic, semantic, and pragmatic characteristics of their students' dialects. Lindfors (1987, pp. 431–434) suggests that the teacher's role should include the following:

1. Provide a variety of language participation activities.
2. Provide and accept a wide range of language variations.
3. Provide literacy activities that meet special communication needs of the classroom community.
4. Observe language with a perspective of seeing behaviors that vary from expectations as possibly making sense from another language perspective.
5. Observe children's participation patterns in different contexts.
6. Observe children's attitudes and interests.
7. Demonstrate ways of using language while maintaining respect for language differences.
8. Respond to what the child is trying to do.
9. Be a learner open to what the children have to teach about their language.

Creating Classroom Environments That Support Language Learning

Teachers are central players in classroom language. Their knowledge about form, content, and use of language provides a beginning foundation for working toward making sense of children's language. We listen with our "mind's ear." The knowledge and beliefs we have about language development guide our interpretations and responses to what we hear. Teachers must be excellent listeners in order to collect information about children's development and to orchestrate experiences to support its growth. Their challenge is to create classrooms where the conditions for language learning are working interactively to support all facets of literacy learning: speaking, listening, reading, and writing. Brian Cambourne's research provides us with a framework for doing just this.

Imagine sleepy Australian families tumbling out of their beds to begin the day: fathers leaving for work, children going to school, and Mum's hooking up bugging devices to their toddlers. Meanwhile, parked down the street a bit, Brian Cambourne, an educational researcher, activates his electronic equipment to begin a day of eavesdropping. For three years, he gathered data about how children learn language in natural settings. What he found gives us an understanding of the conditions that support language learning. In later research, he extended his work to structuring classrooms for literacy learning based on the conditions of learning given in Figure 1-3 (Cambourne, 1988).

IMMERSION

Teachers can create a context where children are *immersed* daily in language—all kinds of language: teacher language, peer language, book language, informal conversation, formal classroom language, and the language of song, rhyme, and story.

DEMONSTRATION

Teachers can engage in language *demonstrations,* which are rich sources of data for children's work in figuring out what phonemes matter in English (phonology) and how to structure complex sentences (syntax and morphology), develop word meanings (semantics), and gain understandings of various social conventions of language (pragmatics).

Reading aloud is one of the most powerful activities teachers can do to immerse their children in demonstrations of language (Morrow, 1983; Teale, 1978). It should happen daily in classrooms. Good literature with simple language structure very close to what the children are speaking and also stories that contain more complex structures should be chosen. By hearing language in a story that is somewhat beyond the language they are producing, children can begin to comprehend those structures that they will produce later. The illustrations and actions of the story put the complex language forms in context and allow children to grasp the meaning even though some of the sentence structure and vocabulary may not be part of their production repertoire. Book language also consists of complete sentences, in contrast to the fragmented language of conversation. Strickland (1973) found that simply including a solid read-aloud program in kindergartens increased African American children's proficiency in standard English language.

Nursery rhymes, number and alphabet books, wordless picture books, nonfiction books, finger rhymes and songs, books about common experiences of young children, and beautiful picture books with immediately engaging stories and illustrations should all be part of the read-aloud program in kindergarten and primary grades. The books can readily become the center of conversation among several children as well as an entire class. An excellent resource is *Children's Literature in the Elementary School* by Charlotte Huck, Susan Hepler, and Janet Hickman (1993).

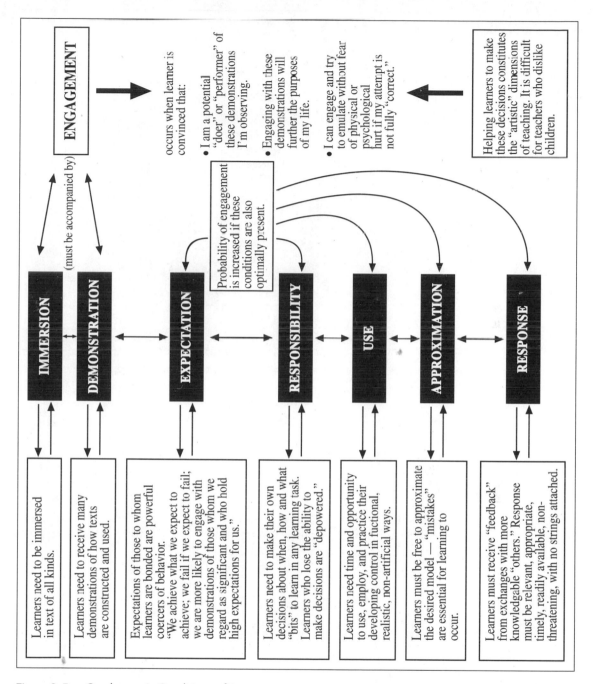

ENGAGEMENT

occurs when learner is convinced that:

- I am a potential "doer" or "performer" of these demonstrations I'm observing.
- Engaging with these demonstrations will further the purposes of my life.
- I can engage and try to emulate without fear of physical or psychological hurt if my attempt is not fully "correct."

Helping learners to make these decisions constitutes the "artistic" dimensions of teaching. It is difficult for teachers who dislike children.

(must be accompanied by)

Probability of engagement is increased if these conditions are also optimally present.

IMMERSION

DEMONSTRATION

EXPECTATION

RESPONSIBILITY

USE

APPROXIMATION

RESPONSE

Learners need to be immersed in text of all kinds.

Learners need to receive many demonstrations of how texts are constructed and used.

Expectations of those to whom learners are bonded are powerful coercers of behavior. "We achieve what we expect to achieve; we fail if we expect to fail; we are more likely to engage with demonstrations of those whom we regard as significant and who hold high expectations for us."

Learners need to make their own decisions about when, how and what "bits" to learn in any learning task. Learners who lose the ability to make decisions are "depowered."

Learners need time and opportunity to use, employ, and practice their developing control in fuctional, realistic, non-artificial ways.

Learners must be free to approximate the desired model — "mistakes" are essential for learning to occur.

Learners must receive "feedback" from exchanges with more knowledgeable "others." Response must be relevant, appropriate, timely, readily available, non-threatening, with no strings attached.

FIGURE 1-3   Cambourne's Conditions of Learning

This book is one of many that could be read aloud in class to stimulate students' thinking and responding.

From *I Went Walking* by Sue Williams, with illustrations by Julie Vivas (Gulliver/Harcourt, 1990).

For children who speak varieties of English that differ from formal English, such as black English or Hawaiian Creole English or English as a second language, teachers may find it useful to share books that allow children to develop comprehension of the standard English structures whose features differ from their own language use (Au, 1993). Children will soon be able to comprehend how two ways of making a statement can have the same meaning. In these contexts, as in all classroom contexts, it is important to maintain respect for the children's natural language. For example, teachers might choose a book like *The Chick and the Duckling* (1988) by Mirra Ginsburg as a model for the inflectional ending *-ing*. This is a story about what happens to a chick who tries to copy a duckling in everything he does.

> "I'm going for a swim," said the Duckling.
> "Me too," said the Chick.

Engagement

Demonstration and *immersion* alone are not enough. Children must be actively *engaged* in their own learning. Cambourne (1988) found that children were more likely to engage after demonstrations (1) if they believed in their own abilities, (2) if they believed there was something in it for them, such as furthering the purposes of their lives in some way, and (3) if they believed it would be enjoyable. Vital to establishing conditions so children will engage is a fourth point: (4) children must believe that it is safe to make mistakes, to take risks. Few of us would willingly participate in something where we make mistakes if we are demeaned, injured, or caused pain in some way. Unfortunately, in many classrooms learning must be right the first time. Children who speak a dialect or mispronounce words in a group class activity and are met with laughter and ridicule, for example, can be so embarrassed that the next time they will take the safe route and become clams. The result is the opposite of what we want. We want children to take risks and feel safe enough to venture into new learning territory.

Expectations

Expectations for learning should be high. Teachers should communicate that they believe children are capable learners. Young children believe they can do anything until somebody tells them something different. The high expectations should be realistically related to children's patterns of development.

Responsibility

The likelihood of keeping children engaged is increased when *responsibility, use, approximation,* and *response* are present. Children as language learners are allowed to make decisions about their learning by themselves. No one predetermines exactly what it is that they should decide to learn next. Instead, the controlled environment and the child's innate ability constrain the possibilities. Children in the same environment will learn very different things. *Responsibility* is another way of saying children own their own learning and make some decisions about how and when to do it.

The idea that learners should take responsibility for their own learning is the condition that is probably most misunderstood. There is a tendency to think this means that teachers don't need to teach. The concern is that "if we let children take responsibility for their own learning, how can we be assured they will learn what's best for them?" (Cambourne, personal interview). The idea conjures up visions of undisciplined, unmanaged classrooms where children do only what they want to do—images of children running wild. But it doesn't mean children can choose not to learn, or that teachers just stand back and let it happen, or that children do only those things that most interest them. It means making choices commensurate with one's level of knowledge and ability. The teacher sets the constraints, and the children make choices within those constraints. A good example of this is the "Plan,

Do, and Review" procedure in the High Scope program (1991). With the teacher's support, the children make oral plans and later written ones for their choice time during the kindergarten day. During their choice times, they can go to different centers around the room and participate in the activities they have selected.

Use

We learn to understand language, how to use it, and to learn through language while *using* it. These three activities occur simultaneously. This is the old idea of practice adapted for today's classrooms. In the past in many classrooms, practice often took place in isolation in well-intentioned, often rote, "drill and practice" formats that emphasized correct responses. Today practice in meaningful contexts emphasizes engagement. The idea is to allow what happens in families to happen in the classroom. We engage children in activities that enable them to use language and, as a consequence, learn it.

Opportunities to talk in classroom settings make an important contribution to children's continuing learning of pragmatics and other aspects of language. Not allowing talk makes learning more difficult. For children to develop proficiency in language use, they need many meaningful contexts for talking: one-to-one with the teacher, in groups with the teacher, and with their peers. Both preplanned and spontaneous language opportunities are necessary. With a class of twenty-five children,

Conversation among children about a book they have enjoyed together is another form of conversation that should be encouraged.

it is impossible to devote equal time to each child, so it is important for teachers to preplan small group interactions related to the curriculum on a regular basis. In these contexts, teachers should be aware of their own response patterns. The tendency is for teachers to allow those students who initiate conversation to talk most. So, by omission, those children who need the most practice may not have the opportunities (Cazden, 1981).

Kindergartens that include *activity centers* are particularly conducive to spontaneous conversation. Centers could include the housekeeping center, book center, office center, art center, block center, and special topics center. Real-life materials should be placed in these centers to engage children in conversations and role playing that reflect their experiences. Children's books, magazines, a telephone, typewriter, computer, paper, pencils, newspapers, advertisements, a variety of empty grocery containers like cereal boxes and canned goods cans, envelopes, stamps and stamp pads are some of the materials that foster literacy conversations (Neuman & Roskos, 1990). First-grade classrooms can also use centers and add a theme center tied to curriculum study. A science center, where children have opportunities to work cooperatively with partners conducting experiments, creates excellent opportunities for children to use language to solve problems.

Teachers provide opportunities for using language in *storytelling* by including wordless picture books in the classroom children's literature collection. Most of these books tell stories through pictures that include all the elements of story structure: character, setting, goal, problem, episode sequence, and resolution. Children can "read" these books with a partner, creating a story for the illustrations. Tomie dePaola's *Pancakes for Breakfast* (1978), a slapstick comedy where papa bear is trying desperately to swat a pesky fly, invites lots of laughter and storytelling. Children will also enjoy inventing stories for the mouse family in Emily McCully's books *First Snow* (1985), *Picnic* (1984), and *School* (1987).

Role playing characters in a favorite folk tale is also an excellent context for using language. Children often pick up some of the book language in their role playing, which contributes to their vocabulary and syntactic development. Some lines that are quickly included in dramatizations of *Henny Penny* (Zimmerman, 1989) are "The sky is falling" and from *The Three Little Pigs and the Big Bad Wolf* (Rounds, 1992), "I'll huff and I'll puff and I'll blow your house down."

Children should also have opportunities to play with the sounds of the language, the phonological system. Although they can produce most of the phonemes of the language by first grade, they are just beginning to manipulate those sounds in conscious ways. Learning *tongue twisters*, for example, helps children identify that words can begin with the same phoneme. *Faint Frogs Feeling Feverish and Other Terrifically Tantalizing Tongue Twisters* by Lillian Obligado (1983) encourages exploration of the concept of the same beginning sounds. Semantic knowledge will also be enhanced as challenging word meanings are worked out in the tongue twister context.

Nursery rhymes, both traditional and contemporary, help the child begin to identify rhyme patterns. Very contemporary teachers may want to share verses from *The Feminist Mother Goose Rhymes* by Judith and Jessica Maxwell (1992), or a nonviolent alternative to Mother Goose, *I Wish I Had a Computer That Makes Waffles* (Dodson, 1978). *Tomie dePaola's Mother Goose* (1985), with its multiethnic illustrations, will appeal to those who prefer the traditional rhymes.

Finger plays and *songs* should be part of the language curriculum as well. Not only do the children practice different syntactic patterns and develop vocabulary, but they also extend their knowledge of phonology. Raffi's song, "I Like to Eat Apples and Bananas" becomes "I like to eat epples and benenes" in the second verse and undergoes more phonemic changes in subsequent verses.

"Show and tell," the traditional event in kindergartens and primary grades, where children bring something from home to show and talk about, provides another classroom opportunity for practicing language in meaningful contexts.

Approximations

Approximations are absolutely basic to learning to talk. We actually enjoy and celebrate babies' incorrect grammar and pronunciation, finding it cute and irresistible. "Dat Mommy nose" eventually becomes "That's Mommy's nose" when the child figures out contractions and possessives and learns how to say the /th/ sound. Parents and teachers know these "mistakes" are temporary and will eventually drop out of children's repertoire. The "mistakes" are more like indicators of what children are experimenting with as they reach for more complex language. They provide insights into how children are figuring out the new-to-them piece of the language puzzle and where they are in their development. Kindergarten teachers will hear many of their children experimenting with the morpheme *-ed,* which is a complicated morpheme after all. It can be pronounced /t/ as in *jumped,* or /-ed/ as in *shouted,* or /d/ as in *cried,* and then there are those irregular verb forms like *went* for the past tense of *go* to make the task even more challenging.

Teachers can do *focused language observations* throughout the year of children's approximations to identify their coping strategies by dividing a standard sheet of paper into boxes equal to the number of children in the class. Children's names are written in the boxes, the date is noted, the paper is attached to a clip board, and then the teacher is ready to make language notes on several children a day until they are all observed. The teacher accumulates a record of some of the language behaviors students are using in the classroom. These observations will be useful in making decisions about materials, language to be modeling, and activities to provide.

Responses and Feedback

Teachers' *responses* and *feedback* to children's approximations are powerful forces in the classroom. Children who are immersed in language and using it in purposeful ways to make meaning are unafraid to make mistakes when the adults in the environment respond to the truth value of the language statements they are making. As teachers engage in conversations with children, they can also model and elaborate on syntactic, semantic, and pragmatic features of language that can help the child grow. These kinds of responses are usually nonthreatening because they are embedded in meaningful activity. Teachers can take lessons from parents about ways to respond to children's language approximations (deVillers & deVillers, 1979).

- Parents tailor the length and complexity of their language to the language ability of their children.
- If the child doesn't seem to understand, parents simplify their language.
- Parents typically respond to the meaning of the language.
- Parents frequently expand or rephrase their children's utterances to fill in grammatical features they left out and supply more information about the situation.

  Child: Kitty eat.
  Parent: Yes, the kitty is eating supper.

- Parents frequently elaborate on their children's utterances.

  Child: Kitty eat.
  Parent: Yes, the kitty is hungry.

- Parents frequently recast sentences by keeping the topic constant while providing a different way to talk about it.

  Child: Kitty eat.
  Parent: What is the kitty eating?

- Parents correct overextensions by providing the correct word for an object, which assists the child's word learning. Parents also correct children's comprehension. These corrections are often accompanied by an elaboration.

  Child: Kitty.
  Parent: No, that's a tiger. He has stripes. We will see him at the zoo.

- When children make grammatical approximations, expansion that includes response to the meaning is more effective than correction of the grammar.

Child: He fall down.
Expansion: Yes, he fell down.
Correction: No, he fell down.

These examples can be guidelines for classroom teachers as they develop responses and provide supportive feedback for children's language. In all instances, children's risk taking is respected, and communication and meaning are the main goal. Brown's (1977) comments to parents about the characteristics of parental speech to young children speak of teachers as well.

Believe that your child can understand more than he or she can say . . . to communicate. To understand and be understood. To keep your minds fixed on the same target. In doing that, you will, without thinking about it, make 100 or maybe 1,000 alterations in your speech and action. Do not try to practice them as such. There is no set of rules of how to talk to a child that can even approach what you unconsciously know. If you concentrate on communicating, everything else will follow (p. 26).

A supportive language environment includes careful attention to immersion, demonstration of language, student engagement, high expectations for performance, student responsibility for learning, frequent and meaningful use of language, acceptance of approximations, and teacher responses and feedback that nurture growth. Teachers can create opportunities for children to engage in many classroom activities that allow them to use all aspects of language in meaningful ways.

Summary

What you have read is a summary, an outline, and a forecast. It is a summary, albeit brief, of a complex, rapidly developing field: language acquisition research. It is a brief outline of some ways this research could affect classroom procedures if teachers are aware of the researchers' findings. And it is a forecast of what you, a classroom teacher, might do with your children to help them build on the language skills they bring to your classroom.

Suggestions for Further Study

1. Visit a kindergarten classroom and make notes about how and to what degree the conditions of learning are being implemented. Which conditions were best met and how? Which conditions need

attention and why? What ideas do you have for strengthening the conditions of learning in the classroom?

2. See if you can locate a parent who will tape record book reading time with his or her child. The child should be one who is not yet decoding text and whose "reading" is talking the story. Transcribe the tape and discuss the parent-child interactions. If you can't locate a parent, you can read aloud to a child instead. Some books to start with are by Eric Carle, Marcia Brown, Mirra Ginsburg, Cindy Ward, and Sue Williams. See the list of children's books for titles.

3. By listening carefully to children's classroom language, you can identify some feature of language that many of them are trying to work out, such as the -ed morpheme. Locate a book that invites the child to join in the reading because it has predictable and memorable text, or a song, nursery rhyme, or finger play, and teach it to the children as a demonstration of the standard use of the form in a meaningful context. Observe children's responses to the aspect of language you have selected. Do not "correct" their language approximations by saying, "That's wrong. Say it this way." Accept approximations. Some of the children will probably continue using their approximations. Other children who are closer to figuring out how the aspect of language works may imitate it in the standard form of the song.

4. Tape record 100 utterances of a kindegarten child. Transcribe and type the utterances, one per line. Then calculate Brown's MLU (page 15) as described in the section of the chapter on syntax. Describe the syntactic structure of each utterance. Then, using the information in the chapter, discuss what kinds of sentence constructions the child can produce in standard form and the coping strategies the child is using for the forms not yet fully understood. What does this tell you about your role of interacting and providing feedback for this child? What does your information tell you about the language you will need to use to be understood?

5. Choose a variation of formal standard English to study such as black English, Hawaiian Creole English, or English as a second language for Spanish-speaking children. Collect information about the ways that form of English varies from standard English and then match children's books to the features of that language to develop a potential read-aloud list for teachers. Chapters in Lindfors (1987) will be helpful in making your interpretation.

6. Select a children's book that focuses on multiple meanings of words or some basic concepts such as position concepts, time, size and weight, numbers and amounts, and shapes. Read and talk about the book with a child. Tape record your experience and interpret the results. What concepts did the child know? What was confusing to the child? Why? How did your language support or interfere with learning?

Suggestions for Further Reading

Au, K. (1993). *Literacy instruction in multicultural settings.* New York: Harcourt Brace Jovanovich.

Au develops a key theme that language is part of culture and discusses how to develop literacy programs grounded in a constructivist model of instruction that respects that culture. She also presents ways to integrate multiethnic literature.

Gleason, J. (1985). *The development of language.* Columbus, OH: Merrill.

This is a collection of papers by different authors that focus in depth on the basic components of language development. It also includes strong discussions of theories of language acquisition, transitions from oral to written language in school years, and language variation in society.

James, S. (1990). *Normal language acquisition.* Austin, TX: pro-ed.

This is a succinctly written up-to-date overview of the basic components of language development.

Lindfors, J. (1987). *Children's language and learning.* Englewood Cliffs, NJ: Prentice-Hall.

Lindfors discusses language structure, acquisition, learning, use in social contexts, and language variation while making strong classroom connections. A special feature of the book is the many examples of children's talk that illustrate the concepts in the book.

Owens, R. (1988). *Language development.* Columbus, OH: Merrill.

This technical book relates language development to child development, the development of the central nervous system, cognitive and perceptual factors, and the social and communicative bases for language. Owens discusses not only basic acquisition but also language disorders.

Pflaum, S. (1986). *The development of language and literacy in young children.* Columbus, OH: Merrill.

After a discussion of language acquisition, Pflaum writes about how to work with language in home and school settings and relates language development to beginning reading and writing experiences.

Taylor, D., & Dorsey-Gaines, C. (1988). *Growing up literate: Learning from inner-city families.* Portsmouth, NH: Heinemann.

The authors visited families who live in an inner city to study the family contexts of young black children living in poverty who were growing up literate. The images of the strengths families provide break many traditional myths.

Taylor, D., & Strickland, D. (1986). *Family storybook reading.* Portsmouth, NH: Heinemann.

Families from varied lifestyles and cultural backgrounds were observed and interviewed to obtain this detailed account of the important role storybook reading plays in family life and in the acquisition of language literacy.

REFERENCES

Angelou, M. (1970). *I know why the caged bird sings*. New York: Bantam.

Au, K. (1993). *Literacy instruction in multicultural settings*. New York: Harcourt Brace Jovanovich.

Benedict, H. (1979). Early lexical development: Comprehension and production. *Journal of Child Language, 6,* 183–200.

Berko, J. (1958). The child's learning of English morphology. *Word, 14,* 303–317.

Bloom, L. (1983). Of continuity, nature, nurture, and magic. In R. Golinkoff (Ed.), *The transition from preverbal to verbal communication*. Hillsdale, NJ: Erlbaum.

Bohannon III, J., & Warren-Leubecker, A. (1985). Theoretical approaches to language acquisition. In J. Gleason (Ed.), *The development of language* (pp. 173–226). Columbus, OH: Merrill.

Boysson-Bardies, B., de Sagart, L., & Durand, C. (1984). Discernible differences in the babbling of infants according to target language. *Journal of Child Language, 11,* 1–15.

Brown, R. (1973). *The first language: The early stages*. Cambridge, MA: Harvard University Press.

———. (1977). Introduction. In C. E. Snow & Ca. A. Ferguson (Eds.), *Talking to children: Language input and acquisition* (pp. 1–21). New York: Cambridge University Press.

Cambourne, B. (1988). *The whole story*. New South Wales, Australia: Ashton Scholastic Pty Ltd.

Cazden, C. (1981). *Language in early childhood education*. Washington, DC: National Association for the Education of the Young Child.

Chomsky, C. (1972). Stages in language development and reading exposure. *Harvard Educational Review, 42*(1), 1–33.

Clark, E. (1971). On the acquisition of the meaning of before and after. *Journal of Verbal Learning and Verbal Behavior, 10,* 266–275.

Corrigan, R. (1975). A scalogram analysis of the development of the use and comprehension of "because" in children. *Child Development, 46,* 195–201.

DeCasper, A., & Fifer, W. (1980). Of human bonding: Newborns prefer their mothers' voices. *Science, 208,* 1174–1176.

deVillers, P., & deVillers, J. (1979). *Early language*. Cambridge, MA: Harvard University Press.

Dore, J. (1978). Representative systems in nursery school conversations: Analysis of talk in its social context. In R. Campbell & P. Smith (Eds.), *Recent advances in the psychology of language: Language development and mother child interaction* (pp. 271–292). New York: Plenum.

Gleason, J. (1985). *The development of language*. Columbus, OH: Merrill.

Gleitman, L., & Wanner, E. (1982). Language acquisition: The state of the state of the art. In E. Wanner & L. Gleitman (Eds.), *Language acquisition: The state of the art*. New York: Cambridge University Press.

Golinkoff, R., Hirsh-Pasek, K., Cauley, K., & Gordon, L. (1987). The eyes have it! Lexical and syntactic comprehension in a new paradigm. *Journal of Child Language, 14,* 23–45.

Halliday, M. (1975). Learning how to mean. In E. Lenneberg & E. Lenneberg (Eds.), *Foundations of language development: A multi-disciplinary approach* (pp. 240–265). New York: Academic Press.

Hatch, E. (1971). The young child's comprehension of time connectives. *Child Development, 42,* 2111–2113.

Heath, S. (1983). *Ways with words: Language, life and work in communities and classrooms.* New York: Cambridge University Press.

High Scope Education Research Foundation. (1991). *Fifth annual high scope registry conference proceedings.* 600 N. River St., Ypsilanti, MI 48198.

Huck, C., Hepler, S., & Hickman, J. (1993). *Children's literature in the elementary school.* New York: Harcourt Brace Jovanovich.

James, S. (1990). *Normal language acquisition.* Austin, TX: pro-ed.

Lindfors, J. (1987). *Children's language and learning.* Englewood Cliffs, NJ: Prentice-Hall.

Litowitz, B. (1977). Learning to make definitions. *Journal of Child Language, 4,* 289–304.

Menn, L. (1985). Phonological development: Learning sounds and sound patterns. In J. Gleason (Ed.), *The development of language* (pp. 61–101). Columbus, OH: Merrill.

Mishler, E. (1976). Studies in dialogue and discourse: 3. Types of discourse initiated and sustained through questions. *Journal of Psycholinguistic Research, 3,* 99–123.

Morrow, L. M. (1983). Home and school correlates of early interest in literature. *Journal of Educational Research, 76,* 221–230.

Neuman, S., & Roskos, K. (1990). The influence of literacy-enriched play settings on preschoolers' engagement with written language. In J. Zutell, S. McCormich, M. Connolly & P. O'Keefe (Eds.), *Literacy theory and research: Analysis from multiple paradigms* (pp. 179–187). Chicago: National Reading Conference.

Owens, R. (1988). *Language development.* Columbus, OH: Merrill.

Pflaum, S. (1986). *The development of language and literacy in young children.* Columbus, OH: Merrill.

Phillips, S. U. (1983). *The invisible culture.* New York: Longman.

Sachs, J. (1985). Prelinguistic development. In J. Gleason (Ed.), *The development of language* (pp. 37–60). Columbus, OH: Merrill.

Stein, N. (1979). How children understand stories: A developmental analysis. In L. Katz (Ed.), *Current topics in early childhood education* (Vol. 2, pp. 261–290). Norwood, NJ: Ablex.

Stein, N. L., & Trabasso, T. (1982). What's in a story? Critical issues in comprehension and instruction. In R. Glaser (Ed.), *Advances in instructional psychology* (Vol. 2, pp. 213–254). Hillsdale, NJ: Erlbaum.

Strickland, D. (1973). A program for linguistically different black children. *Research in Teaching of English, 7,* 79–86.

Teale, W. (1978). Positive environments for learning to read: What studies of early readers tell us. *Language Arts, 55,* 922–932.

Webster's II New Riverside University dictionary. (1984) Boston: Riverside Publishing Company, A Division of Houghton Mifflin Co.

Weeks, T. (1974). *The slow speech development of a bright child.* Lexington, MA: Lexington Books, D. C. Heath and Co.

Wellesley College Center for Research on Women. (1992). *The American Association of University Women report: How schools shortchange girls.* Washington, D.C.: The American Association of University Women Educational Foundation.

Werker, P., & Tess, R. (1984). Cross-language speech perception: Evidence for perceptual reorganization during the first year of life. *Infant Behavior and Development, 7,* 49–64.

White, B. (1975). Critical influences in the origins of competence. *Merrill-Palmer Quarterly, 22,* 243–266.

Children's Books and Records

Brown, Marcia. (1957). *The three billy goats gruff.* New York: Harcourt.

Carle, Eric. (1969). *The very hungry caterpillar.* New York: Philomel.

———. (1990). *The very quiet cricket.* New York: Philomel.

Carroll, Lewis (Charles Dodgson). (1988). *Through the looking glass in Alice's adventures in wonderland* (illustrated by Anthony Browne). New York: Knopf (1865, 1871).

dePaola, Tomie. (1978). *Pancakes for breakfast.* San Diego: Harcourt.

———. (1985). *Tomie dePaola's Mother Goose.* New York: Putnam.

Dodson, Fitzhugh. (1978). *I wish I had a computer that makes waffles.* La Jolla, CA: Oak Tree Publications.

Ginsburg, Mirra. (1988). *The chick and the duckling.* New York: Aladdin Books, Macmillan.

Hill, Eric. (1981). *Where's Spot?* Other Spot books include *Spot's Birthday Party,* 1982; *Spot's First Christmas,* 1983; *Spot's First Walk,* 1981. New York: Putnam.

Hoban, Tana. (1990). *Exactly the opposite.* New York: Greenwillow.

———. (1985). *Is it larger? Is it smaller?* New York: Greenwillow.

———. (1986). *Shapes, shapes, shapes.* New York: Greenwillow.

———. (1987). *26 letters and 99 cents.* New York: Greenwillow.

Hughes, Shirley. (1986). *All shapes and sizes.* New York: Lothrop.

Maxwell, Judith and Jessica. (1992). *The feminist Mother Goose rhymes.* Mt. Vernon, WA: Veda Vangarde.

Mayer, Mercer. (1974). *Frog goes to dinner.* New York: Dial Press.

McCully, Emily. *First snow,* 1985; *Picnic,* 1984; *School,* 1987. New York: Harper & Row.

Obligado, Lillian. (1983). *Faint frogs feeling feverish and other terrifically tantalizing tongue twisters.* New York: Viking Press.

Raffi. *One light one sun.* MCA Records, Universal City, CA, 91608.

Rounds, Glen. (1992). *The three little pigs and the big bad wolf.* New York: Holiday House.

Spier, Peter. (1972). *Fast-slow, high-low. A book of opposites.* Garden City, NY: Doubleday.

Ward, Cindy. (1988). *Cookie's week.* New York: Putnam.

Wells, Rosemary. "Very First Books." *Max's first word,* 1979; *Max's bath,* 1985; *Max's bedtime,* 1985; *Max's birthday,* 1985; *Max's breakfast,* 1985; *Max's ride,* 1979; and *Max's toys,* 1979. New York: Dial.

Williams, Sue. (1990). *I went walking.* New York: Harcourt Brace Jovanovich.

Zimmerman, H. Werner. (1989). *Henny Penny.* New York: Scholastic Hardcover.

Professional Growth

The Society for Research in Child Development, University of Chicago Press,
5720 Woodlawn Ave., Chicago, IL 60637. (317) 702-7470.

This association of 4,500 members is a professional interdisciplinary society composed of such specialists as anthropologists, educators, psychologists, and sociologists, among others. Its work is directed toward furthering research in child development. It publishes *Child Development Abstracts and Bibliography*, a culling of published research from about 275 other English and foreign language journals, reports, and books of this topic. The organization also publishes the *Monograph of the Society for Research in Child Development* three to four times a year, which contains in-depth research studies. It sponsors a biennial convention with exhibits.

Appendix

❀

Replicating Experiments

To understand and appreciate children's coping strategies as they construct language, you will enjoy, as will children, replicating several of the classic language development experiments. It is especially interesting to do the experiments with several children in order to contrast their development as well as to contrast your results with the results of the original study. (The References section includes the information you will need to locate a study.) It is also helpful to do several different experiments with the same child because no single study or task can give a complete picture of a child's performance. For each replication you (a) make notes about the background of the child and the context you were in when you did the replication, (b) write down specifically what the child says, and (c) interpret the results in terms of the characteristics of the child's language development, coping strategies used, and implications for the classroom. Use a tape recorder for better accuracy. Note that the studies suggested for replication include examples of imitation, comprehension, and production tasks.

1. *Morphology.* Create simple black line cartoonlike drawings (stick figures will do) on 3″ × 5″ cards that represent the actions suggested by the production task items Berko (1958) used in her "wug" study. The items are listed below. Pictures of the famous wugs were provided in the chapter as a model to get you started. Make sure that the actions and objects in the pictures are imaginary because children try to make sense of the pictures by fitting them to their background knowledge. For example, you would *not* draw a stick figure of a man golfing and then give the child the task: "This is a man who knows how to naz. He is nazzing. He does it every day. Every day he _____." Many children are likely to reply based on their background knowledge and say "golfs" if golfing is something they know about.

Each task below lists first what is being tested; second, a description of the pictures on the cards; and third, what is said when the cards are presented to the child. Pronunciation is indicated by a phonemic transcription using the General American English Phonemes code presented in Table 1-2.

The Child's Learning of English Morphology
Jean Berko Gleason (1958)

1. *Plural*
   One bird-like animal, then two.
   "This is a wug /wʌg/. Now there is another one. There are two of them. There are two _____."

2. *Plural*
   One bird, then two.
   "This is a guch /gʌtʃ/. Now there is another one. There are two of them. There are two _____."

3. *Past Tense*
   Man with a steaming pitcher on his head.
   "This is a man who knows how to spow /spow/. He is spowing. He did the same thing yesterday. What did he do yesterday? Yesterday he _____."

4. *Plural*
   One animal, then two.
   "This is a kazh /kæʒ/. Now there is another one. There are two of them. There are two _____."

5. *Past Tense*
   Man swinging an object.
   "This is a man who knows how to rick /rik/. He is ricking. He did the same thing yesterday. What did he do yesterday? Yesterday he _____."

6. *Plural*
   One animal, then two.
   "This is a tor /tɔr/. Now there is another one. There are two of them. There are two _____."

7. *Derived Adjective*
   Dog covered with irregular green spots.
   "This is a dog with quirks /kwərks/ on him. He is all covered with quirks. What kind of dog is he? He is a _____ dog."

8. *Plural*
   One flower, then two.
   "This is a lun /lvn/. Now there is another one. There are two of them. There are two _____."

9. *Plural*
   One animal, then two.
   "This is a niz /niz/. Now there is another one. There are two of them. There are two _____."

10. *Past Tense*
Man doing calisthenics.
"This is a man who knows how to mot /mɑt/. He is motting. He did the same thing yesterday. What did he do yesterday? Yesterday he _____."

11. *Plural*
One bird, then two.
"This is a cra /krɑ/. Now there is another one. There are two of them. There are two _____."

12. *Plural*
One animal, then two.
"This is a tass /tæs/. Now there is another one. There are two of them. There are two _____."

13. *Past Tense*
Man dangling an object on a string.
"This is a man who knows how to bod (bɑd). He is bodding. He did the same thing yesterday. What did he do yesterday? Yesterday he _____."

14. *Third Person Singular*
Man shaking an object.
"This is a man who knows how to naz /næz/. He is nazzing. He does it every day. Every day he _____."

15. *Plural*
One glass, then two.
"This is a glass. Now there is another one. There are two of them. There are two _____."

16. *Past Tense*
Man exercising.
"This is a man who knows how to gling /glɪŋ/. He is glinging. He did the same thing yesterday. What did he do yesterday? Yesterday he _____."

17. *Third Person Singular*
Man holding an object.
"This is a man who knows how to loodge /luwdz/. He is loodging. He does it every day. Every day he _____."

18. *Past Tense*
Man standing on the ceiling.
"This is a man who knows how to bing /bɪŋ/. He is binging. He did the same thing yesterday. What did he do yesterday? Yesterday he _____."

19. *Past Tense*
A bell.
"This is a bell that can ring. It is ringing. It did the same thing yesterday. What did it do yesterday? Yesterday it _____."

20. *Progressive and Derived Agentive and Compound*
Man balancing a ball on his nose.
"This is a man who knows how to zib /zib/. What is he doing? He is _____. What would you call a man whose job is to zib?"

---

2. *Syntax and semantics.* It is easy and fun to replicate Hatch's study on the production and comprehension of different syntactic forms using time connectives including *before* and *after* (see page 18). You can use any available objects that would be interesting to the children and are the colors she specifies in the sentences. Children's blocks or small model cars are easy to use. There are two parts to the activity.

a. *Production.* Tell the child, "We are going to play the echo game. I will say something. Then you say it back to me. You will be my echo." Say the first sentence. Ask the child to say it back to you. Continue in the same manner with each item. Write down exactly what the child says.

b. *Comprehension.* Say, "I put some (blocks) on the table. I will say something. Do what I say with the (blocks)." Start with an example to be certain the child knows what to do. You could use an amusing action like "Put the red block on your head" for practice.

3. *Natural language sample.* Collect a sample of a child's natural language by having the child tell the story for a wordless picture book. A book that is especially engaging for most children is *Frog Goes to Dinner* by Mercer Mayer (1974). In the picture story, a boy's pet frog hops into his jacket pocket without the boy's knowledge. When the frog hops out in the fancy restaurant where the family has gone for dinner, he causes all kinds of hilarious chaos. If this book isn't available, refer to the list of wordless picture books provided in the chapter. After you have collected the sample, describe the child's form, content, and use of language and relate your findings to the information presented in the chapter. You could examine the language sample with these questions in mind as well.

a. What kinds of sentence structures was the child using?

b. Were there any overgeneralizations in language use in the telling? What do these suggest about possible new language learning?

c. Were there any other ways the language varied from standard usage? How? What more does this tell you about the child?

d. Were there any phonemes the child was confused about? What were they?

e. How did the child construct meaning for the book? Consider interpretation of pictures, examples of relating background knowledge to the story, and word choice, for example.

f. Where is the child in relationship to age mates? Is the child's language within a range of normalcy? What evidence supports your position?

4. *Practice giving feedback and providing language demonstrations.* Engage a child in an interesting activity and tape record your conversation. For example, you might enter the housekeeping corner pretending to be a guest for lunch and role play with the child. During the conversation, practice recasting sentences, making elaborations and extensions and modeling responses with the main goal in mind—communication. Transcribe your tape and then analyze the conversation by examining the appropriateness of your responses to the child's language and the result of your interaction. How well did you communicate? Keep in mind that experience does not give the whole picture. If you have time, try to have several other conversations with the same child throughout the semester or quarter to see if you observe any differences in the child's language and in your interaction over time.

Two

❀

Understanding Literature As a Base for the Language/Reading Curriculum

We don't achieve literacy and then give children literature; we achieve literacy through literature. . . . Stories are one of the best ways into literacy at the earliest stages of a child's development.

Huck (1989, pp. 258–259)

———

To clarify the reason for a separate chapter on literature in addition to the later chapter on reading, we must identify where these two concerns overlap and where they diverge. The most obvious overlap is that both literature programs and reading instruction are based on children's trade books. The term *trade book* as used here refers to an independent creation by an identified author and/or illustrator, not conceived as part of a sequence designed to teach. The purpose is to entertain or inform. In contrast, a textbook is part of a sequence designed to present a specific pattern of skills or organized body of knowledge.

Literature programs are based on trade books. Reading series, for the most part, are also heavily infused with selections from such books. While five years ago many such series were composed predominantly of stories written especially to teach specific skills, that is not usually the case today. Authors of current reading series now more typically select literature recognized by authorities as exemplary and use it to accomplish objectives of the reading program.

In this particular chapter, we shall not be concerned with a carefully organized sequence of experiences based on textbooks designed to teach children the skills of reading. Rather, we shall examine how sharing trade books with children, an integral activity in early childhood curricula, serves several purposes for young children. The literature program extends and enriches the child's oral language, encourages listening skills, and provides many cognitive and affective opportunities. It also lays a foundation for later, more concrete experiences—a reading program per se—that will help children develop the ability to read print. In fact, in some schools, literature programs that emphasize children interacting with whole books in order to comprehend and respond to what they have read are replacing more traditional sequential, skill-based reading programs.

In the kind of early childhood curriculum described here, literature is central to other language arts activities. It is still unfortunately true that in some classrooms literature is an "extra" to be enjoyed when other more serious responsibilities are finished. The child goes to literature after completing other tasks. This approach is illustrated in Figure 2-1. In contrast, in the program shown in Figure 2-2, literature forms a core from which other experiences can grow. While motivation to listen, speak, read, and write is not limited to literature, books nonetheless are central. With fine books as a core from which other language experiences can grow, the teacher is never at a loss for an effective departure point. Of what importance is regular contact with books? There are many reasons for encouraging young children to listen to books read or to read books themselves.

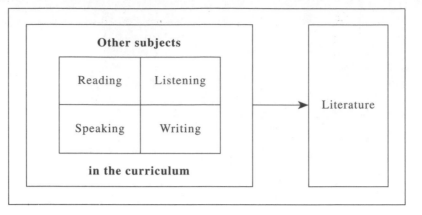

FIGURE 2-1

In more traditional approaches to the curriculum, literature isn't central to the language arts.

REASONS TO READ

The most obvious reason to read is simple enjoyment. Anyone who has ever had the pure sensuous pleasure of following a character through a set of experiences knows this delight. Children are intrigued with the exploits of the young rabbit in *Bailey Goes Camping* by Kevin Henkes (1985). Many youngsters have felt left out when older siblings do something they cannot; Bailey is no exception. Children listen with delight to find out how Bailey, with help from his parents, is able to go camping in his own way. The gentle, humorous watercolors about these personified animals are characteristic of many stories written and illustrated by Henkes. Stan (1991) provides a profile of this artist.

Older children respond enthusiastically to adventuresome *Miss Hickory* (Bailey, 1962). She is by no means as passive as the fact that she is a doll might suggest. Things happen *to* her, but her abilities to respond, to think, and to instigate make her a character young children find a delight.

This reason for reading isn't limited to fiction. We share poetry with children because they can respond so enthusiastically. No one could listen to "Mud" in the collection *Mud, Moon and Me* by Zaro Weil (1992) without laughing out loud about the wonderful sounds the poet develops to describe walking through mud. It isn't important that children understand all the words used. They can delight in the language, a flow of sound through time.

A second reason children read is for diversion from present situations. For many boys and girls, reading offers a temporary means of getting away from problems that may seem insoluble to them, though less than critical for adults. There is no reason to look down on this reason to read, to escape. Even adults need escape from the intensity of current problems, although too few know how effective reading can be in serving this purpose. As Leland Jacobs (1991) put it: "Literary reading can also help the young reader transcend the immediate and the mundane in his or her life" (p. 138).

Devoted readers read because books stimulate the imagination (Brooks, 1992). Effective fiction makes us wonder about the nature of a character, the look of an environment, the reason behind a twist of plot, or the nature of an unspecified outcome. There is much in *Super Cluck* (1991) to cause children to wonder. This is from an "I Can Read Book" series written by Jane and Robert O'Connor. This spritely science fiction mystery features Chuck Cluck, who is so strong he can sneeze the feathers off the other chickens and lift up the chicken coop with his wing. Inadvertently left behind when his egg rolls out of the space ship, Chuck is comfortable with the other more usual chicks, until a shadowy figure wreaks havoc in the henhouse. Using his detective skills, Chuck follows the intruder and in the end rescues the newly hatched chicks. The book is written in prose, although in the scene of the rat dancing around the fire while preparing to make his omelet, he speaks in rhymed poetry (reminiscent of the scene in Rumpelstiltskin). The pleasantly bright watercolor illustrations given definition by a firm black ink pen line are by Megan Lloyd.

Effective nonfiction stimulates us to wonder further as questions are answered and we think of new questions. An example is *Slippery Babies. Young Frogs, Toads and Salamanders* by Ginny Johnson and Judy Cutchins (1991). In three short chapters, the authors present fascinating information about frogs, toads, and salamanders, closing with a brief statement about the danger to these creatures of losing their habitats. Readers learn that among the several thousand bullfrog eggs laid, a "few" are lucky to hatch and survive. Toads can live to be 30 years old. Salamanders can regenerate a missing body part. These and other facts about this class of creatures are presented in clear, easy-to-follow prose, accompanied by equally clear full-color photographs. Young children

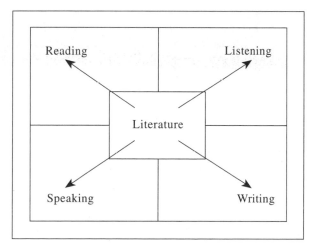

FIGURE 2-2

In the integrated, literature-based curriculum described here, literature is at the core of language arts instruction.

Children's appreciation of literature grows when they share favorite books with each other.

would be fascinated to hear the teacher relate some of these ideas while watching the creatures in the class terrarium.

Another reason we read is to understand ourselves and others. Children whose determination sometimes gets them in trouble can read the message about determination incorporated so skillfully into the saga of *Rufus M.* (Estes, 1943). Any youngster who has ever been thwarted by adults' rules will rejoice in Rufus's circumventing the rule that prevents him (at first) from getting a library card.

We also read to gain an understanding of others who are unlike ourselves. Young Lewis finds out what it is like to be old when he encounters Mr. Madruga in *A Likely Place* (Fox, 1967). He also finds out that, despite the disparity in their ages, they can be friends. A similar cross-generational contact is depicted in *Supergrandpa* by David M. Schwartz (1991), with illustrations in pleasant pastel watercolors by Bert Dodson. In an age when fewer and fewer children have contact with the elderly, such a story as this serves a useful purpose in telling about a 66-year-old Stålfarfar, or "Supergrandpa." He rode over 1,000 miles in Sverige-Loppet, the longest bicycle race in the history of Sweden, where the story is set. Children will learn incidental information about the country; for example, people take trains for long trips, they eat sour milk with lingonberries, and the country has a king and a palace. In a note following this fictionalized account of an actual person and event, the author points out that parents afterward encouraged their children to eat well, exercise, and live a healthy life, so they could "Va' som Stål-farfar," or be like Supergrandpa.

A teacher of Caucasian children expands their experience by reading *Cornrows* by Camille Yarborough (1979). The book celebrates the joy in the African American culture passed from living grandparents to growing children. Narrative and dialogue recount Great Granmaw fixing Mama's hair in cornrows, braids worn by a diversity of people. Native country, social status, and religious beliefs all were symbolized by different patterns. The book tells the history of peoples enslaved and brought to the New World, where the former symbol of pride became one of shame until brave black women reestablished the pride. The chalk drawings by Carole Byard, which depict black people with dignity, enjoying their heritage, are as effective as the prose. More recently, Angela Johnson has helped youngsters understand the similarities that bind us together, no matter the ethnic group, in *Do Like Kyla* (1990). All youngsters have felt the desire to be like an admired older sibling; Johnson explores this in words accompanied by James E. Ransome's thickly painted full-page pictures.

Children Learn Many Aspects of Language

Children also read to understand the *nature of language.* They learn, as the teacher reads or as they read to themselves, about oral and nonverbal language. Boys and girls learn about the dialects of people in different parts of our country in such books as *Strawberry Girl* by Lois Lenski (1945). The author reproduced in detail the dialect of the Florida Crackers, a group of Anglo-Saxon migrants from the Carolinas. At one point the small girl Essie comments: "Pa . . . iffen that cow laps her tongue around the new leaves, she'll twist the bark loose and pull it off. Do we stop her, she might could eat up all them orange trees."

In addition to books that contain American dialects, others use dialects from different countries. Among these is the British English dialect evident in *Alec and His Flying Bed* by Simon Buckingham (1990). Alec calls his mother "Mum," a term more common in England than here. When a neighbor sees him bringing the bed home, he asks, "Moving house, are you, lad?" Later, we get more examples of dialect: "Crikey!" said the man. "Blimey! What is this thing?" Later at supper they have "chips." This fantasy/dream theme picture book might be used to focus on the language differences. It could also serve as a stimulus for children to tell where they would like to travel if they could go anywhere in a dream.

Related to oral language is the nonverbal language that accompanies the spoken word. The author of *The Handmade Alphabet* (1991), Laura Rankin, introduces children to the language of signing with pastel full-page illustrations that show very simply, without a background, an object for each letter. The hands are shown large enough so children can easily see how to make the sign. Children could then be encouraged to learn to sign a word, perhaps their name. Children learn about the stylized gestures perfected by the mime in *The Marcel Marceau Alphabet Book* by George Mendoza (1970). People in other cultures also use gesture, sometimes in highly codified systems that have predetermined meanings, as shown in *You Don't Need Words!* by Ruth Belov Gross (1991).

In addition to oral and gestural language, students learn about *written* language, as when they can see the alphabet used by the Inuit (or Eskimo) people in *Arctic Memories* by Normee Ekoomiak (1988). The text describes daily life in Arctic Quebec, also depicted in paintings and fabric pictures by the author. Children can learn much about games, foods, religious celebrations, shelter, and hunting. In addition to the English text, the information is printed in Inuit. You might photocopy one section, enlarge it on a transparency, and ask children what observations they can make about the language. This book was named an Orbis Pictus honor book, an award given by the National Council of Teachers of English for distinguished nonfiction for children.

Children can see that written language can also be felt, as in *Redbird* by Patrick Fort (1988), in which the words are printed and also presented in Braille, the system of raised dots that blind people use to read. The pictures are also raised so that children can feel the outlines.

Second- and third-graders are old enough to be intrigued with the materials included in the boxed *Fun with Hieroglyphs* by Catharine Roehrig (1990), which includes a brief paperback book explaining how this symbol system worked, as well as twenty-four small, sturdily made stamps and an ink pad, so students can print out their own messages by combining symbols.

Another nonalphabetic way ideas are encoded is through a rebus, in which symbols (like a picture of an eye) stand for words (like *I*). This is illustrated in *Happy Thanksgiving Rebus* by David A. Adler (1991). A simple story told in rebus with full-page accompanying illustrations is followed by the story in conventional text alone. A three-page picture glossary is included. Or you might use *The Cinderella Rebus Book*, retold by Ann Morris with pictures by Ljiljana Rylands (1989). The text with symbols is spread out in different positions on the pages around the colored pencil illustrations. As in the Adler book, the rebus symbols in the glossary are presented in order of appearance.

Words Come to Life

Children can become aware of the qualities of words as they listen to books that play with words. Very young children will chuckle over the sprightly imagination in Patty Wolcott's *Pickle Pickle Pickle Juice* (1991), which plays with some of the words from the old "Peter Piper" rhyme.

Using just ten words, decorated with Blair Dawson's full-color art on every page, the author provides a listening experience that will have youngsters repeating the silly words with delight. The book, from a new series that all have this limited number of words, is especially useful for easing children into other longer but easy-to-read series. Wolcott's *Where Did That Naughty Little Hamster Go?* (1991), with pictures by Rosekrans Hoffman, and her *Eeeeeek!* (1991) in the same series are also useful for listening to language play. Read *Rain Makes Applesauce* by Julian Scheer (1964) to your young listeners, who will revel in the nonsense antic verses and the predictably repetitive refrain "and rain makes applesauce." Pleasant pastel watercolors are crammed with humorous details.

For older, primary-age students, you might use Eve Merriam's *Fighting Words* (1992) to diffuse a disagreement between children, and in the process intrigue them with unusual vocabulary. Young Dale and Leda decide to have a fight, and your young listeners can enjoy the delicious sounds of such words as *balderdash, blunderbuss,* and *booby,* among others. The advantages of such books that encourage language play have been described by Schwartz (1983).

Poems also illustrate the imaginative qualities of words. In the collection entitled *Eric Carle's Animals Animals* (1989), we find such poems as "Quack! Said the Billy Goat" by Charles Causley, in which the poet encodes in words the sounds made by over a dozen animals. Children will enjoy making the sounds as the teacher reads the poem, and this could develop further into a movement experience as children become each of the animals and move as they would move. Brilliantly colored illustrations of tissue paper stroked with additional paint and chalk colors decorate the pages of this collection, which includes over fifty poems by a variety of authors. The book, named an International Reading Association Teachers' Choice winner, also received an American Library Association Notable designation. This fine collection can heighten children's awareness that words are often used in ways that mean more than their literal meanings.

Children can also learn about other times and places. Boys and girls can travel through time to other eras in books that give insight into how people lived and the problems they may have encountered. Such books are available for even the youngest readers or listeners. *Thy Friend, Obadiah* by Brinton Turkle (1969) provides a vivid picture of the sights, smells, and sounds of Nantucket Island in the time of the Quakers. Children discover that Obadiah's problem is a common one, despite the remoteness of the time.

Children may travel to remote parts of our country and even more remote parts of the world in books that give a clear sense of another place. Children on the West Coast of the United States understand the appeal of the rocky shores of New England when their teacher shares the picture book *One Morning in Maine* by Robert McCloskey (1952), an author who captures with authenticity the reaction to a loose, then lost, tooth.

Authors provide penetrating glimpses into places and lifestyles in other countries, although children's sense of geography is not firmly established until they are older. Read *Ba-Nam* by Jeanne M. Lee (1987), which tells of a Vietnamese holiday that may at first seem strange to American youngsters. On Thanh-Minh Day, families visit the graves of their ancestors and burn incense and paper money for the deceased. Young Nan, for the first time taking part in this family celebration, climbs trees with her Keung. Caught by a thunderstorm, startled by the frenzied shrieking monkeys, and frightened by bats, the children are comforted by Ba-Nam. Nan learns how groundless her fears of the old groundskeeper were. In sedate contrast, third-graders get a detail-packed view of life in the Netherlands in *The Wheel on the School* by Meindert DeJong (1964), from the pen of a prolific author who writes remembrances of his own childhood.

Nonfiction Intrigues Children

Children read in quest of information. Often the facts in trade books are more compelling than similar material in texts. Trade books offer writers more freedom than do textbooks, which are usually conceived in sequential order, with concepts and vocabulary carefully controlled for maximum readership. Trade books can afford to be more selective in the concepts they present, more imaginative in the treatment of the subject, and more sophisticated in the vocabulary and language patterns they use. Information books correlate usefully with early childhood curriculum areas of social studies, math, science, art, and music.

Related to social studies, consider using *As the Crow Flies* by Gail Hartman (1991). This introduces the idea of maps as representations of experiences. In five simple segments (i.e., "As the eagle soars . . . ," "As the rabbit hops . . ."), we see each of the birds or animals in turn traveling a short route. This is depicted in individual pictures and then on a composite "map" by Harvey Stevenson. At the end, each composite map is in turn compiled into "The Big Map" showing all the five segments. The brightly attractive, uncluttered pages form a predictable rhythm in each segment, as each separate part of the route is shown, followed by the symbolic form. It would be interesting to use this as a pattern and have youngsters make their own maps. Some books, like this one, deal with a single concept, presenting supporting detail that enriches the basic idea. No story per se is told, but rather facts are marshalled to teach a concept.

In addition to learning about our own culture, an important strand of social studies programs is studying other cultures. *Corn Is Maize—The Gift of the Indians* by Aliki (1976) describes how Indians discovered and used corn. The simple, straightforward text also tells how corn came to be an important food throughout the world. Pictures by Aliki clearly show the sequence of planting, growing, and harvesting corn. To introduce this work to young children, a teacher could plan an experience with corn meal. If you are in a school where you can use the kitchen, make corn meal muffins with your children. Use a box mix, or get the corn meal and follow a recipe. If you cannot use the school kitchen, make corn meal muffins at home for children to eat during snack time.

Cooking experiences are useful contexts in which language develops. After beginning with corn meal muffins as described above, you could move into *Country Bear's Good Neighbor* by Larry Dane Brimner (1989), which includes a more complex recipe for children to make apple cake. The book is effective in motivating the thinking skill of predicting, and afterward children can use their own language to talk about the directions given, their listening skills in following the recipe steps, and their encoding skills in making pictures and adding words for an experience chart after baking and sampling the product.

There are many new math books that present complex concepts so young children can understand them. Telling time is a part of the early childhood curriculum, and *Time to . . .* by Bruce McMillan (1989) follows a kindergarten youngster throughout the day, from when he wakes in the morning until it's time to go to sleep. The clock's little hand counts each hour of Brian's day in this colorful photographic essay by McMillan, whose books are consistently full of realistic, clear pictures.

There is a plethora of such books from which to choose. *Off and Counting* by Sally Noll (1984) uses highly symbolic forms to teach the words *four, five,* and so on. Using a simplified two-dimensional artistic style, Nancy Hellen in *The Bus Stop* (1988) teaches the words *second, third, fourth,* and so on. In bright, highly intense colors, with dye-cut holes for the eyes, Lois Ehlert in *Fish Eyes* (1990) teaches simple addition (i.e., "2 jumping fish plus me makes 3"). In remarkably lifelike illustrations, Carol Schwartz shows youngsters the multiplication processes author Joy N. Hulme describes in *Sea Squares* (1991)—for example, "4 seals are quite complete, with 16 flippery feet." Children learn a lot about denizens of the sea, and the book could serve well as a model for students to make their own multiplication book about other animals.

There are an amazing variety of science books for young children. Some of these introduce children to the natural world around them, like Ann Schweninger's *Autumn Days* (1991), which has enough text so that teachers will need to read it to youngsters. It deals with human activities (i.e., preserving fruit), changes in animals (how crickets are affected), chemical phenomena (ways leaves change colors), and activities children can do (make a leaf wreath). The author/artist has arranged these ideas in different-sized panels on the page, and while sometimes the text is in blocks, at other times it is in speech balloons.

From *Sea Squares* by Joy N. Hulme, with illustrations by Carol Schwartz (Hyperion, 1991).

Schweninger's usual personified animals tell an interesting story, whether it reinforces what children experience—for those who live in a northern climate—or introduces a new experience—for children from a southern climate. Second- or third-graders could read this compact book themselves, although teachers of younger children might find it useful with their group.

Wasps at Home, with text and photographs by Bianca Lavies (1991), illustrates how effective books with large full-color photographs can be in helping young children experience something vicariously. Few children can get close enough to wasps to understand their body structure, nesting habits, larvae state, feeding patterns, and other aspects of the life cycle, shown here so dramatically. With photographs on nearly every page, many of them at least a half-page in size, Lavies shows viewers marvelously clear details usually unseen. The book is one in a series of superb photographic studies, which also includes books on armadillos and praying mantises. You could compare this book with the section in *Insect Metamorphosis. From Egg to Adult* by Ron and Nancy Goor (1990). The book includes extraordinary, large, full-color photographs that will intrigue child readers/viewers, including information on paper wasps and female braconid wasps. In these, as with other science books, the attempt is not to teach a lot of factual information in an organized, conscious way. Rather, the purpose is to capture children's interest, using the authors' ability to write interestingly about unfamiliar topics so children will want to learn more. The large photographs common in the best of this sort of book are guaranteed to attract and hold students' attention.

Art books for children are also plentiful. Some books deal with art elements, like *The Shapes Game* by Paul Rogers (1989), in which the abandoned, playful exploration in opaque, flat colors is reminiscent of the most lighthearted work of the French painter Henri Matisse. *Shapes* by Meredith Dunham (1987) ties children's developing awareness of this art element to language. The words for each shape are given in English, French, Spanish, and Italian. *Colors* by Philip Yenawine (1991) is from a series of four books that are remarkable for their clear language and the many full-color reproductions of art works. Some books about art cast their information in quasifictional format, like *Visiting the Art Museum* by Laurene Krasny Brown and Marc Brown (1986), which brings a family into contact with paintings by such artists as Pablo Picasso and Henri Rousseau. Similarly, in *Katie's Picture Show* by James Mayhew (1989), the youngster first sees and then enters paintings by such artists as John Constable and Pierre Auguste Renoir.

Finally, there are many music books worth sharing with children. These are of two types. The first is books that *include* music. Sometimes these contain a poem, illustrations, and music so children can sing the song. Author John Langstaff has done several of these for early childhood educators, like *Frog Went A-Courtin'* (1955). Marilyn Singer's *Will You Take Me to Town on Strawberry Day?* (1981) is another example. More recently, Chris Conover has added to this genre with her charmingly intricate pictures for *Froggie Went A-Courting* (1986), as has Carol Jones in providing illustrations for *This Old Man* (1990). In this book, a die-cut hole on one page encourages children to guess what is being talked about by looking through the hole to the following page. In both books, music is provided so teachers can teach the song to children. Primary-grade children enjoy learning some of the seven songs included in *The Diane Goode Book of American Folk Tales and Songs* (Durrell, 1989); the book includes tales from multiethnic sources. Full-piano accompaniments are provided in Ashley Bryan's *All Night, All Day* (1991), subtitled *A Child's First Book of African-American Spirituals*. Children will enjoy both the music and the cheerfully segmental paintings.

The second type is books that are *about* music. For example, *What Instrument Is This?* by Rosmarie Hausherr (1992) is a fine way to introduce children to the instruments of the orchestra. On the first page in each sequence, the instrument is described—for example, "What instrument looks like a shiny boa constrictor with a wide open mouth?" This opening section includes a full-color photograph of a child playing the instrument. The following page gives more complete factual information and shows an adult playing the instrument in a black and white photograph. The book includes common instruments like the guitar, and less well known ones like the bagpipe. These "Bags of Sound" and other instruments are also described in Neil Ardley's *Music* (1989) from a series called "Eyewitness Books." The full-color photographs are excellent, and teachers can paraphrase the text, which is more complex than children can read themselves. The advantages of using these and other kinds of books about music are described by Lamme (1990).

OUTCOMES OF LITERATURE PROGRAMS

In addition to the preceding reasons why children read, the teacher has other purposes in planning a literature program. These relate to aspects of literature and language of which children may be unaware. They form an additional rationale for implementing literature programs as central to the curriculum.

We read aloud to share with children their *literary heritage*. Literature, a reflection of culture, transmits the mores and values of society. In the process of reading to children, teachers share a literary legacy of value.

Folk tales, for example, transmit cultural values about conflicts between good and evil. Often these values are conveyed through stock characters who exemplify certain qualities. The evil stepmother, a recurring character, the jealous stepsister, the kindly father, the wicked witch, and the simpleton are characters used to teach specific values. In commenting about the usefulness of such stories, Chukovsky (1973) noted

> the value of such tales in developing, strengthening, enriching, and directing children's capacity for creative thinking and imaginative responses (p. 214).

He goes on to assert that

> the child who listens to fairy tales feels like an active participant and always identifies himself [*sic*] with those characters who crusade for justice, goodness, and freedom (p. 219).

Teachers have many tales available from the European tradition. An example is *Snow White* (1991), retold by Josephine Poole in a darkly elegant set of pictures by Angela Barrett, to which children will return again and again. In addition to retellings of such well-known tales, there are increasingly available editions of tales from other parts of the world. *The Orphan Boy* (1990) by Tololwa M. Mollel is an example. This tale from the Maasai people who live in Kenya and Tanzania is illustrated with full-page and larger paintings, including remarkable textures done by Paul Morin. Tales from Native American cultures are increasingly more available. *The Rough-Face Girl* by Rafe Martin (1992) is actually an Algonquin Indian version of Cinderella. The illustrations by David Shannon unobtrusively include much authentic detail.

In addition to reading aloud to an entire group as described above, teachers plan time to reread books, if not to the whole class, then to the small group of children who have asked to hear a story again. Research studies indicate that repeated stories generate (1) more talk, (2) more complex questions, (3) more in-depth responses, and (4) greater interest in reading the story independently (Morrow, 1988; Yaden, 1988).

A second major reason teachers plan literature programs is for the effect they have on *children's own language*. There is much evidence that children who are read to and who have access to quantities of literature develop earlier linguistically. In addition, such boys and girls develop more sophisticated language than children who are not read to regularly.

Chomsky (1972), on the basis of her study of children from the ages of 6 to 10, endorsed using literature in the language arts/reading curriculum.

> Results indicate that exposure to the more complex language available from reading does seem to go hand in hand with increased knowledge of the language. The child could be read to, not restricted to material deemed "at his level" to get out of them whatever he may. In general, . . . the effort should be toward providing more and richer language exposure, rather than limiting the child with restrictive and carefully programmed materials. In this way the child would be permitted to derive what is accessible to him from a wide range of inputs, and put it to use in his own way. This approach would seem to be more closely in accord with the nature of language acquisition (p. 3).

The preceding position statement is buttressed by several research studies indicating more specifically the types of language growth that occur when children are immersed in books. Students' *interest* in reading increases. Pfau (1966) directed a two-year program involving first- and second-graders. In addition to the regular basal reading program, students in the experimental classrooms participated in a forty-five-minute-per-day recreational reading program using a selection of 100 trade books housed in the classroom. A control group participated in the regular basal program. In all four measures of reading interest, the experimental group was significantly superior to the control group.

Students' *ability* in reading also increases. Porter (1969) had high school juniors read aloud to elementary-school children. The program showed positive results for both groups in the measures of reading achievement used.

Cohen (1968) assessed the impact of a program on *vocabulary* development and reading achievement for second-grade retarded, minority students of low socioeconomic status. After nine months, the experimental group improved significantly over the control group in word knowledge, quality of vocabulary, and reading comprehension. Huck (1992) also commented on the benefits of reading aloud on a regular basis.

In addition to the effects on reading and vocabulary identified above, exposure to literature appears to make a difference in children's writing ability (King & McKenzie, 1988). Children become more fluent writers as their exposure to literature increases.

Research studies have indicated some concrete types of growth that occur when children experience literature. Teachers need to use books that have richer language than the children themselves use, even though results may not always appear immediately. It is important to continue providing such language experiences even though there is no indication that the child understands or uses the language. There is research evidence that such linguistic experiences if "not attended or assimilated at the moment may be stored for retrieval at a later, more opportune time when the backlog of experience is sufficient to make them meaningful" (Stross, 1978, p. 755).

The Teacher As Book Selector

In such a program as this, one of the most critical teacher roles is that of book selector. When students can read or look at books on their own, we emphasize freedom of choice. In the organized group sharing we do with children, however, it is important that teachers choose fine books because students' own choices may not expose them to the best-quality literature. Critic/author Cameron (1976) believes the romantic notion of children's innate good taste is faulty. She doubts that most children, especially those who have not been exposed to a great deal of literature, can make intelligent aesthetic choices: "It would seem to me that children *generally* speaking in the early years have no particular taste as the word is applied to aesthetics. . . . When they are in good health they are small engines of energy . . . open to all appeals to the senses and extremely vulnerable to influence." As we expose children to the kinds of literature-based programs described in this book, we enable them to make increasingly sophisticated judgments about books.

A teacher's main responsibility is to read many different kinds of literature to children for many different purposes. We read all kinds of things to children because they tend to like what they have heard before (Fisher & Natarella, 1979). Teachers should read some less immediately popular forms of literature to classes, and then in the process these may become more popular. A related issue in selection is date of publication, as teachers seek a balance between old favorites and more recently published books. Throughout this book we have included many of our old favorites, which we imagine are books you already know. In addition, however, we have included many books published recently, in an effort to encourage you to share newer books for program balance.

Seeing Through Children's Eyes

In selecting books for children, it is important to try to see a book as they will see it. While it is obviously impossible for adults to respond as children will, to anticipate how children may respond is possible. Such an attempt may help us to avoid thinking that a book is excellent while children find it dull. Adults' reactions have often been notably off the mark. One writer reminds us of the difference between adult and child tastes in recalling "the initial reaction to Maurice Sendak's *Where the Wild Things Are* (1963), a book many adults decided would frighten the preschooler. Time has proved the adults wrong."[1] This author suggests that those who select books for children must read *reviews*, which are brief examinations of the strengths and weaknesses of individual books. Reviews can be found in such periodicals as *The Horn Book Magazine, School Library Journal, The New Advocate,* and *The Five Owls,* among others. These are often accumulated into collections, as in *The New York Times Parents' Guide to the Best Books for Children* (Lipson, 1988). In addition, teachers and librarians must read *critiques,* which set individual books in the context of other books of a similar type or in the total body of the writer's work. This is particularly evident in *Collected Perspectives: Choosing and Using Books for the Classroom* (Moir, Cain & Prosak-Beres, 1990).

A teacher uses reviews and critiques written by other adults and also his or her own judgment. Do *you* think a particular book is clever, self-consciously cute, or simply dull? Can you articulate—at least to yourself—why you think so?

A fine way to check your own perception is to compare it with the perception of the children you teach. A major focus in this program is eliciting responses to literature. Seeking candid responses to a book is not easy, but it is facilitated by the kinds of questions you ask. Do not ask children, "Did you like this book?" since the question is unlikely to elicit a useful response. Compliant children will dutifully nod their heads yes. The obstreperous boy or girl will say no simply to catch your attention.

Instead, when you have finished reading a book to children, simply say, "Tell me what you are thinking." This opens the way for a diversity of responses:

1. Relating the book to some personal experience
2. Relating the book to another they've heard[2]
3. Commenting on an unfamiliar or pleasant-sounding word
4. Expressing admiration for a character
5. Raising a question about what might happen next in the story

[1] See Mae Durham Roger, "Afterward: Creativity and Critics," in *Wilson Library Bulletin,* October 1978, pp. 170–171. The author also makes another provocative contention: that there are useful books, popular books, and fine literature, and few books are all three.
[2] Helping children think about a book in relation to another they've heard or read is what moves beyond experiences with isolated books into an integrated *program* of literature. Do this, for instance, by reading aloud an established favorite, *Mr. Grumpy's Outing* by John Burningham (1971), and then asking children to think about how it is similar to or different from Frank Asch's *Moonbear's Canoe* (1993). You could make a chart with children about their observations concerning these two related stories.

6. Reacting to the way the teacher read it
7. Expressing a personal like or dislike for the story
8. Asking to hear it read again

These by no means exhaust the responses you will get when you ask, "Can you tell me what you were thinking?" They do illustrate, however, why this approach is so much more productive than simply asking children if they enjoyed the story. Listening carefully to children's responses can help teachers see the book as children do.

Finding Quality Books

The dilemma of selecting the best from among the rest is pointed out by Hurst (1991), who comments: "We didn't like the hollow, made-for-easy-reading stories in old basals. We wanted more and better . . . reading materials . . . real literature." But as we find out, some new children's books are really just old basal-type stories masquerading in new clothing.

For example, *The King's New Clothes* (1987) by Patricia and Fred McKissack is wooden, simplified language that will not interest most readers. It is a truncated basal story in a separate cover. We must really look for more imaginative language than this eviscerated retelling includes. When basal reading series included stories like this, we deplored them. Just because they're now appearing as books, we must not be misled by them. Another trade book with this sort of impoverished language is *Cat Is Back at Bat* by John Stadler (1991):

> The cat is back at bat.
> An ape in a cape has a scrape.
> A shark hears a bark in a park.
> A raccoon will soon be on the moon.
> A pup in a cup goes up.

Yes, it is true that the words are embellished by the amusing drawings done by the author. But does this compensate for the paucity of language? We think not.

In contrast to this sort of thing, we look for books like *How Do You Make a Bubble?* by William Hooks (1992), which is strongly supportive of early efforts to read because of its predictable structure achieved through repeated sentences. The rhyming words make this an interesting story as well. Stories can be delightfully wacky, like *The Day the Goose Got Loose* by Reeve Lindberg (1990), with full-page, full-color illustrations by Steven Kellogg. Throughout this book-length narrative poem, the title is the repeated refrain, which children can say along with the teacher. Reading the print for these words follows naturally.

Using Literature with Children

Once the teacher has chosen good literature, the problem remains what to do with it. Enjoying literature for its own sake does not necessarily exclude having a closer look at it. A major task for teachers is to plan ways to engage children with literature. In fact, as one writer rather acerbically said, "Teachers cannot justify their salaries on the basis of being mere purveyors of stories" (Johnson, 1979). Those of us who work with students from the time they enter school until they leave the primary grades have many ways to elicit responses to books. With the very youngest children, these are limited to oral responses, but for older primary children, responses can sometimes be written.

Books and Sounds

A major way to interest children in the sounds around them is to read books that describe sounds. Many authors have incorporated environmental noises into their books in creative ways. In *Farmer Palmer's Wagon Ride* (1974), author/illustrator William Steig uses many aural words, including "zizzing-zazzing, and chirring-whirring of the heat charged insects" and the "dramberamberoomed" and "bom-BOMBED" sounds of the thunder.[3]

Another possibility is *Crocodile Beat* by Gail Jorgensen (1988), which is full of such sound words as "Quack Quack Quackity," "Boom-Boom-Boom-," and "Chitter-chatter Chitter-chatter Chitter-chatter." Each of the animals makes its own sound as they notice that the crocodile moves from awaiting his prey to doing something about it! Brilliantly colored tissue paper collages full of imaginative textures enhance the story line. Use such books with children. Then discuss with them why these words are effective aural descriptors. Or have boys and girls suggest other combinations of sounds they feel describe such environmental sounds as insects and thunder. What is the sound of a rushing brook? What words could we make up to recapture the sound of sandal soles slapping on cement? Look for books that allow children to make up their own sound words.

Oral Language

Children enjoy exploring ways they can use their voices. Conscious understanding of *pitch, stress,* and *juncture* (pause) can lead to more effective speaking. A way to begin developing verbal flexibility is to have

---

[3] Many helpful suggestions about "Classroom Uses for the Books of William Steig" are given by Richard F. Abrahamson in *The Reading Teacher,* December 1978, pp. 307–311. Each of Steig's books is annotated, and specific suggestions for using the books are included.

children experiment with sounds. This can often be done in the context of a piece of literature. Try reading *The Doorbell Rang* by Pat Hutchins (1986) to your children. There is much dialogue in this book, which can be a context within which to explore these three elements of paralanguage. After sharing the entire story with your children, modeling the effective use of pitch, stress, and juncture, select a few sentences and explore how they might be said differently by different people. For example, "Perhaps you'd better eat them before we open the door" can be said in a variety of ways, depending on which of the words is emphasized. The sentence sounds different if the stress is on the word *perhaps,* on the word *you'd,* on *before,* or on *open.*

In addition to such stories, choose some books that encourage children's participation through cumulative rhymes boys and girls can say with you. After sharing books that contain repeated refrains, move on to books that include more complex cumulative rhymes. In these, a brief one- or two-line verse is added to each succeeding repetition until a lengthy story is accumulated.

Such a cumulative rhyme is found in *The House That Jack Built* by Jenny Stow (1992), which is accompanied by imaginative, casual pictures that depict this old rhyme in a new setting: the Caribbean where the illustrator lived. An even more complex accumulation of ideas is presented in *The Ornery Morning* by Patricia Brennan Demuth (1991), which is an example of a *chaining* tale. It all begins when Rooster refuses to crow. Because of that, Mama Cow refuses to give milk, Hen refuses to lay an egg, Horse refuses to pull the rake, and so on. This

From *The Ornery Morning* by Patricia Brennan Demuth, with illustrations by Craig McFarland Brown (Dutton, 1991).

accumulates to a seven-line verse, at which point Daughter thinks of a solution to reverse the chain and get the animals to cooperate. The illustrations by Craig McFarland Brown are done in a watercolor wash, given definition by an overlay of many small black ink dots indicating shadow and texture. Another example of a chaining tale that is useful in helping children understand this concept is *Hugh Can Do* by Jennifer Armstrong (1992), in which young Hugh wants to go to the city to make his fortune but doesn't have a coin to pay the tollbooth man. By trading goods and services with a variety of people, all linked together, he's able to accomplish his goal.

Children will delight in saying such verses with you as you read, repeating whatever they can remember. Some children will repeat most of the lines; others will recall only a word or two. It makes no difference because each will benefit from the experience of being involved actively with the literature instead of simply listening passively.

Such predictable rhymes or stories are useful in beginning reading. Although the activity is primarily oral, at times teachers provide print copies for children to follow along. Because sections are repeated over and over, boys and girls can begin to identify these recurring sections in print, giving them a positive feeling that they can read. Following along the print as they say the repeated refrain enhances students' understanding of the relationship between speech and print.

Choral Reading

Begin choral reading very simply with young children, who will enjoy saying a single line with you. One author tells of having boys and girls in a day care center say with her, "Eeee! The [animal's name] is really old."[4] Each segment of the Ghanaian animal fable she told closes with this line. By the time the segment is over, children will know which animal name to insert as they say chorally the single line. In contrast, late-primary-age children can easily be involved in an oral interpretation of *Molly Whuppie*, retold by Walter de la Mare (1983). Fluent readers can take the roles of Molly, the giant, his wife, and the King (reading from parts the teacher makes by photocopying and highlighting with marker what the children are to speak). Then all the children can be involved in saying the two repeated refrains. Provide time for children to study these illustrations individually. The highly stylized full-color pictures by Erroll Le Cain are full of fascinating details that need to be seen close up.

[4] See Stella Dennis (1979), "Tell an African Fable with Your Children's Help," *First Teacher*, *1*(5), 6. Published monthly, this tabloid-size newspaper features recurring columns written by teachers of young children, illustrated with photos. Graphics show practical ideas about things to make. Write to *First Teacher*, P.O. Box 13081, Fort Lee, NJ 07024.

Dramatizing

Children can also respond to literature using both their voices and their bodies as they dramatize poems or stories. You could use a book like *Sometimes I Feel Like a Mouse* by Jean Modesitt (1992), and ask children to move like the "horse galloping," the "squirrel skittering," and the "swan floating," among others in this book that explores feelings. Children enjoy being the spider and Miss Muffett in the simple poem. Or use "Over in the Meadow," which features a variety of animals. Half the children can dramatize the animal movement, while the other half can say the poem with the teacher. Longer than poems, many short stories also contain opportunities for dramatizing. A particularly appropriate story is *Annabelle's Un-Birthday* by Steven Kroll (1991). Second-grader Annabelle is suffering first-day jitters before going to her new school; looking forward to going to her grandmother's after school provides something secure to hold on to. Although the day at school is quite pleasant, Annabelle gets herself in a predicament, which Grandmother helps her solve; in the process she teaches her granddaughter an important lesson in honesty. This humorous account of a commonplace event and its uncommon outcome provides many opportunities for dramatizing. The actions include: laying out clothes for the next day, eating breakfast before going to school, opening the door to the new room, painting in the art class, getting in the elevator to go up to Grandmother's, passing the dishes of ice cream, and playing hide and go seek, among others. Children can pantomime each of the actions as the teacher reads the story. Then let the students redo the sequence of action to see whether they can tell the story without words. Another base for dramatization is *The Witch's Hat* by Tony Johnson (1991), which includes a repetitive text and easy language. More suggestions about dramatizing and choral reading are included in Chapter 4.

Visual Responses

Some books present visual challenges to children. Illustrators sometimes hide objects for children to find. One example is *The Adventures of Simple Simon* by Chris Conover (1987), a visual interpretation of the tradition rhyme. Use this as a group experience to develop visual acuity, as children look for and then talk about what they have observed in the pictures. This artist does remarkably detailed, realistic illustrations of many small animals, and children are intrigued to notice the types of animals depicted, the costumes they are wearing, and the objects they are using.

Another more elaborate visual search is motivated by *Three Jovial Huntsmen* by Susan Jeffers (1973). A generous-sized double-page spread provides the adaptor/illustrator with ample space to show the three obtuse huntsmen. In their proper British hunting attire, they search high and low, missing myriad denizens of the forest. Rabbits, quail, opossums, and others are skillfully tucked into the detailed black ink drawings with pleasant watercolor wash. Children chuckle over the hunters' lack of observation skills as they themselves find what the hunters cannot.

Some books of nonfiction also encourage children to look carefully for what is hidden in the pictures. For example, in *Look! The Ultimate Spot-the-Difference Book* by April Wilson (1990), the illustrator shows viewers twelve different regions of the world. Each of the two facing illustrations is slightly different from the other. Sometimes the difference is in the large center illustration; at other times it is in the smaller panels that border each center picture. Children will, in the process of hunting for differences, incidentally learn much information about various climates because of these exact renderings. This book is fine for sharpening children's observation skills. At the back of the book a color-coded diagram shows each of the differences.

Other suggestions for visual and plot comparisons are given in a useful small paperback by Coody (1992).

COMPARISON ACTIVITIES

Plot-pattern comparisons are useful to sharpen children's perceptions about variation in literature. One author (Scott, 1978) suggested that aesthetic awareness develops as children realize that stories are more than their outlines and that home—away—home again is a recurrent pattern. Probably the best known of such stories is *Where the Wild Things Are* (Sendak, 1963), although many stories follow this pattern. Two are *Daisy* by Brian Wildsmith (1984) and *The Star Grazers* by Christine Widman (1989). In *Daisy,* the author/illustrator uses an old device, the half-page inserted between two full ones, which—when flipped—advances the action. This time Wildsmith works in a large (9¼″ × 12″) format, telling the tale of a cow that has wanderlust. Quite a different story, though the same pattern, is evident in *The Star Gazers,* an account of young Jacob's fantasy adventure high in the sky. Read a pair of such stories to students. Have them list the plot sequences on the board so the plots can be compared. Moss (1984), in a book of literature-based units useful for teachers, provides many questions a teacher can use to help children think about ways in which stories are like and unlike each other. She feels that comparing stories, helping children discover relationships, is important so that children can eventually take over the responsibility for asking themselves questions about literature. Her literature units provide many interesting possibilities for teachers of young children.

Studying the Book

How does a book get made? Anyone who has ever watched an author or illustrator talk with children knows how fascinated children are with this process. A unit study of *The Book* is a valuable experience for young children. Introduce this by bringing in many different kinds of books: a replica of an early American hornbook, a pop-up book (Noelle Carter, 1991), a Braille book, (Virginia Allen Jensen and Polly Edman, 1979), a shape book (Moira Kemp, 1991), a scroll book, and an accordion-fold book (Marie Angel, 1991). Using these for motivation, identify with children the parts of a book, providing such terminology as *binding, endpaper, spine,* and *title page.* Then use an array of picture books to help children notice differences in size, shape, placement of illustrations and type face, and style of illustration. Following this, the teacher can share rudimentary information about how a book is manufactured.

There are now books and other media that describe the process of book production. "How a Book Is Made" shows artist Ann Grifalconi as she created the art for her book, *The Ballad of the Burglar of Babylon* (available from Media Plus, Inc., 60 Riverside Dr., New York, NY 10024). Three filmstrips are accompanied by records dealing with the topics of *Editorial Art Production, Printing,* and *Binding.* Ali Mitgutsch (1986) describes the process in *From Picture to Picture Book.* For older children *A Book Takes Root. The Making of a Picture Book* by Michael Kehoe (1993) offers a more complete description of the processes involved, augmented with close-up full-color photographs.

Composing

Both oral and written composing by children can grow from experiences with literature.

To involve children in oral composing, you might use a book such as *Sitting in My Box* by Dee Lillegard (1989). Read and enjoy this with your children; then use the pattern it provides for children's own composing. The pattern is:

> Sitting in my box.
> An _____ knocks.
> "Let me, let me in."
> So we both move over.

After saying this the way the author wrote it, ask children to substitute the names of other animals that could be used. The large-scale, closeup pictures by Jon Agee are a pleasant accompaniment to this simple text that is useful to oral composing.

Upper-primary children should on occasion be given opportunities to write based on a piece of literature. Children in second and third grades tried their hand at parallel-plot construction (Stewig, 1977). Their teacher read them a version of "The Gingerbread Boy," and together they listed the plot elements on the chalkboard. Children then wrote their own stories following the pattern presented in the original story.

An Integrated Approach

This chapter has considered literature as integral to the language arts curriculum in early childhood. This concept was presented as a separate chapter to facilitate a detailed consideration of literature, although the program recommended is one that integrates many types of language experiences. In the following chapters, each area of the language arts is treated separately. This is done, again, merely to provide a depth of focus. It is not to suggest isolated time periods devoted to listening, speaking, reading, and writing. The most successful programs integrate the language arts to create a unified learning experience in which children's language grows naturally from topics of interest to them.

Integrating language arts is not a new idea, although until whole language enthusiasts began championing it, curricular integration was not widespread. Some time ago, Harbert and Reed (1977) described how they integrated literature into their classrooms. Children's interest was motivated by a display of books about the topic of time. Both children's and adult books were included, with the latter providing many illustra-

Daily opportunities to read and explore good literature should be a part of every early childhood program.

tions for study even though the texts themselves were too difficult for boys and girls to read. Construction activities in the woodworking area and in the art room involved listening to directions, discussing projects orally, and then writing accounts of how clocks and sundials were made. A classroom visitor (the owner of a clock shop) and a field excursion (to the bell tower of a college campus) similarly demanded several language skills. Children wrote information pieces (including metric measurements) about processes involved in making clocks. They also wrote imaginative compositions involving time.

These teachers had a clear understanding of how listening, speaking, reading, and writing skills can develop in an environment in which children are studying many facets of a topic. The impulse is strong to use each skill, to gather information, to plan together, to record what was done, and to express ideas imaginatively. It is a far more natural, more meaningful way to master language competencies than is learning in isolation. In the next chapters we shall examine each of these areas separately in order to emphasize fully the possibilities that exist. No attempt should be made to schedule separate blocks of time for each area in the early childhood curriculum.

Communicating with Parents

Our major concern here is with how teachers can use books as an integral part of the curriculum in school settings. We cannot assume children come to school with a rich background in literature; that is an ideal but not common experience. Rather, we need to ensure that the curriculum we provide is book-rich.

Another responsibility is to communicate to parents the importance of books in the lives of their children. Part of a teacher's efforts is devoted to educating parents about the importance of books. One way to do this is to talk informally with parents during conferences or when they are visiting the classroom about the kinds of learning books stimulate. Another way might be to do a program for the parent-teacher group about books. A fine film to use is *What's So Great About Books?* (available from Cypress Films, P.O. Box 4872, Carmel, CA 93921). This demonstrates in convincing fashion the need to begin early. The main focus is on simple, inexpensive techniques for sharing books with children, techniques open to all parents. The critical nature of this informal sharing and its effects on success in reading is discussed. The book by Allison and Weston (1993) is a particularly effective one to recommend to parents. The kinds of informal literacy play it advocates emphasize the importance of literature.

Teachers may hesitate to advocate much involvement with books for parents in lower socioeconomic classes because of the high cost of hardback books. While it is true that production costs of such books have priced them beyond the reach of many parents, most publishing companies also sell paperbacks. Parents usually can afford these modestly priced books. A simply worded letter to parents which children can take home might be helpful in encouraging book ownership. One author has effectively extolled the virtues of paperback books:

> When a book doesn't cost much to begin with, it can be rolled up and carted around in a pocket, words can be underlined and pictures embellished with a pencil or crayon. . . . [The book] can be loved and totally enjoyed in whatever manner the child wishes. Inevitably, it will become torn, dog-eared or even lost, yet this will not cause friction between you and your child.[5]

The following list gives several paperback book clubs teachers can use in the classroom to encourage book ownership.

1. The Best Book Club Ever
   61 Jericho Turnpike
   Jericho, NY 11753 — Ages 2–7

2. Carnival Book Club
   P.O. Box 6035
   Columbia, MO 65205-6035 — Grades K to 2. No obligation to order; bonus points for certain dollar amounts ordered; hardcover and paperback

3. Grow-With-Me Book Club
   Garden City, NY 11503 — Ages 2–7

4. I Can Read Book Club
   1250 Fairwood Avenue
   Columbus, OH 43216 — Ages 4–8

5. Junior Library Guild
   100 Pine Avenue, Dept. CNA
   Holmes, PA 19043 — Seven categories, including preschool, primary, easy reading, and intermediate; hard cover

6. Parents' Magazine's Read Aloud and Easy Reading Program
   Box 161
   Bergenfield, NJ 07621 — Ages 4–8

7. Scholastic Book Services
   Write for their *Reader's Choice* catalog, including books in paperback and book and record combinations — Ages 6–8

[5] See DayAnn McClenathan, "An Open Letter to Parents," *Early Years,* November 1979, p. 33. You might paraphrase some of the many valid ideas this author includes in language appropriate to the educational background of the parents to whom you are writing.

8. Weekly Reader Children's Book   Ages 5–7
   Club
   1250 Fairview Avenue
   Columbus, OH 43216

In addition, teachers can support children's librarians in public libraries, who often make special efforts to get children signed up for their own library cards.

SUMMARY

Children's language grows from within and from without. As Chapter 1 suggested, teachers who are aware of the amount of language children bring to school can enhance boys' and girls' language potential. By planning experiences that involve students in using oral and written language to question, organize, reflect, and respond, teachers develop the language within.

Another cornerstone of language development is language from without. The teacher's language model, also mentioned in Chapter 1, is an example of an external motivation to language growth. Another rich source is children's literature, the focus of this chapter. The basic premise of the program described in this book is that literature for young readers forms a core from which other language experiences can grow.

Children can read (or listen) for enjoyment, to escape, for the imaginative stimulation that results, to understand themselves and others, to gain understanding of language, to learn about other times and places, and in quest of information. Teachers plan literature-based language arts/reading programs for other outcomes, which include an understanding of the literary heritage. As a result of such a program, teachers notice increased linguistic ability as children's vocabulary, reading interests, and reading achievement expand.

A critical task in such a program is book selection, as we read reviews of books and compare these with our own and with children's reactions.

Having chosen a good piece of literature, we decide what to do with it. Sometimes we seek oral participation, using books that encourage children to use their voices in creating sound effects or say part of a refrain with the teacher. More extended experiences in choral reading are also possible. Such verbal involvement leads naturally to informal dramatization. Teachers also use books for developing visual sensitivity, as boys and girls look at an illustration or a pair of pictures and then use oral language to describe what they see and how such stimuli are alike or different. Both oral and written composing can also grow from experiences with books.

Such activities as these were described separately in this chapter to emphasize the many possibilities available. Separate chapters about such discrete language activities as listening, speaking, and composing are also included in this book. This chapter closes, however, with the strong position statement that an integrated approach is the most logical one during the early childhood years. Any book can be the core for a unified variety of experiences in which students will listen, speak, read, and write if the book has been wisely chosen. There is no need for separate time blocks when teachers develop their ability to see and develop myriad possibilities that interrelate with one another.

Suggestions for Further Study

1. The contention in this chapter is that reading series today include the work of respected authors. Take a basal book at your grade level in each of two series. Make a list of authors from the table of contents. Compare this list with the index of names in such standard works about children's literature as *Children's Literature in the Elementary School* by Charlotte S. Huck and colleagues (Fort Worth, TX: Harcourt Brace Jovanovich, 1993) or *Children and Books* by Zena Sutherland (Glenview, IL: Scott, Foresman, 1986). How many of the authors of selections in the basal series books are recommended in books about children's literature?

2. Use the film *The Mime of Marcel Marceau* (Learning Corporation of America, 711 Fifth Ave., New York, NY 10022). It is a fine introduction to *The Marcel Marceau Alphabet Book*, mentioned in this chapter. On successive days, make a list with your boys and girls of words for a particular letter of the alphabet, as done in the book. Stress verbs that begin with that letter. Then let children choose a word from the list you have made and pantomime it for the rest of the children to guess.

3. A variety of fairy tales can help students identify likenesses and differences. Some parents (and early childhood educators) wonder about using such folk literature with children because of the violence in the tales. Clearly the most impressive statement about this issue is Bruno Bettelheim, *The Use of Enchantment: The Meaning and Importance of Fairy Tales* (New York: Knopf, 1976). Another examination of this issue is presented by Carl-Heinz Mallet in *Fairytales and Children* (New York: Schocken Books, 1984). Read what these authors have to say. Do you agree or disagree? Why?

4. Children's book critics are not always infallible. (See the comment in the chapter about the initial reviews of *Where the Wild Things Are*.) Look up reviews on Sendak's latest book. You could use recent issues of *Book Review Digest* (published ten times per year by H. W. Wilson Company, 950 University Avenue, Bronx, NY 10452). This resource

will tell you where the Sendak reviews appeared. Read the book itself, and compare your own reaction with that of the reviewers. Be sure to include reviews from such educational periodicals as *Language Arts* and such literary periodicals as *The Horn Book Magazine*.

5. The chapter recommends using a particular version of *The House That Jack Built,* although others with illustrations by different artists are available. Find at least three different versions to use with children. Share each, and ask boys and girls to tell you which they prefer and why. What insights can you gain about students' visual preferences from this experience? This process is described more fully in "Book Illustration: Key to Visual and Verbal Literacy" by John Warren Stewig in *Using Literature in the Elementary Classroom* (Urbana, IL: National Council of Teachers of English, 1989, pp. 52–74).

6. Try using poetry as a base for choral reading. Ideas for how to begin are included in "Choral Reading: Who Has Time? Why Take Time?" by John Warren Stewig (Arlington, VA: ERIC Document Reproduction Service No. 165 110, October 1978). Many usable poems are included in *To The Zoo* by Lee Bennett Hopkins (Boston: Little, Brown, 1992).

Suggestions for Further Reading

Bettelheim, B. (1969, March). The care and feeding of monsters. *Ladies Home Journal*, p. 48.

This article is an interview between this leading proponent of the psychoanalytic approach and three mothers who represent varying concerns about monster books. Bettelheim is skeptical about books that offer monsters, believing children who read these feel they are in control of the monsters. One mother raises the question of whether picture books portray worse monsters than children may have in their own minds. Bettelheim explains his feeling that old-fashioned fairy tales (which came out of an adult's fantasy) are more valid than modern stories (which represent adults' views of what a child's fantasy is). The article is interesting for Bettelheim's comments on Maurice Sendak's *Where the Wild Things Are*.

Bettelheim, B. (1977). *The uses of enchantment. The meaning and importance of fairy tales.* New York: Vintage Books.

A brilliant, albeit idiosyncratic tour de force, this book describes the author's psychoanalytic view of why fairy tales are absolutely necessary for young children. His analysis of tales (some familiar, but others quite unfamiliar to most readers) is heavily sexually oriented. His recommendation of the original, not the expurgated, version will concern some early childhood educators. Nonetheless, the thinking is incisive. His point that the tales are unreal but not untrue is a subtle distinction but a significant one. His indictment of modern writing for children may help lead teachers away from some of the shallow stories for boys and girls into more significant literature.

Burke, E. M. (1977, November). *Fascinating children with words through trade-books.* A paper presented at the Annual Meeting of the National Council of Teachers of English. Arlington, VA: ERIC Document Reproduction No. 149 362.

The author begins by contending that great literature is more than the sum of its parts. Children are fascinated by the poetic elements of English (rhyme, rhythm, alliteration) and by wordplay. To choose literature solely by these elements, however, defeats the purpose of selecting good books. When these elements are present in a book in addition to a good plot, children can reflect upon the language. The ability to reflect upon language, called *metalinguistic awareness*, is encouraged when sounds and letters intrigue the ear and eye because they are audibly and visually pleasing.

Among recommended books rich in alliteration is Mary L. O'Neill's *What Is That Sound?* (New York: Atheneum, 1966). Among books mentioned that are rhythmic is Maurice Sendak's *Chicken Soup with Rice* (New York: Harper & Row, 1962). Rhyme makes literature a "participatory sport rather than a spectator one" as children are encouraged to join in with a rhyming response.

Other types of specialty books include alphabet books, which show children the components of language, and books that demonstrate peculiarities of words, such as Eve Merriam's *Small Fry* (New York: Knopf, 1965), which presents the names of baby animals. Specific books containing antonyms, synonyms, and homonyms are also suggested.

Engelhardt, T. (1991, June). *Reading may be harmful to your kids. Harper's Magazine*, pp. 55–62.

Although this article doesn't deal specifically with books for early childhood, it does provide many insights into publishing in general. The author opens by documenting the doubling of children's titles published yearly and the quadrupling of sales. He then goes on to raise his issue: What is it that children are reading? His analysis of children's bestseller lists, reflecting a mall culture, is that the books are deficient in such literary elements as setting, characterization, and style. The culture, which views children's books as a product to be marketed, has fueled a boom different from the book boom of the 1960s, when federal money directed to libraries in fact stimulated new authors to explore new topics with imagination. The current boom is stimulated by publishing executives who were raised on television. It caters to parents who are also accustomed to the homogenized plots of television. The current book boom is dominated by series books designed for girl readers, characterized by two-dimensional characters following predictable adventures that always end happily. Cranked out to specifications that don't allow for individual creativity, these series are as bland as fast food and reflect, in Engelhardt's view, a depressing bleakness.

The author contrasts the conditions today with the ferment of the 1960s, when writers such as S. E. Hinton, Virginia Hamilton, and Louise Fitzhugh came to prominence. The writers of individual—not series—novels, like Gary Paulsen, are today forced to take on the characteristics of series novels in order to compete in the marketplace. Many of the plots of even fine novelists thus become disturbingly similar to scripts for soap operas. All of this is directly the result of an adult culture that sees children primarily as consumers and caters to children who see themselves as consumers. As children's book publishing burgeons, children grow up with "junior versions of adult products, adult anxieties, adult fears, and adult shadows," but these are carefully controlled, systematized, and sanitized so children never really encounter genuine adults. The author feels it is indeed children who are thus the losers.

Fisher, M. (1975). *Who's who in children's books.* New York: Holt, Rinehart & Winston.

If you don't know who Edward Ardizzone, Peter Asbjornsen, and Aesop are, this compact paperback reference will tell you. Ardizzone is the illustrator of *Tim All Alone,* Asbjornsen is the collector of the tales in *East of the Sun and West of the Moon,* and Aesop is the obscure Greek slave who collected and retold the brief animal tales called fables. This type of knowledge is of itself of limited usefulness, but the related commentary in each entry is compelling reading. The book provides plot synopses, fascinating evaluative comments, and the author's personal responses to books.

Hirsch, E. D., Jr. (1991) *What your first grader needs to know.* New York: Doubleday.

From a series of resource books extending through sixth grade, this outlines what Hirsch and his committee of teachers and administrators consider fundamental in six areas: language arts; geography; world and American civilization; fine arts, at only nineteen pages the shortest section in the book; mathematics; and natural sciences. Hirsch is careful to state and restate that this is "not meant to be the whole of the school curriculum," nor is the content included to be "stressed above other forms of knowledge." Despite this reasonable caveat, many will misinterpret his attempt to identify the common knowledges to which he feels all children should have access. Making sure that all children, minorities included, have access to this learning, which he sees as critical to success, is more democratic than current approaches that overlook the fact that advantaged children come to school knowing much of this material. He points out that given an average 180-day school year, using just fifteen minutes a day, a teacher could go over everything in the book three times. This is not simply a text-only approach; throughout the book Hirsch includes simple suggestions for activities to involve children in hands-on experiences. The literature section includes Mother Goose rhymes, stories, fables, and myths.

Horner, C. T. (1978). *The single-parent family in children's books.* Metuchen, NJ: Scarecrow Press.

Annotated bibliographies of children's books dealing with specific topics are plentiful. This is typical of the best available. Children in intact families can read about children unlike themselves; those growing up in single-parent families may gain insights and reassurance as they read about children in similar situations.

Horner analyzed the content of over 200 books that deal with single parenthood resulting from death, divorce, prolonged absence, illegitimacy, and orphans/wards of the court. The annotated titles are classified by cause, predominant parent, author, subject, and suggested grade level. Also included is a multimedia bibliography of related materials.

Livingston, M. C. (1974, March). Children's literature—In chaos, a creative weapon. *The Reading Teacher,* pp. 534–539.

The author opens with the assumption that disorder and confusion mark our times. A nostalgic view of the "good old days" is not helpful, either personally or in books, because it is unrealistic. She points out that literature that launders Mother Goose or fairy tales, deleting what adults find scary or harmful, actually does children a disservice. Modern stories that present bland conflicts in which good always prevails are similarly unhelpful. These deprive children of knowing that "there are matters of courage, or fortitude . . . available to them to fight the evils which exist."

The converse of the type of book described above is the new approach in which "all values of the past have been thrown overboard. . . . Any sort of language, and/or diction, is permissible—any sort of morbid situation . . . is presented." The author sees this new trend as destructive.

In between these two positions, she suggests we cease to think of the "right" book for children and seek instead to match the book with the child for whom it is appropriate. Eschewing prescriptivism, Livingston suggests we must seek books that allow children their rights of private discovery and passionate digression.

Travers, P. L. (1975). On not writing for children. *Children's Literature, 4,* 15–22.

The respected author of *Mary Poppins* reflects on why she writes and speculates on the reason other authors write. She concludes that few authors consciously write specifically for children. She argues eloquently that labeling books for specific age levels is ridiculous, for who can judge what child will be moved by what book and at what age?

Walker, George H., Jr., & Kuerbitz, Iris E. (1979, Summer). Reading to preschoolers as an aid to successful beginning reading. *Reading Improvement,* pp. 149–154.

This study grouped thirty-six students in grades 1 through 3 according to the frequency with which they heard stories (every day, every other day, or once per week). It was found "that more frequent reading to preschoolers resulted in greater personal interest in storytime activities." Furthermore, those children who participated in frequent and regular storytime experiences throughout their preschool years had greater success in beginning reading than those children with infrequent storytime experiences.

References

Allison, L., & Weston, M. (1993). *Wordsaroni. Word play for you and your preschooler.* Boston: Little, Brown.

Brooks, B. (1992). Imagination, the source of reading. *The New Advocate, 5*(2), 79–85.

Cameron, E. (1976). A question of taste. *Children's Literature in Education, 21,* 59.

Chomsky, C. (1972, February). Stages in language development and reading exposure. *Harvard Educational Review,* pp. 1–33.

Chukovsky, K. (1973). The battle for the fairy tale: Three stages. In V. Hamilton (Ed.), *Children and literature. Views and reviews* (pp. 213–220). New York: Lothrop, Lee & Shepard.

Cohen, D. H. (1968, February). The effect of literature on vocabulary and reading achievement. *Elementary English,* pp. 209–217.

Coody, B. (1992). *Using literature with young children* (4th ed.). Dubuque, IA: Brown.

Fisher, C. J., & Natarella, P. A. (1979). Of cabbages and kings of what kinds of poetry children like. *Language Arts, 56*(4), 381–385.

Harbert, M., & Reed, M. (1977, October). Language and learning through authentic experiences. *Insights into Open Education,* pp. 6–11.

Huck, C. S. (1989). No wider than the heart is wide. In C. S. Huck & J. Hickman (Eds.), *Children's literature in the classroom: Weaving Charlotte's web* (pp. 251–262). Needham Heights, MA: Christopher-Gordon.

————. (1992). Literacy and literature. *Language Arts, 69*(7), 520–526.

Hurst, C. O. (1991). Digging deeper in literature. *Teaching K–8, 21*(1), 70–72.

Jacobs, L. B. (1991). Teaching the language arts. *Teaching K–8, 21*(1), 138–139.

Johnson, T. (1979). Presenting literature to children. *Children's Literature in Education, 10*(1), 35–43.

King, M. L., & McKenzie, M. G. (1988). Research currents: Literary discourse from a child's perspective. *Language Arts, 65,* 304–314.

Lamme, L. L. (1990). Exploring the world of music through picture books. *The Reading Teacher, 44*(4), 294–299.

Lipson, E. R. (1988). *The New York Times parents' guide to the best books for children.* New York: Times Books.

Moir, H., Cain, M., & Prosak-Beres, L. (1990). *Collected perspectives: Choosing and using books for the classroom.* Norwood, MA: Christopher-Gordon.

Morrow, L. (1988). Young children's responses to one-to-one story readings in school settings. *Reading Research Quarterly, 23,* 89–107.

Moss, J. (1984). *Focus units in literature: A handbook for elementary school teachers.* Urbana, IL: National Council of Teachers of English.

Pfau, D. W. (1966). *An investigation of the effects of planned recreational reading in first and second grade.* Unpublished Ph.D. dissertation, State University of New York at Buffalo.

Porter, E. J. (1969). *The effect of a program of reading aloud to middle grade children in the inner city.* Unpublished Ph.D. dissertation, The Ohio State University, Columbus.

Schwartz, J. I. (1983). Language play. In B. Busching & J. Schwartz (Eds.), *Integrating the language arts in the elementary school* (pp. 81–89). Urbana, IL: National Council of Teachers of English.

Scott, J. C. (1978, April). Running away to home—A story pattern in children's literature. *Language Arts,* pp. 471–477.

Stan, S. (1991), November/December). Conversations. Kevin Henkes. *The Five Owls,* p. 31.

Stewig, J. W. (1977). Encouraging language growth. In B. Cullinan & C. Carmichael (Eds.), *Literature and young children* (pp. 17–38). Urbana, IL: National Council of Teachers of English.

Stross, B. (1978, September). Language acquisition and teaching. *Language Arts,* pp. 751–755.

Yaden, D. (1988). Understanding stories through repeated read-alouds. *The Reading Teacher, 41,* 556–560.

Children's Books

Adler, David A. (1991). *Happy Thanksgiving rebus.* New York: Viking Press.

Aliki. (1976). *Corn is maize—The gift of the Indians.* New York: Thomas Y. Crowell.

Angel, Marie. (1991). *Woodland Christmas.* New York: Dial Press.

Ardley, Neil. (1989). *Music.* New York: Knopf.

Armstrong, Jenny. (1992). *Hugh can do.* New York: Crown.

Asch, Frank. (1993). *Moonbear's canoe.* New York: Little Simon.

Bailey, Carolyn. (1962). *Miss Hickory.* New York: Viking Press.

Brimner, Larry Dane. (1989). *Country bear's good neighbor.* New York: Orchard Books.

Brown, Laurene Krasny, & Brown, Marc. (1986). *Visiting the art museum.* New York: Dutton.

Bryan, Ashley. (1991). *All night, all day: A child's first book of African-American spirituals.* New York: Atheneum.

Buckingham, Simon. (1990). *Alec and his flying bed.* New York: Lothrop.

Burningham, John. (1971). *Mr. Grumpy's outing.* New York: Holt, Rinehart & Winston.

Carle, Eric. (1989). *Eric Carle's animals animals.* New York: Philomel Books.

Carter, Noelle. (1991). *My pet.* New York: Viking Press.

Conover, Chris (Reteller). (1986). *Froggie went a-courting.* New York: Farrar, Straus & Giroux.

————. (1987). *The adventures of Simple Simon.* New York: Farrar, Straus & Giroux.

DeJong, Meindert. (1964). *The wheel on the school.* New York: Harper & Row.

de la Mare, Walter. (1983). *Molly Whuppie.* New York: Farrar, Straus & Giroux.

Demuth, Patricia Brennan. (1991). *The ornery morning.* New York: Dutton.

Dunham, Meredith. (1987). *Shapes: How do you say it?* New York: Lothrop, Lee & Shepard.

Durrell, Ann (Collector). (1989). *The Diane Goode book of American folk tales and songs.* New York: Dutton.

Ehlert, Lois. (1990). *Fish eyes.* San Diego: Harcourt Brace Jovanovich.

Ekoomiak, Normee. (1988). *Arctic memories.* New York: Henry Holt.

Estes, Eleanor. (1943). *Rufus M.* New York: Harcourt, Brace.

Fort, Patrick. (1988). *Redbird.* New York: Orchard Books.

Fox, Paula. (1967). *A likely place.* New York: Macmillan.

Goor, Ron and Nancy. (1990). *Insect metamorphosis. From egg to adult.* New York: Atheneum.

Gross, Ruth Belov. (1991). *You don't need words!* New York: Scholastic.

Hartman, Gail. (1991). *As the crow flies. A first book of maps.* New York: Bradbury Press.

Hausherr, Rosmarie. (1992). *What instrument is this?* New York: Scholastic.

Hellen, Nancy. (1988). *The bus stop.* New York: Orchard Books.

Henkes, Kevin. (1985). *Bailey goes camping.* New York: Greenwillow.

Hooks, William. (1992). *How do you make a bubble?* New York: Bantam Little Rooster.

Hulme, Joy N. (1991). *Sea squares.* New York: Hyperion Books for Children.

Hutchins, Pat. (1986). *The doorbell rang.* New York: Greenwillow.

Jeffers, Susan. (1973). *Three jovial huntsmen.* Scarsdale, NY: Bradbury Press.

Jensen, Virginia Allen, & Edman, Polly. (1979). *Red thread riddles.* New York: Philomel Books.

Johnson, Angela. (1990). *Do like Kyla.* New York: Orchard Books.

Johnson, Ginny, & Cutchins, Judy. (1991). *Slippery babies. Young frogs, toads and salamanders.* New York: Morrow Junior Books.

Johnson, Tony. (1991). *The witch's hat.* New York: Bantam Books.

Jones, Carol (Ill.). (1990). *This old man.* Boston: Houghton Mifflin.

Jorgensen, Gail. (1988). *Crocodile beat.* New York: Bradbury Press.

Kehoe, Michael. (1993). *A book takes root. The making of a picture book.* Minneapolis: Carolrhoda Books.

Kemp, Moira. (1991). *Baa, baa, black sheep.* New York: Lodestar Books.

Kroll, Steven. (1991). *Annabelle's un-birthday.* New York: Macmillan.

Langstaff, John. (1955). *Frog went a-courtin'.* New York: Harcourt, Brace.

Lavies, Bianca. (1991). *Wasps at home.* New York: Dutton Children's Books.

Lee, Jeanne M. (1987). *Ba-nam.* New York: Henry Holt.

Lenski, Lois. (1945). *Strawberry girl.* Philadelphia: Lippincott.

Lillegard, Dee. (1989). *Sitting in my box.* New York: Dutton.

Lindberg, Reeve. (1990). *The day the goose got loose.* New York: Dial Press.

Martin, Rafe. (1992). *The rough-face girl.* New York: Putnam's.

Mayhew, James. (1989). *Katie's picture show.* New York: A Bantam Little Rooster Book.

McCloskey, Robert. (1952). *One morning in Maine.* New York: Viking Press.

McKissack, Patricia and Fred. (1987). *The king's new clothes.* Chicago: Children's Press.

McMillan, Bruce. (1989). *Time to. . . .* New York: Lothrop.

Mendoza, George. (1970). *The Marcel Marceau alphabet book.* Garden City, NY: Doubleday (out of print).

Merriam, Eve. (1992). *Fighting words.* New York: Morrow Junior Books.

Mitgutsch, Ali. (1986). *From picture to picture book.* Minneapolis: Carolrhoda Books.

Modesitt, Jeanne. (1992). *Sometimes I feel like a mouse. A book about feelings.* New York: Scholastic.

Mollel, Tololwa M. (1992). *The orphan boy.* New York: Clarion Books.

Morris, Ann (Reteller). (1989). *The Cinderella rebus book.* New York: Orchard Books.

Noll, Sally. (1984). *Off and counting.* New York: Greenwillow.

O'Connor, Jane and Robert. (1991). *Super cluck.* New York: Harper & Row.

Poole, Josephine (Reteller). (1991). *Snow White.* New York: Knopf.

Rankin, Laura. (1991). *The handmade alphabet.* New York: Dial Books.

Roehrig, Catharine. (1990). *Fun with hieroglyphs.* New York: The Metropolitan Museum of Art/Viking.

Rogers, Paul. (1989). *The shapes game.* New York: Henry Holt.

Scheer, Julian. (1964). *Rain makes applesauce.* New York: Holiday House.

Schwartz, David M. (1991). *Supergrandpa.* New York: Lothrop.

Schweninger, Ann. (1991). *Let's look at the seasons. Autumn days.* New York: Viking Press.

Sendak, Maurice. (1963). *Where the wild things are.* New York: Harper & Row.

Singer, Marilyn. (1981). *Will you take me to town on Strawberry Day?* New York: Harper & Row.

Stadler, J. (1991). *Cat is back at bat.* New York: Dutton.

Steig, William. (1974). *Farmer Palmer's wagon ride.* New York: Farrar, Straus & Giroux.

Stow, Jenny. (1992). *The house that Jack built.* New York: Dial Books for Young Readers.

Turkle, Brinton. (1969). *Thy friend, Obadiah.* New York: Viking Press.

Weil, Zaro. (1992). *Mud, moon and me.* Boston: Houghton Mifflin.

Widman, Christine. (1989). *The star grazers.* New York: Harper & Row.

Wildsmith, Brian. (1984). *Daisy.* New York: Pantheon Books.

Wilson, April. (1990). *Look! The ultimate spot-the-difference book.* New York: Dial Press.

Wolcott, Patty. (1991). *Eeeeeeek!* New York: Random House.

———. (1991). *Pickle pickle pickle juice.* New York: Random House.

————. (1991). *Where did that naughty little hamster go?* New York: Random House.

Yarborough, Camille. (1979). *Cornrows.* New York: Coward, McCann & Geoghegan.

Yenawine, Philip. (1991). *Colors.* New York: The Museum of Modern Art/Delacorte Press.

Professional Growth

The Work of the Children's Literature Assembly of the National Council of Teachers of English

Contact:

Miles Myers, Executive Director
National Council of Teachers of English
1111 Kenyon Road
Urbana, IL 61801
(217) 328-3870

This is a subgroup of the NCTE, a parent group with 120,000 members that focuses particularly on the interests of people involved with children and young adult literature. During the annual convention and the spring conference of the NCTE, this group often features as speakers authors and illustrators of children's literature. During the year it publishes lists of recommended books, gives awards, and publishes *The Journal of Children's Literature*. It provides a network of people interested in techniques of teaching literature, in researching various aspects of it, and in materials related to children's books.

THREE

Understanding Listening As Part of an Integrated Program

All teachers are actors. . . . All great actors are great listeners. Listening is just as important in being a teacher.

Murray (1989, p. 33)

A teacher of kindergarten, interested in helping her children focus on environmental sounds, read Margaret Wise Brown's *The Quiet Noisy Book* (1993) to her children. Together they compiled a chart of sounds in their classroom. Then she asked the boys and girls to listen intently as they went home that night, so they could report sounds they'd heard the next day. When her 5-year-olds started to contribute their ideas, they said among other things: "I heard grass growing," "I heard myself thinking," and "I heard germs walking." We can smile at the imaginative quality of these youngsters' responses. They do indeed remind us that children live in a sea of sound, surrounded by information and pleasure they take in through their ears. One task of the school is to capitalize on children's natural interest in the aural world and engage them in activities to sharpen their listening skills.

Almost from the moment newborn infants are laid in their cribs, they are intently at work taking in information through human beings' most-used receptive channel—the ears. Although this first listening is crude compared with the sophisticated, inferential listening adults do, it is a beginning. As children grow, their listening abilities develop while the children sense, sort, and begin to act upon the sounds they receive.

By the time children go to school, they have listened for countless hours, largely on their own initiative. As with speech, most children receive little direct instruction in the home about how to listen. Although most listening habits are assimilated unconsciously, rather than being taught, children have learned the necessity of listening to learn. In this as in other areas, however, there are marked differences in how much children have learned.

In some homes, children are encouraged to listen.[1] Parents listen and respond to what the child says. Mothers and fathers answer insistent requests for labels, "What's that?" Dinner time is an occasion for talking and listening. The groundwork is laid, albeit unconsciously, for the idea that listening is a courtesy paid to the speaker. Duker (1969, p. 749) pointed out: "Generally it is agreed that parents who listen to their children tend to be the best teachers of good listening habits."

In other homes, little premium is put on listening. Children from some lower-socioeconomic-class homes have poorly developed hearing (Roche & Siervogel, 1980). Their families are sometimes fragmented because of instability and seldom gather for leisurely exchange of talk. If the home environment is crowded with young children, it is usually permeated with noise. Passive watching of television too often substitutes for active aural-oral interchanges between child and adult. Apparently children from such surroundings sometimes "tune out" the noise, and consequently their listening skills develop slowly. In addition, such children do less well on listening tests even after instruction (Feltman, 1967).

[1] Last and DeMuth (1991) provide a list of many helpful activities teachers can suggest that parents do at home to improve children's listening abilities.

Even children who are usually listened to will get a chuckle from Martha Alexander's book, *Even That Moose Won't Listen to Me* (1988), in which young Rebecca tries to warn everyone in her family about the "giant moose" in the backyard. Her brother Gregory, her dad, and mom are all too busy, so Rebecca tries to solve the problem herself and finally succeeds in doing so. Imagine her family's surprise when they see the moose damage to the garden. Then it is Rebecca who is too busy to tell them what happened. This is a delightful turnabout in Alexander's usual pleasantly simple watercolor illustrations.

A Distinction in Terms

A distinction must be made between two terms: *hearing* and *listening*. Although these are often used interchangeably, they refer, in fact, to two distinctly different abilities. *Hearing* refers to the physical reception of sound waves through the ear. Most people can hear, with the exception of those who unfortunately suffer some structural or neurological defect. *Listening* refers to the processes of both hearing and *responding*, as the listener reacts to the physical stimuli or uses the information she or he has heard.

There are many ways to think about or classify types of listening. The number of these classifications and the accompanying terminology vary with each writer. Which classification system is used makes little differ-

From *Even That Moose Won't Listen to Me* by Martha Alexander, with illustrations by the author (Dial, 1988).

ence; the important thing to remember is that, while most young children with whom you work can hear, few are good listeners. This is the reason your responsibility as a teacher of listening is important.

Some years ago Strickland (1969) identified four different types of listening characteristic of both adults and children. *Marginal* listening is the kind children in an open classroom do when they go about their own work yet are still aware that others in the classroom are doing other tasks. A major component in the early childhood language arts curriculum is *appreciative* listening, in which classes listen to the teacher or perhaps to a tape or record as a story or poem is presented. *Attentive* listening is essential when teachers are giving instructions or directions and when children themselves are participating in discussions or planning sessions. Finally, *analytic* listening is used when children need to detect an author's purpose, analyze point of view, or compare what the speaker is saying with what the listener already knows. Specific activities designed to encourage attentive and analytic listening are described later in this chapter.

The Child As Listener in School

As any kindergarten teacher can tell you, there is a wide difference in listening abilities among children. This difference remains apparent at all grade levels, and the spread seems to widen as children grow older. Who is likely to be a good listener?

Before children can be effective listeners, they must be able to hear adequately. A continuing job of every teacher is to be alert for signs of hearing problems because between five and ten percent of all students may be hearing impaired (Greene & Petty, 1975).

At the start of a school year, as the teacher begins to work with a group, one task is to determine whether any children in the room have a hearing problem. This is important at any age or grade level because hearing problems may develop at varying times. A child's loss may not have been detected by previous teachers especially if it only recently became apparent. Detecting hearing problems is not simple. Different boys and girls may:

1. Have trouble hearing different types of sounds
2. Hear with different efficiency at different times because of such physical conditions as being overly tired
3. Manifest their hearing problem in different ways

The teacher looks for signs indicating that, rather than being inattentive, the child may have a hearing impairment that needs referral to a specialist. The following symptoms may be exhibited:

1. Trouble hearing /th/ words, which contain the softest sound in the language.

2. A problem hearing consonant sounds, as they are softer than the vowel sounds in words.

3. Trouble understanding long sentences. Children with hearing problems can usually cope only with short sentences (van Riper, 1978).

4. Problems in voice production, including:
   a. abnormal pitch, intensity, or quality of the voice
   b. unusual speech rhythm
   c. persistent articulation errors (Travis, 1971)

5. Trouble distinguishing between different phonemes.

6. Memory-span problems and difficulty remembering sequences. The sequence activity suggested later in this chapter, for example, would prove difficult to children with hearing problems.

7. Frequent gestures to make ideas or wants known

If such signs are evident, the teacher refers the child to the speech and hearing therapist employed by the school system or suggests to parents the need to take the child for a hearing test. The teacher makes such recommendations even though some children suspected of having hearing problems may simply be poor listeners. "According to some ear specialists, it may be that more than half of proclaimed deafness is nothing more than inattention" (Lundsteen, 1979, p. 28). If hearing tests reveal no pathological problem with the child's hearing, the teacher must help the child listen attentively. Children whose listening skills are underdeveloped are a major focus of this chapter.[2] Even among children whose hearing is judged "normal," there is a wide range of differences in listening ability. What types of children may the teacher expect to listen well?

The child who is intelligent is likely to be a good listener (Duker, 1969, p. 749). Although the exact nature of this relationship is uncertain, several researchers have found a significant relationship between listening skills and general intelligence. The child who is a good reader is also apt to be a more skilled listener than other children (Brown, 1965). Since both reading and listening are receptive language skills, such a relationship is logical and is, in fact, borne out by research studies. In pointing out the relationship between listening and reading, E. D. Hirsch, Jr. (1991), reported that by seventh grade, "the ability to

---

[2] For those children whose hearing is impaired, special attention beyond the training of the classroom teacher is required. For a teacher with such a child in the room, the following may be of help and may serve as a reference to recommend to parents: *Listen! Hear! For Parents of Hearing-Impaired Children* is a brief ten-panel brochure that gives stage-by-stage guidance for parents in helping such children, aged 0 to 6, develop speech, audition, and cognition. It is available from the Alexander Graham Bell Association for the Deaf, 3417 Volta Place NW, Washington, DC 20007.

read and the ability to listen have reached exactly the same level." He goes on to say that if a child learns to listen well in the early grades, that child will normally be reading well later.

In addition to reading ability, children who have well-developed background knowledge, or internalized schema about the topic, are apt to be more effective listeners. Samuels (1984) talks about this cognitive attribute, among others, as critical because it allows child listeners not only to grasp the message but also to make inferences about the topic. Less easy to assess is a quality identified by Hyslop and Tone (1989); empathy in the listener. They point out that effective listeners are more likely to care about both the message and the speaker. Gender differences are not as apparent in this language skill as they are in some others. Hollow (1955) found no significant differences in listening ability between boys and girls in her 200-child sample after six weeks of instruction in a sequential listening program.

Listening Demands

People frequently react to comments about the need for improving listening skills by wondering why this is a concern. Since everyone listens, why worry about it? One valid reason for helping children improve their listening skills is that we listen a large part of our lives, both in school and as adults.

A study done in schools indicates the importance of listening in the lives of children. Wilt (1950) studied 568 children in sixteen classrooms, investigating the amount of time spent in each of the language arts. She found that children listened fifty-eight percent of their time. In addition, she studied the relationship between what *actually* happened and what teachers *thought* happened in the classrooms. She discovered that children spent an average of more than two and a half hours listening during a five-hour school day. This is especially interesting, since the amount was more than twice that estimated by teachers. Though the Wilt (1950) study is by now old, it has not been replicated on a large scale. What are conditions like in schools now? It is safe to assume that children spend a good part of their school lives listening. The amount of time spent listening to a teacher in a group setting may have diminished; however, recent emphases on individually guided instruction, cooperative learning, and whole language may actually have increased the amount of time children spend listening to each other as they work in such programs. In fact, Wolvin and Coakley (1988) estimated that students spend more than half of each school day engaged in listening.

Another comment on the amount of listening children do was provided by Delamont (1976): "About two-thirds of the time that teachers and pupils are in the classroom someone is talking. About two-thirds of that talk is done by the teacher, and about two-thirds of the teacher's talk is for organizing."

A small study investigated the amount of time devoted to the various language arts in the classrooms of 266 teachers (van Wingerden, 1965). Of these respondents, 52.9 percent reported there was "little" direct, planned listening instruction in their program. Perhaps this is because so little of curriculum guides and elementary language arts textbooks is devoted to listening instruction. Because this is the case, teachers too seldom know how to teach listening. This chapter will point out some ways teachers can work to improve listening skills.

Children listen much of the time they are in school. Is this also true in adult life? An early study pointed out clearly the importance of listening in the lives of adults. Rankin (1928) discovered that sixty-eight percent of his subjects' waking hours were spent in some form of communication. Following are the types and percentages:

1. Listening, forty-five percent of the total

2. Speaking, thirty percent of the total

3. Reading, sixteen percent of the total

4. Writing, nine percent of the total

Although this study was done with a small sample, more recent studies done with larger samples have replicated the results, showing the validity of Rankin's pioneer work in this area (Bird, 1955; Breiter, 1957). If the study were replicated today, what would be the results? Because of the increase in such passive entertainment as television watching, the percentage of time spent listening has probably increased. We do not know for sure, but apparently, to function well both in school and in the adult world, we need well-developed listening skills.

Such skills are increasingly called into use in important areas. One study indicated that fifty-eight percent of the public's political information was gathered from newspapers and magazines (Bois, 1966), while the remaining forty-two percent came from radio and television. With the brevity and (some say) the bias of electronic media, it is apparent that critical listening is of utmost importance to our society. With the increase in television viewing, the percentages have probably reversed since the study was reported.

Yet another reason for stressing the importance of listening is that much content is lost after listening occurs. It has been estimated that, only one week after listening to an oral presentation, the average listener has forgotten twenty-five percent of what was heard. After a month's interval, fully fifty percent of what had been retained is lost. Thus, we need to listen well because we lose much of what we have heard.

Problems with Listening

In addition to heavy demands for listening and evidence that there are wide differences in listening abilities, some features of the act of listening itself create problems. One of these is the nature of the listening process. Earlier it was mentioned that children who are good readers often are good listeners. This relationship is logical because both reading and listening are receptive skills. There is a fundamental difference between the two, however. A listener usually cannot control either the rate of presentation or the number of repetitions. In reading, we can control both. If something makes no sense, one can read and then reread again, pausing to consult a dictionary to determine the meaning of a crucial word. Listeners don't have that luxury. Ephemeral words are spoken at a rate the listener does not choose, and it is often impossible to hear the same thing over again. It is true that tape recordings or records allow listeners to control the number of repetitions; however, in more common situations, when listening to a person speak, the listener must "catch it on the wing" (Anderson & Lapp, 1988).

The converse problem—of the speaker going so slowly that the listener loses interest—has also been noted. Common estimates are that we can listen comfortably at rates up to twice as fast as a speaker can speak. This discrepancy has been investigated by researchers who demonstrated that people can listen at rates up to 450 words per minute (Orr, Friedman & Williams, 1965). This study made use of mechanically compressed speech, eliminating the problem of high pitch that usually results when records or tapes are played at too fast a speed. Although the ability to listen and comprehend compressed speech has been established, no use of this technology has been made at the elementary school level at this time.

Is Improvement Possible?

Children listen with varying effectiveness, but many demands to listen are placed on all children. So the question is: Does direct instruction in how to listen result in improved listening ability? Several research studies have indicated that listening is a teachable skill. These were summarized by Duker (1968) in a book useful to teachers. Duker surveyed over 1,300 studies and concluded that considerable agreement exists among researchers: Listening can be taught, and the results of such teaching can be measured. A study by Childers (1970) is representative of those demonstrating the value of teaching listening skills. Using a large group of children ($N = 111$) including a wide variety of intelligence levels, Childers tested listening ability before and after a series of lessons designed to increase listening skills. Children in all groups improved their listening skills significantly. Jalongo (1991) is among those who continue to believe that focused lessons on specific listening skills can help students become better listeners.

Listening is a necessary skill that can be improved. Many teachers want to help their children do this. How does one go about the task? There are basically two approaches to listening instruction: (1) use of a commercial program and (2) creation of a program by the classroom teacher.

Commercial Programs

Some teachers want the help provided by commercial programs, which have as a distinguishing feature their highly sequential, organized nature. Such programs identify a specific set of listening subskills to be improved, often specify procedures for teacher and pupils, and typically make provisions for evaluating how well the skill is learned. The programs are usually based on a set of tapes or records, sometimes supplemented by visual materials. The best of such programs include pre- and posttests so teachers can assess which of the children need further instruction.

Typical of an effective commercial listening kit is "Listening to the World," available from American Guidance Service (4201 Woodland Road, P.O. Box 99, Circle Pines, MN 55014-1796). A lesson manual guides the teacher in uses of the audiocassettes, song cards, gameboards, and other manipulatives through a carefully planned sequence of ninety lessons that focus on the characteristics of sounds, auditory attention, hypothesis testing, and auditory memory. Like other such materials, this kit includes a sequence of experiences field-tested before the kit was produced and a wide range of professionally produced materials—everything necessary to teach the program. Materials like this, when well done, make it much easier for a teacher to teach listening. Spiegel (1990) gave some criteria useful in evaluating such programs.

Teacher-Made Programs

Commercial programs provide a solution to the problem for teachers who are insecure about their own knowledge about listening, or who feel they have too much content to prepare in too short a time. No such program, however, meets the specific needs of the children in a particular classroom as effectively as can one that is created especially by the teacher in that situation. A major contribution by experts in holistic approaches to early childhood education has been their insistence that the most effective planning is done at the classroom level by the teacher who knows a particular group of children. A major advantage of such a teacher-made program is its flexibility. As teachers sense children's listening interests, they can alter and adapt the sequence of experiences to the needs of the particular group. Some sample listening experiences are included here to show the types of activities possible. These should not be followed prescriptively but may suggest some ideas to try once you determine your children's listening needs. Perhaps the sequence will encourage you to think about other experiences you can plan for your group.

Setting the Stage

Whether in preparation for a separate listening lesson or while giving directions in a subject-matter-related lesson, it is crucial that the teacher set the stage for careful listening. Much inattentive listening occurs because the speaker proceeds without preparing the listeners adequately, without guiding the listeners' attention (Friedman, 1978).

Before beginning, make sure to compensate for any physical distractions. This suggestion seems self-evident, but in actuality, children are often required to listen in less than ideal conditions. Lundsteen (1979, p. 28) commented: "It is not uncommon for children to be expected to listen far beyond the time of their likely attention span with lawn mowers going or children playing outside the window, with noise-amplifying flooring, sweltering weather [un-air-conditioned], or over-heating— every imaginable kind of inhibition to attention."

As a teacher, you need to be aware that children have grown accustomed to shutting out sounds. Ecologists express growing concern about noise pollution; children are among others shutting out the high-level noises that pervade our atmosphere. It is not surprising that people shut out sounds because the overall loudness of environmental noise is doubling every ten years. Quiet eludes us. In addition to loud noises, we are constantly bombarded by the ubiquitous mechanized music that fills the spaces in restaurants, elevators, and waiting rooms. That noise is among the less offensive that intrudes on us; many noises in our environments approach deafening level.

Even in school children *must* tune out. The task of finishing an assignment while other children, perhaps no more than fifteen feet away, are reading orally is not an easy one. The increasing number of open-space schools with fewer walls has made listening more difficult. Since children have learned to ignore sound, when you are planning a lesson in which they must listen, you will need to set the stage carefully so that they can listen.

In addition to setting the stage, it is important that teachers set the *expectation* of listening attentively. Frequently children ask over and over again to have simple directions repeated. When the teacher acquiesces, the result is less efficient listening habits. It is crucial that you establish in children's minds that directions and instructions will be given once and only *once*. Naturally this way of giving instructions cannot be established precipitously. Some warning must be given, and practice in listening attentively must be provided.

The teacher can easily talk with the children, perhaps pointing out that she or he has had to repeat instructions several times and alerting children to the fact that she or he does not intend to continue doing so. Teachers can systematically reduce the number of times they repeat directions until each is said only once. This method encourages careful listening to all instructions. Another effective way to encourage careful listening is to ask a child to repeat what has been said. Give a direction and then ask a child to say it again in his or her own words. Ask for a child by name after giving the instructions, so all will listen in case they may be called upon.

Children also need to be prepared by being informed about the *purpose of listening*. Some brief introduction, perhaps stating what the lesson is about, the nature of the instructions, and why the children are to listen, will help establish the purpose (Anderson, 1989). The teacher does not entreat children to listen "because listening is important" but rather "because when I finish giving the directions, there are three activities you are to do." This procedure puts listening into a very practical framework. Children begin to realize that, unless they listen, they will not be able to accomplish the task. Funk and Funk (1989) pointed out the value of asking children to listen *for* something, not *to* something, as a critical distinction.

What should be done with the child who does not listen, even though directions are repeated only once? The remedy is to maintain the policy, telling the child to find out from some other child what the instructions were. The bother of being interrupted by a child who has not listened soon annoys others who have, and they are not slow to let the non-listener know they do not want to listen for the other child.

Probably one of the most significant ways a teacher encourages good listening habits is by being a good listener. Brent and Anderson (1993) remind us of the importance of the teacher as model. It is unreasonable to ask others to do something we ourselves don't do. Yet too often teachers, preoccupied with many tasks, ignore the child who is speaking or reading. A student teacher once personified such preoccupation in a negative way. While a child was reading orally during reading groups, she got up from her chair, walked halfway across the room, wrote on the chalkboard an additional direction she had forgotten, walked back, and sat down again at the reading table. You can imagine the child's feelings! Not only did this event reinforce the child's idea that what he was doing was not important, but it further reinforced the idea that listening was not important to that teacher. We keep in mind Cazden's (1981) warning that "it is . . . common for teachers to cut off genuine curiosity and a spirit of inquiry by not listening" (p. 91).

Teachers of culturally diverse children must remember that evidence of listening varies from culture to culture. Hall (1969) commented that members of a cultural group manipulate such things as posture and eye contact in a particular way that a teacher from a different cultural group may not understand. Information about such differences in European cultures has existed for some time. Other groups' evidences of listening have not been widely studied. Hall warned that teachers of Mexican American, Puerto Rican, and African American children must be aware that ways of showing one is listening may vary with these cultures. Basically, the informal rule for black culture goes somewhat as follows: If you are in the same room with another person or in a context where the person has ready access to you, there are times when there is no need to go through the motions of showing him or her you are listening because that is implied automatically. Sensitive teachers will do their best to learn what the culturally induced manifestations of listening are in order to facilitate learning.

A Sequence of Skills

One approach to refining listening skills is for the teacher to develop a listening strand in the early literacy program. What follows is a sequence of skills that may be used as the basis for a listening program, though it is not intended that any class would necessarily follow the sequence completely or in this exact order. Working closely with a group over an extended time, the teacher can easily determine whether children are profiting from a particular segment and can then condense, expand, or eliminate it. What *is* important is that teachers think about a sequence of skills, for as Devine (1982) said: "Listeners may derive meaning from larger structures of spoken discourse, but teachers . . . can best *teach* the total process by focusing on one or two skills at a time" (p. 4).

Listening to Natural Sounds   It is beneficial to begin a sequence of listening experiences by heightening children's awareness of the sounds around them. You could introduce this concept by reading *Soft and Noisy* by Judy Hindley (1992) to your class. This book introduces mechanical sounds like a clock, natural sounds like wind, inside sounds like pot lids clanging, outside sounds like airplane noises, loud sounds like cars screeching, and soft sounds like the gurgle of bathwater, among others. These sounds, transcribed in conventional letters, will encourage children to make the noises themselves. The pleasant two-dimensional pictures are by Patrice Aggs.

From *The Quiet Noisy Book* by Margaret Wise Brown, with illustrations by Leonard Weisgard (HarperCollins, 1993).

Many books explore the world of environmental sounds. For instance, *Rumble Thumble Boom!* by Anna Grossnickle Hines (1992) relates in large letters that are part of the illustrations the sounds that frighten the young narrator during a storm. He and his dog are *both* frightened, so they end up cuddled with Mom and Dad, shown in dark illustrations highlighted with white chalk. Other books that focus on environmental sounds are Lucy Cousins's *What Can Rabbit Hear?* (1992), a lift-the-flap book for preschool children, and Craig Brown's *City Sounds* (1992) for primary-age classes, done in this illustrator's distinctive pointillism approach. Finally, four books that have delighted many children are now once again available. Margaret Wise Brown during the 1930s and 1940s wrote *The Noisy Book* and followed that with *The Quiet Noisy Book, The Seashore Noisy Book,* and *The Summer Noisy Book,* all originally illustrated by Leonard Weisgard. All four were reissued in 1993.

After enjoying books like these, you might have children stop everything they are doing and simply listen to all the sounds around them. The group can then discuss the sounds they heard, listing them on the chalkboard. We make such a list even with preschool children, who can read only a few words or none. This is done to reinforce in the children's minds the relationship between saying words and writing down ideas. Such informal linking of thought and print lays important groundwork for later, more formal literacy experiences.

A group of primary children compiled the following list of environmental sounds:

Sounds Inside the Room	Sounds in Me	Sounds Outside the Room
Creaking	Getting mad	A mail truck
A chair moving	Scratching	A cat meowing
The clock	Teeth grinding	Birds flying
Putting a pencil down	Breathing	A hawk making a noise
Bumping		Trees moving
Sniffing		Bell on tape for filmstrip
The heater blower		in room next door

In addition to listening to sounds in the room, children can go on a sound walk. Divide the children into pairs, one of whom wears a blindfold. The other child's task is to lead the blindfolded child safely around the school. The children reverse roles after a short time and then return to the room to talk about the sounds they heard. First-grade children dictated the following:

> We went to the bathroom. I heard the sink, and flushing the toilet, and that paper thing. I heard everyone talking in Miss _____'s room. We went to the gym. I heard Mr. _____ blow his whistle and talk. I heard a pencil drop on a desk in our room. I heard somebody putting on his jacket in the hall. He wiggled his jacket and I heard it.   (*David*)

> I heard kids yelling in the gym. I heard Mr. _____ talking. We went in the bathroom. I heard somebody going potty, and I heard the toilet flushing. We went to the music room. I heard the kids singing, and they were playing songs on the record player. I heard when I banged the door with my foot. We went through the halls. I heard some people talking. When I was back in our room, I bumped into somebody's chair, and I heard it.   (*Connie*)

A follow-up to such an in-school activity is to ask children to listen carefully to sounds around them after they leave school. The trip home and activities during the evening can provide the basis for group sharing the next day. One teacher of kindergarten children asked students to do this. The next day the children drew pictures of their favorite sound. As she labeled the pictures for her students, the teacher found one had drawn "birds flocking," another "flowers opening," and yet a third the sounds of "the sun shining." While these latter two are probably more imaginary than actual, they do illustrate children's involvement with the activity.

A group of second-graders listed the following sounds they heard on the way to school:

Sounds on the Bus

Stomping feet

Brakes squeaking

Driver telling children to turn around and sit down

Snowballs hitting the bus

Tires going over rocks

Directionals ticking

Sounds Outside the Bus

Shoveling snow

Cars passing

School bell

Child falling down

To make the activity of listening to sounds more complex, have children listen at different times, to focus attention on the fact that our sound environment varies. Listen in September, in January, and in May to emphasize how sounds differ according to *time of year*. Listen at 9:30 A.M., at 11:30 A.M., and at 2:30 P.M. to emphasize how sounds differ according to *time of day*. Finally, listen on a bright, sunny day and on a cloudy, overcast day to emphasize how sounds differ according to *atmospheric conditions*. *Listen to the Rain* by Bill Martin, Jr., and John Archambault (1988) is particularly useful to point out the many subtle ways rain sounds vary.

One group of first-graders dictated the following sound story during the first week of February:

We heard footprints. They sounded scrunchy because of the snow on the ground. It was a creaky sound. We heard a big noise like a rocket in the sky. We heard an airplane up in the sky. It was a buzzy sound. We heard someone put on their motor in a car. We heard a car's wheels moving in the snow. We heard the truck slam the door. We heard it beep its horn, and the mailman went past with the truck. We heard a snow blower. We heard the thing scraping on the road. We heard the tractor shoving the snow off. We heard the trees blowing because it's windy. We heard the trees knocking each other. We heard a chain clicking on the pole.

A group of second-graders made the following time-of-day charts with their teacher:

Sounds at 8:55 A.M.

Buses roaring outside

Kids in snow shouting

Chairs being lifted off desk tops

Papers shuffling

Sounds at 10:00 A.M.

Quiet sound in room

Heater rattling

Halls are quiet

Teacher's voice in room across the hall

Sounds at 12:55 P.M.

Children stomping snow from feet

Loud talking and laughing

The "on-duty" lady yelling to be quiet

"Shuussh!" sound

Galoshes dragging down hall

Sounds at 3:20 P.M.

Bell ringing

Kids running to get outside

Buses running but not moving

Teachers' voices

Janitor's broom

To help children focus on sounds, the teacher could turn on a cassette recorder at several different times of the day, and later have children listen to the tape. Or each child in class could make a list of sounds at some time at night. Then they'd enjoy Diane Goode's *I Hear a Noise* (1988) about the little boy who can't fall asleep because of a noise.

Listening to Created Sounds   To begin, cover a large cardboard box with colored construction paper and label it "Our Sound Box." Put into the box several objects that make noises. Some of these should be very familiar—for example, a scissors. Others can be objects that make less familiar sounds. Make the sound and have the children guess what the object is. As you are doing this, focus the discussion on the nature of the sound. If it was made by a scissor, ask:

How do you know what it is?

What is the sound like?

What words can you use to tell about the sound?

How is this sound different from other sounds?

Kindergarten children gave these descriptions:

1. *Keys* as "sounds like banging together" and "sounds like a tambourine"
2. *Paper ripping* as "like when you open wrapping paper" and "sounds like a zipper zipping"
3. *Bell ringing* as "sounds like when you hear reindeer in the sky"

First-graders described:

1. *Masking tape* as "sounds like a kiss" and "sounds like going downhill on a sled"

2. *Stapler* as "sounds like a ball going bump-bump, bump-bump" and "you can hear it go up and down"

3. *Buttons* in a jar as "makes a shaking noise like a rattlesnake"

Second-graders made these comments:

1. *Crumpling piece of paper* as "cards being shuffled," "sandpaper rubbing," and "crunching a styrofoam cup"

2. *Keys* as "metal that's loud" and "my dad lets me play with his, so I know for sure"

3. *Charm bracelet* as "not so loud as the keys, must be thinner metal" and "could be tiny keys"

The following transcription is from a transitional first-grade room (for children spending an additional year between first and second grades). It shows how the teacher uses this listening activity as a stimulus for oral language.

Teacher: Today, boys and girls, we are going to play a listening game. I put different things into this sound box, which make different kinds of sounds. Some of the things you may recognize right away. You could say, "I know what this is." For other sounds, you may say, "Oh, what could that be?"
Child: Yeah, some can be hard and some can be easy.
Teacher: Yes, some of them may be easy for you to tell. If others are hard to tell, maybe you can tell Ms. Maertz what they remind you of. You could say, "It sounds like. . . ."

(Bell sound)

Teacher: What?
Child: A bell.
2nd Child: It went "ding."
Teacher: Did it sound like anything else to someone?
3rd Child: Silver.
Teacher: Silver. What is silver?
Child: Color is silver.

(Keys)

Teacher: Kate, what does that sound like?
Child: It sounds like keys.
2nd Child: To drive a car.
Teacher: Yes, you do need keys to drive a car.
3rd Child: It sounded like shaking.

(Rhythm instrument)

Child: Sounds like sticks.
Teacher: Gerald, what does it sound like to you?

Child: Sounds like they were being hit together.
Teacher: Kenneth, what does it sound like to you?
Child: Snapping together.
Child: They have a brown color on them.
Teacher: How did you know they had a brown color? Could you hear that, or did you know that?
Child: I knew that.
Teacher: Now this next one is very difficult. You'll need to listen quite carefully.

(Sandpaper blocks)

Several children: It's a spray.
Teacher: Martha, what does that sound like to you?
(No response)
Teacher: Jennifer, what does that sound like to you?
Child: It sounds like spraying.
Child: It sounds like sandpaper.
Teacher: And what does it sound like the sandpaper was doing?
Child: It made noise.
Teacher: You're all showing me, but what kind of sound did it make?
Child: It sounds like it's rubbing.
Teacher: It sounds like sandpaper was rubbing. Good. Now listen very carefully to the next one.

(Beanbag)

Child: A rattle.
Teacher: A rattle? What else could it be?
Child: Beans shaking.
Teacher: Beans shaking. Very good. I heard someone else say something. Who else had an idea?
Child: It sounds like a maraca.
Teacher: What's inside a maraca.
Child: Maracas are made out of seeds.
Teacher: OK. What kind of sound does it make?
Child: Some kind of shaking sound.

Such an activity can sensitize children to rather minimal differences among sounds as they enjoy being "sound detectives." Eventually children can tell the difference between the sound made when a metal lid is opened (for instance, the kind on a Band-Aid box) and the sound made when a plastic lid is opened (for instance, on a refrigerator storage box). Later children will enjoy contributing objects to the sound box. Encourage them to bring an object from home that can be shared through the sound box. In this sort of activity, we are motivating children to think about the *source* of the sound (i.e., an airplane), the type of *action* that makes the sound (i.e., scraping), or the words that *describe* the sound (i.e., click). Moffett and Wagner (1992) feel that taping such sounds in short and simple sequences can provide useful practice for children.

Listening to Voices In a gamelike format, children can listen to voices to determine who is speaking. This is one of the goals of the listening program—to discriminate speech sounds—in a curriculum guide from the Philadelphia Public Schools (Division of Early Childhood Education, 1984). With very young children, use the following poem:

> *Little Tommy Tittlemouse*
> *lives in a little house.*
> *Someone is knocking*
> *Oh Me! Oh My!*
> *Someone is saying,*
> *"Is it I!"*

Have children cover their eyes. The teacher walks around, saying the verse, and taps one child on the shoulder who says the last line. Then the children guess who was speaking. After listening to their peers repeat the phrase, some kindergarten children recognized the voices:

Mark's voice, "because it is loud and low"

Darrell's voice, "because it is crumbly, bumpy, and different"

Jermaine's voice, "because it is black and gargley"

Jimmy's voice, "because it goes and stops, goes and stops"

Chris's voice, "because it is fast, and it goes high and low"

With older boys and girls, a different approach is useful. Again, the children close their eyes while the teacher walks quietly around the room, stopping to tap one student on the shoulder. After returning to the front of the room so children cannot deduce from the direction of her or his voice who the child might be, the teacher has the child say three or four sentences and the other children guess who said them. It is a simple activity, but it does encourage careful listening, particularly because the only clue the children have is an aural one.

A second-grade teacher who tried this game with her students reported that the children loved it and nearly always guessed the voices, even when the children who were speaking tried to disguise their voices. Among the comments boys and girls volunteered in identifying the speakers were these:

"I know him so well he can't fool me."

"She says some sounds different, so I knew."

"His voice is hollow-sounding."

"She always talks so fast you know it's her."

"His voice is so low, I couldn't miss him."

Such audio materials as records or tapes of people reading can also be used. Select a poem from the record Mother Goose (Caedmon Records, Item CPN 1091, HarperCollins 10 East 53rd St., New York, NY 10022), featuring readings by Cyril Ritchard, Celeste Holm, and Boris Karloff. Listen with your children to Karloff's reading of "There Was a Crooked Man," for instance, and have them tell you what the voice was like. Children often respond by saying it was *creepy* or *scary,* which is indeed true. Then ask:

What makes the voice sound that way?

How is his voice different from the way people usually speak?

Is there anything different about the speed (or pitch or some other aspect) that is unusual?

Developing Words to Describe   In the preceding and other listening activities, the teacher is working to, as Moffett and Wagner (1992) said, "increase and refine vocabulary" (p. 217), to describe sounds students have heard. This is slow to develop; some of the less specific words come first: "It was a loud sound" or "It was a soft sound." On the other hand, children can be led to see that we can describe the following aspects of sound:

Several children can listen to a professional reading of a book on tape in the listening corner.

1. *Pitch*—the highness or lowness of the sound. Comparisons can be made, and when three sounds are heard, the use of such words as *high, higher, highest* or *low, lower, lowest* can be encouraged.

2. *Timbre.* Children should be encouraged to describe the quality of the sound. Is it a *soft* sound, a *harsh* sound, a *raspy,* or *singy* sound? These terms may sound rather imprecise, but the point is to encourage children to put into words the sense impressions they have taken in through their ears. For the teacher to insist on the one word that seems most appropriate would defeat the purpose of the experience.

3. *Duration.* All sounds can be characterized as constant or intermittent, and children can be asked to describe this aspect of the sound. If it is intermittent, can the pattern of sound and silence be described in words? Many listening activities of this nature can be planned with the music teacher, who will be happy to suggest experiences in which children listen to various musical instruments. If your school has no music teacher, consult any of the elementary music series, looking especially at the listening sections provided.

4. *Components.* Some sounds are made up of distinct segments—separate parts that can be distinguished from one another. For instance, when pushed down slowly, the stapler we used in one classroom made three distinct sounds.

Listening for Sequence   It is simple to encourage attentive listening in quasi-game situations by having children listen to sequences and then tell or write what they have heard. Preschool and kindergarten children can listen to simple sequences made by rhythm instruments and then tell what they heard. The teacher might play a sequence: bell, then drum; bell, drum, drum; or drum, drum, bell. This can be done first in the open and later behind a small screen to focus the attention on listening. Play the sequence and then call on one of the children to tell what it was. After you play the sequences for a while, involve the children by allowing the child who responds correctly to play the next sequence. The sequences can become more involved as children's ability increases.

With older children, you may read a string of numbers: 2, 7, 11. Begin with a short string and gradually increase its length. Read the sequence evenly at first, and then try patterning with the voice: 2, 1 / 4, 3, 4; or 3, 2, 1 / 2, 5 / 7. Encourage children to discuss such questions as: Which way is easier to remember—when the numbers are read evenly, or in a patterned sequence? Children find that the challenge of listening and remembering the sequence is an enjoyable experience, and attentive listening is encouraged. What you are doing here is developing aural memory, the ability to retain something heard.

With primary-age children, try sequencing a simple series of directions, which you read while children listen and then respond. When you begin, three directions may be enough; see how far you can extend this. A sample series might include the following directions.

Write:

1. Your middle name
2. Our classroom number
3. The name of the street you live on

With older children who have had more practice, a sequence might include the following directions.

Write:

1. Your age
2. The number of years you've lived here
3. Your mother's first name
4. Your favorite food[3]

Listening to Anticipate   The ability to anticipate is closely linked to the ability to extract meaning while listening. A child may learn to anticipate when presented with a piece of poetry in which some of the words are left out. The purpose of the exercise is to encourage children to use whatever clues they can garner in trying to guess what the missing word might be. The teacher might read the following poem and leave out the boldface words. Children are then encouraged to offer their suggestions about what word might logically fit into the blank based on what they have heard until then.

CAT
by Mary Britton Miller
(in Chapman, 1986)

The black cat yawns,
*Opens her **jaws**,*
Stretches her legs,
*And shows her **claws**.*

Then she gets up
And stands on four
*Long still **legs***
And yawns some more.

---

[3] Other sequence activities are included in "'Huh? Wadja Say?' Index of Better Listening," *Instructor*, October 1974, pp. 59–68. Additional activities recommended include listening for detail, for main ideas, and to make inferences. The many suggested activities are arranged roughly by level of difficulty, and many of the simpler ones can be used by primary teachers.

She shows her sharp teeth,
She stretches her lip,
Her slice of a tongue
Turns up at the **tip.**

Lifting herself
On her delicate toes
She arches her **back**
As high as it goes.

She lets herself down
With particular care,
And pads away
With her **tail** *in the air.*

Don't insist that children give the one word the poet chose. There is often more than one possible answer. The teacher encourages boys and girls to discuss the reasons they think their answer is more likely. When kindergarten through second-grade children participated in this activity, they suggested the following possibilities (enclosed in brackets below):

The black cat yawns,
Opens her _____ [eyes, mouth, the nails on her feet],
Stretches her legs,
And shows her _____ [teeth, face, ears, tail wiggling].

Then she gets up
And stands on four
Long still _____ [pipes]
And yawns some more.

She shows her sharp teeth,
She stretches her lip,
Her slice of a tongue
Turns up at the _____ [ceiling, sky, moon].

Lifting herself
On her delicate toes
She arches her _____ [nose, body, head]
As high as it goes.

The poem is available in a collection of poems by Jean Chapman (1986) divided into eight sections. Each section is introduced with a black pencil drawing by Peter Parnall. In addition to this listening experience, you might read several of the poems in this collection, which includes only cat poems, and ask children to think and talk about which one of them is their favorite.

In addition to listening for missing words, students can listen for missing phrases. In the following poem, for example, children need to listen attentively to gather information about the pattern of the poem so they can anticipate what will come next. They are to fill in the boldface lines.

THE MYSTERIOUS CAT

by Vachel Lindsay
(in Hall, 1985)

I saw a proud, mysterious cat,
I saw a proud, mysterious cat,
Too proud to catch a mouse or rat—
Mew, mew, mew.

But catnip she would eat and purr,
But catnip she would eat and purr,
And goldfish she did much prefer—
Mew, mew, mew.

Did you ever hear of a thing like that?
Did you ever hear of a thing like that?
Did you ever hear of a thing like that?
Oh, what a proud mysterious cat.
Oh, what a proud mysterious cat.
Oh, what a proud mysterious cat.
Mew . . . mew . . . mew.

After giving children such initial oral experiences in listening to anticipate, teachers often provide copies of the material, which can then be used for read-along experiences, a literacy activity that reinforces the relationship between oral and written language. The preceding poem is available in a large collection that includes poems from 1640 through the contemporary poet, Jack Prelutsky. It is a fine resource for teachers, though not for children because there are no illustrations.

Listening to Determine Meaning   Sometimes teachers prepare children for listening by discussing the meaning of unfamiliar words in advance. At other times, you can encourage children to listen carefully to determine meaning from context. You might read the following from a skillfully written book illustrated with remarkable closeup photographs. In *Backyard Hunter. The Praying Mantis* (1990), author Bianca Lavies writes:

It is September, and this male Chinese
mantis has shed his skin for the last
time. His final molt exposed fully grown
wings, folded down his back. Now he can fly.

After enjoying the book together, go back to this segment of text, rereading it and in addition perhaps viewing it on an overhead projector, so you can talk with children about the meaning of the word *molt*, a term most children won't know. Often in a piece of text, the meaning may not be entirely clear. The purpose when beginning such exercises is not to pin down one specific meaning. Rather, encourage children to think about what they have heard, discuss the evidence on which they have based their answer, and determine which is the most likely possibility. The materials to motivate such listening and discussion can be made up by the teacher, or they can be drawn from literature.

The teacher might read *Theodore and the Talking Mushroom* by Leo Lionni (1971), about a timid mouse named Theodore who gained confidence in a devious way. The teacher could then engage children in a discussion about some of the words used. Try using the following section:

> "Quirp!" said the mushroom.
> "What does it mean?" asked Theodore's friends, dumbfounded.
> "It means," said Theodore, "that the mouse should be venerated above all other animals."
> The news of Theodore's discovery spread quickly.
> His friends made him a crown.
> Animals came from far away with garlands of flowers.
> Wherever he went he was venerated above all other animals.

Rather than trying to pose some specific alternatives, simply ask children to tell what they think the word *venerate* means based on what they have heard. Children thought it meant Theodore should be "the most important," "the leader of the animals," and he "was smart because he understood what the mushroom said." Other words included in the book along with ideas suggested by first- and second-grade listeners are given here:

fluttering	"It means something is falling." "It goes down in slow motion." "It's waving just like water jumping up."
bewildered	"They were happy, then sad." "They didn't know what to say."
dumbfounded	"It means they were being dumb." "It means they do not know what it was." "They never saw anything like that before." "They had questions about it inside themselves."
garlands	"That means it is a lot of flowers." "Big hunks of flowers." "This means strings of flowers."
fraud	"It means that you are being mean." "He told a story." "It ain't real." "A two-timer and a double crosser."

Older primary children may have the skills to look up a word in a dictionary to find other aspects of its definition.

Critical Listening A more sophisticated kind of listening requires that children listen critically to answer questions posed about the material. Many times a shared listening experience may culminate naturally in some discussion questions. In this case, as in the case of a written question the child is to answer, the teacher's goal is to move beyond mere factual questions to ones that require more involved thinking processes.

After second- and third-graders have listened to *Backyard Hunter. The Praying Mantis* (1990) by Bianca Lavies, it is natural to ask them content questions:

How many antennae does a mantis have?

Where does this insect get its name?

What purpose does the mantis's skin serve?

All of these questions are in fact answered in the text. We need to go on to more sophisticated questions, however, that will stimulate children to think about what they have heard:

How is this insect like or unlike another that you know about?

Given the conditions necessary for the mantis, do you think they could live where we live?

What signs could you look for that would tell you if a praying mantis was in your yard?

Even more interesting would be to set this text in the context of another book that describes the same insect. For example, we could use the section on "Praying Mantids" from *Insect Metamorphosis. From Egg to Adult* by Ron and Nancy Goor (1990), which provides a briefer look at the same insect. Children could then be encouraged to make two group lists on the chalkboard, indicating the information they learned from each book.

In addition to using such factual materials, at times the teacher uses fiction when attempting to encourage critical listening. The ability to draw inferences, to extend ideas beyond the basic story, is a skill that develops slowly. While discussing a story the class has shared orally, the teacher is motivating children to use what they have heard to answer higher-level questions that were not given in the story.

The teacher might use the disarmingly original story of *The Bat Poet* who, unlike his brothers, has aspirations to write poetry (Jarrell, 1964). He encounters an audience for his writing in a neighboring mockingbird. After reading the entire story for the children, the teacher might ask questions to encourage the children to listen to make inferences. Some responses from first-grade children are included in brackets immediately following the question.

1. How do you think the bat might react if he encountered someone in trouble on his nightly flights? ["He would help, because he's so nice to the other animals." "He would try to get the things off the animal." "He would let his tail loose."]

2. What does the story tell you about the bat's personality? ["He was a nice person because he was giving poems to other animals." "He was nice to the mockingbird because he said a poem." "Kind, because he told a story to the chipmunk."]

3. Do you think the mockingbird was genuinely interested in the bat's poems? What clues do you have? ["No, he didn't like the poems." "The mockingbird wanted him not to do it." "He just didn't like it, no matter what he said."]

4. Would he have reacted differently if the poems hadn't been as well written? ["He would tell the bat it's bad." "He would say it was good." "I don't know." "He was interested because the poem was about him."]

This sort of listening to a wide variety of literature is supported by Wells (1986), who reported on a longitudinal study he did in England in which he found "the most important literacy activity as measured by later test scores was listening to stories read aloud" (p. 159).

Teachers Evaluate Themselves

In this, as in other curriculum areas, the teacher is a model for children to emulate. Teaches may unconsciously foster poor listening habits among children. Because listening habits, like much habituated behavior, often remained unexamined, a checklist for teachers is given here.

How Effective Am I As a Planner?

1. Do I realize children have difficulty listening attentively for long periods of time? Can I plan my sequence of learning activities with variety so that listening is a pleasant and not overly lengthy task?

2. Do I plan my presentation carefully so children listen to one thing at a time? Are my instructions planned with clarity so children can easily understand them?

3. Are my explanations carefully given throughout, clearly and concisely? Have I planned more than one way to say something, so if children do not understand the first time, I am prepared with an alternative? Have I used language fully, rather than relying on context? Saying, "Hand me that one" may be clear when the child is sitting at the same table and can see the object. But saying, "Hand me the wider blue book with the red letters and picture on its cover" is better. It models precision in speech that encourages good listening.

4. Do I plan some times during the day when an individual child may come to me and share something orally? Do I work to establish a rapport that encourages such oral sharing and listening?

How Effective Am I As a Presenter?

1. Do I encourage good listening by limiting the amount of talking I do? Studies of the amount of talking teachers do found that two-thirds of the time, it is the teacher who is talking. One study of classroom interaction revealed that in an hour, on average the teachers generated eighty questions, and all the students in class together generated two questions (Dillon, 1988).

2. Do I use changes in pitch, tempo, and volume of my speaking? Can I manipulate these paralinguistic elements to hold the children's attention? Do I also consciously use kinesic to add richness to my speech?

3. Do I give children time to think when I ask a question? Can I endure some "empty spaces" while children cope with the verbal problem I have presented? Or does silence threaten me so that I have to fill it up with talk?

4. Do I wait to get the attention of all children before I begin to speak? Do I have eye contact with the majority of listeners before I begin?

5. Do I remember to give some positive response to each speaker without needlessly summarizing or paraphrasing what he or she has said?

6. Do I make sure that when only one child has difficulty understanding, I clarify for that child later, rather than interrupting the train of thought of all the children while I explain?

7. Is my speech free of repeated expressions or phrases that are unnecessary or offensive? Two that are common among teachers are "You know . . ." and "Listen. . . ."

8. Do I listen attentively to children when they talk and express my interest and appreciation in what they say?[4]

The above lists are not to suggest that the teacher's major job is that of presenter or dispenser of information. Such was the case fifty years ago, but ideas about the teacher's role are changing. Nonetheless, at times a teacher does present information, and such presentation ought to be as effective as possible. Thinking about the above questions may help the teacher increase effectiveness.

[4] A highly apparent part of paying attention is eye contact. A survey of 350 elementary children showed that the largest number chose "She looks at me when I am talking" as the way they knew they had the teacher's attention. See Charles Galloway and Truman Whitfield, "Hey, Did You Really Hear That Kid?" *Instructor*, October 1976, pp. 84–86.

Table 3-1

Self-Evaluation Checklist

	Yes	No	Needs Reflection
Am I defeating good listening by talking too much?			
Do I realize that children have difficulty listening attentively for a long period of time?			
Do I vary my style of presentation in order to encourage children to listen?			
Do I expect children to concentrate on too many things at a time?			
Do I give children time to find the answer to one question before another is asked?			
Do I ask open-ended questions that do not require right or wrong answers?			
Are my explanations clearly presented?			
Do I try not to repeat what each child says, but rather require the class to concentrate on the child speaking?			
Am I taking too much time in explaining to one child while others lose interest?			
Do I try not to repeat phrases or expressions so often that they become ineffective and monotonous?			
Do I treat the children's opinions with respect?			
Am I getting the full attention of the class before giving information?			
Do I make myself available for listening? Do children feel free to come to me with their problems and know they will have my undivided attention?			

Checklist

Another approach to evaluation is presented in Table 3-1 by Dwyer (1989).

Beyond individual reflection on their own skills related to teaching listening, Lundsteen (1984) suggested ways groups of teachers could make schoolwide efforts to improve instruction.

Children Evaluate Themselves

It is often helpful, in listening, as in other areas, to encourage children to evaluate themselves. Discussions about what group members think constitutes a good listener can begin at the kindergarten level, and children can draw up lists that may be posted in the classroom and reviewed periodically (Brent & Anderson, 1993).

In the early years, such a list is often quite simple. The following list was drawn up cooperatively by a kindergarten class and their teacher.

Am I a good listener? If so, I:

1. Look at the person who is talking
2. Don't talk until it is question time
3. Think about what the person is saying
4. Keep my hands and feet quiet

It is readily apparent to an adult, of course, that such criteria do not necessarily ensure attention listening. It is very possible to be listening attentively while not looking at a speaker. Even at this level, however, when we are trying to build listening habits, it is more *likely* that good listening will occur if the child listener maintains eye contact with the speaker.

As children become older, the list of points included on the chart can become more sophisticated. A third-grade class drew up the following list:

Do you think you are a good listener? If you are, you do these things:

1. Get ready to listen.
2. Anticipate the speaker's idea. Listen for cues the speaker gives.
3. Listen for a summary. If the speaker doesn't give one, make one yourself.
4. Take brief notes on information talks.
5. Think of questions to ask the speaker. What else do you want to know?
6. Think about how what the speaker has said is like or unlike what you already know.

In recommending such checklists as an important ongoing evaluative procedure in integrated language programs, Stibbs (1979) pointed out that these serve three purposes. This British educator felt checklists that children themselves develop and then use are appropriate for diagnosis, recording progress, and personal judgment.

This child-author is reading her story aloud to her classmates, who listen and respond with questions and comments.

SUMMARY

Listening could be called the most elusive of the language skills. A distinction, too seldom made, exists between hearing and more complex listening. Listening problems that require specialized attention do exist in the early childhood years, although most children fall within a normal range. These normal abilities are used to meet the early and continuing demands to listen well. Listening skills are the skills most used by both children and adults. Few children experience a regular sequence of lessons planned to enhance listening skills, despite research showing that these skills can be improved. One means of improvement is the commercial listening kit materials available. Another approach is for teachers to design a listening strand for the integrated language arts/reading program. The major portion of this chapter presented a program of listening skills. After setting the expectation that children will listen, linked with clearly stated purposes for listening, teachers can lead children through a sequence of listening experiences of increasing difficulty. Children should listen to environmental sounds, to created sounds, and to voices as they develop a vocabulary to describe what they have heard. More complex activities involve students in listening to sequence, to anticipate, to determine meaning, and finally to think critically. The chapter concluded with a section on teachers evaluating themselves. To write and read about an aural skill can be frustrating, but we have done so in the hope that you will translate these ideas into a vital listening component in your literacy program.

Suggestions for Further Study

1. Select a story or piece of informational writing of interest to you. Practice reading it aloud until you are satisfied with the results. Make a tape of your reading. Wait a week or so, and then listen critically to the recording. Is it the kind of reading to which children would listen with interest? If not, what aspects of your presentation need work?

2. Plan a short lesson and teach it to a group of children, recording it on either audiotape or videotape. The advantage of videotape is that it allows you to monitor your use of kinesics. Review the recording. How effectively does the presentation encourage attentive listening? Which elements need more work?

3. Electronic music piped into most public places is so pervasive that we seldom notice it. Yet it can be considered pollution. Check your telephone book to see if there is a supplier of such sound in your community. Call and arrange an interview with one of the staff. What rationale is given for such music? Can the people who provide this service also provide documentation about its value? On what basis do they justify this service to those who consider using it?

4. Many people are concerned about noise pollution. You might be interested in reading about this problem. See David Lipscomb, *Noise: The Unwanted Sounds* (Chicago: Nelson-Hall, 1974). Sections in longer, more technical books also speak to this problem. For instance, "Noise" in *Environmental Hazards to Young Children* by Dorothy Noyes Kane, pp. 74–90 (Phoenix: Oryx Press, 1985), details effects on physical health and cognitive development, as well as pointing out reasons children are at special risk. You might also see "The Effects of Noise on Man" in *Conference on Noise Abatement Policies*, pp. 23–32 (Paris: Chateau de la Muette, 1980); or see "Effects of Noise on People" by P. B. Wilkins in *Noise and Vibration* (eds. R. G. White and J. G. Walker), pp. 805–825 (New York: Wiley, 1982).

5. Is the average classroom a quiet place in which to listen and work? In preparation for a visit to a school to answer this question, read what several authors have said about this. R. A. Hager, in "Open Education: A Look at the Subtleties," reports that there is a higher noise level to be dealt with in this popular approach to education (ERIC document #322567, 1990). W. G. Neill, in "Orchestrating the Soundscape," warns that people don't realize the dangers of excessive noise because it is pervasive and invisible [*Science and Children*, October 1982, *20*(2), 15]. And A. Eagan, in "Noise in the Library:

Effects and Control," reports that even in this usually quiet place, too much noise intrudes [*Wilson Library Bulletin*, February 1991, *65*(6), 44–47]. Then observe in the school and note the sources of noise pollution. Think up some ways these could be controlled, if not eliminated.

6. The Montessori approach is based on education of the senses, including listening. Read about the work of this pioneer educator. Her approach to developing listening skills is described in *The Montessori Method*, pp. 203–206, 209–214 (Cambridge, MA: Robert Bently, 1964). You could contrast Montessori's suggestions for listening activities with those you have seen in early childhood classrooms.

7. Research reports quoted in this chapter assert there is no significant difference between boys and girls in listening ability (Hollow, 1955). Contrary evidence is presented in Larry L. Barker, *Listening Behavior*, p. 45 (Englewood Cliffs, NJ: Prentice-Hall, 1971). Read both of these, and then observe in a preschool classroom. Can you notice any overt differences between boys and girls in to whom they listen, how much they listen, and how they show they are listening?

Suggestions for Further Reading

Berg-Cross, L., & Berg-Cross, G. (1978, March). Listening to stories may change children's social attitudes. *The Reading Teacher*, pp. 659–663.

> This study explores the effect of listening to picture books that expressed social values (with regard to sex role stereotyping, friendship, death, and risk taking) had on children's social attitudes. One hundred twenty children took pre- and posttests to measure their attitudes. Four picture books were read to each child individually. No discussion took place while the story was being read or afterward, but spontaneous questions from the child were answered.
>
> The attitude change from pre- to posttest was significant. Across all stories, students changed well over half their answers on the two tests. Results indicated that the expressed attitudes and values of 4- to 6-year-olds can be significantly changed by the children's listening to and looking at a picture storybook that espouses different attitudes. This attitude change occurred even without discussion, a finding contrary to previous research. The socializing aspect of these books suggests that parents and teachers should take more seriously the books they introduce to children.

Bryant, J. E. (1970). Listening centers: A sound investment in education? *Journal of Learning Disabilities*, *3*, 156–159.

> Most articles that describe listening centers as a means to individualization of listening instruction are favorable; this article raises some questions about the idea.

Devine, T. G. (1978, January). Listening: What do we know after 50 years of research and theorizing? *The Reading Teacher*, pp. 296–304.

> The author reports on nearly three dozen pieces of writing about listening, ranging in date of publication from 1926 to 1977, and concludes that, though much is known about listening, little is done about it. He describes listening tests; teaching techniques;

the relation to intelligence, to reading, and to thinking; and the status of listening instruction in the United States. His comment on skills sequences is revealing. Although many of these make logical sense, very few of them have been validated through research.

Hamacheck, D. E. (1971). How to get your child to listen to you. How to listen to your child. *Today's Education, 60,* 33–48.

This is an excellent resource for teachers—because it will cause them to reexamine their listening behavior—and to recommend to parents. Written in easily readable, concise fashion, the articles have a practical emphasis.

Hennings, D. G. (1990). *Communication in action* (4th ed.). Boston: Houghton Mifflin.

In her usual highly readable style, the author opens with a classroom anecdote to illustrate the types of listening, with clarifying examples of each type. The strength of this writing, as in Henning's earlier books, is the practicality of her classroom activities. There are simple, introductory activities included, as well as more complex critical listening skills for older children. She deals with appreciative listening and closes with a helpful checklist teachers can use in monitoring how children's skills are developing.

Herman, W. L. (1967). The use of language arts in social studies lessons. *American Educational Research Journal, 4,* 117–124.

During the six-week unit topic, the author had three judges record what went on in fourteen randomly selected fifth-grade classrooms. Results showed that in these social studies classes, children were engaged in listening and speaking 78.8 percent of the time and were reading only 13 percent of the time. Children who were slow learners were called on significantly fewer times than were bright children.

Konopa, V., & Zimering, S. (1972, March). Noise—The challenge of the future. *Journal of School Health,* pp. 172–176.

The detrimental physical and psychological effects of noise on people, especially the effect of teenagers listening to loud rock music, are described in scientific detail understandable to the lay person. Citing this as the most noise-exposed generation ever reared in the Western World, the authors describe government efforts to control noise through legislation and industry efforts to provide less noisy work environments. The authors conclude with efforts individuals can make to help control noise. A bibliography is included.

Lamberts, F., Ericksen, N., Blickhan, J., & Hollister, S. (1980, April). Listening and language activities for preschool children. *Language, Speech and Hearing Services in Schools,* pp. 111–117.

Opening with a summary of the kinds of language growth that are related to listening skill (including growth in sentence length), the authors point out that children have greater difficulty learning to attend to auditory than to visual information. They comment on the dearth of available auditory training materials for young children. Then they describe a set of materials, including pictures, slides, and cassette tapes, that they developed. In addition to matching pictures, students view a sequence of pictures, listen to a sequence of sounds, and cross out the missing sound. The authors reported that when they used these materials with preschool children, the combination of sound and pictures made it possible to maintain the attention of children even when materials were used repeatedly over long periods of time. Lamberts and her colleagues felt these materials help balance the predominantly "eye-biased" elementary curriculum.

Lundsteen, S. W. (1969). Critical listening and thinking: A recommended goal for future research. *Journal of Research and Development in Education, 3,* 119–133.

The author points out that research and writing in this area are confused and confusing. The lack of agreed-upon definitions is partly the cause; she based her work on Russell's definition. The article reviews the significant research, including that of Kellogg, Saadeh, and Reddin, and contains a review of her extensive research. She identifies the need for teachers to develop their own critical listening skills so they can help children improve this skill.

Russell, D. H., & Russell, E. F. (1979). *Listening aids through the grades.* New York: Bureau of Publications, Teachers College, Columbia University.

Updated by Dorothy G. Hennings, herself an author of several imaginative texts, this handy paperback still contains the most comprehensive collection of listening activities in existence. It has been expanded to include 232 activities, divided generally into kindergarten, primary, and intermediate grade sections and into levels of listening skill. The introduction is interesting because of its analysis of the similarities and differences between reading and listening.

Strother, D. B. (1987, April). On listening. *Phi Delta Kappan, 68*(8), 625–628.

Readers can compare the types of listening identified by Strickland, described earlier in this chapter, with the categorization system presented in this article. Strother includes a brief summary of listening research, points out that there are now some new tests of listening, and presents status information about the states that are developing plans to comply with P.L. 95-561, passed in 1978, which specifies the need to include speaking and listening among the basic skills. The article concludes with a section on classroom strategies; the material on how to use the "extra time" available because of the difference between how fast people talk and how fast we can listen is interesting.

Winn, D. D. (1988, November). Develop skills as part of the curriculum. *The Reading Teacher, 42*(2), 144–146.

Rather than thinking about planning a listening curriculum or locating a commercially available one, Winn suggests that the teacher and children can together plan a set of listening experiences that will reflect the kinds of listening the children really do in the classroom. Winn describes a process in which children chart, over time, the variety of listening skills they use. Then the teacher can plan direct instruction experiences to develop the skill, moving in a following stage to provide practice experiences across the curriculum.

Suggested Books for Children

Baylor, Byrd. (1978). *The other way to listen.* New York: Scribner.

This poetic text consists of short, conversational responses to nature. Peter Parnall's distinctive settings and insightful portraits depict an old man and a young boy as they speak together of the need to take time to listen. The boy learns to listen with the old man's help. Alone, he hears a sound he cannot write down because it would not make a word. The book is, once again, Parnall's insightful tribute to the idea that spareness is effective. The minimal lines in the sketches are brightened with yellow orange. The short text is equally spare, without an unnecessary word.

Bilezikian, Gary. (1990). *While I slept.* New York: Orchard Books.

Full-page, soft-hued illustrations are presented above the simple text, often a single phrase on a page. The child hears animal sounds (the cat who meows) and inanimate sounds (the bed that creaks), among others. Use this book with children as motivation to write a sound story about their house sounds.

Branley, Franklyn M. (1990). *High sounds, low sounds.* New York: Thomas Y. Crowell.

When doing a listening unit, it is often possible to interest upper-primary children in the science of sound. Branley's book does an admirable job of making complex matters simple; the experiments he suggests will intrigue children. The illustrations, done in Paul Galdone's usual relaxed style, are a valued and integral part of the book.

Bridwell, Norman. (1991). *Clifford's animal sounds.* New York: Scholastic.

In sturdy board book format, with seven double-page openings, this book follows the little red dog's exploration of the farm animals, each of whose sound is represented in a word. Simple pictures in bright solid colors are outlined in a black ink outline and presented with only minimal backgrounds, which won't distract young listeners. With only minimal encouragement, they will want to make the sounds along with the adult reader.

Brown, Craig. (1991). *My barn.* New York: Greenwillow.

In his pleasantly vivid pastel full-page pictures, author/artist Brown evokes a bucolic look at the sounds made by fourteen different animals the unnamed farmer looks after. From loud sounds (i.e., the donkey's hee hawww) to soft sounds (i.e., the peep peep of the baby chick), from large and small animals—all will encourage children to make the sound along with the reader. These are rural sounds, and a follow-up activity might engage children in doing a similar book about sounds in their environment.

Brown, Margaret Wise. (1993). *The summer noisy book.* New York: Harper & Row.

The story of little Muffin, an appealing pooch of indeterminate origin, and the sounds he hears on his way to the country and while he is there. To involve the children, the story gives the sound and then asks them to guess what makes that sound. Cheerful pictures in full color by Leonard Weisgard are a happy addition. This is from a series of books: see *The City Noisy Book, The Country Noisy Book, The Indoor Noisy Book,* and *The Quiet Noisy Book* (1993).

Dubov, Christine Salac. (1991). *Ding dong! And other sounds.* New York: Tambourine Books.

From a series of board books, this features very clear backgroundless photographs of children using various objects (bell, maracas, triangle, and cymbals among others) to make sounds. In the end, the individual children come together in a group to make music. Others in the series—*Knock! And Other Sounds* and *Oink! And Other Sounds* (same publisher, same year)—also feature full-color photographs by Elizabeth Hathon.

Isadora, Rachel. (1985). *I hear.* New York: Greenwillow.

Useful in motivating conscious awareness of environmental sounds, this simple book with just two sentences on each page features an unnamed young girl still in her crib. She hears sounds and describes them ("I hear a bird. Chirp, chirp"), she identifies the source ("I hear footsteps. It's Mommy and Daddy"), and she draws conclusions from what she hears ("I hear the kettle whistle. Time for breakfast"). All of this is accompanied by soft-focus chalk drawings by the author/artist. Use this book to motivate a discussion of the sounds children hear around them in their homes.

Lemieux, Michele. (1984). *What's that noise?* New York: Morrow.

For this gentle story of a bear trying to determine what an unfamiliar noise is, the author provides large watercolor and pastel illustrations of a woodland environment. Bear knows the noise isn't the "squeak-squeak" of the mice, the "peep, peep" of the baby birds, the "ribit, ribit" of the frogs, the "chock, chock" of the woodcutters' axes, the "creak-splash" of the old mill, or the "splash" of the apple he threw into the pond. The unfamiliar "thump-bump" sound continues through all his attempts to find out what it is. It isn't until the snow begins to fall that he finds out what the noise is, and it makes him happy to know what it is as he falls asleep for the winter. After enjoying this book with a group of children, have them listen so carefully that they can hear their own hearts beat. Is there any other sound they can hear that is even softer than that?

Martin, Bill, Jr., & Carle, Eric. (1991). *Polar bear, polar bear, what do you hear?* New York: Henry Holt.

Using the tissue paper streaked with paint that he began using in his collages some time ago, Carle here creates blocky-shaped, sharp-edged animals on backgroundless pages to accompany the simple, repetitive text. The lion hears a hippopotamus "snorting," the hippo hears the flamingo "fluting," the flamingo hears the zebra "braying," and so on. In all, there are nine different sounds, ending with the children, who are imitating all the sounds the various animals have made. Use the book to encourage children to make the sounds, talk about other words that might describe the sounds, and think about how to describe sounds made by other animals not included in this book.

McGovern, Ann. (1967). *Too much noise.* Boston: Houghton Mifflin.

Two-color illustrations with black ink lines tell the story of an old man in an old house that creaked, squeaked, and made many other noises. After suggestions from the Wise Man didn't work, the old man solves his own problem.

Parnall, Peter. (1989). *Quiet.* New York: Morrow Junior Books.

The illustrator, respected for his subtly understated drawings, here uses just a few colors placed sparely on the page to show the values of being silent, to hear the sounds of nature. The unnamed young boy lies quietly in the grass, listening to the sound of his breath, bumblebees droning, a mouse rustling under nearby leaves, wind whispers in the pines, and a chickadee pecking up a seed. He is able to hear these and other wonders because he can be quiet and really listen. This book is a fine motivation for children to listen to the small sounds in their own environments.

Richardson, Joy. (1986). *What happens when you listen?* Milwaukee, WI: Gareth Stevens Publishing.

In simple and brief picture book format, the author explains some complex phenomena about how sound is produced and transmitted. The author has devised several easy-to-do experiments using readily available materials/objects to help children understand aspects of sound such as the vibrations caused by sound. Diagrams showing various parts of the ear are large and clear. The book concludes with a brief bibliography, a list of sources to which children may write for further information, and an index, making the book useful as a basis for a report on listening.

Rylant, Cynthia. (1986). *Night in the country*. New York: Bradbury Press.

Artist May Szilagyi's softly focused chalk drawings sweep across the full, double-page spreads, enhancing this book about environmental sounds written in Rylant's usual condensed, poetry-like prose. She tells of the many small sounds to be heard: the dog's chain clinking, an apple dropping from the tree, a mother raccoon licking her babies, and the frogs growing quiet as the dawn approaches. Use this with children and encourage them to listen carefully to night noises so they can contribute to a group list the following day.

Shapiro, Arnold L. (1991). *Who says that?* New York: Dutton.

To make the youngest children aware of the sounds of animals in their environments, this book features very simple two-word rhymed couplets, interrupted at intervals with the longer line, "But boys and girls make different noise!" The pictures showing common animals like cats and less common ones like coyotes are done in simplified flat shapes defined with firm black pen lines. Children's noises include talk, shout, sing, chuckle, whisper, giggle, snicker, laugh, holler, and scream. These could be used as the base for a vocabulary experience as you talk about how these terms are different from one another.

Showers, Paul. (1991). *The listening walk*. New York: Thomas Y. Crowell.

A little boy, his pipe-puffing father, and their old dog walk around the city. Sometimes the noises are soft: the sound of the dog's toenails on the sidewalk; sometimes they are loud: the boom of a jet. Always they are fascinating to the little boy, who uses his ears to sense the city in an unusual way. The pictures by Aliki, though limited in color, are fresh. Showers's *Ears Are for Hearing* (same publisher, 1993) offers much useful information about how sounds are produced, received, and processed.

Taylor, Barbara. (1991). *Hear! Hear! The science of sound*. New York: Random House.

This useful paperback includes many simple science experiments beginners can perform, presented on visually appealing pages with color on each page. The information and pictures are grouped into categories like: "Sound and Music," "Drums, Scrapers and Shakers," and "Sound Messages." The participation experiences are simple enough for young children to do with materials easily found in schools, although the teacher will need to read and paraphrase the text.

Tresselt, Alvin. (1991). *Wake up, farm!* New York: Lothrop.

In a reissue of a book first published in 1955, here smartly dressed in new watercolors by Carolyn Ewing, child readers/listeners become aware of the myriad sounds that are common in an environment that may be unfamiliar to many children today. The rooster's cock-a-doodle-doo, the hen's cluck, cluck, cluck, and the duck's quack, the pig's oink, the goose's honk, the turkey, the donkey, the sheep, the pigeons, the tabby cat, the dog, the bees, and the cows: all contribute to a symphony of sound, all of which takes place before the little boy goes down to breakfast.

Ziefert, Harriet, & Gorbaty, Norman. (1984). *Baby Ben's go-go book*. New York: Random House.

> Typical of the kind of board book that has proliferated recently, this is made up of eight heavy cardboard "pages" laminated with a smooth surface, featuring simple illustrations and a brief text on each page. In this case, the baby explores sounds made by a car, a dump truck, a tug boat, an airplane, a train, and finally the baby himself. The full-color and ink line illustrations are two dimensional, and the text is simple enough so that children will soon learn it and enjoy repeating it while they make the sounds of the objects. Another example is *Animal Noises* by Sally Kilroy (New York: Scholastic, 1983), which features fourteen different animals and their sounds.

Zolotow, Charlotte. (1987). *If you listen*. New York: Harper & Row.

> This book is a pleasant, impressionistic treatment of the variety of sounds a young girl hears as she follows her mother's advice to listen to church bells, a fog horn from a river miles away, one petal falling off a rose, and a train rushing by in the night, among other sounds. The chalk illustrations by Marc Simont are as appealing as the text, which deals obliquely with the small girl listening because she is lonely for her absent father.

Zolotow, Charlotte. (1989). *The quiet mother and the noisy little boy*. New York: Harper & Row.

> Sandy, the little boy, likes noise so much that he "made it all the time." He talked in a loud voice to his mother, his father, and his dog. He even talked to himself in a very large voice. He played records, opened his drawers, went through doors that made noises, ran with his barking dog, and was only quiet when he was reading books or doing puzzles. His mother wishes for a bit of quiet, but when the little boy goes to visit his cousin, she notices how strangely quiet the house is. When the little boy and his cousin return, mother notices that the cousin is even noisier than her child is: Roger is a veritable tornado of noise! Thank goodness—Roger finally goes home, and the little boy is delighted to sit down quietly to do a puzzle with his mother. Pleasantly casual watercolor and crayon drawings by Marc Simont enliven the text.

References

Anderson, L. M. (1989). Classroom instruction. In M. Reynolds (Ed.), *Knowledge base for the beginning teacher* (pp. 101–115). New York: Pergamon Press.

Anderson, P. A., & Lapp, D. (1988). *Language skills in elementary education*. New York: Macmillan.

Bird, D. E. (1955, April). Are you listening? *Office Executive, 40*, 18–19.

Bois, J. S. (1966). The art of listening. In S. Duker (Compiler), *Listening: Readings* (pp. 43–47). New York: Scarecrow Press.

Breiter, L. R. (1957). *Research in listening and its importance to literature*. Unpublished master's thesis, Brooklyn College, New York.

Brent, R., & Anderson, P. (1993). Developing children's classroom listening strategies. *The Reading Teacher, 47*(2), 122–126.

Brown, C. T. (1965, June). Three studies on the listening of children. *Speech Monographs, 32*, 129–138.

Cazden, C. B. (Ed.). (1981). *Language in early childhood education* (rev. ed.). Washington, DC: National Association for the Education of Young Children.

Childers, P. R. (1970, Summer). Listening ability is a modifiable skill. *Journal of Experimental Education, 38,* 1–3.

Delamont, S. (1976). *Interaction in the classroom.* London: Methuen.

Devine, T. G. (1982). *Listening skills schoolwide: Activities and programs.* Urbana, IL: ERIC Clearinghouse/NCTE.

Dillon, J. T. (1988). *Questioning and teaching. A manual of practice.* New York: Teachers College Press.

Division of Early Childhood Education. (1984). *Standardized curriculum.* Philadelphia School District, ED #288 624.

Duker, S. (1968). *Listening bibliography* (2nd ed.). Metuchen, NJ: Scarecrow Press.

———. (1969). Listening. In R. L. Ebel (Ed.), *Encyclopedia of educational research* (pp. 747–751). New York: Macmillan.

Dwyer, J. (Ed.). (1989). *'A sea of talk.'* Portsmouth, NH: Heinemann.

Feltman, A. (1967). *The effect of reinforcement on listening skills of the culturally deprived.* Unpublished master's thesis, The Ohio State University, Columbus, OH.

Friedman, P. G. (1978). *Listening processes: Attention, understanding, evaluation.* Washington, DC: National Education Association.

Funk, H. D., & Funk, G. D. (1989). Guidelines for developing listening skills. *The Reading Teacher, 42*(9), 660–663.

Greene, H. A., & Petty, W. T. (1975). *Developing language skills in the elementary schools.* Boston: Allyn & Bacon.

Hall, E. T. (1969). Listening behavior: Some cultural differences. *Phi Delta Kappan, 50,* 379–380.

Hirsch, E. D., Jr. (1991). *What your first grader needs to know.* New York: Doubleday.

Hollow, M. K., Sr. (1955). *An experimental study of listening comprehension at the intermediate grade level.* Unpublished Ph.D. dissertation, Fordham University, Bronx, NY.

Hyslop, N. B., & Tone, B. (1989). Listening: Are we teaching it, and if so, how? *Bulletin of the Association for Business Communication, 52* (2), 45–46.

Jalongo, M. R. (1991). *Strategies for developing children's listening skills* (Phi Delta Kappa Fastback Series #314). Bloomington, IN: Phi Delta Kappa Educational Foundation.

Last, E., & DeMuth, R. J. (Eds.). (1991). *Classroom activities in listening and speaking.* Madison: Wisconsin Department of Public Instruction.

Lundsteen, S. W. (1979). *Listening—Its impact on reading and the other language arts.* Urbana, IL: National Council of Teachers of English.

———. (1984, February). How to assess your listening needs. *Curriculum Review,* pp. 22–23.

Moffett, J., & Wagner, B. J. (1992). *Student-centered language arts, K-12* (4th ed.). Portsmouth, NH: Boynton/Cook Publishers.

Murray, T. M. (1989, Fall). Cull: The man and his issue. *Childhood Education, 66*(1), 33–34.

Orr, D. B., Friedman, H. L., & Williams, J. C., et al. (1965). Trainability of listening comprehension of speeded discourse. *Journal of Educational Psychology, 56,* 148–156.

Rankin, P. T. (1928). The importance of listening ability. *English Journal, 17,* 623–630.

Roche, A. F., & Siervogel, R. M. (1980). *Longitudinal study of children's hearing: Its relation to noise and other factors.* Presented at 100th meeting of the Acoustical Society of America. Abstract in *Journal of the Acoustical Society of America,* Suppl. 1, p. S89.

Samuels, S. J. (1984). Factors influencing listening: Inside or outside the head. *Theory into Practice, 23*(3), 183–189.

Spiegel, D. L. (1990). Materials for developing listening skills: A review of five criteria. *The Reading Teacher, 43*(9), 674–676.

Stibbs, A. (1979). *Assessing children's language.* London: Ward Lock Educational/The National Association for the Teaching of English.

Strickland, R. G. (1969). *The language arts in the elementary school.* Lexington, MA: Heath.

Travis, L. E. (Ed.). (1971). *Handbook of speech pathology.* New York: Appleton-Century-Crofts.

van Riper, C. (1978). *Speech correction.* Englewood Cliffs, NJ: Prentice-Hall.

van Wingerden, A. (1965). *A study of direct, planned listening instruction in four counties in the state of Washington.* Unpublished Ph.D. dissertation, Washington State University, Pullman, WA.

Wells, G. (1986). *The meaning makers.* Portsmouth, NH: Heinemann.

Wilt, M. E. (1950). A study of teacher awareness of listening as a factor in elementary education. *Journal of Educational Research, 43,* 626–636.

Wolvin, A., & Coakley, G. (1988). *Listening* (3rd ed.). Dubuque, IA: Brown.

Children's Books

Alexander, Martha. (1988). *Even that moose won't listen to me.* New York: Dial Books for Young Readers.

Brown, Craig. (1992). *City sounds.* New York: Greenwillow.

Brown, Margaret Wise. (1993). *The noisy book.* New York: HarperTrophy.

———. (1993). *The quiet noisy book.* New York: HarperTrophy.

———. (1993). *The seashore noisy book.* New York: HarperCollins.

———. (1993). *The summer noisy book.* New York: HarperCollins.

Chapman, Jean. (1986). *Cat will rhyme with hat.* New York: Scribner.

Cousins, Lucy. (1992). *What can rabbit hear?* New York: Tambourine Books.

Goode, Diane. (1988). *I hear a noise.* New York: Dutton.

Goor, Ron, and Goor, Nancy. (1990). *Insect metamorphosis. From egg to adult.* New York: Atheneum.

Hall, Donald. (1985). *The Oxford book of children's verse in America.* New York: Oxford.

Hindley, Judy. (1992). *Soft and noisy.* New York: Hyperion Books for Children.

Hines, Anna Grossnickle. (1992). *Rumble thumble boom!* New York: Greenwillow.

Jarrell, Randall. (1964). *The bat poet.* New York: Macmillan.

Lavies, Bianca. (1990). *Backyard hunter. The praying mantis.* New York: Dutton.

Lionni, Leo. (1971). *Theodore and the talking mushroom.* New York: Pantheon Books.

Martin, Bill, Jr., & Archambault, John. (1988). *Listen to the rain.* New York: Henry Holt.

Professional Growth

The Work of the International Listening Association

Contact:

Dr. Charles Roberts, Executive Director
c/o Center for Information and Communication Science
Ball State University
Muncie, IN 47306
(317) 285-1889

This association of 500 members includes representatives from education, business, industry, and government, all of whom are interested in some aspect of the study and development of effective listening. It conducts research on listening in regard to educational, cultural, and other areas, exchanging information on teaching methods and materials. It sponsors workshops and seminars as well as an annual conference. The association publishes the *International Listening Association Journal* and *The Listening Post.*

FOUR

UNDERSTANDING ORAL LANGUAGE AS PART of AN INTEGRATED PROGRAM

. . . narrative (storying, storytelling, storymaking) should be located at the center of the learning process in the classroom and should be more fully explored in all subjects of the curriculum.

Gallas (1992, p. 172)

This chapter will focus on enriching the oral language competencies that children bring to school. Linguists agree that most boys and girls are in command of the basic structures of their language before they come to school (John & Moskovitz, 1970). Children have used their listening skills to hear and master the sounds of English. They have acquired an impressive array of syntactic constructions (Yawkey et al., 1981). Young children have experimented with a variety of ways of expressing ideas (see Clay, 1975). They have used language to serve all the functions for which adults use it. While there still are some significant gaps in the skills children possess when they enter school, basic linguistic competency is essentially established for many children (Chomsky, 1969). Our task, therefore, is to provide an array of experiences that move students beyond such basic competency to more masterful fluency. Teachers provide experiences that challenge children to extend, enrich, and elaborate the language patterns they already command.

The Primacy of Oral Language

Some common but often overlooked facts reveal why linguists have identified oral language as *the* language. This form and not the written form, which is symbolization removed from the actual language, merits our attention for several reasons. Oral language is (1) the most commonly used mode of expression—used more frequently than written language by adults; (2) the first form a child learns and, for many children, the mode in which they feel most secure; and (3) the form all peoples develop. Of the 2,796 languages in the world, all have an oral form, whereas only about 153 have a written form (Pei, 1984).

Oral Language in the Curriculum

Children need to go beyond basic language skills to develop oral fluency, yet only recently have school language arts curricula begun to reflect the importance of talk. Preschool and kindergarten teachers have long known that children need opportunities to talk. Once students enter traditional first-grade classrooms, however, the amount boys and girls are allowed to talk is often sharply constrained because talking has had a low priority in education (Lange, 1981). Neither elementary textbooks nor curriculum guides give teachers enough encouragement for developing this aspect of language; in most, written language still predominates. These materials rarely have a deliberate sequence designed to develop oral skills in a coherent, planned way. In recent years, teachers have been finding the encouragement they need in the burgeoning literature about whole language approaches to education, although Strickland and colleagues (1989) said that "the language curriculum of the school is much more likely to emphasize reading and writing—not talk" (p. 193).

Probably one reason for the minimal emphasis on oral language is that, to date, too little has been done to identify the separate components of oral fluency. Research has not provided clear-cut answers for the following questions:

1. What specific oral competencies should children have as a result of the oral fluency strand in an early literacy curriculum?
2. What are the most efficient ways of developing the desired competencies? What experiences, problems, and challenges should children encounter to develop oral fluency?
3. What kinds of evaluation of oral fluency are appropriate? How can we measure the specific competencies to determine whether our program is effective?

Walter Loban (1966, p. 99), in a fresh and direct article written especially for classroom teachers, commented on the problem of evaluating oral language: "Until anything is evaluated it is unlikely to receive much emphasis in the total teaching scheme. 'Give me the power to evaluate and I will control the curriculum,' is a memorable saying. The boundaries of the curriculum inevitably shrink to whatever is evaluated, and at the present time oral proficiency is scarcely evaluated at all." Although Loban's article was written some time ago, it is still well worth reading. What makes Loban's comments especially pertinent is that Moffett and Wagner (1992), over twenty-five years later, still assert that schools prefer reading and writing to speaking and listening because "oral language activities are too hard to test in the customary ways" (p. 9).

There seem to be two reasons for this evaluation problem. The first is the *complexity* of the oral message, and the second is its *transitory* nature. Any oral message is made up of a wide range of components: the basic oral sounds, the paralinguistic elements, and such little-recognized components as gestures and kinesics. Thus, analyzing oral communication is a more complex task than analyzing written communication. The transitory nature of oral communication militates against effective evaluation. Once a message is frozen in writing, it can be considered at leisure, reexamined, and pondered. Unless one has audio- and videotape equipment for preserving both verbal and nonverbal aspects of oral language, evaluation is almost impossible. Once something is said, it is lost. Until teachers can find the time to tape students' oral communication so these data can be analyzed later, effective evaluation will remain limited.

Where to Begin: Informal Conversation

The nursery and kindergarten teacher's role is to encourage children's spontaneous oral language while helping increase their skill in using words to say what they want to say. Most young children are eager to talk with the teacher, with other children, and in small group situations. Thus, the most important thing the teacher does to increase oral fluency is to demonstrate interest in what children want to share.

The teacher does this in several ways. Children must have a listening ear as often as they need it. If the teacher is elbow deep in mixing fingerpaints, it is absolutely crucial to suggest another (and more appropriate!) time for the child to share his or her ideas. Thus, the teacher may say something like, "I can't talk with you right now, Bobby, or the paint will dry out, but come and sit by me when we have milk and I can listen then." It is admittedly true—in fact, almost inevitable—that by milk time, which may be only ten minutes away, the child will have forgotten what he wanted to say. Nonetheless, the teacher has established in the child's mind that what he has to say is significant, even if something prevents the teacher from listening at the exact moment the idea occurs.

When children role-play real situations, such as working in an office, authentic oral language develops.

Another way teachers demonstrate to children the importance of oral language is by the informal conversation groups they form and encourage. Draw two to six children together, perhaps to observe something, to reflect upon someone's idea, to share part of a book, or to help solve a problem. The purpose is to provide a milieu in which children learn the delight of and, incidentally, some of the informal rules that govern small group conversation or discussion. Neal (1987) offered a possible sequence of conversation experiences for children.

Most early childhood teachers want to facilitate this type of informal conversation and discussion. The same is not, unfortunately, always true of teachers of other grades. What are the values of informal conversation groups, and why should all teachers encourage them?

Many values accrue from such informal conversations. Frequently, the *self-concept* is strengthened as the child learns to interact with a group of peers. The child learns to cope with situations verbally instead of withdrawing into silence or having a tantrum, which may have sufficed at home. Another value is the *language learnings* that may occur as children find out, for example, that their ideas may be clear to them but may not be equally clear to listeners. *Conceptual learnings* are another value of these groups—for instance, when one child talks about a topic another child has never encountered, discusses an unfamiliar aspect of a familiar topic, or suggests another way of viewing a topic.

Any and all of these learnings can and do occur without the teacher being in the group. The teacher can help expand and relate any learnings that are occurring, but the teacher is not the crucial element in the group. As Britton (1985) said so well, there are many talkers in any elementary classroom, and teachers who regard themselves as *one*, but not even the most important one, will allow children to learn on their own.

Although these values from small group conversations are clear, it is still rare to see much time specifically set aside for such activities beyond the kindergarten level. Because parents assume everyone can talk, too few understand why oral language is a basic skill. Not enough early childhood teachers can explain fluently why time set aside for talk is critical.

Play corners are commonly used to motivate informal conversation among young children. Unfortunately, such corners too frequently remain unchanged. The objects (kitchen equipment, clothes for dressing up, and other real things to encourage language use) are the same from the beginning of the year to the end. It is wise to vary the equipment in the play corner (Dodge & Frost, 1986). In addition to the ubiquitous housekeeping equipment, teachers can change the corner's equipment so it is a role-playing center, garage/repair shop, hospital, shoe shop, or beauty salon, among other possibilities (Riley, 1991). Morrow and Weinstein (1982) pointed out why a library play corner should be part of early childhood classrooms. Their research indicated clearly that altering the classroom environment to make such a choice possible increases the literacy involvement of children.

More Formal Conversations: Group Sharing Time

Often at the beginning of a day, early childhood teachers draw their entire group together in a time designed to reestablish a feeling of community, to give children a chance to talk about important things that have happened since yesterday, and to plan the day's activity. This sharing time has much potential, and the language learning it offers to young children is wide-ranging and long-lasting. Surely, when teachers work in this context, they are helping students develop abilities that are of much use in adult life, for all adults engage in variations of this technique in sharing with peers something that delights us and in planning cooperatively what needs to be done.

For this sharing time to be of maximum effectiveness, teachers should follow these guidelines:

1. Give undivided attention to what is going on. Although the temptation may be great to balance the attendance register or to enter information on health records, the teacher always gives each sharer his or her full attention. This activity is *informal*, but it is also *directed* at first. It is not free and spontaneous in the beginning. Such qualities are learned, and the teacher has to guide the discussion by making appropriate comments (Higginbotham & Reitzel, 1977), asking leading questions, perhaps holding part of the article being shared for the child. The teacher is an active, not a passive, participant. As children develop the skill of taking part, the teacher's role lessens. By the time the practice has served its purpose, eliciting a free flow of discussion, the teacher will be involved only minimally.

2. Develop the ability to ask intelligent, probing questions, not such questions as "Who gave you the book, Tom?" or "When did you get the fire truck, Anne?" These elicit one- or few-word replies and don't help expand oral fluency. Rather, ask such questions as "What else can you tell us about the truck, Anne?" or "Have you heard any other stories like the one in Tom's book? How are they like each other?" or "What do you suppose you might have done if the same thing had happened while you were at the parade?" Such questions are not easy to ask, but this skill can be developed.

Sharing time focuses on children's language, although the teacher should feel free to participate by sharing information about a hobby or perhaps a trip. At times the teacher invites classroom visitors who provide language stimulus. One kindergarten teacher had an "Old-Fashioned Day," inviting grandparents to share. Some came prepared only to tell of days gone by; others brought pictures or showed how to churn butter. One played a guitar and sang a song learned during an Appalachian childhood. Similarly, a third-grade teacher invited a retired teacher who had worked with Hopi children in the Southwest. He brought souvenirs, including drawings students had made. It was a valuable language-interaction experience enjoyed by both the retired teacher and the children, who were on the edge of their seats as he told of daily life in an Indian school.

It is important for teachers to attend carefully during sharing time because different narrative styles are apparent in ethnic groups. Cazden (1986) reported that children's narrative style is more "topic-centered" in Caucasian children and more "topic-associating" in African American children. This reflects differences in other aspects of black oral style. Cazden and others found that white teachers found topic-associating stories hard to follow and inferred that the speaker was apt to be low-achieving, whereas black teachers responded positively to both kinds of stories and their narrators.

The Importance of Questions

Anyone who intends to teach should be able to ask stimulating, open-ended questions, but research has demonstrated that such is not necessarily the case. Some early research by Gall (1970) showed that the ability is neither native nor easy to develop. Cliatt and Shaw (1985) as well as Snydam (1985) have continued this line of thinking, documenting

The child is explaining the picture and story she developed individually after a group brainstorming session about winter. The teacher and the other children will ask her questions about her work.

the importance of open-ended questions in stimulating children's curiosity. More recent research has been on the feasibility of teachers encouraging children to ask their own questions before beginning a unit of study (Jacobs, 1991). In commenting on the pervasiveness of teachers' questioning, Dillon (1988) reported that questions constitute sixty percent of teacher talk but only one percent of student talk. He introduces a book on this topic with a quote designed to make us reflect on this pervasive but often unconsidered aspect of classrooms: ". . . questioning by teachers is an exercise of power and control—and thus limits authentic discussion and discourages questioning by students" (p. ix). To change this, his first chapter focuses exclusively on questioning by students themselves.

Researchers have also studied the effects of waiting for responses to questions. Rowe (1974) established that when teachers increase the wait times beyond the usual average of about one second to at least three to five seconds, pupils: (1) increase the length of their responses, (2) offer more alternatives, (3) ask more questions, (4) interact more with other pupils, and (5) appear more confident in replies. Tarlington and Verriour (1991) reported similar helpful outcomes of increasing wait times when children were dramatizing.

Responding to Stories   Teachers of young children sometimes make the mistake of asking the wrong question after reading a story. To ask "Did you like the story?" does not accomplish anything. Most children, eager to please, will answer yes. For the one or two obstreperous children who want to attract attention, their emphatic *no* serves their purpose but not the teacher's. The question encourages a yes/no response but does not encourage thinking. A better question is "What were you thinking as you listened to the story?" Responding children can (1) give a value judgment, sharing their feeling about the story; (2) link the story to another they've heard; (3) relate the story to their own lives; (4) react to the teacher's reading of the story; or (5) comment on the pictures that accompany the story (Stewig, 1988).

A third-grade teacher read *Franklin Stein* by Ellen Raskin (1972) to her class. Afterward she asked children to tell what they were thinking. Some responses were "Franklin Stein should make a girl pet for Fred. He should also invent a way to keep his sister's mouth shut" (*Trenny*). "The title gave a different feeling than the story actually did. I thought that Fred would turn out to be a sort of Frankenstein" (*Fonna*). "I was wondering what Fred's friend would look like" (*Ricky*).

Teachers can use questions to provide practice in *elaborating* part of a story. Sometimes children can be encouraged to think about relatively minor elements in a tale. In *Goldilocks and the Three Bears* by Lorinda Cauley (1981), the walk the bears take while waiting for the porridge to cool is briefly mentioned. One second-grade teacher read the story to her class, and then used these three questions:

1. "Where did they go?" ["They went to New York City." "The three bears went to a lake." "They went down the block."]
2. "Who did they meet?" ["They met an elephant, a lion, and a tiger escaped from a zoo." "They met a man in a boat who was fishing." "They met a lady selling cars."]
3. "What did they do?" ["They went to look for a house to live in in New York." "They went fishing, and they looked down to the bottom of the lake." "They searched for a new car."]

Teachers use questions to stimulate discussion about many topics. Research justifies discussing literature with children; such discussion expands vocabulary and many other language abilities, as Huck (1992) pointed out. Roser and colleagues (1992) showed that language charts, which record the discussions primary children have had about literature, document the link such discussions make between reading and oral language.

Developing Describing Competencies

Many different activities can lead to oral fluency. Describing is one competency that can be expanded and enlarged as the teacher helps children toward fluency.

Describing People   Children enjoy the opportunity to observe people and then use words to create oral descriptions. (Such activities may culminate in written activities for older students.) For the primary child this is essentially a two-step procedure. First, the teacher works on simple describing. Tell children to secretly pick a friend and observe that friend in spare moments. Later, each child can give an oral description while others guess the identity of the child being described. Among first-grade children who dictated descriptions was Eugene:

> He's got some black boots, and he's got a green shirt with yellow stripes and red stripes. He's got some big teeth in front, and he's got a tooth missing. He plays outside. He chases the girls. We play a whole bunch of games outside. He likes to play with the second-graders, and the second-graders play King-of-the-Mountain. He likes to color, and he shares crayons with me.

A second-grade class tried their hand at a similar experience, and Debi said:

> My friend has blond hair. She doesn't wear glasses. She has gray eyes and long bangs. She is in the room 102 Warm Fuzzy Crew. She is my best friend and I am her best friend. I know her for a long time—since kindergarten. She has a big family. There are seven in her family. She lives near me. I walk to her house and we have fun. We play house.

When beginning, simply have the children observe randomly. Accept and encourage all reporting. After children have developed some facility in this, help them categorize or organize the descriptors they have been using as an aid to further improvement. Ask "What kinds of things about the person have we been including in our descriptions?" and list the answers. When posted in the room, the list will help children develop this skill.

A slightly more involved task is *comparing*. The child can choose two "subjects," observe their likenesses and differences, and give an oral impression of both children.

Describing Objects   Students can be challenged to describe objects, which presents a different sort of task. Bring in a large box with objects in it and allow a child to describe one of them for the rest of the children, who can guess what the object is. It is important to remember that even though this can be a delightful game, the main purpose is *not* the guessing but rather the developing of describing competencies. Therefore, at some time after children have enjoyed playing the "game," the teacher draws from them a list of elements that should be included in a good description.

In addition, at some time during this activity, the teacher helps children understand that descriptions can be made in two different ways: *finite* and *comparative*. The sample statements in Table 4-1 indicate how various elements might be described.

Describing Pictures   Pictures are one type of object that can be described. Because they are more complex visually than most objects,

Table 4-1

Finite and Comparative Descriptions

	Finite	Comparative
A.	Size "The object is about six inches long."	"The object is about as long as a water glass is tall."
B.	Color "It's blue with a lot of black mixed in it."	"It's the color of the sky just before a thunderstorm."
C.	Texture "It's made of lots of small peaks arranged close together in a regular pattern."	"It's like a rough kind of sandpaper."

they deserve special attention as motivation in developing describing skills. At first, teachers and students can talk about the visual qualities of pictures. One kindergarten teacher read *One Wide River to Cross* by Barbara Emberly (1966). Later, while having her boys and girls use very dull woodcutting tools to make their own block prints,[1] the following conversation ensured:

Tina: I made a woodcut design for you!
Ms. Weis: How can you tell it's a woodcut?
Tina: The letters are kinda' squarish, 'cuz it's hard to do curvy lines on wood.
Ms. Weis: Did you remember that from the book?
Tina: No, but when you were showing us how to make the Christmas card design. . . .
Ms. Weis: Oh, and what else tells you that it's a woodcut?
Tina: Well, there's some little lines around the letters because the wood sometimes gets in the way.
Ms. Weis: Do you remember what we called that?
Tina: No.
Ms. Weis: Well, some people call it the scrap.
Tina: Oh, yeah . . . the scrap.
Ms. Weis: Can I have this lovely design?
Tina: Sure, I'll make you another one if you want!

Later, teachers can consciously use pictures as a discussion stimulus. Reproductions of artists' paintings are a rich motivation to talk. Children are shown the pictures and encouraged to move through a three-step procedure: first simple *describing,* then *comparing* two illustrations, and finally *valuing.* This last term means stating a preference. The teacher is developing the fluency that enables a child to say, "I like this picture because. . . ." As adults we often make statements beginning "I like . . . ," but only rarely do we move to the more sophisticated statement including a fluent reason for this preference.

A kindergarten teacher, working with mostly Caucasian children from lower-middle-class backgrounds attending a whole-day program, introduced two versions of the same story. She used *Three Blind Mice* with pictures by Paul Galdone (1987) and another version with pictures by Victoria Chess (1990). On the first day, after the teacher read the story, children were asked to simply tell what they noticed about the pictures or the story. On the second day, they made a comparison/contrast chart (see Table 4-2).

On the third day, children studied both books to decide which they preferred. Then they came to the teacher individually and dictated a statement. Some preferred Galdone:

[1] This particular teacher felt comfortable having her children use woodcutting tools. If you don't, you could do the project using potato prints. This technique is effectively described in *Potato Printing* by Helen R. Haddad (New York: Thomas Y. Crowell, 1981).

I like this part [when they ask the host for food] when they were not scared. I liked the part [when they slept in the hay stack] when they're sleeping good. I liked this part when they scratch their eyes and the cat scratched the mouse.   (*Ashley*)

TablE 4-2

How They Are *Different*

Chess	Galdone
Cover illustration:	
Mice are wearing clothes	Mice are wearing only scarves; walking on grass
Second mouse holds comb	First mouse holds comb
Mice can still see	They are blind already
Inside illustrations:	
Flowers are all the same (purple)	Flowers are all different colors and shapes
Mice sleep outside in a field in grass	They sleep under a haystack in straw
The host at the inn has a wife	No wife is shown or mentioned
Mice are standing on part of the well; one is picking up a nutshell	Can't see the well; nutshell is there but no one is picking it up.
Host, farmer, and wife are all mice	Host, farmer, and wife are all humans
Cat is not shown, though "wanted" picture of it is hanging on the wall	Cat is shown, close up
Mice look at themselves "in a glass"	Mice look at themselves "in a pond"
Chemist (a mouse) gives them "never too late to mend" salve	Dr. Hare gives them magic salve
Inside view of mice in their new house (no explanation of how they got it)	Outside view of them building their thatched house
Text:	
"Pined" for some fun	"Wished" for some fun
"Hid themselves"	"Made a leap"
"Lost their minds"	"Couldn't find their way home"

How They Are *Alike*

1. Mice are dressed in the same colors (red, yellow, and blue).
2. More of the words are the same than are different.

From *Three Blind Mice* by
John W. Ivimey, with illustrations by Victoria Chess
(Little, Brown, 1990).

> I like this one when they go to say "hi" to the guy [rabbit]. I liked when they put that stuff on their eyes. I like the cover because this guy has a big comb and I like the colors of their scarves.   (*Ben*)

Others preferred the version by Chess:

> I liked the part [when they jumped out of the window]. I liked it because he's holding the comb.   (*Brett*)

> Because he's got a little comb and they're stepping on a branch [on the cover]. I liked the part when they cut the tails off.   (*Brian*)

The teacher was surprised at how definite the children were when picking their favorite version. Although they had never done this sort of activity before, she found that even those children who didn't have much to say quickly and firmly chose their favorite. Evidently, children enjoyed choosing and then telling about their choice.

Almost any picture can stimulate describing skills (Stewig, 1986). The rationale for moving children through a sequence of increasing difficulty in developing skills of describing, comparing, and valuing may be helpful to teachers interested in doing such a program. Using illustrations from children's books is an easy way to develop these skills. Hough, Nurss, and Wood (1987) cautioned that to move children beyond simple reporting of what they see into more complex language functions like reasoning, projecting, or predicting, teachers must be willing to provide "consistent, intentional interaction" (p. 9).

From *Three Blind Mice* by John W. Ivimey, with illustrations by Paul Galdone (Clarion, 1987).

Describing Voices   A kindergarten teacher used a record, "Mother Goose" (by Cyril Ritchard and others), with her class. She asked children to listen to and then describe the voices. A recording of "The Crooked Man" was read by Boris Karloff. Children commented: "It sounded scary." "It is an ugly voice." "It was down a little." After listening to "The Three Little Kittens" read by Celeste Holm, children said: "It sounded wavy." "Her voice went up and down." "She sounded like a baby."

Describing the Environment   At times we might ask children to tell about part of their environment. Students can describe home or school. A teacher in Wisconsin, where seasons bring strikingly different kinds of wind, used *Gilberto and the Wind* by Marie Hall Ets (1963) with her boys and girls. After she used the book/tape kit with the class,[2] children dictated their reactions to the wind. Jeff dictated:

> I like when it hits me, and I like when it blows me back. Then I like when I ride my bigwheel; it pushes my bigwheel back. When I don't have a hat my face gets cold, and when I get in the house my face gets warm. When I shoot the cans up in the air and it comes down, it pushes, and it goes up in the air, and the wind blows it down. I like to play in it when the leaves is way up in the air. I like to catch 'em and crunch 'em, and when they are writing a name

---

[2] Several manufacturers produce such kits, which provide an aural interpretation to go along with the visual and printed text. This kit is available from Live Oak Media, P. O. Box AL, Pine Plains, NY 12567. Like others in this series, this includes a paperback copy of the book and a read-along cassette (one side without a page-turn signal for more confident readers, the other with a signal so less secure readers can follow along).

out in the wind, it makes them mess up. I like when we are playing kickball. When I don't kick it, the wind kicks it.

Field Excursions   When teachers plan field trips, they are setting up a situation in which questions are critical and children can use their describing competencies (Mangieri, Staley & Wilhide, 1984). Oral language is central as children draw up a list of questions to which they would like answers as a result of the trip. During the excursion, students should be encouraged to ask questions of the host/guide or resource person, of the teacher, or of other adults who are helping supervise. When they return to the room, children need time to dictate group chart stories or to tape record individual impressions of the experience. In so doing, they can describe what they saw, felt, smelled, touched, and tasted during the experience. All the while, they will be using their listening skills as they interact verbally with others. An informal oral report to younger children might be an appropriate culminating activity for upper-primary students.

Children Create Beauty with Their Voices

More time is now spent in the passive consumption of electronic media than on arts created by the individual. Thus, suggesting that children need time to explore and extend the range, power, and expressiveness of their voices is apt to go unheeded. Yet children can indeed create beauty with their voices. This section makes some specific suggestions to help children achieve great satisfaction from the expressive qualities of their voices. Engaging children in what Stoodt (1988) called *aesthetic* oral experiences is the necessary other half of a total program, balancing informational purposes for speaking.

Oral Reading

The teacher reads to the class each day for a variety of purposes, including sharing a wide spectrum of literature children might not otherwise encounter. Equally important is to provide a model of an adult as reader so students may see this activity as pleasant. Reading for even five minutes a day results in a vast quantity of literature being shared during the year. If you were to read just one poem a day for an entire school year, children would encounter about 180 poems, more than most children encounter in their entire elementary school career. If you read prose for just five minutes per day, sharing about five or six pages, imagine how many books children could encounter in a year! Neither plan would be good as described because a program of reading must include a variety of forms. The figures are included simply to make the point that vast quantities of literature, of whatever form, can be shared with children if teachers do this on a regular basis.

Encouraging Effective Oral Reading As with storytelling, the purpose of oral reading is not only for children's passive pleasure. It extends to involving upper-primary children in reading to the group. This is not reading around the circle in reading class, but more expressive creation—choosing something the child likes to share with others. To make this more effective, the teacher through discussion draws from children some things an effective oral reader does. These can be formalized in a chart posted in the room. Children might identify some of the following: Readers (1) establish eye contact with listeners before beginning, (2) tell something interesting about the selection (perhaps why they like it) before beginning, (3) have practiced enough so the selection can be read fluently without excessive dependence on the book, and (4) use their voices effectively to catch and hold interest. With younger children, this point may be identified very simply: "His voice told us when he ended a sentence." With older children, it will be discussed in more sophisticated fashion: "She stressed the important words" or "He used the pauses effectively." It is not necessary to discuss oral reading techniques with the entire group; not all children will be ready to begin oral reading at the same time. Work with a small group, but post the chart where everyone can see it. It will stimulate other children's interest.

The teacher should help children select something to read, keeping in mind their reading ability and what has been read in class recently. We want to make this as pleasant an experience as possible for all children.

Provide time for practice. Students need time alone to practice, to manipulate pitch, stress, and juncture in a variety of ways to bring life to the printed word.

Provide time for students to evaluate their own work before they read aloud (Gunderson, 1991). Make available an easily operated cassette tape recorder. Children find listening to themselves as revealing as adults do; they are sure to find different ways to read material as a result of using the recorder. Or encourage children to practice in pairs before reading for the class.

Help a child evaluate his or her performance by asking questions. Find time to listen and ask questions: "Where do you feel you read especially well?" "What things about your reading in this section (or sections) are particularly good?" "Where do you have trouble getting the reading to turn out the way you want it to?" "What things make trouble for you there?"

Najimy (1983) reported on having children develop checklists for what makes an effective oral reader. Before starting on a project in which they would select and then prepare a story they enjoyed for others to hear, children thought about what they liked in an oral reader and drew up a cooperative group list. They could then practice and evaluate their own reading using the checklist.

Storytelling by the Teacher

The ultimate purpose of sharing stories orally is to establish in children's minds that these activities are worthwhile. The final goal is to motivate children to assume responsibility for the activity. The teacher provides a model by learning stories and telling them to children.

Selecting a Story to Tell   Choose a story that captures your imagination (Sutherland & Arbuthnot, 1984). Read through several stories and then set the project aside. After a while one or two of them will come back to you; you should probably learn one of these.

Preparing the Story   There are three basic steps in preparing the story.

1. *Units of action.* First, divide the story into *units of action* (Stewig, 1990a). You will notice that most stories seem to divide into easily definable series of actions or episodes. These can be summarized in brief note form, and the sequence can be learned. For most people, this is a more efficient way of learning the story than trying to memorize it.

The Talking Eggs by Robert D. San Souci (1989), a Caldecott Honor book, illustrates how a story can be divided into units:

Unit One: Her mother sends Blanche to the well to fetch water. While there, Blanche meets an old woman and gives her a drink.

Unit Two: When Blanche gets home, both mother and sister Rose berate Blanche for being so slow in returning that the water is warm. Blanche, frightened, runs away into the woods.

Unit Three: There Blanche encounters the same old woman, who invites her home after cautioning her that she must not laugh at anything she sees.

Unit Four: At the old woman's house, many strange things happen: Blanche sees chickens of every color with varying numbers of legs; she sees a cow with two heads and corkscrew horns. Inside the house, even stranger things occur: the old woman removes her head to comb her hair; when Blanche boils the old beef bone she is given, the pot fills with thick stew; one grain of rice fills the mortar; they watch the rabbits dance in front of the house.

Unit Five: The next morning, the old woman tells Blanche to help herself to eggs from the henhouse, warning that she should choose only those that say, "Don't take me." Blanche does as she is told.

Unit Six: On the way home, again following instructions, Blanche throws the eggs over her shoulder and is amazed that all sorts of wonderful things spill out of the eggs.

Unit Seven: At home, overcome with envy over Blanche's riches, her mother and Rose plot that Rose will go into the woods and meet the woman, so she can get fine dresses and jewels.

Unit Eight: After encountering the old woman, Rose goes to her house but disobeys all the woman's instructions. No magical happenings occur.

Unit Nine: After taking the eggs she has been told to leave behind, Rose starts home. When she throws the eggs over her shoulder, awful things spring out of the eggs. She rushes home, only to discover that Blanche has gone to the city. Neither Rose nor her mother ever see the old lady again.

2. *Exact wording.* The second task in preparing a story is to identify sections that need to be memorized verbatim. In this story, we use the rich language drawn from the story's Creole background to retain the unique flavor of the time (late nineteenth century) and place of origin (Louisiana). For example, Rose and her mother talk about going off to fancy balls wearing "trail-train dresses"; the old woman tells Blanche, "You got a spirit of do-right in your soul"; Rose resists going into the woods, "lookin' for some crazy ol' aunty." In addition to language like this from Creole origins, other words that are standard English may be unfamiliar to children. The old woman *plaited* her braids. She used a *mortar* and *pestle* and cooked in a *skillet*. The rabbits did the *cakewalk*. It would be inadvisable to change these to simple, more commonly known words—like substituting *dance* for *cakewalk*—because in doing so, we lose the story's distinctive flavor.

3. *Learning the story.* Memorizing a story in its entirety is indeed formidable, especially when demands for more "practical" activities press upon us all. The delightful thing is that most stories have only a few short sections that need to be learned exactly. Stories are more interesting if the teller learns the essence and allows it to unfold in a slightly different way each time (Nessel, 1985). After identifying the units of action and memorizing some exact wordings, the third step in learning a story is to write the units of action on index cards and carry them with you. Whenever you have a few minutes, you can review the action sequence. Reread the cards—perhaps while waiting for a red light, a doctor's appointment, or the elevator. I find it usually takes me about three or four days to learn a story.

Gestures   Judicious use of gestures can enhance a story. In the story used here, while saying, "She began to toss the eggs one at a time over her left shoulder," it is very logical to make that gesture, especially when telling the story to very young children, to help focus their attention. Each individual can use good judgment in this matter.

Music   An additional way to enhance the telling of stories is to create simple tunes for songs the characters sing. When we tell an old Italian folk tale about Giricoccola to children, we teach them the simple melody in Figure 4-1. They can sing along as the character in the story, the moon, sings. The story is now available in a picture book format (Stewig, 1993).

Such simple tunes are easy to create and serve two purposes. First, they capture children's attention and provide for active involvement. Even very young children enjoy singing along with the storyteller. In this story, the song is sung five times, and even though the 4-year-olds with whom I worked could not really learn it, they enjoyed singing some of the words. Second, such songs reinforce the idea that creating music, along with other art forms, is a logical school activity. You can teach these songs to your class before you tell the story by simply sing-

From *The Moon's Choice* by John Warren Stewig, with illustrations by Jan Palmer (Simon & Schuster, 1993).

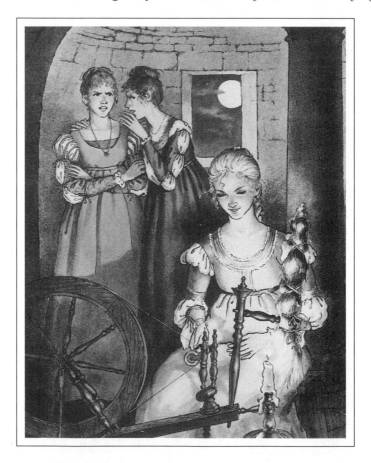

FIGURE 4-1

A simple melody like this can be made up, and children can sing along with the teacher.

ing the song or by playing the melody on an instrument. The final goal is not the teacher as performer, but rather the child as composer of simple tunes. Music educators (Paynter & Ashton, 1970) say that students enjoy making up melodies. When a melody composed by a group of children can be used in storytelling, it provides an additional impetus to create (Stewig, 1990a).

Children As Storytellers

The teacher's goal is to encourage children to tell their own stories. The kindergarten teacher encourages spontaneous talk at many times during the day. This can be telling brief anecdotes or stories about current or remembered experiences. At first these may be only two to six sentences long, but they lay the groundwork for more formal storytelling activities later. In addition to encouraging children to tell their own stories, teachers often use literature to inspire stories.

Retelling the Tale   With very young children, a useful stimulus to oral language is retelling a favorite story in their own words (Preece, 1991). One kindergarten teacher read *Two Greedy Bears* by Mirra Ginsburg (1976). After children enjoyed the amusing story of bears who are bested by a wily fox, students dictated these retellings:

> The cubs were walking. They were hungry, and they saw this cheese under the plant. They didn't know how to split it, and they were fighting between it.

Then the fox came and then he split it. Every time it was bigger, and then he took the other piece of it to make it smaller, and that other piece gets bigger. He chewed more off it, and the other piece was bigger until it was almost all gone and they just had a little part left. They got thirsty, and then they saw water. They wanted to drink more, and they started to fight over it. They just started to drink, and they drank so much they got a stomachache, and they went to sleep for a while, and then they woke up and they felt better.   (*Joe*)

The two bear cubs went out to see the world and one said, "I'm thirsty," and the other one said, "I'm thirstier." And so they drank some. The other drank some more and some more, and then they stopped. One said, "I've got a stomachache." The other said, "I've got a bigger stomachache," and then they fell asleep. When they woke up they felt better. And then one said, "I'm hungry," and the other said, "I'm hungrier," and they began their hunt. Then they found a big piece of brown cheese. The bear cubs did not know how to divide it into two. They thought that when they would break it, each would be bigger than the other. And then came a fox and he broke it in half, but he was to make sure that one was not bigger than the other, so he took a bite out of one, then the other was bigger. Then he took another and the other was bigger. Then he ate up all the cheese except two little crumbs and then he said, "Happy appetite." Then the two bear cubs ate the piece of cheese and then the end.   (*Leslie*)

Translating from Pictures to Words   One way to encourage children to tell stories is to have students make up words for wordless picture books. These books have a fairly tight story structure, so it is easy to provide verbal descriptions of them.

A second-grade teacher used the book *Bubble Bubble* by Mercer Mayer (1973). Pleasant watercolor and ink illustrations depict an adventuresome little boy who gets more than he bargained for when he begins blowing soap bubbles. Afterward, children who wanted to dictated their own words. Joy contributed this:

One day a little boy was walking through an area with all kinds of bubbles. The bubbles came right in front of him. He jumped on a box and he saw all kinds of bubbles. He saw a magic bubble maker. He could buy it for only 25 cents. He bought it. He went home and showed it to his mother. Then he started blowing a bubble tree. All of a sudden he saw a kangaroo out of bubbles in front of him. When he ran with the bubbles in front of him, he saw all kinds of stuff made of bubbles. Then he made all kinds of stuff with the bubbles—a plane, snake, shoe, and a flower. The snake was awful mean. It almost bit him. Then he made a big fat cat, and the snake got awfully sad because he had no one to play with. The cat chased after the snake. Then the cat started chasing after him. Then he made an elephant and scared the cat away. Then the elephant stamped at him. Then he made a mouse and it scared the elephant away. He had fun popping all of the things he made. All of a sudden he dumped his bubbles on the ground and he threw the bubble maker away. But when he dumped his bubbles on the ground, a dragon came up. But he was walking away.

In a combination first/second grade, the teacher used *Time to Get Out of the Bath, Shirley* by John Burningham (1978). Realistic pictures on one page and fantastic pictures on the opposite page tell this amusing story. Shirley shrinks in size and slips down the drain, entering a world of castles, knights, and jousting. After children looked at the wordless book, they dictated a group story:

First of all, Shirley shrank. Then she hopped on the duck and went down the drain. (She had to shrink a lot in order to fit through the strainer which keeps the soap out.) Then she went out the waterfall and she must have grown, or else she would be so small that someone would step on her. Wearing only a towel and holding onto a leaf, she let her rubber duckie go down a waterfall. Still in the towel, Shirley rode a horse through the forest with a prince. In the light of the full moon, the witch was spying from behind the tree, while two other witches were watching her spy. When morning came, she raced two other horses. The king and the queen were on the other horses. Off they rode to the kingdom, and the king and queen got married. After blowing up two ducks, they rode the ducks down the river to Alabama for their honeymoon. On their honeymoon, they had a fight. Then Shirley knocked down the king and won the fight. Up she went through the drain into the tub. (This story is truly out of this world!)

In addition to using wordless picture books as a stimulus to compose, such books can also be used to determine whether children are ready to begin more structured reading experiences. When children's oral language in dictated stories begins to approximate more formal language (book talk), the child is probably ready for more direct instruction in reading. With older children, dictated stories give teachers insight into their ability to infer (Jett-Simpson, 1976). Hudson-Ross, Cleary, and Casey (1993) show, in classroom transcripts, the values of what teachers can learn by studying what children say during dictation experiences.

Dictating the Ending   A particularly effective way to elicit dictation is to read a story to an exciting place and then ask young children how they would finish it (Stewig, 1990b). The activity can be done in a group, or individual children can complete the tale. Then the actual ending can be compared and contrasted with the suggested ones.

A teacher read *The Strange Disappearance of Arthur Cluck* by Nathaniel Benchley (1967), in which a chick named Arthur is lost. Ralph the owl helps search, to no avail. Finally, "he looked in the farmhouse window, and saw a bowl of colored eggs." After this, Eric was among the second-grade children who dictated endings:

Ralph looked in the bowl, but he couldn't find Arthur. Then he saw something in the bushes. It was a squirrel. "Will you help me find Arthur?" he asked. The squirrel said yes, and they went searching in the farmhouse again. They couldn't find him, but his mother heard something while she was sleeping. Ralph gave up. So did the squirrel. The mother looked around where she heard the noise. It was in the hay. She picked up the hay; there was Arthur. The End.

Old Mother Hubbard by Lisa Amorso (1987) also works well for this purpose. Involve children in problem solving by reading only the first verse to them. Then ask them what Old Mother Hubbard did so her poor dog wouldn't have to go hungry. Some first-graders came up with these solutions: "She remembered she had buried a bone in the ground, just in case her cupboard was bare" (*Hayes*). "So she went to the woods. She searched under the trees and found a dinosaur bone" (*Jennifer*). "So she went to the woods and caught a squirrel and killed it. She cooked it, and got the bones, and gave it to her dog" (*Slaven*). For children who have enjoyed this rhyme, share with them the elaborations of the dog's adventures in *Old Mother Hubbard's Dog Dresses Up* (1990) and three other titles in the series by John Yeoman and Quentin Blake. These fanciful extensions of the characters into other places and activities show how an author can develop a basic idea beyond the original source of the idea.

Another effective story for this purpose is *Dorrie and the Witch Doctor* by Patricia Coombs (1967). A first-grade teacher read part of it and then asked children what would happen next. Joseph dictated: "The witch doctor gives Dorrie a witch potion, and she hiccups because there are cobwebs in it." Danny dictated: "The doctor might have to sleep over. In the night, Aunt Agra might turn the doctor into a sandwich, so she could eat him for lunch, because she thinks Dorrie is fooling about being sick. Then she'll get very sick, and her mother will say angrily 'Aunt Agra, you get out of this house!'" Note the syntax in the second twenty-eight-word sentence. Perfectly formed, it is far more elaborate than Danny, or most first-graders, could encode in handwriting. Children who enjoy this story would be interested in the other nine books in the series still in print, including *Dorrie and the Pin Witch* (1989).

Extending a Story   Extending a story is a useful and more difficult activity than story completion. When children have been engrossed in a particular story, ask a question that will take them beyond the end of the tale. In *Mooch the Messy* by Marjorie W. Sharmat (1976), the author tells of an appealing rat who revels in his disorderly housekeeping until his tidy father arrives for a visit. Mooch reforms, the two clean up his tunnel, and the story ends on a positive, organized note. Some teachers read the story and then asked children, "What did Mooch do after his father left?" Students enjoyed providing endings, some of which showed that Mooch had not completely reformed! "Mooch kept it neat for the next time Dad came. You never know when he will come back again" (*David, first grade*). "He went home and kept his tunnel neat because his father said he was coming back. His father kept sending him letters saying he was coming, and so Mooch kept his hole clean" (*Nora, second grade*).

Constructing a Parallel Plot   In this technique, useful in motivating either oral or written composition, a literature model is provided. With the teacher's help, children extract the plot. Specific details are stripped away, and the level of abstraction is raised so units of action can serve as a basis for a story by children. The plot is then fleshed out with new details—setting, characterization, and resolution—which are the children's own.

Some stories have very simple structures. In "The Gingerbread Boy," for example, the plot line is (1) an old person makes a food; (2) the food runs away; (3) the food encounters someone (either person or animal, depending on version) who wants to eat it; (4) the food escapes; (5) actions 3 and 4 are repeated differing numbers of times; and (6) the food is captured and eaten. There are small variations in the plot line, depending on which version is used. You might want to use the version "Johnny-Cake," found in *Tales from the Enchanted World* by Amabel Williams-Ellis (1987) with elegantly detailed full-color and black and white illustrations by Moira Kemp.

The plot of *Periwinkle* by Roger Duvoisin (1976) is more elaborate. A giraffe cannot find a friend because no one speaks her language. Although she meets Lotus, the frog, who can communicate with her, Periwinkle discovers the course of friendship does not always run smoothly. The units of action are (1) main character is sad because it is different; (2) main character meets another character who is different in the same way; (3) they are pleased with each other but disagree; (4) each goes his or her own way; (5) they reconcile; (6) they disagree again; (7) a danger threatens the first character, who is saved by the second character; and (8) they reconcile and agree to be friends.

After a second-grade teacher read this story to her students, she helped them identify the plot elements listed above. Then children dictated this group story:

> Yacup, the unicorn, was sad. "I wish I had someone to hiccup with; I'm lonely."
> "I hiccup," said a voice high above. Yacup jumped and galloped about. "Where are you?"
> "I'm here in the treetop. I'm Jigup."
> "I hiccup and I am lonely. I have no one to hiccup a song with."
> "Where did you learn to hiccup?"
> The owl said, "I saw a child hiccup and learned to hiccup watching him. Where did you learn to hiccup?"
> The unicorn said, "I caught a cold from a dinosaur and he was hiccuping and I caught the hiccups. Fly down and sit on my back and we can hiccup together."

So the owl flew down and sat on Yacup's back.

"You hiccup too much."

"You hiccup too loud."

"You hiccup in my ear."

"Stop it."

"Stop, stop."

"O, go jump in a tree."

"Gladly!"

So Yacup jumped up as far as he could.

"Ouch, ouch," yelled Yacup. "I'm caught in the branches."

Poor unicorn was trapped—branches all around—scratching him, his ears, his tail, his eyes. Suddenly came a loud noise. A jet was flying low and with the propellers cut the branches. Down fell Yacup and wandered back to his silent woods.

No one to hiccup with. . . .

No one to listen to him . . .

"Maybe I should have listened better with Jigup." Off Yacup galloped to listen to Jigup's hiccups.

"I'm sorry I didn't listen to you," said Yacup when he saw Jigup.

"I'm sorry I was mean to you," said Jigup. So Jigup flew down on Yacup's back.

"Please tell me about yourself."

"No, I want you to tell me about yourself."

"You first."

"No, you first."

Jigup hiccuped and said, "I'm wasting my time. First you hiccup too loud; now you only want to listen."

"Since you feel that way, get off my back," said Yacup. He bucked up and off fell Jigup.

Before Yacup could fly away, a hawk flew down and started to carry Jigup. Yacup charged after the hawk and. . . .

"Thank you, Yacup, for saving me."

"I'll just rest for a minute in the tree." So Yacup went back to his silent wood. He thought for a while and said, "The trouble with Jigup and I—we didn't take turns." So he walked back to the tree and called: "Let's be friends. We must talk to each other. Tell me where you learned to hiccup."

So Jigup said, "I heard a boy hiccuping and I learned. How did you learn? He was a good boy and fed me some food."

"I learned when I lived in a castle and all the people hiccuped there. They were very kind to me and took good care of me."

And so Yacup and Jigup went on hiccuping, always taking turns. They learned to hiccup a song and were very happy.

Asking "What If" Questions   Another effective way to elicit stories from children is to pose "what if" questions (Torrance & Meyers, 1970). The teacher can present one of these either early in a day or in the week, and provide time later for children to tell their story to answer the question. The goal in making up "what if" questions is to provide an open-ended structure. This might seem to be a contradiction of creativity, but such is not the case. The fact that a question *is* posed adds structure to the storytelling, but the open-ended nature of the question encourages the child's creativity.

Recently college juniors created the following "what if" questions:

1. What if when you stepped outside your house all the other people in the world had disappeared?
2. What if everything that you touched melted?
3. What if you could be anything in your kitchen?

Here are some stories told by the children with whom this set of "what if" questions was used:

1. "I'd cry, and I would run around yelling and screaming. I would be scared because I would think that what got them would get me too. So I would run back into my house and hide in the clothes hamper. I would keep on screaming." (*Sue, second grade*)
2. "Once upon a time, I was eating ice cubes. And I went to bed and my bed melted. And I turned off my lamp and my lamp melted. Then the next morning I turned on the television and my television melted. I was going to read a book and my book melted. Then I was going to school and my whole school melted. The teachers melted, and don't forget the kids melted. And then I cut myself and my whole Band-Aid melted. I was gonna make a story up and my papers melted. And then I was gonna write something on the chalkboard and the whole chalkboard melted. And then I was going to go to my collection of bugs and then my bugs melted. And then I was going to paint something and then my painting stick and my painting jar and my painting paper melted. And then I was going to go outside and play with my swings and then my whole swing set melted because I sat on it. And then I was going to sleep by the fireplace and then the fire melted all the ice that I had in my body. And whatever I touched came normal again." (*Erick, first grade*)
3. "If I could be frosting, I could be put on a cake. If I could be some tea, I would turn myself back and drink the tea. If I were a chair, I would wait until someone would come and sit on me. If I were a box of cereal, I would eat myself. Then I would turn myself back into what I was. Then I would turn myself into everything in the kitchen and I would hide from my mom. When she comes in, I would grab her and say, 'Peek-a-boo.' Then I bet she would say 'Ahh!'" (*Dionna, first grade*)

Once they understand the procedure, children can create their own "what if" questions; they delight in doing this.

Increased Oral Fluency   One advantage of story dictation is that it allows students to express themselves more fluently than they can in writing. Even among children who have mastered the skill of encoding thought in manuscript letters, oral expression is almost always more coherent and extended. A teacher of a transitional first grade read a variant of *Stone Soup* by Iris Van Rynbach (1988) to her children and then asked them, "What did the soldier do after he left the town where he made the soup?" Children printed their responses. Later that week, the teacher reread the story—at the children's request. Then she asked those who wished to dictate their answers to tell a response as she wrote it down. In both pairs of responses that follow, note the more abbreviated response when the child was writing.

Handwritten: He came to a house. He asked for a big container. He put the stone in. All the people put vegetables in the soup stone container. (*Jennifer*)
Dictated: "He went to another village. He called for a big container. He put the stone rock in the soup and he tasted it. He needed some vegetables to put in the stone soup, and all the family got some vegetables. They put them in the stone soup. He tasted it again. They ate it. He gave the stone to them in case they needed it. He went away." (*Jennifer*)

Handwritten: He kept walking and walking until he got to another village to teach them how to make soup. (*Joe*)
Dictated: "Then he was walking, and then he came to another village, and the family didn't have no food. So he made some food with his stone soup, and then he said if they had any carrots and they had none but he had some. Then he served it out. Then everybody like it, so he gave the stone soup to them." (*Joe*)

This discrepancy is common and continues throughout the primary grades. To encourage the full expression of children's ability to compose, we must provide dictation experiences even though we also teach students to encode their thoughts in writing. Hall (1986) offers other ideas about engaging children in dictation.

Choral Speaking

Choral speaking and *choral reading* are two terms that are used interchangeably to mean saying a piece of poetry as a group. Providing a rich diet of poetry as part of the oral reading program is one of the best ways to develop interest and enthusiasm for the art of choral speaking. With poetry, as with some other forms of literature, reading aloud is the most effective way to experience it. Poetry is not effective read silently. Teachers need to transform poems from a thing in space into sounds in time because "it is the performance of the poem which *is* the poem" (Salpen, 1964).

The early childhood teacher, reading many poems to children, will discover them repeating some of the words or perhaps even a phrase or two. The teacher should encourage this repetition, but participation at this level remains simple. Groups enjoy saying simple rhymes together, perhaps from *Mother Goose*.[3] If appropriate, the teacher helps them learn to say a poem orally, but formal work in choral speaking is more logically a concern of the primary and intermediate grades.

Children may be divided into many types of groupings for choral reading: unison, refrain and chorus, dialogue or antiphonal, line-a-child, or solo voice with choir (Stewig, 1981). Any teacher with a good poetry anthology will find useful poems, but some are suggested here in case you have never tried locating poetry for this purpose.

For *unison* reading, you might like to try "January Thaw" by Eve Merriam, in a collection entitled *Fresh Paint* (1986).

For *refrain and chorus,* the repeated line "chucka-choo, chucka-choon" in *There's a Train Going by My Window* by Wendy Kesselman (1982) is effective.

For *dialogue or antiphonal* reading, try *The World Turned Upside Down* by Marcia Sewall (1986), in which half of the children say the verse up to the semicolon and the other half say the remainder.

For *line-a-child,* try "Monday's Child Is Red and Spotty" by Colin McNaughton in *For Laughing Out Loud,* selected by Jack Prelutsky (1991).

For *solo voice with choir,* use "Let's Go to the Wood" in *This Little Pig-A-Wig* by Lenore Blegvad (1978).

As a composer decides which instrument will play a specific part in a musical score, so the teacher decides—at least at the beginning—which children will say what lines. Children will soon have ideas of their own about how the poem should be divided. The teacher encourages these ideas and takes the time necessary to try out the variety of ways boys and girls suggest. A group of children recently evolved the following way of dividing this poem as the way they liked best, after experimenting with several different ways of saying it:

[3] There are innumerable versions of *Mother Goose* verses. Those in *The Orchard Book of Nursery Rhymes,* chosen by Zena Sutherland (New York: Orchard Books, 1990), are accompanied by the meticulously detailed illustrations of Faith Jaques, whose "Illustrator's Notes" at the end of the book are particularly informative. Watercolor and ink line illustrations by Maryann Kovalski accompany *Sharon, Lois and Bram's Mother Goose* (Boston: Atlantic Monthly Press, 1985), which includes music for piano. Use *The Glorious Mother Goose,* selected by Cooper Edens (New York: Atheneum, 1988), for the historic array of thirty-eight artists whose work was originally published between 1870 and 1933. Also featuring multiple artists (over sixty) is *Tail Feathers from Mother Goose* (Boston: Little, Brown, 1988), a panorama of contemporary illustrators.

THE GOBLIN

By Rose Fyleman
(Cole, 1984)

| Group 1 | Groups 1 & 2 | Groups 1, 2 & 3 |

A goblin lives in our house, in our house, in our house,
[All children]
A goblin lives in our house all the year around.
Bob: *He bumps*
Jane: *And he jumps*
Mary: *And he thumps*
Ted: *And he stumps.*
Tim: *He knocks*
Al: *And he rocks*
Liz: *And he rattles at the locks.*

| Group 1 | Groups 1 & 2 | Groups 1, 2 & 3 |

A goblin lives in our house, in our house, in our house,
A goblin lives in our house all the year around. [All children]

Marking the Poem   Teacher and children together can make decisions about where they want the voices to get louder or softer, where to say a line faster or slower, and other interpretive decisions. With upper-primary-grade children, a rudimentary marking system sometimes makes it easy to remember how children want to say a poem. For example, you could use— / to indicate a slight pause and // would show a complete stop. Indicating where voices get louder, using <, or where voices get softer, using >, helps children remember how they want the poem to sound. For a second-grade teacher's description of how she helped children mark and then rehearse poems they had chosen to read for their class, see the helpful article by Lenz (1992).

Creating Verbal Obbligatos   Many poems lend themselves to the creation of verbal obbligatos. The term *obbligato*, borrowed from music, means a persistent background motif. Usually this refers to a repeated theme played by an instrument against the major melody in a piece of music. In choral reading, it means having some children repeat words or sounds at patterned intervals to heighten the mood or evoke the image. In "Trains" (Sutherland & Arbuthnot, 1984, p. 51), for example, some children may repeat the words *clickety-clack* in a rhythm they have created as the rest of the students say the poem. One group of children with high voices repeats the *clickety-clack* in one rhythm while another group with lower-pitched voices repeats the same words at a different rhythm. This provides a background while the third group says the poem.

Other poems that lend themselves readily to the enhancement of obbligatos are the cat poems in Nancy Larrick's *Cats Are Cats* (1988). Experimenting with *mew, meow,* and other cat sounds in different pitches and different rhythms can result in a very rich obbligato background for the poems. A more involved background is necessary for "Three Little Puffins" (Sutherland & Arbuthnot, 1976, p. 74), which mentions panting, puffing, chewing, and chuffing—all in one poem! Children enter with enthusiasm into planning this intriguing collection of sounds as they vary rhythm and pitch to create an obbligato that may surpass the poem in interest.

As children create obbligatos, they get wrapped up in the excitement of creation and performance. Tape recording an early effort allows children to reflect and discuss. As the students listen and reshape, the piece moves from its tentative beginnings to a finished choral experience, alive as only children's imaginations can bring something to life.

Readers Theatre

In readers theatre, individual children read roles (Bauer, 1987). As material for readers theatre, teachers need fairly short selections with sufficient dialogue to involve children. *Gumshoe Goose* by Mary DeBall Kwitz (1991) and *Mo and His Friends* by Mary Pope Osborne (1991) are examples of books that work well for this purpose. Each is composed of several short chapters told mostly through dialogue of the animal characters. Children could be helped in groups to select one of the short chapters (each complete in itself), assign and practice parts, and then do the reading for other children. Part of the Dial "Easy-to-Read" series, these are in paperback format. Teachers could get two copies and rip them apart so children could cut out and mount the illustrations. One child could hold up the illustrations in sequence as the other readers present the story. Although illustrations are not usually considered part of a readers theatre presentation, including them adds additional interest to the presentation.

Drama in the Classroom

Young children engage in dramatic play even before they enter preschool. Informally they assume roles—mother, father, and other adults they observe—and they interact with peers in "trying on" adult roles. Dramatizing is a sturdy plant, but it needs to be encouraged because of the language growth it stimulates. As Schickendanz (1978) pointed out, children generate more verbal language during dramatic play than in any other situation. Wise teachers build upon the potential for language learning by structuring experiences to bring children and drama and books together.

Seltzer (1989) has suggested that a careful observation of children's behavior during role playing can suggest ways to structure more formal drama experiences for children. The following role-play observation guide developed by Seltzer can be useful in learning more about children's beginning dramatizing.

Role-Play Observation Guide (Seltzer, 1989, pp. 24–25)

Child _____

Activity _____

Observing a role-play episode, do you see the child doing the following?

Behavior	Notes
1. Pretending to be someone else	
2. Sharing with others	
3. Using one object (prop) to stand for another	
4. Using actions and sounds as substitutes for the real thing	
5. Using words to represent a make-believe setting or situation	
6. Talking with others within the context of role-playing	

Story Dramatization   We often begin with simple movement experiences. For example, there are many movement possibilities in Michael Rosen's *We're Going on a Bear Hunt* (1989) which has pleasantly large, full-color watercolor illustrations by Helen Oxenbury. The mother, father, and children must go through long wavy grass ("swishy swashy"), a deep cold river ("splash, splosh"), thick, oozy mud ("squelch, squerch"), a big dark forest ("stumble trip"), a swirling, whirling snowstorm ("hoooo woooo"), and a narrow gloomy cave ("tip-toe, tiptoe") until at last they come face to face with their quarry. Then the entire sequence reverses—only much more rapidly(!)—until the entire family is safe under the covers in bed. Talk with children about

Children have chosen a favorite part in a story they've read to use as the basis for a dramatization.

how they could use their bodies to show each of the action words, and then they can make the motions they've devised as you read the poem.

Dramatizing a poem or story is one of the most natural and rewarding ways a teacher brings young children and literature together (Davies, 1983). In the process of enacting literature, children develop deeper understanding, express their reactions, and learn about the process of dramatization. What is story dramatization? Very simply, it is helping boys and girls take a story and plan ways to use their bodies and voices to enact it. This requires children to make decisions in order to effectively translate a printed story to a living mode incorporating voice, gesture, and body movement. The goal is the knowledge children gain about literature and drama and their ability to work together in relating them. The purpose is *not* to involve students in learning lines written by adults or to create a performance for the enjoyment of an audience.

Creative Drama   Story dramatization is only one type of creative drama. A variety of activities—rhythmic movement exploration through pantomime, characterization, making up original stories—all are included under the general term *creative dramatics*. Despite this diversity, some common qualities of dramatic experiences can be identified. One distinguishing quality is *inclusiveness*. All children can participate by taking an idea and reacting spontaneously. The key word is *opportunity:* teachers make a genuine attempt to involve all children, including allowing timid or unresponsive children to play inanimate objects if this gives them security. One kindergarten child may prefer to be a rock in the old stone wall when the rest are being mice gathering for the winter while interpreting *Frederick* by Leo Lionni (1967). The same is true of older children. When using "The Sandhill Crane" (Austin, in Adams, 1972), two third-grade children were unfamiliar with the animals described in the poem, so they devised a creative way of working together to be the dam opening, letting water into the swamp.

The teacher has a plan for each session. Because of the *ongoing* quality of drama, however, the session is not a failure if the exact purpose is not reached in that particular session; other sessions are coming later. Suppose the class is dramatizing *Red Riding Hood* by Christopher Coady (1991). The main purpose might be to help children sense and portray the scariness of the forest and the way the trees, growing closely together, allow only dimly filtered light to sift through to the forest floor. Imagine, however, that as the teacher worked on mood with children, they became fascinated with the threat of the wolf. Portraying the devious wolf creeping behind Little Red diverted one class from the teacher's intent. He was not dismayed by the deviation because he could lead another session on mood later. Perhaps for a second session, the leader could use another version of the same tale (Hogrogian, 1967; Zwerger, 1983).

There is a *recurring* quality to drama because certain ideas or organizing elements pervade all dramatic experiences. These include mood, plot, characterization, rhythm, and unity (Lud & Ulrich, 1980). Because these recur, older students, who may have had drama for some time, are as concerned with them as kindergarten children. The following example uses characterization. We read "Snakes and Snails" by G. T. Hallock (Sheldon, 1966), discussed how snakes move, and delighted in moving through the mind-created swamp grasses as threatening snakes. One particular group of kindergartners, however, was ready to progress beyond simple movement to more complex characterizations, so we stopped and talked about snakes. Some questions we considered were: (1) How might a heavy, fat, old rattler, steeped in the sun, move? (2) How might she or he be different from a lithe, young grass snake? (3) If you were hungry, how would you move differently than if you were full of a foolish mouse dinner? These and other questions stimulated children to think of differences, and we were on our way to a simple understanding of characterization.

Children should have characterization experiences at each grade level. At the upper levels, we might use the nonsense rhyme about the old lady who was so silly she swallowed an entire menagerie (Westcott, 1980) and explore such questions as: (1) What is the old lady really like? (2) Was she always as silly as she is now? (3) What kinds of problems could she have? How might she react to these problems? After discussing her peculiarities, children could be divided into groups of four, with two groups working together. One group invents a problem for the hungry old woman; the other creates her response, thereby establishing their concept of her character. This activity challenges children to think more deeply, expanding and developing their characterization. In the poem, the woman is two-dimensional, a silhouette set against a series of bizarre behaviors. Older students can examine her thoughts and attitudes, the reasons for her behaviors, and her responses to problems and people. In the process, they can create several different versions of the old lady. After enjoying that experience, using the film "I Know an Old Lady Who Swallowed a Fly" gives children a chance to think and talk about how the story in this format, with color and animation, is different than in book format.[4]

Creative drama is a *process* for elementary children, rather than a content area with specific grade or level expectations. For college-age students and teachers, there is content *about* drama to be learned (McCaslin, 1990), but this is less important with young children. Children do indeed learn about such things as characterization, mood, plot, conflict, and rhythm, but they learn about these dramatic techniques with any materials. It does not matter whether the leader uses *Snow White* by Paul Heins (1974) or *Cinderella* by Diane Goode (1988) to develop ideas about characterization. The leader might use *The Sleeping Beauty* (Hyman, 1977; Yolen, 1986) for mood development. If none of these interests the group, the teacher may choose an entirely different story.

Components of Drama   Drama sessions are made up of four basic components:

1. *Material.* Ideas used to motivate the session usually appeal to children's senses. There are many kinds of motivations: pictures, real objects, conflict lines, and minimal situations, among others. Here our primary concern is literature.

2. *Discussion-questioning segment.* After (or while) the teacher presents the motivation, spontaneous discussion occurs, carefully directed by the teacher's judicious use of questions to uncover possibilities in the material.

3. *Playing an idea.* This stage varies in complexity with the children's age and dramatic experience. Sometimes this is a simple pantomime of one activity, such as opening a birthday present; at other times it is more complex, such as playing an entire story children have created.

---

[4] The film is available from International Film Bureau, 332 S. Michigan Ave., Chicago, IL 60604; 6 minutes, color/sound, featuring folk singer Burl Ives accompanying himself as he sings the old song.

4. *Evaluation.* In this stage, children are encouraged to consider what they have done and decide which aspects pleased them and which could have been more effective. Self-evaluation is a basic goal of drama. Last (1990) provides a helpful section on evaluation, including some assessment checklists in a curriculum guide that includes a strong early childhood component. This kind of material is helpful, for as Genishi (1992) said:

> . . . no one has proven that language-based activities like dramatic play, often a feature of whole language programs, contribute in measurable ways to school learning . . . assessing such activities . . . is as much a challenge . . . as describing developmentally appropriate curricula (p. 107).

Preparing for Drama: Creating Dialogue   To enhance children's ability to create dialogue, it is often helpful to use part of a story and ask them to talk as if they were the characters. In *Owl at Home* by Arnold Lobel (1975), the author tells the amusing tale of Owl, not too bright but nonetheless a hero. Owl has a problem he cannot solve that keeps him awake at night. After reading the story, the teacher demonstrated how to "become" one of the characters. She was Owl and chose one of the more verbal children to be Chipmunk. By structuring the situation this way, she showed her first-graders what she wanted them to do. The following dialogue was created by two children after the introductory demonstration:

Owl is asleep in his chair when he is awakened by a knock on the door.

Owl: I thought I heard someone knocking on the door. I'm going to get my bathrobe. I'm coming! I'm coming! (*Opens door.*) Hi, Deer, come in.

Owl and Deer sit down.

Owl: How come you came so early?
Deer: 'Cause I wanted to visit you. I thought you would be up.
Owl: It's so early in the morning!
Deer: You usually are the first one up. How come you are still sleeping?
Owl: What time is it?
Deer: I don't know. I have no watch.
Owl: It's one o'clock!
Deer: Do you usually sleep till one o'clock?
Owl: I usually wake up at 10:30.
Deer: It's past 1:30. What was wrong last night? Why couldn't you sleep?
Owl: When I was in bed, I saw these two things. I got up to turn on the light. I saw nothing, and I turned out the light. Then I turned it on again, and I saw the two bumps.
Deer: Then what?

Owl: I got out of bed. I turned off the light. They came back. I got under the covers. I got my head under the covers. Then when I got into bed, it was scary. Then I started jumping on the bed. It was starting to crack, and the bed broke. My bed crashed. I got trapped under it. I got out. I went downstairs.

Deer: Then what? Did I come? You musta' bumped your head and musta' lost your memory, right?

Owl: I heard some noise, and I got up in the morning. I sat down in the chair. I got tired again, and I sat down and went back to sleep.

Deer: Do you want me to go now?

Owl: Yes.

Deer: OK.

Owl: Goodbye. Don't forget to see me again some other day. (*Deer leaves.*)

Levels of Dramatizing   In thinking about literature dramatization, two terms are crucial: interpreting and improvising. The term *interpreting* may seem a cumbersome way of saying *act out*. Frequently teachers respond by saying, "But I do that all the time in my reading classes." There is an important distinction between interpreting a story and improvising on one.

Many teachers do make extensive use of interpreting literature in reading classes, in such forms as assigning children to read each character's part or allowing the group to enact a story without relying on the book. In these activities, a crucial element is successful and accurate interpretation, enactment, or re-creation of the author's statement and intent.

The teacher might work with "The Fox and the Grapes" by Claire Littlejohn (1988), asking children how they could convey the anger of the thwarted fox using sounds and body movements. In this case, children are interpreting the fable. The teacher might also ask the children, "What might have happened if the grapes *had* fallen into the fox's paws?" Here children are being asked to extend, extrapolate, and enrich the basic material with their own ideas, moving from simple interpreting to more sophisticated improvising on literature. Another example may clarify the distinction. Allowing children to choose parts and enact a story is doubtlessly valuable. In *King Midas and the Golden Touch* by Eric Metaxas (1992), children revel in impersonating the greedy king and his pathetic daughter.[5] But teachers, though they may sense that

[5] A useful section on such materials is "Myth and Dramatization" in *Competency and Creativity in Language Arts: A Multiethnic Focus* (by Nancy Hansen-Krening, Reading, MA: Addison-Wesley, 1979, pp. 190–195). The emphasis is on drawing from children's own cultures—here as a basis for drama, elsewhere as a basis for speaking and writing. Each section begins with a rationale followed by annotated references and lesson plans that are imaginative.

children are learning from such an experience, too frequently move to more practical considerations after simple interpretation.

Improvisation is the major emphasis in creative dramatics. Different from interpretation, it involves going beyond the basic material. Using this theme, children could respond to a variety of questions: (1) Why do you imagine the king was so greedy? What might have made him this way? (2) How did his daughter happen to be so sweet, having been raised alone in the castle with her father as an example? (3) In what other ways could he have solved his problem? The teacher might use these questions to stimulate discussion; others may be used to encourage children to "act out" their responses. Mature classes can create episodes that might occur before, during, and after the basic story. In these ways, the class moves easily from interpretation to improvisation, with children drawing from within themselves ideas, feelings, and conclusions based on but not found in the story.

A Session with Rumpelstiltskin   The group of third-grade children sat entranced as their teacher read the old Grimm tale of Rumpelstiltskin in a version with elegant full-color paintings by a Russian artist, Gennady Spirin (Sage, 1991). Several children knew the story, but this was a first attempt to dramatize it. To begin, the teacher helped the class find units of action or scenes to play. This is critical because young children cannot do a story effectively in its entirety. Rather, the plot—a complex unit of events flowing freely from introduction to climax— must be segmented into smaller units for dramatizing. The class discovered the following sequence of events: (1) At the castle, the king commands the miller's beautiful daughter Rose to spin straw into gold; the little man appears and strikes a bargain with Rose; the little man begins to spin straw into gold. (2) The next morning the king is delighted by the gold; he leads Rose to a larger room with the same command; he departs. (3) The girl is despondent; the little man reappears; Rose gives him the ring and he begins to transform the straw. (4) The king rejoices in the gold; he takes the miller's daughter to a still larger room and commands her to spin. (5) The little man reappears; the bargain for Rose's first child is set; he spins the straw into gold. (6) The next morning Rose marries the king. (7) Almost one year later in the queen's bedroom, the little man reappears and gives Rose three days to learn his name. (8) The queen tries to guess his name to no avail; the queen quickly sends messengers "to every corner of the land" in search of names. (9) The following day, the queen tries to learn his name from servants and neighbors; the little man reappears, but the queen's efforts are to no avail; the second day, the same thing happens. (10) The next evening, the messenger reports what he has observed; the little man reappears and the queen guesses his name with the messenger's help; the little man stamps his foot through the floor and vanishes.

To ease children into enacting the scenes, the teacher led a series of pantomime tasks, including the king hunting in the woods, the king showing the miller's daughter the straw, the daughter weeping, the little man spinning, the king rejoicing over the gold, the king and the miller's daughter being married, Queen Rose caring for her child, and the little gray-haired man stamping himself in two. Each child had a chance to practice each pantomime task.

Then the teacher divided the children into groups of four, allowing each to choose which child would be the miller, the daughter, the king, and Rumpelstiltskin. The teacher and her aide oversaw as each group worked in its space in the room, joining the sequence of pantomimes into a scene. Another day, the children redid the same scenes because the teacher knew the value of this. As Spodek (1985) said: "Simple dramatic presentations can be repeated. Children can be encouraged to try new roles, playing them in their own way" (p. 57). Later, the class was encouraged to string the scenes together to tell the entire story. When the teacher sensed they were ready, she encouraged them to add dialogue they needed to advance the plot. No emphasis was put on memorizing, and children were encouraged to make the dialogue as natural as possible. When students were satisfied with their action and dialogue, they shared the story. In the discussion that followed, the teacher asked:

Which were the best parts of our interpretation?

What things helped make the story clear?

Were there places where we could convey the idea more clearly? What would help us do that?

This was a beginning story dramatization or interpretation of literature for this particular class. Later the teacher could have encouraged children to extend, elaborate, or enhance the story by considering these questions: Why did the miller live alone with his daughter? What had happened to the mother? Did the king and the miller's daughter really live happily ever after? What was their life like a year after the story ended? How would the story change if Rose could really spin straw into gold? How would it end if the servant hadn't learned the name?[6] Such questions, a basis for discussion and planning, help children move to more sophisticated story improvisation. Additional enrichment opportunities could include reading a different version (Zelinsky, 1986) and encouraging children to compare and contrast the two. The units of action and pantomime tasks integral to the story would be quite differ-

[6] Asking children to create a different ending for a story can be useful. A student teacher working with 4-year-old Spanish-speaking children in a day care setting shared "Little Miss Muffett" and asked how the poem might have ended differently. One child said Miss Muffett could have taken a giant stick and squished the spider; another that she could get her dog to eat the spider up—two imaginative alternatives!

ent. Paley (1981), who continues to teach kindergarten while she writes about her experiences, has provided very helpful material about the relationship among literature, children's dictation and writing, and drama.

SUMMARY

Children bring to school a vigorous oral language shaped by the language of the home and adequate for most of their purposes. The task of the school is to expand on these oral competencies and in some cases to add standard English to the child's home language. Informal conversations and more formal "share and tell" call on the teacher's ability to use questioning techniques to draw out boys' and girls' oral language. Structured experiences in developing describing competencies enhance native oral abilities. Oral reading by the teacher provides needed literary language experience. Such reading leads naturally into storytelling, first by the teacher and then by students. Choral reading experiences enhance the appreciation of poetry while also developing the expressiveness of students' voices. Finally, story drama is critical in early childhood education.

The rewards are many: increased understanding and freedom of response to literature, development of drama skills, growth in language competencies, and increased ability to portray ideas through pantomime and gesture. Children respond willingly to experiences in story drama; the challenge that results from translating the printed page into spoken word and gesture can be rewarding for both children and teacher.

SUGGESTIONS FOR FURTHER STUDY

1. The statement in the chapter that oral language is *the* language is an oversimplification. Record some speech and transcribe it. What elements of speech cannot be transcribed? What can we communicate in writing but not in speech?

2. Describing is one oral language component considered in this chapter. Another is fluency—stringing thoughts together coherently. Identify more components and make up activities to develop them in children.

3. Select a book you enjoy and plan several questions related to the book that require children to operate on levels other than recall.

4. Children's taste in poetry differs from teachers'. See C. Ann Terry, *Children's Poetry Preferences: A National Survey of Upper Elementary Grades* (Urbana, IL: National Council of Teachers of English, 1974) and Carol J. Fisher and Margaret A. Natarella, "Of Cabbages and

Kings: Or What Kinds of Poetry Young Children Like," *Language Arts, 56,*(4), April 1979, pp. 380–385. How is what these authors say reflected or contradicted by children's responses when you read poems to them?

5. Storytellers communicate through gestures as well as with voices. Follow the steps outlined in the chapter for learning a story. Tell it to children and tape record your telling. Then tell it to another group and have someone videotape it. What things about your effectiveness can you learn from comparing the audio and videotapes? To prepare, you might find it helpful to read "Using Storytelling to Promote Language and Literacy Development" by Jackie Peck, in *The Reading Teacher, 43*(2), November 1989, pp. 138–141. After giving some general principles of working with storytelling, the author describes more specifically how she engaged third-graders in studying this art and preparing stories to tell.

6. Make up ten "what if" questions. Use them with children to motivate storytelling. Record and analyze the results to determine which questions were effective and which were not. Why?

Suggestions for Further Reading

Britton, J. (1971). *Language and learning.* Coral Gables, FL: University of Miami Press.

Britton (like Halliday, below) defines three stages of oral language development: *expressive speech*, largely egocentric; *transactional stage*, with dialogue used to inform, persuade, teach, and learn; and *poetic speech*, in which individuals react to the total, including past experiences. These phases move from language as participant to language as spectator. Adults can be both. As spectator, says Britton, "there is an increasing ability to handle the possibilities of experiences."

Haley-James, S. M., & Hobson, C. D. (1980, May). Interviewing: A means of encouraging the drive to communicate. *Language Arts,* pp. 497–502.

The article reports on a planned sequence of interviews through which first-graders improved listening, speaking, reading, and writing skills. Guidelines are provided for teachers interested in such a program.

Halliday, M. A. K. (1975). *Learning how to mean, explorations in the development of language.* London: Edward Arnold.

The author analyzes ways children develop oral skill in different functions of language. Halliday says: "The early development of the grammatical system has been thoroughly explored. What has been much less explored . . . is how the child learns dialogue." Language acquisition and development pass through three stages: *origin of language, transition stage,* and a stage he calls "into language." Adult language occurs without being tied to the immediate environment. The functions of language are developed by the same author in *System and Function in Language* (London: Oxford, 1976), including instrumental (satisfying needs), regulatory (controlling others), interactional (cooperating), personal (expressing the self), heuristic (organizational), imaginative (creating), and representational (informative) functions.

Maguire J. (1985). *Creative storytelling.* New York: McGraw-Hill.

Starting with the assumption that storytelling is "a uniquely powerful way of providing children with life-enhancing mental images," this storyteller provides an informal, warmly convincing affirmation of this art. There is a strong section on types of stories, on finding different stories for different listeners, and on making up one's own stories from experience. Throughout the book there are boxed-page and double-page features on various topics, like "The Trickster," and a feature that recurs throughout the book, "Pathways to Storytelling." The section on "what if" questions reinforces comments made in this chapter. Two older books, useful despite their age, are Eileen Colwell's *A Storyteller's Choice* (New York: Henry Z. Walck, 1965) and Ruth Sawyer's *The Way of the Storyteller* (New York: Penguin, 1977).

Smith, J. (1979, October). Classroom help for the non-verbal and speech delayed child. *Early Years,* pp. 74–76.

The article focuses on environmental and functional causes of delayed speech (or mutism). Easy, informal teaching procedures help the classroom teacher assess the nonverbal strengths and weaknesses of students and identify children who should be referred for more intensive evaluation. Informal tests include auditory discrimination and memory, phonetic knowledge, verbal skills, and self-concept assessment. Activities are included to elicit speech from the child who is organically and functionally able to speak but does not.

Szasz, S. (1978). *The body language of children.* New York: Norton.

Teachers rarely notice children's physical clues to how they feel; they tend to focus on verbal responses and gross motor behavior. The superb photography in this book creates empathy with the subjects, with the text providing a lexicon of nonverbal communications. Szasz clearly states she knew what caused the response she captured on film. By adding words to the photographs, she hopes to provide a guide to the interpretation of children's behavior. Her success in doing so is impressive.

Suggested Books for Children

Gantos, Jack. (1989). *Rotten Ralph's show and tell.* Boston: Houghton Mifflin.

In a hilarious adventure of the scruffy cat Ralph and his devoted owner Sarah, children get a convincing child's-eye view of the problems of coming up with something to take for this common classroom activity. After Ralph makes it impossible for Sarah to take either her violin or her stamp collection, she does the dangerous thing and takes Ralph. In school Ralph wreaks havoc and as a consequence ends up wearing the dunce cap. But Sarah loves him anyway; at the end they enjoy a special cake together. In *Show and Tell* by Elvira Woodruff (1991), the other kindergarten children think that Andy brings the most boring things to share, until the day he brings in a small bottle of bubbles. What happens is anything but boring! *Jason Goes to Show-and-Tell* by Colleen Sutherland (1992) is another look at the topic. For older children, *Roommates and Rachel* by Kathryn O. Galbraith (1991) is a very funny account of bringing baby Rachel to share with the class.

Richardson, Joy. (1986). *What happens when you talk?* Milwaukee: Gareth Stevens Publishing.

This useful information book explains the physical aspects of producing sounds, both vowels and consonants. There are clear diagrams of such things as the voice box and the shape of the lips in making sounds (including aspirated and unaspirated consonants). There are several simple experiments that can be done with commonly available equipment and that demonstrate aspects of sound, how it varies, and how it is transmitted. The book closes with a bibliography, a list of sources to which children can write for more information, and an index.

References

Bauer, C. F. (1987). *Presenting readers theatre.* New York: H. W. Wilson.

Britton, J. (1985). ERIC/RCS report: Building a language-rich environment. *Language Arts, 62,* 95–99.

Cazden, B. (1986). Classroom discourse. In M. C. Wittrock (Ed.), *Handbook of research on teaching* (3rd ed., pp. 432–463). New York: Macmillan.

Chomsky, C. (1969). *The acquisition of syntax in children from two to ten.* Cambridge, MA: MIT Press.

Clay, M. (1975). *What did I write?* Portsmouth, NH: Heincmann.

Cliatt, M. J., & Shaw, J. M. (1985, November/December). Open questions, open answers. *Science and Children, 23*(3), 14–16.

Davies, G. (1983). *Practical primary drama.* London: Heinemann Educational Books.

Dillon, J. T. (1988). *Questioning and teaching: A manual of practice.* New York: Teachers College Press.

Dodge, M. K., & Frost, J. L. (1986). Children's dramatic play. *Childhood Education, 62*(3), 166–170.

Gall, M. D. (1970). The use of questions in teaching. *Review of Educational Research, 40,* 707–721.

Gallas, K. (1992, March). When children take the chair: A study of sharing time in a primary classroom. *Language Arts, 69*(3), 172–182.

Genishi, C. (1992). Developing the foundation: Oral language and communicative competence. In C. Seefeldt (Ed.), *The early childhood curriculum: A review of current research* (pp. 85–117). New York: Teachers College Press.

Gunderson, L. (1971). Reading and language development. In V. Frose (Ed.), *Whole-language. Practice and theory* (p. 161). Boston: Allyn & Bacon.

Hall, S. E. M. (1986). An approach to dictation with young children. *Insights Into Open Education, 18*(7), 2–7.

Higginbotham, D., & Reitzel, A. (1977). *The emergence of decentration in children's social speech.* ERIC Document No. 144 408.

Hough, R. A., Nurss, J. R., & Wood, D. (1987, November). Tell me a story: Making opportunities for elaborated language in early childhood classrooms. *Young Children,* pp. 6–12.

Huck, C. S. (1992). Literacy and literature. *Language Arts, 69*(7), 520–526.

Hudson-Ross, S., Cleary, L. M., & Casey, M. (1993). *Children's voices. Children talk about literacy.* Portsmouth, NH: Heinemann.

Jacobs, S. E. (1991, April 3–7) *Putting children's questions first.* Paper presented at the annual convention of the American Educational Research Association, Chicago, ERIC Document No. 333332.

Jett-Simpson, M. (1976). *Children's inferential responses to a wordless picture book: Development and use of a classification system for verbalized inference.* Unpublished Ph.D. dissertation, University of Washington, Seattle.

John, V. P., & Moskovitz, S. (1970). Language acquisition and development in early childhood. In *Linguistics in school programs* (pp. 167–215), The sixty-ninth yearbook of the National Society for the Study of Education, Part II. Chicago: University of Chicago Press.

Lange, B. (1981). ERIC/RCS report: Directing classroom communication. *Language Arts, 58,* 729–733.

Last, E. (Ed.). (1990). *A guide to curriculum planning in classroom drama and theatre.* Madison, WI: Wisconsin Department of Public Instruction.

Lenz, L. (1992). Crossroads of literacy and orality: Reading poetry aloud. *Language Arts, 69*(8), 597–603.

Loban, W. (1966, March). Oral language proficiency affects reading and writing. *The Instructor,* pp. 97ff.

Lud, M., & Ulrich, J. (1980, March). The hidden drama in your classroom. *Early Years,* pp. 64–65+.

Mangieri, J. N., Staley, N. K., & Wilhide, J. A. (Eds.). (1984). *Teaching language arts. Classroom applications.* New York: McGraw-Hill.

McCaslin, N. (1990). *Creative drama in the classroom.* New York: Longman.

Moffett, J., & Wagner, B. J. (1992). *Student-centered language arts, K–12* (4th ed). Portsmouth, NH: Boynton/Cook Publishers.

Morrow, L. M., & Weinstein, C. S. (1982, November). Increasing children's use of literature through program and physical design changes. *The Elementary School Journal, 83*(2), 131–137.

Najimy, C. (1983). Children writing books for children. In B. Busching & J. Schwartz (Eds.), *Integrating the language arts in the elementary school* (pp. 64–69). Urbana, IL: National Council of Teachers of English.

Neal, C. (1987). Speaking as a language art. In C. R. Personke & D. D. Johnson (Eds.), *Language arts instruction and the beginning teacher: A practical guide* (pp. 12–20).

Nessel, D. D. (1985, January). Storytelling in the reading program. *The Reading Teacher,* pp. 378–381.

Paley, V. G. (1981). *Wally's stories.* Cambridge, MA: Harvard University Press.

Paynter, J., & Aston, P. (1970). *Sound and silence.* Cambridge, MA: Harvard University Press.

Pei, M. (1984). *The story of language.* New York: New American Library.

Preece, A. (1991). Supporting storytelling with "talking sticks." *Reading Today, 8*(4), 24.

Riley, M. T. (1991). Environments that make a difference. Lubbock, TX: Institute for Child and Family Studies, Texas Tech University, ERIC Document No. 345881.

Roser, N. L., Hoffman, J. V., Labbo, L. D., & Farest, C. (1992). Language charts: A record of story time talk. *Language Arts, 69*(1), 44–52.

Rowe, M. B. (1974). Wait-time and rewards as instructional variables, their influence on language, logic and rate control: Part 1. *Journal of Research in Science Teaching, 11,* 81–84.

Salpen, D. (1964). *A study of an oral approach to the appreciation of poetry.* Unpublished Ph.D. dissertation, University of Minnesota, Minneapolis.

Schickendanz, J. (1978, September). "You be the doctor and I'll be sick": Preschoolers learn the language arts through play. *Language Arts*, pp. 713–718.

Seltzer, D. A. (1989). *Assessment and early childhood education.* Overland Park, KS: Research and Training Associates, Inc., ERIC Document No. 330446.

Sheldon, W. (1966). *The reading of poetry.* Boston: Allyn & Bacon.

Snydam, M. N. (1985, February). Research report: Questions. *Arithmetic teacher, 32*(6), 18.

Spodek, B. (1985). *Teaching in the early years* (3rd ed.). Englewood Cliffs, NJ: Prentice-Hall.

Stewig, J. W. (1981, September/October). Choral speaking: Who has time? Why take time? *Childhood Education*, pp. 25–29.

———. (1986). Books in the classroom. *The Horn Book, 62*(3), 363–365.

———. (1988). *Children and literature.* Boston: Houghton Mifflin.

———. (1990a). Participation storytelling. *The CLA Bulletin, 16*(1), 4–7.

———. (1990b). *Read to write.* Katonah, NY: Richard C. Owen.

Stoodt, B. D. (1988). *Teaching language arts.* New York: Harper & Row.

Strickland, D. S., Dillon, R. M., Funkhauser, L., Glick, M., & Rogers, C. (1989). Research currents: Classroom dialogue during literature response groups. *Language Arts, 66*(2), 192–197.

Sutherland, Z., & Arbuthnot, M. H. (1984). *Children and books.* Glenview, IL: Scott, Foresman.

———. (Revisors). (1976). *Scott, Foresman anthology of children's literature.* Glenview, IL: Scott, Foresman.

Tarlington, C., & Verriour, P. (1991). *Role drama.* Portsmouth, NH: Heinemann.

Torrance, F. P., & Meyers, R. F. (1970). *Creative learning and teaching.* New York: Dodd, Mead.

Yawkey, T. D., Askov, E. N., Cartwright, C. A., Dupuis, M. M., Fairchild, S. H., & Yawkey, M. L. (1981). *Language arts and the young child.* Itasca, IL: F. E. Peacock.

Children's Books

Adams, Adrienne (Compiler). (1972). *Poetry of Earth,* p. 39. New York: Scribner (out of print).

Amorso, Lisa (Ill.). (1987). *Old Mother Hubbard.* New York: Knopf.

Benchley, Nathaniel. (1967). *The strange disappearance of Arthur Cluck.* New York: Harper & Row.

Blegvad, Lenore. (1978). *This little pig-a-wig.* New York: Atheneum.

Burningham, John. (1978). *Time to get out of the bath, Shirley.* New York: Thomas Y. Crowell.

Cauley, Lorinda Bryan (Reteller). (1981). *Goldilocks and the three bears.* New York: Putnam.

Chess, Victoria (Ill.). (1990). *Three blind mice.* Boston: Little, Brown.

Coady, Christopher. (1991). *Red Riding Hood.* New York: Dutton Children's Books.

Cole, Joanna. (1984). *A new treasury of children's poetry,* p. 172. New York: Doubleday.

Coombs, Patricia. (1967). *Dorrie and the witch doctor.* New York: Lothrop (out of print).

———. (1989). *Dorrie and the pin witch*. New York: Lothrop.

Duvoisin, Roger. (1976). *Periwinkle*. New York: Knopf (out of print).

Emberley, Barbara. (1966). *One wide river to cross*. Englewood Cliffs, NJ: Prentice-Hall (out of print).

Ets, Marie Hall. (1963). *Gilberto and the wind*. New York: Viking Press.

Galbraith, Kathryn O. (1991). *Roommates and Rachel*. New York: McElderry Books.

Galdone, Paul. (1987). *Three blind mice*. New York: Clarion.

Ginsburg, Mirra. (1976). *Two greedy bears*. New York: Macmillan.

Goode, Diane (Transl.). (1988). *Cinderella*. New York: Knopf.

Heins, Paul. (1974). *Snow White*. Boston: Little, Brown.

Hogrogian, Nonny. (1967). *The renowned history of Little Red Riding Hood*. New York: Thomas Y. Crowell.

Hyman, Trina Schart. (1977). *The sleeping beauty*. Boston: Little, Brown.

Kesselman, Wendy. (1982). *There's a train going by my window*. New York: Doubleday (out of print).

Kwitz, Mary DeBall. (1991). *Gumshoe goose*. New York: Dial.

Larrick, Nancy (Comp.). (1988). *Cats are cats*. New York: Philomel Books.

Lionni, Leo. (1967). *Frederick*. New York: Pantheon Books.

Littlejohn, Claire. (1988). *Aesop's fables*. New York: Dial Books for Young Readers.

Lobel, Arnold. (1975). *Owl at home*. New York: Harper & Row.

Mayer, Mercer. (1973). *Bubble bubble*. New York: Parents' Magazine Press.

Merriam, Eve. (1986). *Fresh paint*. New York: Macmillan.

Metaxas, Eric. (1992). *King Midas and the golden touch*. Saxonville, MA: Picture Book Studio.

Osborne, Mary Pope. (1991). *Mo and his friends*. New York: Dial.

Prelutsky, Jack (Selector). (1991). *For laughing out loud*, p. 27. New York: Knopf.

Raskin, Ellen. (1972). *Franklin Stein*. New York: Atheneum (out of print).

Ritchard, Cyril, et al. (Readers). *Mother Goose*. Caedmon Records, TC 1091.

Rosen, Michael. (1989). *We're going on a bear hunt*. New York: McElderry Books.

Sage, Alison (Reteller). (1991). *Rumpelstiltskin*. New York: Dial.

San Souci, Robert D. (1989). *The talking eggs*. New York: Dial.

Sewall, Marcia. (1986). *The world turned upside down*. Boston: Atlantic Monthly Press.

Sharmat, Marjorie W. (1976). *Mooch the messy*. New York: Harper & Row.

Stewig, John Warren. (1993). *The moon's choice*. New York: Simon & Schuster.

Sutherland, Colleen. (1992). *Jason goes to show-and-tell*. Honesdale, PA: Boyds Mills Press.

Van Rynbach, Iris. (1988). *The soup stone*. New York: Greenwillow Books.

Westcott, Nadine Bernard (Ill.). (1980). *I know an old lady who swallowed a fly*. Boston: Little, Brown.

Williams-Ellis, Amabel. (1987). *Tales from the enchanted world*, pp. 96–101. Boston: Little, Brown.

Woodruff, Elvira. (1991). *Show and tell*. New York: Holiday House.

Yeoman, John, and Blake, Quentin. (1990). *Old Mother Hubbard's dog dresses up*. Boston: Houghton Mifflin.

Yolen, Jane (Reteller). (1986). *The sleeping beauty.* New York: Ariel Books/Alfred
    A. Knopf.
Zelinsky, Paul. (1986). *Rumpelstiltskin.* New York: Dutton.
Zwerger, Lisabeth. (1983). *Little red cap.* New York: Morrow.

Professional Growth

The Work of the American Alliance for Theatre and Education

Contact:

Roger L. Bedard, Executive Director
Theatre Department
Arizona State University
Tempe, AZ 85287-3411
(602) 965-6064

This association of 1,500 members is open to education professionals
who are interested in theatre for youth and informal classroom drama.
It encourages standards of excellence in drama/theatre education for
young people by providing a network of resources, support, advocacy,
and access to programs and projects that focus on drama as part of the
human experience. It conducts regional workshops and festivals,
bestows awards, and has an annual convention. Two publications, *The
Drama/Theatre Teacher* and *Youth Theatre Journal,* provide interesting
reading for teachers concerned about drama.

Five

Understanding Reading As Part of an Integrated Program

And goodnight to the old lady whispering hush.

Goodnight stars, goodnight air, goodnight noises everywhere.

Brown (1947)

These words echo in the memories of many children as their parents or other significant adults tucked them into bed after reading Margaret Wise Brown's classic book *Goodnight Moon* (1947). This is where reading begins. Literacy experiences during the first years of life, before children enter preschool or kindergarten, are already shaping their attitudes toward reading and laying the foundations for formal reading instruction. What is reading? What are the characteristics or patterns of reading development? How can you use the patterns of reading development? What can be the design of a reading program? What are the key literacy events for reading instruction? These are the main questions we will explore in this chapter.

What Is Reading?

There are much debate and argument about the definitions of reading. Some say it is a process where children first learn letters and then sounds to go with letters. Knowing this, children can "sound out" words, which allows them to read more and more difficult texts (Gough, 1972). Often this is referred to as a "bottom up" model of reading. Others argue that reading is primarily a process of constructing meaning,

Daily opportunities to read independently support children's growth and development.

during which words and letter-sound relationships are learned. This is frequently referred to as a "top down" model of reading (Goodman, 1976).

The position taken in this book is that neither definition describes the whole picture; it is much more complex. Neither the "top down" nor the "bottom up" model explains the reality of the kinds of behaviors children demonstrate while learning to read or while reading. Children demonstrate both "top down" and "bottom up" behaviors in interesting combinations much like you do when you read. Imagine the following scenario:

> Your roommate calls across the room, "What is c-h-e-v-i-o-t? What does it mean?"
>
> "What?" you ask, and he spells it again while you write it down: "cheviot." "/Ch-e-v-e-ot/?" It is not likely you will be able to pronounce it correctly simply by sounding it out. Once you have pronounced it, you aren't certain you are correct unless you have heard it before. If you happen to pronounce it correctly but don't know its meaning, you are stuck again. "Why don't you look it up in the dictionary?" you ask.
>
> "I left it in the car," your roommate replies.
>
> This moves you into a search mode. "Where did you see the word? Bring me the book. I need to see the sentence or paragraph it's in." Your roommate brings the book, from which you read "The cheviot of the peasant's coat was tattered and worn." You still may not be certain about how to pronounce the word, but you have some idea of its meaning. "Well . . . it's describing the coat. It must be some part of a coat or the kind of material it's made of," you reply.
>
> "That's what I thought. But I'd never seen the word before so it knocked me for a loop. Dr. Wordsmith is big on vocabulary. Do you think that's a word he would put on a test?" asks your roommate.
>
> "I don't know. To cover your bases, you better get your dictionary out of the car or borrow one tomorrow. But you can figure out enough of the meaning to keep reading the book," you answer.

Even this simple example of one aspect of reading—problem solving for an unknown word—requires the reader to work at both letter knowledge and meaning levels where the main goal is to construct meaning. The roommate recognized he had lost meaning when he didn't know a word. In your efforts to help, you drew on your background knowledge about strategies for letter-sound relationships and constructing meaning from text. You both tried to decide whether the exact meaning and pronunciation of the word were necessary to understand what the sentence meant.

Reading is both an interactive process between the reader, the text, and context (Rummelhart, 1985) *and a transaction* (Rosenblatt, 1978). It is the things readers do to orchestrate meaning making for a text. This relationship is illustrated in Figure 5-1 (Wisconsin Department of Public Instruction, 1986). Readers bring varying background knowledge (including knowledge about how language works, as discussed in Chap-

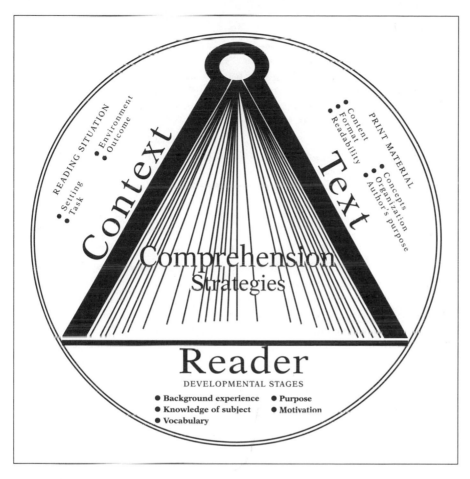

FIGURE 5-1

Wisconsin Model
for Reading
Comprehension

ter 1), experiences (including attitudes and emotions), and levels of maturity to each reading context and text. They use strategies, or plans of action, to bring together what they know and feel with the text and the demands of the reading situation. Text, context, and reader act on one another. In particular, the relationship between reader and author is analogous to a transaction where each contributes (Rosenblatt, 1978). The reader brings his or her knowledge, experience, and maturity level to the reading but so does the author, who expects to influence the reader's construction of meaning for the text. Author's meaning meets reader's meaning, and in the process, the reader constructs new meaning in negotiation with the author.

Factors in the text itself, such as its structure and organization, also influence readers' construction of meaning. Short sentences, long sentences, paragraphs with topic sentences, paragraphs without topic sentences, the relationships of illustrations to the text, the amount of text on a page, poetic forms, fiction, and nonfiction are a few examples of text characteristics that influence this process. Familiar structures are easier than unfamiliar ones, just as well-organized text is easier to comprehend than poorly organized text.

The context for reading is the situation the reader is in at any particular time. A reading-for-pleasure context is very different from a study reading context. The roommate in the preceding scenario would probably have skipped "cheviot" if he were reading for pleasure. However, the context was studying for a class where the instructor valued vocabulary, so the roommate adjusted his reading to the demands of the situation. The beginner who is reading aloud for the teacher and then reading to herself in the library corner will approach these two situations differently as well. The reading task demands, physical environment, and social settings are all part of the context.

Within the social context, parents, teachers, and peers can influence how readers approach reading and their feelings about it. Many university students recall "round robin reading" where they took turns reading aloud in front of the class with no preparation. Students who were accurate oral readers loved it because they received positive feedback. Those who were inaccurate hated it because it was another opportunity to fail. Subsequently, many such oral readers have negative feelings about reading today and do not enjoy it.

Home contexts for reading also have a powerful impact on children as developing readers. Children whose parents read to them are, on the whole, more successful in school (Taylor & Strickland, 1986; Teale, 1981). Both parents and teachers have the power to influence children's reading and their perception of themselves as readers for a lifetime.

At this point you may be wondering where skills fit into this description of the reading process. Skills fit into the reader section of the model. They are part of the knowledge the reader has about print, vocabulary, and text structure. Most of you probably think of the skill worksheets you did on such topics as phonics rules, antonyms, homonyms, cause/effect relationships, and main idea. If you stop to think about it, these are bits of information or knowledge that are only helpful if they can be used to solve problems while constructing meaning during reading. These bits of knowledge serve readers' strategies for figuring out words and constructing text meaning. Knowing when and where to use and not to use these bits of information puts them under strategic control. Children use strategies they know to construct meaning for texts (Paris, Lipson & Wixson, 1983). Beginners gradually learn to coordinate the multiple facets of the reading process. Let's examine some of the characteristics of children's journey toward accomplished reading next.

What Are the Characteristics of Reading Development?

Reading development is like language and writing development. When we discussed language development, we learned that although children's development generally falls into broad sequential patterns, there is a great deal of variability in the rate and detail of development. Some children develop faster than others and some learn certain details before others. Consequently, children the same age exhibit a range of developmental characteristics. Children are problem solvers who construct rules to make sense of what they are hearing in their environment. Many of those rules (coping strategies) look like mistakes because they work in some instances and not others. If children are in an environment where the conditions of learning (see Figure 1-3) support their problem solving, then these rules increase in accuracy and gradually evolve into highly efficient and effective strategies that allow children to produce and comprehend most forms of their oral language. These developmental characteristics are also true of learning to read.

What Are Patterns of Reading Development?

Patterns of development are loose collections of literacy behaviors that represent children's growth. Like the descriptions of language development in Chapter 1, descriptions of reading development are not all-inclusive. At best, they are an oversimplification because of the complexity of the reading process. However, we know enough from years of research to be able to describe its developmental progression in our culture in general terms (Adams, 1990; Chall, 1983; Department of Education Wellington, 1985; Fisher, 1991; LaBerge & Samuels, 1974; O'Donnel & Wood, 1992; Sulzby, 1985; Teale & Sulzby, 1986).

Let's turn now to one set of descriptions that characterize this unfolding development. As you read the descriptions, notice there are two parts: (1) a general description of the reading behaviors children are working on during a particular pattern of development, and (2) a description of a few behaviors that, when they appear, indicate advancement toward the next pattern of development. These are indicators of the "cutting edge" of learning and are particularly important to teachers in deciding how to focus instruction. These "cutting edges" of learning are usually observed when children are working with instructional materials that are at a "just right" level, meaning children can recognize ninety to ninety-five percent of the words and can comprehend seventy percent of the material.

EMERGENT READERS

Snuggled safely in their parents' arms, children respond to books and stories as meaningful parts of their lives. Parents model reading, and from these demonstrations children begin to identify how books work: that there are stories in them to be discovered with each turning of the page. Then they have to try it for themselves. Holding books upside down and babbling while turning pages, stopping occasionally to nibble on some page corners, children discover books. Boys and girls will learn the front and back of the book, to look at the left page first and then the right (when reading English), that pictures illustrate the story and print tells it, making mistakes along the way until they "get it."

As children acquire oral language, they move from babble reading to pointing and naming pictures and making comments about the action of the pictures. Next comes simple "readings" that sound like children's oral language. Some youngsters carry on monologue conversations with books. Simple oral language-like "readings" evolve into written language-like "readings" where children incorporate remembered fragments of the printed story in their readings. For example, a child who was reading *Horton Hatches the Egg* by Dr. Seuss (1940) was overheard doing an oral language-like reading interspersed with the book language, "I meant what I said and I said what I meant, an elephant's faithful, one hundred percent." Several months later, this same child was heard doing a verbatim memorized "reading" of the book, not paying any attention to the print but taking her cues from the illustrations. In fact, she had it so well memorized that she could "read with her eyes shut" like in Dr. Seuss's book by the same name (1978). This evolution of book reading is taking place from birth to kindergarten for most children.

At the same time they are figuring out how books work and progressing in their picture-governed reading, emergent readers are beginning to develop some phonemic awareness. Phonemic awareness is when children develop the concept that words can be segmented into sound units. This may be very obvious to an adult, but to a child the notion that words are made up of sound units doesn't fit their view of the world. Things like trains, whistles, and dogs make sounds. Consider how Mike made sense of the rhyming game his mom and dad introduced while traveling to Yellowstone Park. "We are going to play the rhyming game, Mike. We are going to try to think of as many words as we can that sound the same." Mom says, "Rat." "Sat," says Dad. Mom says, "Cat." "Now it's your turn, Mike. What do you say?" "Fluffy!" To Mike, this game involves associating something meaningful to the word. Fluffy, the family cat, is his most important association with *cat*. For emergent readers, their beginning phonemic awareness is hearing rhyme and a few consonant sounds at the beginnings of words (Adams,

THE FAMILY CIRCUS®   By Bil Keane   FIGURE 5-2

11-17
Copyright 1981
The Register and Tribune
Syndicate, Inc

"One more guess, Mommy, then if you're still
wrong I'll have to tell you what it is."

1990). This awareness is developed through oral language, not print language at this time.

Children will be meeting print in other ways in print-rich environments. Television, magazines, billboards, signs, messages, all kinds of books, labels, computers—they are surrounded by it. As young as 3 years of age, they are able to "read" the signs for their favorite fast foods. They don't read by attending to the letters alone but by recognizing the complete sign, which includes the design elements, in its total environment (Goodman, 1984). If the sign is reduced to print only, it would be a puzzle to them. In a videotape, a researcher showed a child the label for Coke with its logo and asked him to read it. He confidently read, "Pep-si-cola, Pep-si-co-la" (Goodman, undated). This child had probably overgeneralized soft drink labels and coped with all of their variability by calling all of them Pepsicola. Pepsi was probably the common soft drink in his home. When the same child was given the word alone, he had no idea what it represented.

Children experiment with putting messages on paper, beginning with scribbles (see Figure 5-2) and pictures and gradually advancing forms that look more and more like letters. Their writing reflects their thinking about stories, letter formation, word formation, and letter-sound relationships. (See Chapter 6 for a full discussion.) Print awareness for

Table 5-1

Emergent Readers

Some Key Behaviors	Indicators of Advancement
Focus mostly on pictures	Attention shifts to print
Develop directionality	Memorized story readings
Begin to develop phonemic awareness	
Develop understanding of conventions of reading	
Do pretend reading	
Begin to write and name letters	
Construct story meaning	

books grows out of exploration of print through writing for many children.

While children are engaged in this marvel of learning, teachers will be observing to see how they are working out the foregoing aspects of reading. Teachers will also observe for the "cutting edges" of learning, which indicate advancement to the next pattern of development. Two *key indicators* are: (1) children are easily able to do memorized story "readings" for new predictable books after hearing them read a few times, and (2) most important, they realize that print tells the story so they begin to make attempts to decode it (Clay, 1991a; Sulzby, 1985). A summary of the emergent pattern is presented in Table 5-1.

Transitional Readers

Transitional readers shift their attention to trying to make sense of print, recognizing that words are the record of the story. Like P. J. in "The Family Circus" cartoon in Figure 5-3, they recognize the relationship between illustrations and print. They may refuse to read for a time because "they don't know the words" (Sulzby, 1985). This is the same child who, as an emergent reader, was happily doing perfectly or near-perfectly memorized "readings" of favorite books. As transitional readers begin to read, they still rely heavily on the pictures to remember the story. They recognize some sight words and use their knowledge of some initial consonants in combination with pictures to figure out words as one of their main coping strategies.

They are also developing the ability to match individual spoken words with the same words in print. Since they are still trying to get a clear idea of the concept of "word," their earliest attempts at voice/print match will be to use a common coping strategy that shows they believe

THE FAMILY CIRCUS®   By Bil Keane   Figure 5-3

11-3
Copyright 1986
Cowles Syndicate, Inc.

"The pictures show what happens in
the story, and the words
are the play-by-play."

words are the syllable beats of the language. In the sentence "The alligator went snap!" there are seven syllable beats. By applying the syllable beat strategy, children expect seven words, and so they will run out of text as they point to the words according to syllable beat while reading. Phonemic awareness continues to develop as do written forms of print.

Key indicators of a shift to the next pattern are (1) voice/print match for one-syllable words, and (2) students' increased efforts to figure out words and attempts to use letter-sound relationships beyond the initial consonant (Clay, 1991a). This is done in the context of making sense of stories. The transitional pattern is summarized in Table 5-2.

Beginning Readers

Beginning readers know that print tells the story. They are trying to work out how to orchestrate the cues available in any text for figuring out words. Those four cueing systems are (1) meaning, (2) visual cues, (3) sound-symbol relationships, and (4) structure/grammar. Each cueing system can be used to cross-check the others while a new word is figured out (see Figure 5-4).

Meaning cues include prior knowledge of the topic, memory for previous readings of the text, information from the text surrounding the unknown word, the pictures, and the text structure. The reader uses meaning cues to check whether the reading attempt makes sense.

Table 5-2

Transitional Readers

Some Key Behaviors	Indicators of Advancement
Begin to recognize some sight words	Voice/print match
Use pictures and some initial consonants to figure out words	Begin to try to use most letters to figure out words
Still rely on memorization of story	
Predict from pictures	
Spelling is semiphonemic (see Chapter 6)	
Construct story meaning	

Visual cues are those images or partial images of words stored in memory that help the reader answer the question: Does that look right? For example, children may see a word and realize, "I don't know this word but I've seen that word before." Often children search for the word in the preceding text or where they remember seeing it. When they find it, they read the familiar text that contains the word and then return to their place and read the same word. They have enough visual memory to know they have seen the word but no other knowledge about how to work it out. (Transitional readers and beginners use this strategy if allowed to do so.) Conventional sentence markers such as capital letters and periods are other examples of visual cues. There are also words children simply recognize at sight by using their visual memory. As their visual knowledge increases, children can recognize letters and spelling patterns that are the same in words. When they are advanced beginners, they are able to look at words and think of other words that look like them as a visual strategy for decoding.

Sound-symbol relationships typically are thought of as phonics cues. As children's phonemic awareness increases, so does their knowledge of individual letter-sound relationships. The beginning reader pays attention to individual letters and tries to "sound them out." The advanced beginner looks at common spelling patterns, or letter clusters, that reappear with frequency in English words.

Structure/grammar cues are what children know about the English language. Speakers of English, as we learned in Chapter 1, expect language to behave in certain ways consistent with its established patterns. If readers know the language they are reading, they will know how English sentences should be stated and expect the printed sentences to behave the same way. They will be able to answer the question: Can we say it that way? Speakers of other languages and English dialects bring the syntax of their language to reading, so they make "mistakes" that

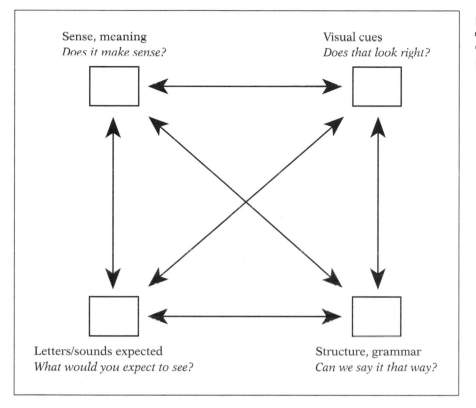

FIGURE 5-4

Cues for Decoding
(Clay, 1993b)

Sense, meaning
Does it make sense?

Visual cues
Does that look right?

Letters/sounds expected
What would you expect to see?

Structure, grammar
Can we say it that way?

are actually correct grammar in their own language. A logical coping strategy for these readers is to apply what they know about the order of the language they speak when they attempt to read standard English. This also explains, for example, why it is easier for native speakers of Spanish to learn to read in their own language (Cummins, 1981; Verhoeven, 1987).

The challenge for beginning readers is to use these strategies together to cross-check. A word must make sense, look right, and sound like English. Children who are cross-checking will self-correct many of their reading miscues. We are delighted to see this self-correcting behavior when it occurs. It is the kind of independent problem solving we expect to occur gradually during beginning reading.

Many beginners can't manage all of the cues at once. Typically, in classrooms where storybook reading is central, the first coping strategies many children use are "Say what makes sense" and "Say what sounds right." The result is miscues (mistakes) that overemphasize meaning and language cues and disregard visual and letter-sound cues. In the following example the text was "The lion roared." The child read the text "The tiger roared." The child mistook the meaning cues from the picture of the lion for a tiger and used her sense of meaning to predict the word. However, she did not cross-check with print because there are no letter resemblances between "tiger" and "lion."

Text:	The lion roared.		
Child miscues to meaning:	√	tiger	√
		lion	

[*Note:* The √ indicates that the child read the word correctly. This notation system, popularized by Clay (1993a), is called running records. It is based on Goodman's (1969) miscue analysis.]

As children acquire more knowledge of letter-sound relationships and visual cues, their main coping strategy may shift to "Look at the letters. Sound them out." They are likely to use visual and letter-sound cues and ignore meaning and sometimes the grammar too. In the following example, the text was "Little Bear cried." The child read it "Little Bear c-c-r-id" pronouncing the "i" as a short /i/ (rhyming with *lid*) and did not self-correct.

Text:	Little Bear cried.		
Child miscues by using letter-sound cues:	√	√	c-c-r-id
			cried

Finally, students start to integrate the cueing systems and use them as checks against each other to confirm the pronunciation of words and their meaning. In the following example, the text was "Jill wore yellow socks." The child read it as "Jill wore yellow shoes-socks." Here the child cross-checked meaning and structure against the visual and letter-sound cues (Jett-Simpson & Leslie, 1994).

Text:	Jill wore yellow socks.			
Child cross-checks:	√	√	√	shoes-socks
				socks

Interestingly, in kindergarten classrooms where letter-sound relationships make up the reading program, children tend to use letter-sound strategies before meaning strategies. The instructional environment does affect children's reading behaviors.

When you are observing readers, you'll notice that children's reading isn't quite this clear and simple. Children will make a variety of miscues that show they are attempting to use different kinds of cues. What teachers must do is observe readers' miscues and ask themselves: What cues are the children using? What cues do they need to use to cross-check? Teachers guide children to cross-check by asking appropriate questions.

Table 5-3

Beginning Readers

Some Key Behaviors	Indicators of Advancement
Focus on meaning cues	Cross-checking
Focus on letter-sound relationships	Begin to see spelling patterns
Begin to use more than one cue at a time	
Expand sight word knowledge	
Begin to self-correct	
Develop phonemic awareness	
Spelling includes some semiphonemic and phonemic spellings; standard spelling is increasing (see Chapter 6)	
Construct story meaning	

Does it make sense? Does that look right? What would you expect to see? Can we say it that way? (See Figure 5-4.) If the child makes a meaning miscue like in the tiger/lion example above, the teacher could focus the child on a visual cue by pointing to the word *lion* and saying, "You read this as *tiger*. Does that look right?" The question focuses the attention and gives the child the opportunity to self-correct. The teacher asks the question if she or he knows that the child can use at least the initial consonant as an aid in figuring out the word. It is pointless to ask the question if the child doesn't have that knowledge.

As an outgrowth of reading lots of stories, beginners increase their sight word vocabulary significantly. They also attempt more complex temporary spellings in their story writing. Spelling patterns in their stories tend to be a combination of correct spellings of some words and temporary spellings that are semiphonemic (/kt/ for *cat*) and phonemic (/kat/ for *cat*).[1] Most stories read during this time are about familiar topics and written in structures that support comprehension so they are effective in encouraging children to use all cueing systems.

The *key indicators* of movement into the advanced beginner pattern are that children (1) use all the cueing strategies, though not consistently, in at least a partial cross-checking system, and (2) *begin* to use familiar letter clusters (spelling patterns) to work out unknown words. See Table 5-3 for a summary of this pattern.

[1] Cambourne (1987) recommended the term *temporary spelling* rather than *invented spelling*. The connotations of *temporary* are more transitory and therefore easier for parents to accept.

Table 5-4

The Most Common Phonograms (Adams, 1990, pp. 321–322)

ack	eat	ice	ock	uck	unk
ain	ell	ick	oke	ug	
ake	est	ide	op	ump	
ale		ight	ore		
ail		ill	or		
ame		in			
an		ine			
ank		ing			
ap		ink			
ash		ip			
at		ir			
ate					
aw					
ay					

Note: Nearly 500 words can be derived from these phonograms.

Advanced Beginners

Beginning readers become *advanced beginners* when they begin *chunking,* a term popularized by Clay (1993b). To chunk they must see patterns or letter clusters and use them to figure out new words. A number of chunks or letter clusters frequently appear together in English. Some are *consonant blends* (two or more consonants that frequently appear together) such as *bl, scr,* and *st; digraphs* (two or more consonants that, when combined, produce a new sound) such as *sh, ch, wh,* and *ng; diphthongs* (sounds that blend two separate vowel sounds) such as *oi, oy, ow,* and *ou; prefixes* such as *un-* and *tele-; suffixes* like *-ing, -ed,* and *-ly;* and *compound words* like *into* and *today.*

Children can also use their knowledge of remembered words and word parts to figure out new words by analogy. Let's say the new word is *frog.* A child's thinking could go something like this:

Oh. That looks like "dog" but it starts like "from." I know—"frog"!

The *phonograms* (letter clusters that are the basis for word families or rhyming words) *at, an, un,* and *et* are very important chunks to learn for increasing reading proficiency. In learning them, children also learn many of the patterns and sound correspondences for vowels. The most common phonograms are presented in Table 5-4.

An advanced beginner might use chunking as *one of the strategies* in a cross-checking process to figure out a word like *licking* in the sentence "The dog was licking the pizza pan." The thinking could go something like this:

Table 5-5

Advanced Beginners

Some Key Behaviors	Indicators of Advancement
Develop chunking strategies	Effective chunking
Develop cross-checking strategies	Consistent use of cross-checking
Refine self-monitoring	Consistent self-monitoring
Phonemic and standard spelling	
Construct meaning	

Oops, I don't know that word. I'll read to the end of the sentence. It's something the dog is doing to the pizza pan, starts with /l/, ends with /-ing/, and this is /ick/—Licking! That makes sense.

Moving from processing unknown words letter by letter to recognizing common letter combinations or chunks greatly increases readers' efficiency. Advanced beginners continue to refine decoding and comprehension strategies as they build their independence in self-monitoring and cross-checking. Spelling patterns in writing are usually a mixture of phonemic temporary spellings and standard spellings by this time, which is the transitional stage of spelling development (see Chapter 6).

Key indicators of a pattern shift are that readers use chunking effectively and become independent cross-checkers. As part of chunking, they develop strategies for working with vowel patterns. They cross-check the basic cues—meaning, visual, letter-sound, and structure/grammar—against each other for congruity in their attempts at problem solving during reading. They self-monitor their comprehension and decoding, and their reading sounds more fluent as they read increasingly difficult material. Spelling is transitional (see Chapter 6). A summary of the pattern of advanced beginners is given in Table 5-5.

Consolidators

Consolidators work to become *automatic* (LaBerge & Samuels, 1974) in coordinated strategy use through cross-checking and self-monitoring. They are firmly consolidating most aspects of reading acquisition at this time. As they become more automatic, fluency increases and word recognition becomes more rapid. Not many new reading behaviors appear during this pattern because these readers are giving most of their attention to making what they know efficient and automatic. Consolidators continue to develop the use of background knowledge and inferential

Table 5-6

Consolidators

Some Key Behaviors	Indicators of Advancement
Work to become automatic with strategies	Become automatic
Work to greatly increase sight words	Silent reading speed exceeds oral reading speed
Learn to handle more difficult texts	
Construct story meaning	

thinking abilities such as prediction and sense of story structure for comprehending stories. Critical to development is sustained practice, or lots of reading, particularly of easy books, to establish this automaticity.

Consolidators are venturing into unfamiliar territory with some of their reading because reading materials are no longer designed to be about only familiar topics. Lack of background knowledge about a topic seriously interferes with effective strategy use, and strategies will break down.

Key indicators that reading is consolidated are: (1) automatic cross-checking and self-monitoring are in place, and (2) silent reading speed exceeds oral reading speed. See Table 5-6 for a summary of consolidators.

Accomplished Readers

Accomplished readers have good control of basic decoding and self-monitoring strategies. They know when they are comprehending, recognize when comprehension breaks down, and know how to remedy most breakdowns. They have control over the basic reading process and are now focusing more attention on applying this knowledge in a wide variety of familiar and unfamiliar contexts. They are also refining and adding to their existing strategies. For example, they can use text organization as a cue to identifying what information the author considered important. These readers develop strategies for how to comprehend more complex text structures, how to handle unfamiliar topics, and how to increase their word meaning vocabularies. Their main work is to apply their reading abilities to comprehending a wide range of literature and content materials, while they are developing critical reading abilities and refining their appreciation of literature. Table 5-7 is a summary of this pattern.

Table 5-7

Accomplished Readers

Some Key Behaviors	Indicators of Advancement
Control cross-checking strategies	Ability to be flexible in multiple reading settings
Self-monitor	
Develop word meaning vocabulary	Can move from novice to more expert reading behaviors with unfamiliar topics
Develop strategies for complex text structures	

What Is the Relationship Between Patterns of Reading Development and Grade Levels?

Any kindergarten or primary teacher could have children representing *each* pattern of reading development in a single classroom, though not in equal numbers. Although kindergartens will probably contain mostly emergent and transitional readers at the beginning of the year, it is also likely that there will be a few beginners, advanced beginners, and perhaps even a consolidator or accomplished reader in a class. The mix will change throughout the year and throughout the elementary school years. In Figure 5-5, the darkened area on each grade level bar estimates where the mass of students is likely to be developmentally for each grade level. You will notice there are dots on either side that represent children in earlier or later patterns of development. There will always be a range of individual differences. Just because a child enters a kindergarten, first, second, or third grade classroom doesn't mean the child is at the same place developmentally as the other children.

This range of individual differences is initially overwhelming to many teachers. Why does it exist? The children entering kindergarten today are a more heterogeneous group than the kindergarten children of even a decade ago. Not only do they develop at different rates, but they also have different literacy experiences. Some come with no school-like experiences. Many children have experienced educational television like "Sesame Street." Others may have had several years in highly academic settings. There are also significant differences in cultural and linguistic experiences, socioeconomic backgrounds, and family structures, which comprise their background knowledge and learning experiences (Gullo, 1992).

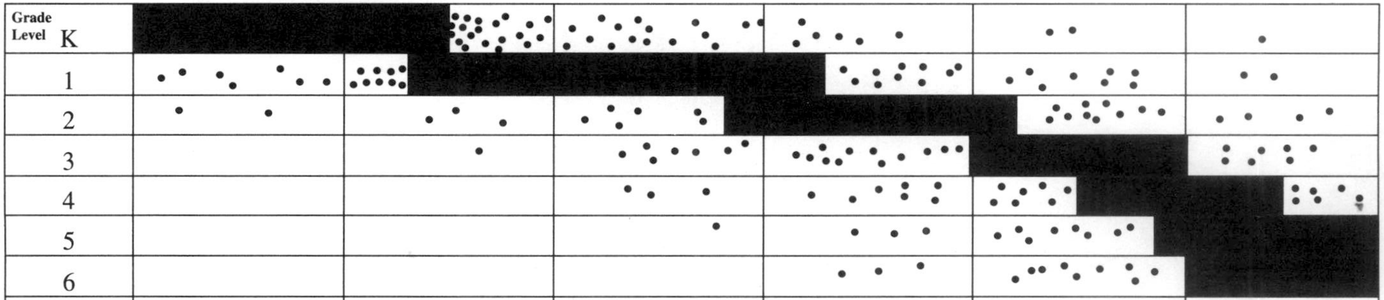

	Emergent Readers	Transitional Readers	Beginning Readers	Advanced Beginning Reading	Consolidating Readers	Accomplished Readers
Patterns of Development	• Focuses on pictures • Develops directionality • Begins phonemic awareness • Develops understanding of conventions of print • Does "pretend reading" • Begins to write and name letters	• Begins to recognize some sight words • Uses pictures and some initial consonants to figure out words • Still relies on memorization of story • Predicts from pictures • Begins to spell semiphonemically	• Focuses on meaning cues • Focuses on letter/sound cues • Begins to use several cues at a time • Expands sight word knowledge • Begins to use cues to self-correct • Develops phonemic awareness • Spelling includes some semiphonemic and phonemic spellings; standard spelling is increasing	• Develops chunking strategies • Develops cross-checking strategies • Refines self-monitoring and self-correction • Transitional and standard spelling	• Works to become automatic with strategies • Increases sight words • Handles more and more complex text	• Controls cross-checking strategies • Self-monitors • Develops more word meaning vocabulary • Develops strategies for complex text structures
	Indicators of Advancement: • Attention shifts to print • Memorized story retellings	**Indicators of Advancement:** • Voice/print match • Begins to try to use most letters to figure out words	**Indicators of Advancement:** • Cross-checking cues • Begins to *see* spelling patterns	**Indicators of Advancement:** • Effective chunking • Consistent use of cross-checking • Consistent self-monitoring and self-correcting	**Indicators of Advancement:** • Becomes strategic • Silent reading speech exceeds oral	**Indicators of Advancement:** • Ability to be flexible in multiple reading settings • Moves from novice to more expert reading behaviors with familiar topics

FIGURE 5-5   Relationship of Grade Level to Patterns of Reading (Jett-Simpson & Leslie, 1994)

How Can You Use Patterns
of Reading Development?

Observe Children's Assets

Knowledge of developmental patterns can direct teachers' observations toward children's assets. Observers have a choice. They can look for things children can't do, or they can observe what children can do and what new learning is emerging. The developmental patterns described here are designed to focus attention on assets—growth patterns. What teachers believe and know to be important characteristics of reading are what they will notice during observations. The more we know about the reading process and the more we keep our minds open to new information we observe in children, the better we will be able to describe children's reading development and make appropriate instructional decisions.

Let's consider the impact of the teacher's point of view, asset or deficit, on observations of children at both ends of the developmental continuum. Children who enter kindergarten demonstrating more advanced literacy behaviors have a decided advantage because they will be perceived as more mature and intelligent. Frequently, teachers respond to them more positively than to children who are in the emergent pattern of development. The more advanced children get extra materials and positive attention, such as extra time in the reading corner, opportunities to read to students in another class, and chances to read the "new" books. In many programs, they are placed in a top reading group where they are encouraged to self-correct their miscues by making sense of the text, and they are allowed more time to read than their counterparts (Allington, 1983).

Conversely, children who demonstrate less developed reading behaviors may be classified as "remedial" before they have had an opportunity to demonstrate their abilities. They are not valued for their assets: what they know and can do. Often these children don't have access to the physical and social experiences that support maximum development. They are frequently placed in low reading groups. When they make miscues, they are asked to sound out words (not encouraged to cross-check), meaning is not emphasized, and they are not provided as much time to read (Allington, 1983). The physical and social school experiences created for young children can result in an educational situation where "the rich get richer and the poor get poorer" (Stanovich, 1986).

Observe Students' Reading Behaviors

The descriptions of patterns of reading development can guide observations of student reading behaviors that indicate growth. Although children will be demonstrating a wide range of reading behaviors, some of which are inconsistent from context to context, teachers must be particularly alert for the "cutting edges" of learning that indicate advancement. When children attempt to work on characteristics of reading called "indicators of advancement," they are moving to the next pattern of development. Teachers may notice that children seem to regress at times. Often this indicates that they are trying to incorporate some new learning into their knowledge. What teachers thought was learned may be dropped for a while in the interests of focusing on the new learning, only to reappear later (Clay, 1991a).

To develop a composite picture of a child's reading behaviors, teachers need to observe the child in a variety of reading and writing contexts over time. This is done best by integrating observations, which are one form of assessment, with instruction. One simple system many teachers have used is to divide the class into equal observation groups for each day of the week so a regular observation pattern is established. They attach self-adhesive mailing labels to a clipboard and write name, date, context, and reading behavior on a label each time they observe some interesting reading behavior. If some children not on the day's list demonstrate some "breakthrough" reading behavior, notes are taken for them, too. At the end of the day, the labels can quickly be placed in a three-ring binder notebook indexed with children's names. After several observations, teachers can begin to interpret patterns of development.

Provide Developmentally Appropriate Instruction

Knowledge of patterns of reading development and reading process is the foundation for developmentally appropriate instruction. We observe so we know what to teach. Knowledge of patterns of reading development helps teachers identify where readers are developmentally, so instruction can be matched to their needs and teachers can avoid expecting too much or too little (Bredekamp, 1987). For example, a teacher who has observed that many of her children are trying to work out where to start reading on a page and what direction to track the print will know these children aren't going to make much sense of instruction about using spelling patterns (chunks) as a word analysis strategy. Such children aren't even paying attention to word analysis yet. The optimal focus of a lesson for these children would be to model directionality and where to start on the page. With the teacher's instructional support, these children will be able to successfully track print. Instruction, then, is directed toward supporting emerging literacy learnings.

Select Materials

Knowledge of patterns of reading development provides information for guiding teachers in selecting appropriate instructional materials for read-

Lion, Lion,
what do you hear?

I hear a hippopotamus
snorting in my ear.

From *Polar Bear, Polar Bear, What Do You Hear?* by Bill Martin, Jr., with illustrations by Eric Carle (Holt, 1991).

ers. Several types of books are particularly supportive of the learning-to-read process: predictable books, alphabet books, and series designed for developing readers. Predictable books contain a variety of different combinations of repeated patterns: rhyme, pictures, plot structure, refrains, familiar cultural sequences like seasons, days of the week, and months of the year, and sentence patterns. A well-known predictable book is *Brown Bear, Brown Bear, What Do You See?* by Bill Martin, Jr. (1992), a perennial favorite, where the illustrations and text inseparably build the story.

> *Brown bear, brown bear*
> *What do you see?*
> *I see a red bird looking at me.*
>
> *Red bird, red bird*
> *What do you see?*
> *I see a yellow duck looking at me.*

Once children catch on to the pattern, the story is easy to remember and work out because of all the cues or scaffolds the story gives to the problem solving. In particular, emergent, transitional, and beginning readers are supported in reading by the predictable structures. However, teachers should gradually decrease the predictability of just-right-for-learning books so students don't develop the misconception that reading is just identifying the pattern and memorizing it. Martin wrote *Polar Bear, Polar Bear, What Do You Hear?* (1991) with the same kind of predictable pattern.

Alphabet books can be very useful to emergent and transitional readers who are working out letter names and how letters look. Children can learn some of the sound-symbol associations for letters, as well as expand their vocabulary and enjoy the interesting ways authors present the alphabet. Alphabet books aren't simply depictions of simple things in the environment that represent a letter, like apples and balls. Jan Garten's *The Alphabet Tale* (1994) invites readers to predict the next animal to appear by anticipating the next letter in the alphabet and examining the clue—the tip of an animal's tail. Children will be entranced with the rhythm of *Chicka Chicka Boom Boom* by Bill Martin, Jr., and John Archambault (1989), the story of letters that meet at the top of the coconut tree and tumble to the ground when the tree is overloaded. Undaunted, they untangle themselves and start over again. Lois Ehlert's (1989) brilliant fruit and vegetable collages in *Eating the Alphabet* invite children to identify familiar items and to learn about some new delectable edible items. A food theme could be continued with *Potluck* by Anne Shelby (1991), in which action-packed pictures show children representing many ethnic groups coming to the potluck with a variety of food offerings. An obvious follow-up to reading these books would be to have a tasting party.

As teachers use more children's literature as the base for reading programs, there has been an increase in the number of series published by trade book publishers, designed not only to fulfill the functions of children's literature described in Chapter 2 but to support developing readers as well. Beginning readers and advanced beginners can find books that match their interests and abilities among the many titles. The Frog and Toad books by Arnold Lobel are classic beginning-to-read books that have won awards for excellence in literature. One of these books, *Frog and Toad Together* (1972), was named an Honor Book for the Newbery Award, given annually by the American Library Association for the author of the most distinguished contribution to literature for children. Lobel's *Frog and Toad Are Friends* (1970) was an Honor Book for the Caldecott Medal, given annually to the most distinguished American picture book for children. It is possible for books to fulfill the dual function of being good literature for children and supporting the process of learning to read. Not all books match the standard set by Lobel. As discussed in Chapter 2, a number of books in beginning-to-read series fail on both counts: they are neither good literature nor very successful for teaching reading. It is important to review beginning-to-read books as carefully as you would any other literature.

From *The Alphabet Tale* by Jan Garten, with illustrations by Muriel Batherman (Greenwillow, 1994).

Sharp eyes and sharp teeth—
Run first and look later.
    This is the tail of an . . .

The classroom library should represent children's range of reading abilities so that every child can find books that are "easy," "just right for learning" and "challenging." Easy books are those that children can read with strong comprehension, at least eighty percent, and word recognition of around ninety-five percent or better. They build confidence and fluency. Just-right-for-learning books are ones with which children may need some help from a peer or the teacher to read successfully (comprehension at least seventy percent and word recognition at least ninety percent). With just-right-for learning books, students make enough miscues to stretch their learning by applying known and new problem-solving strategies. Challenging books are those that children cannot read at this time in their reading lives but that they will be able to read independently some day. Challenging books can also be books that have information-laden pictures with captions that children explore to gain information (Clay, 1993b; Hansen, 1987).

Decide How to Teach

Knowledge of patterns of reading development and reading process provides the basis for deciding how to teach. Teachers decide how to teach reading based on knowledge about learners, the reading process, and

patterns of reading development. The teacher creates a rich literacy learning environment with the students where instructional methods and experiences are carefully selected to meet learners' needs. The methods and learning experiences should be part of a classroom environment that meets the conditions of learning as presented in Figure 1-3: immersion, demonstration, engagement, expectation, responsibility, use, approximation, and response. From our point of view, there is not a single systematic set of procedures for all children at all levels.

What Can Be the Design of a Reading Program?

Common Approaches

You may have heard of the basal reader approach, intensive phonics approach, literature approach, whole language approach, or language experience approach, to mention a few of the most common labels for ways reading instruction has been presented. We will briefly describe each of these approaches and then explain the approach we are recommending.

The Basal Reader Approach   Many of you probably learned to read using a basal reader. Simply put, a basal reader approach consists of a set of books that contain a collection of stories, articles, and poems that are graduated in difficulty by grade level with an accompanying manual for the teacher to follow and seatwork materials for students in workbook, journal, or blackline master format. Teachers' manuals contain very detailed sets of directions about how to teach the materials. Basals have been developed to represent both "top down" and "bottom up" points of view, although all basal series contain attention to phonics in some way.

It is important to note that basal readers are assembled by groups of authors, publishers, and marketing people who are not part of your classroom. They are assembled for imagined children at each grade level. Children and teachers have little input into structuring the learning experiences if the program is followed as assembled. The emphasis is placed on teaching the materials. If followed unquestioningly, the reading program is being directed by outsiders.

Intensive Phonics Approach "Bottom up" basals are called *intensive phonics programs*. There is a great deal of emphasis on isolated phonics instruction and work at the word level. Typically, stories in these basals are written to carefully control the letter-sound relationships. A beginning text might be something like this: "The cat sat on the mat. The cat is fat. The fat cat sat on the mat." There is little resemblance between natural language and this contrived text.

Several different sets of packaged commercial intensive phonics materials are available that focus exclusively on letter-sound relationships and their rules. These can be purchased independent of any basal reader program. In such programs, skills are taught in isolation and are not linked to strategic learning. These programs often are used in addition to a basal series.

Literature Approach This label can apply to several different ways of structuring a program. In some cases it refers to basal series called literature basals. Rather than teaching stories written exclusively for the basal, these basal series contain stories originally found in children's literature. In some cases they are abridged for the basal, and in others the stories and illustrations remain intact. More emphasis is placed on constructing story meaning than on learning phonics.

The label *literature approach* can also apply to the use of a single novel in packages frequently called literature units. A unit is likely to include a summary of the story, activities for introducing the book, comprehension questions, and follow-up activities. Often the instruction plan that accompanies the literature unit is very similar to the basal reader teachers' manuals. Clearly, it is difficult to provide for a range of reading abilities using a single novel.

Literature approach can also refer to a program where students are all allowed to select the books they want to read based on their interests and abilities. The classrooms where there is self-selection are typically grounded in a whole language philosophy.

Whole Language Approach   Whole language is not really a particular method. It is a philosophy based on a set of beliefs about the learner: (1) learning is a social process, (2) learning is best achieved through direct engagement and experience, (3) learners' purposes and intentions are what drive learning, and (4) learning involves hypothesis testing. In addition, it is based on principles of language development, such as those discussed in Chapter 1, and reading and writing processes as transactions of meaning (Edelsky, Altwerger & Flores, 1991). The teacher's central role is to collaborate with the children in their learning and to create environments for supporting it, much as Cambourne described in his conditions for learning in Figure 1-3. If you were to observe in whole language classrooms, you would be likely to see students engaged in a variety of literacy experiences from classroom to classroom because no one set of experiences defines whole language. However, a common element would be reading and writing authentic texts. It would also be clear from observation that the classrooms consistently apply the beliefs described above.

Language Experience Approach   In the language experience approach, children dictate a caption or story for some experience they have had. The teacher writes what the children say and then reads it back, inviting them to join in. The teacher has the children do different activities with the text and invites them to read back. There are whole-class stories created as well as individual stories. Children's first reading material is from their oral language (Hall, 1981).

A Balanced Learner-Centered Reading Program

A balanced learner-centered reading program is probably closest to whole language and rests on the same beliefs stated above. In addition it is based on the following premises:

1. Reading is an interactive and transactional process.
2. Reading progresses in patterns of development.
3. The reading environment should meet Cambourne's (1988) conditions of learning (Figure 1-3)
4. Instruction is determined from children's needs and patterns of development.
5. Reading should be the main activity during the reading period.
6. Writing should be integrated in the reading period.

To meet the stated premises, we propose a program that is organized around key literacy events. Within these key events, teachers can select teaching methods they identify as most appropriate to students' patterns of development, which may include some language experience and phonics instruction. Teachers also demonstrate reading by participating in the key literacy events, modeling reading and writing, and demonstrating problem-solving strategies for word analysis and comprehension. They select literacy experiences that actively involve children and provide opportunities for modeling. Teachers also model purposes for reading such as pleasure, information, and research.

Students will have opportunities to engage in reading independently, with a partner, in small groups, and with the whole class while immersing themselves in reading. It is recognized that there is something to be gained from working both alone and with others. Students are expected to learn and to assume responsibility for their learning to the degree that they are able to do so given their maturity.

Mistakes are honored as attempts to problem solve and considered essential to learning. This means that teachers respond to these mistakes as approximations of the desired model, giving just enough feedback so students can complete solving the problem on their own. Word-perfect reading is not the goal. As well as easy texts, children need to work in just-right-for-learning texts, so that they will make mistakes that provide opportunities for stretching the learning. For example, the teacher might respond to a child's miscue in the following way:

Child reads: A lion is not a monster. (*The text says "A tiger is not a monster" and pictures a tiger on the page.*)
Teacher responds: Try that again.

Child reads it the same way.

Teacher responds: Look at the picture. What do you see?
Child: A tiger.
Teacher: What would you expect to see at the beginning of tiger?
Child: Tiger—t.
Teacher: Point to the word *tiger.*

Child points to the word and automatically rereads correctly.

With another child who made the same miscue, the scenario may be different; for example:

Child reads: A lion is not a monster. (*The text says "A tiger is not a monster" and pictures a tiger on the page.*)
Teacher responds: Try that again.
Child: Oh, that's a tiger.

Child points to the picture and then reads the text correctly.

In each example, the teacher suggested strategies the child could use to problem solve on her own. The first child needed to be directed to a number of strategies before she figured out the word. The second child needed only a single nudge. Teachers adjust their feedback to match children's needs and provide material children can use to optimize their learning.

What Are the Key Literacy Events for Reading Instruction?

A balanced learner-centered reading program should include key literacy events. Some events are best used with certain patterns of development, whereas others are appropriate for all learning because of their flexibility. These literacy events will be discussed and related to children's patterns of reading development. First, we will discuss key literacy events directed primarily by the teacher, and second, we will describe key literacy events that are mainly managed by children.

Teacher-Directed Literacy Events

Teacher-directed literacy events include the shared book experience, creating texts with children, guided reading, individual and small group conferences, mini-lessons, and teacher read-alouds.

Through the shared book experience, a teacher can build a positive beginning reading experience for all students.

The Shared Book Experience—Using "Big Books"

Picture the following classroom scene. Displayed on an easel is a big book (a text enlarged so that it is several feet tall and wide) with the teacher seated next to it, pointer in hand. Children are sitting on a rug close to the teacher and the book so that everyone can see the illustrations and print. The teacher begins to read the story while pointing to the text. The children are invited to join in by talking about the pictures, predicting what is going to happen next, chiming in with the teacher's reading on the predictable parts, and enjoying a good story. The shared book experience has begun.

The shared book experience is a natural transition from parents' laps to school reading for emergent, transitional, and beginning readers. Conceptualized by Don Holdaway (1979) in response to the increasing diversity of the population of children attending New Zealand schools, the shared book experience was designed to replicate in the classroom the natural coziness of home bedtime stories. This rich, interactive literature environment welcomes all children immediately into the "literacy club" (Smith, 1988). Children view themselves as readers and are given opportunities to participate and make connections through literature irrespective of their socioeconomic, cultural, or linguistic backgrounds. Youngsters can immerse themselves in big book reading, expecting that they can eventually "do it alone." In this risk-free environment, everyone can successfully participate at his or her own developmental level.

Selecting Big Books   Selecting big books requires attention to several important text characteristics. Above all, they should be good stories: ones that delight, tantalize, capture children's interest, and invite immediate engagement. Because one of the goals is for the story to stick in memory so that children can do partially or fully memorized "readings" of the book when the lesson is finished, it is important to look for books that have some combination of the following: (1) rhyme, (2) rhythm, (3) illustrations that illuminate and enhance the text, (4) repetition, which reinforces the constancy of print, and (5) predictability.

Cookie's Week by Cindy Ward (1988) provides predictability based on the days of the week, repeated sentence patterns, repeated cause/effect relationships, and repeated plot pattern. The text is also clearly supported by the illustrations.

> *On Monday, Cookie fell in the toilet*
> *   There was water everywhere!*
> *On Tuesday, Cookie knocked a plant off the window sill.*
> *   There was dirt everywhere!*
> *On Wednesday. . . .*

A House Is a House for Me, by Mary Ann Hoberman (1986) includes lots of rhyme and rhythm.

A hill is a house for an ant, an ant.
A hive is a house for a bee.
A hole is a house for a mole or a mouse
And a house is a house for me!

The preceding examples are enlarged texts of books originally written as trade books for children.

Another major category of big books is those written specifically as instructional texts for teaching beginning reading. They are available from such publishers as Rigby and Richard Owen. The lovable mascot of one publisher (Wright Group) is Mrs. Wishy Washy by Joy Crowly (1986), a woman who honors cleanliness above all, to the extent that she shoos her farm animals out of the mud and gives them a thorough bathing. To the readers' delight, the animals return to their mud puddle in the end with the exclamation "Oh lovely, mud!"

The following section provides a framework that could be used by teachers when developing the shared book literacy event. How the teacher works with it should constantly be adjusted to children's changing needs.

An Instructional Framework for the Shared Book Experience— Teaching with "Big Books"   These activities are done on the first day:

1. *Warmup.* Begin the period with some brief warm-ups such as finger plays, songs, and a reread of a favorite big book. Let the children choose.

2. *Introduce the new big book.* Invite the children to discuss the front and back covers of the big book to identify story clues. Point to, identify by label, and read the title, author, and illustrator. "The title of our book today is . . . ." Children will gradually learn the terminology through teacher modeling.

3. *Read the book for the first time.* The purpose of the first read is enjoyment! Read the story with joy and enthusiasm, pointing to the text and inviting the children to participate. Invite children to talk about what is happening in selected illustrations to clarify confusing parts of the story, use the illustrations and text to predict what will happen next at strategic points in the story, and join in with the reading as they catch on to how the story is developing. The most powerful end result is a spontaneous shout of "Read it again!" Throughout the reading, teachers will be demonstrating voice/print match, directionality of print, where to begin reading on the page, and reading itself.

4. *Read it again.* Invite the children to participate as in the first reading, and give them opportunities to talk about their personal reactions to the story.

5. *Have children read small copies of the big book.* It is important to have about six small copies of the big book to use as a follow-up. Make the little versions available for the children to read on their own sometime during the day. The books could be placed in the book corner to be available during center time for as long as the children remain interested.

6. *Have children read the big book.* Another favorite center during choice time is the big book easel. Children delight in playing school with the big book, either alone or with a small group of friends.

7. *Have children listen to the story on tape.* This follow-up activity can be part of the center set-up. It is especially useful for children who want to hear the story again and again.

8. *Observe the children.* By observing the children's responses throughout the lesson and their independent reading in the centers, teachers can identify behaviors that indicate patterns of reading development described previously. In particular, teachers watch to see if children like the book; to determine whether they are reading the pictures, demonstrating directionality and other concepts of print, or beginning to try to read the print; to see if they have voice/print match; and to determine the degree to which they are memorizing the story. If teachers watch and listen carefully, observation will yield direction for tomorrow's shared book experience. Teachers take notes on self-adhesive mailing labels placed in each child's section of an observation notebook at the end of the day and throughout the year.

On the second day, the teacher begins the shared book experience time with the warm-up as described above. The next step is to reread yesterday's book and do a focused mini-lesson at the sentence or word level. Reread the story, and as you reach highly predictable spots in the story, be silent and let the children take over the reading. This is the time for a few mini-lessons, such as modeling reading strategies appropriate to children's patterns of development, to facilitate children's development. The teacher provides for individual differences by carefully selecting children to participate who need the guided practice with some aspect of reading. While the lesson might be practice for one child, it is a new demonstration of what to do for other children in the group. Following are some examples of skills, strategy, or comprehension mini-lessons that teachers can embed and weave into the rereading. Teachers can demonstrate and explain and then invite the children to do the activities.

Concepts of Print

1. Take turns pointing to the story text as it is read to practice voice/print match and directionality. The teacher can assist children who

are confused by holding the pointer and doing it with them. (*emergent readers*)

2. Work with concepts of print by having a child point out where to start reading on the page, and show with the finger how to continue the reading. (*emergent readers*)

3. Practice right-to-left page turning. A child who needs the practice can be designated official page turner. (*emergent readers*)

4. Match sentence strips to selected story sentences. (*emergent and transitional readers*)

5. Match some word cards to selected words in the story. (*emergent and transitional readers*)

6. Have children frame words, phrases, and/or sentence patterns they know with their hands. (*transitional and beginning readers*)

Phonemic Awareness and Letter-Sound Relationships

1. Predict a letter at the beginning of a word. (The teacher could say, "Say *monkey* with me. Monkey. What do you expect to see at the beginning of *monkey*?" Children answer. Then have someone point to the word on the page. (*transitional and beginning readers*)

2. Identify the rhyming words. (*emergent and transitional readers*)

3. Think of other words that rhyme with a rhyming word pattern in the story. (*emergent and transitional readers*)

4. Choose a consonant or a spelling pattern from the story and develop a word wall chart. For example, at the end of *The Hungry Giant* by Joy Crowly (1980), he yells "Ow! Ow! Ow!" Children could develop a word wall chart for words that can be made with /ow/. To do this write the key pattern at the top of a 12″ × 18″ sheet of paper and have the children use the pattern to generate other words. Model one to begin: "This is a pattern that is in other words. For example, what word would we get if we put a *c* in front of the /ow/?" Write the words generated on the chart as well. Post the chart on the wall for children's quick reference in figuring out words independently when they are reading. When the wall is too full of these charts, remove the ones the children have well under control. (*beginning and advanced beginning readers*)

Meaning Making

1. Tell favorite words or sentences from the story and point them out. (*transitional, beginning, and advanced beginning readers*)

2. Have children make their voices reflect the cues in exclamation marks, questions, and commas. (*all readers*)

3. Think of other words that would make sense at a particular spot in the story. (*all readers*)

4. Do group dramatizations of parts of the story.   (*all readers*)

5. Invite children to relate the story to their own experiences.   (*all readers*)

6. Do a group retelling by inviting the children to remember what comes next in the story.   (*all readers*)

Cross-Checking Strategies

1. Model think-alouds on what strategies can be used to figure out hard words in the story: reread, read on, check to see what makes sense, if it sounds right, if it looks right, and if the letter-sound patterns are what one would expect to see.   (*beginning, advanced beginning, and consolidating readers*)

2. Model strategies for making sense when meaning breaks down: reread, read on, look at the pictures, think of possible meanings, and ask a friend for help.   (*beginning and advanced beginning readers*)

What next? At this point teachers may choose to simply integrate the big book into the group of familiar big books for rereading during warm-up time while continuing to make the small versions available in the book center. Many teachers like to take a big book that is working well and extend it by integrating the activity into the rest of the day's activities.

EXTENSION ACTIVITIES

The best extension activities relate directly to the story. It is also important to keep in mind that what the children need to practice and experience most during reading is reading. The following examples integrate reading and writing.

Innovations on the story involve making up a new version of a story or a new verse for a song or poem following the basic pattern of the original. (This procedure is commonly labeled a language experience activity by some educators.) Class big books can be made easily by having each child contribute an illustration and innovation. For *Cookie's Week* by Cindy Ward (1988), the innovation could be a class book titled *Our Week*. Each child could choose a day of the week, describe an accident they had, and illustrate it. For example: "On Monday, Tanisha stepped in a mud puddle. There was mud everywhere."

Since there will be more children than days of the week, there will be multiple pages for some days. (Be sure that all days are covered.) Precut the pages so that they are staggered widths, with the Monday pages the narrowest and Sunday pages the full width of a large sheet of paper, so the book can be assembled in a waterfall pattern. Then each time the children read the book, they can create a new story sequence by choosing different examples of days of the week.

While the children are making illustrations, the teacher can circulate through the classroom and transcribe children's dictations on their illustrated pages. Or if there is a computer in the classroom, have the children take turns dictating to the teacher to get printouts of their text to be glued on their illustrations.

Simpler texts, like *Yuck Soup!* by Joy Crowly (1986), will require only a one-word change to create an extended text. In the story, some strange green outer space creatures are making soup out of very inedible things. On each page another item is tossed in the soup: "In go some thistles. In go some toothbrushes." Of course when they taste the concoction at the end, they say "Yuck!" To innovate, all the children need do is think of something "yucky" to go in the soup, as illustrated in the following example:

> In go some worms.
> In go some turnips.
> In go some garbage.
> In go some toothpicks.
> Yuck!

Children could illustrate their statements. These could be bound into a big book or become a wall story on a long hall outside the classroom door.

Wall murals are also an interesting way for children to respond. For *A House Is a House for Me* by Mary Ann Hoberman (1986), children could choose an animal to draw beside its house, to be cut out and placed on a wall mural that focuses on places animals live. These drawings could be accompanied by speech balloons where the animals tell what kind of house is for them by borrowing a sentence pattern from the story, "A hive is a house for a bee."

Retelling stories through creative drama, puppets, or flannel boards are other effective extensions. Stewig and Buege (1994) suggest several ways drama can grow from reading.

Integrating Activities into Centers   Teachers select books for the shared book experience that relate to a theme of study, integrating them with the rest of the curriculum. Activities that relate to the story content can be integrated into the book center, the listening center, the writing center, a word play center, and a theme center such as a hands-on science center. These will be described more fully in Chapter 7.

Creating Texts with Children   There are typically a number of opportunities throughout the day to create texts with the children. One way was illustrated in the discussion of the shared book experience, where the teacher works to help children create a spin-off version of the big book. Children also enjoy doing versions of favorite songs, which can be written on charts for group reading during music time.

Language experience methodology is a second way to create texts with children. It is particularly effective with emergent, transitional, and beginning readers. As discussed earlier, this approach involves using children's language to create a text about an experience (Hall, 1981). Teachers provide common experiences such as field trips, like a trip to a pumpkin farm, and classroom experiments, like churning butter. Afterward the teacher engages the children in conversation about their experiences and asks them what they want to write about them. As selected children dictate their sentences, the teacher writes them on chart paper and invites children to assist with the spelling, to help them apply their knowledge of letter-sound relationships. The teacher and the class reread the chart story as a group. Individual copies can be printed on the computer so each child can have one. Extension activities like those discussed for the shared book experience are provided as follow-up.

Guided Reading

When you read the title of this section, many of you probably remembered what reading was like for you in school, when you sat in an ability-level reading group with a basal reader in hand focusing on the new story. You probably recall that your teacher, who followed a script in the teacher's manual, presented the new words, asked a few questions, and then asked you to read the page to find out. . . . Someone in the group would read aloud while the teacher corrected the pronunciation errors. Next, the teacher would ask a few questions about the page, and the cycle would be repeated for each subsequent page. This was, and still is, called the directed reading activity, which is accompanied by "round robin" reading where each student takes a turn reading aloud. It is a highly teacher/textbook-controlled activity that reinforces teacher dependence and is based on the assumption that knowing how to pronounce the words before reading and then getting them right while reading are the goals of reading. This is *not* the "guided reading" we will describe here.

Introducing the Story   The purpose of guided reading is to give enough support to readers so they can read a new story *independently* at the first reading. Transitional readers, beginning readers, and advanced beginners benefit most from guided reading. (Emergent readers are served well with the shared book experience.) Guided reading is most effective with groups of four to eight children.

Instead of using a script from a teacher's manual, teachers choose a book children will be able to read successfully at a just-right-for-learning level with an appropriate introduction that will be referred to here as a "talk-through." What goes into the introduction depends on the relationships among the following factors (Clay, 1991b):

The difficulty of the text:

   the complexity of language structure in the text

   the complexity of the story structure

   the number of unfamiliar concepts or new knowledge

   the amount of support illustrations provide for the text

What the children can do and are trying to do (their patterns of development):

   knowledge of strategies

   ability to use oral language

   what is known about print

   knowledge of the world (background knowledge)

   knowledge of story structure

"Book introductions are an authentic social interaction about the new book, but when they provide an orientation to novel features of stories . . . they are a kind of teaching" (Clay, 1991b, p. 267). To the observer, they will sound more like conversations or story "talk-throughs." They are not a "telling," as in your school experiences, but rather a "drawing in," which invites children to be active participants and contributors in constructing meaning. Although teachers can anticipate what may need introducing, it is only through interaction with the children that the introduction can take full shape as it is adjusted to their observations and responses.

Based on knowledge of children and the text, teachers plan talk-throughs to match the children's needs. When children have a small number of reading strategies under control, the talk-throughs are rich. But as children advance in their development and gain more control over their own reading, teachers gradually reduce the content of talk-throughs to a minimum and encourage children to do more and more of the talk-through on their own. The goal is to gradually turn the procedure over to the children so they are independently talking through new books. Of course, stories that are familiar or ones children can read independently are not introduced. Children read these stories on their own.

It is impossible to describe talk-throughs in terms as specific as those scripted teacher's manuals your former teachers used because they are dynamic and no two are the same. They are constantly adapted to students' needs. Generally speaking, they could take the following shape (Clay, 1991b):

1. State the topic, title, and characters.
2. Encourage children to predict the story from the cover and from illustrations throughout the book.

3. Draw from children some experiences they can relate to the text; probe to find out what children know.

4. Create an overview of the story with the children.

5. Work with any conceptual confusions.

6. Use novel features of language of the text.

7. Intentionally weave in a particular sentence pattern two or three times and have the children repeat it to get a bit of practice with difficult language (rehearsal).

8. When appropriate, address letter-sound relationships of first or last letters or letter clusters and the pronunciation of unusual names.

9. Demonstrate strategies appropriate to the children's patterns of development.

10. Have children talk about how they know what they know.

11. Accept partially correct responses (approximations) and build on them.

12. Tighten the criteria of acceptability.

13. Present new knowledge and have children work with it.

During the whole process it is important to remember that "the overview of the story is like a conversational exchange, and the attention to detail should not dismember the flow of the story" (Clay, 1991b, p. 267). "The teacher's role is to keep the learner at the cutting edge of his or her competencies" (p. 272). The teacher pushes for independent problem solving and gradually passes all control to the reader. An example of a talk-through is provided in Table 5-8 to illustrate one possibility.

Reading the Story for the First Time Children are provided with their own copies of the story. After the introduction, children are invited to make their first attempt at reading the story independently. This is an important time for teachers to carefully observe for the problem-solving strategies children are using successfully and attempting to use. These observations can be woven into the class work after the first read. The teacher moves briefly from child to child, prompting, encouraging, and responding to approximations while they work out the stories. Keep in mind, however, that word-perfect reading is not the goal. Children should be making miscues if the book is "just right" (at least ninety to ninety-four percent word recognition and with at least seventy percent comprehension) because the book will have some difficult parts to challenge and stretch their abilities—keeping them on the "cutting edge" of learning. Teachers focus on the problem-solving strategies children are using to work out the book: rereading, reading on, using the cueing systems (meaning, visual, letter-sound relationships, and language structure), noticing picture cues, self-correcting, and cross-checking. We

Table 5-8

Example of a Guided Reading Literacy Event—The Talk-Through

T.	The title of this book is *What Could a Hippopotamus Be?* *(Teacher points to the title.)* It is written by Mike Thaler. The pictures are by Robert Grossman. *(Points to names.)* Look at the cover of the book. What ideas do you get for what the story could be about?
Ss.	(Possible responses.) A hippo. Look, he's a fireman.
T.	What makes you think that?
Ss.	I saw a fireman. He has a fireman's hat like that, and there's the hose and a ladder.
T.	Hippopotamus is trying to figure out what he can be. Let's look at this page.
Ss.	He's in a fireman's hat. He's going to put out a fire.
T.	What do you think? Do you think he can be a fireman?
Ss.	(Answers.)
T.	Why do you think that? *(Then teacher turns the page.)*
Ss.	*(The children will see that Hippopotamus broke all the rungs of the ladder and fell down. There is only one word on this page—"No." It is likely that some of the children will know it and call out "No.")*
T.	What do you think will happen next? *(Responds to children's ideas.)*
T.	*(Turns page.)* Hippopotamus wonders if he can be a sailor. What does a sailor do? Let's say "sailor" together. What would you expect to see at the beginning of *sailor*?
Ss.	S.
T.	*(Points to the word sailor.)* What do you think happened to Hippopotamus?
Ss.	Look, he fell in. It says "No."
T.	*(The question-answer structure of the story will probably be established by now so that the children will easily predict what happens to hippo throughout the story.)*

want to see the children taking risks, trying to resolve reading challenges when they meet them. That is what is meant by successful reading here.

Thinking About and Working with the Text   After the first read, invite children to give their comments and opinions. Appropriate follow-up activities should be done that match children's patterns of reading development. Probably only one of these would be done with a story.

1. *Think-aloud strategy*. Have the children talk about how they figured out hard parts in the story and what they did when they got stuck. Both teachers and children can demonstrate think-alouds for problem solving. For example, the teacher could model by saying something like the following about a specific word in the story: "Here's what I do when I come to a hard part like a word I don't know. First, I read on and think about what it could mean. I look at the picture for some clues. I ask myself, what would make sense? Then I look closely at the word. What do I know about this word? What patterns do I see? Then I try out what I think the word is in the sentence. I think and cross-check by asking myself, does it make sense? Does it sound right? Does it look right? If yes, I keep reading. If no, I try again."

2. *High-frequency words*. Sometimes the hard part is a high-frequency or basic sight word, such as *a, the, is, are, and,* or *was*. These serve grammatical functions in sentences and have no physical referents in the world. If the children can't figure out the word, you can have the children participate in a two-minute activity. Tell them the word; then have them look closely at it, go quickly to the chalkboard, write the word, and run their finger under the word as they say it. Then have them erase and repeat the procedure. You can vary the activity by having them write it large or small. Next have them look at their text and skim the pages to see how many times the word appears in the story and talk about where else they have seen the word. Encourage the children to practice the word in the word play center by typing it on the typewriter or computer and building it with magnetic letters. If the children are reading a variety of books and writing, they will have many other opportunities to work with these high-frequency words. It is useful to keep a group list of these words on the wall as you work with them, to which children can refer when reading and writing independently.

3. *Letter-sound relationships and patterns*. Just as with the shared book experience, you can focus on some letter-sound relationship or spelling pattern from the story that can be the basis for developing a word wall chart. See the example for *The Hungry Giant* story in the section on the shared book experience.

Rereading the Story   Children can now return to the story and take control as readers by rereading independently or with a partner. Youngsters will need to be taught how to be good partners, letting the reader take time to work out challenges without the listener calling out the word. The listener can encourage the reader to "try that again" when the reader makes miscues that don't make sense. A good whole-class mini-lesson could focus on how to be a good reading partner.

Responding to the Text   Children may enjoy responding by rereading the book, writing a spin-off version of the story, dramatizing it, or engaging in any of the language arts activities described in Chapter 2 on literature. But it isn't always necessary for teachers to plan a language arts response to the book. In many cases, rereading the book and taking it home to read to the family are enough. Successful reading of a story can be its own reward.

Individual and Small Group Conferences

Once children reach the point where they are able to select their own books and read them independently, they can begin to participate in individual or small group conferences (about three or four children). Usually teachers can begin this when children reach the beginning reader pattern of development. *Small group conferences* can be conducted as part of the readers workshop. During these conferences, it is the reader's responsibility to prepare by reading the book, plan how to summarize the story, and select a short section to read aloud to the listeners. The reader invites children listening in the group to make comments and ask questions about what was shared. The teacher keeps the discussion going and models questions and comments. Sample questions might be (Routman, 1991):

Why did you choose that book?

What did the story make you wonder about?

How does the character feel about . . . ?

Were there any hard parts? What did you do?

One of the goals of the small group sharing times is to develop conversational book discussions (Newkirk & McClure, 1992).

A more formal version of the small group conference is called *literature circles* or *literature groups* (Peterson & Eeds, 1990). One way to organize literature groups is for teachers to tell the students a little about three books to pique their interest. Students then sign up for the book of their choice for literature group study. Children read and discuss assigned sections of the book and respond personally to them. Then teachers guide a discussion of literary elements that are particularly powerful in the stories, such as character, story structure, plot, setting, point of view, time, and mood, for an in-depth exploration of the books (Keegan & Shrake, 1991).

Individual conferences are structured like small group conferences. The reader prepares by reading the book, planning a story summary, and selecting part of the book to read aloud to the teacher. The teacher is the listener who makes comments about what the child has shared and asks honest questions to understand the child's response and gain insight into the strategies the child used while reading the book. Teachers can easily integrate assessment with the conference by taking notes on the child's attitudes, interests, and demonstrations of learning. This is also an opportune time to note the difficulty of the material for the child: easy, just right for learning, or challenging. From the observation information, teachers can identify topics for mini-lessons to meet the common needs of students and determine whether students need assistance in selecting reading material.

Mini-Lessons

Many little lessons can be tucked into key literacy events. The teacher's role is always to observe what the children are doing and respond in ways that encourage them to problem solve. This might include helping them identify clues they have missed, demonstrating strategies, nudging children to try more difficult tasks, and helping them understand what part of a task they have right, for example. Each of these interchanges, whether during a shared book experience, individual or small group conferences, whole-class share times, guided reading, or partner reading, is a small teaching lesson that helps the children do it on their own—to develop independence.

At times the teacher presents a mini-lesson to the whole class. These focus on concepts useful to all students, not narrow topics that might apply to only a few children. Atwell (1987) suggested that these lessons focus on classroom procedures, strategies, or literature study. The teacher could demonstrate a think-aloud strategy children can use for figuring out unknown words, or discuss what characteristics readers might expect in Steven Kellogg's books, or what constitutes a folk tale. Again, ideas for the focus of these lessons come from careful observation of children's patterns of reading development, knowledge of the learning-to-read process, and the content of materials under study.

Teacher Read-Alouds

Teacher read-aloud time, which should take place in every classroom, every day, is often the favorite time of day. It is a time to relax, enjoy a good story, and come together as a community of learners. Laughing together, worrying together, wondering together, and even weeping together bond members of a class in the shared experience.

As discussed in Chapter 2, listening to stories can affect children's language development by increasing their knowledge of more complex linguistic structures, as well as increasing their comprehension of more challenging vocabulary. The impact of literature can be seen in children's writing when they incorporate book language and story ideas into their own stories.

What teachers choose to read aloud should represent a range of books, including books that the children could read independently and those that challenge their listening comprehension. Books should represent many genres of children's literature: poetry, folk and fairy tales, realistic fiction, and nonfiction. Books that tie to thematic units and curriculum topics can also be included. Teacher read-aloud time is a good place to introduce to children books that they are less likely to pick up on their own but are excellent stories. Often the result of the teacher's reading is that children want to read the books on their own. These books should be accessible for this purpose.

Child-Managed Literacy Events

Child-managed literacy events include sustained silent (or noisy) reading, partner reading, whole-class sharing, and responding to literature. These are opportunities for students to practice reading and to demonstrate their comprehension and interpretation of what they have read.

Independent Reading—SNR and SSR

The major form of independent reading that should be integral in all classrooms for children in all patterns of reading development is sustained silent reading (SSR). This is a time when children choose books they want to read independently—to practice reading by reading. Typically, twenty minutes are set aside during the day when everyone, including the teacher, reads. Sustained noisy reading (SNR) often precedes SSR. Most emergent, transitional, and beginning readers read quietly to themselves, but not silently, during independent reading time.

Originally, SSR was developed as a way to give children time when they could simply enjoy reading without having to do related assignments. When studies began to reveal how little reading went on during reading classes, SSR became more central to reading class as well. Gambrell (1984) reported that during an average twenty-seven-minute direct instruction lesson in first grade, the average amount of time given to contextual reading was a total of two minutes of silent reading broken into two one-minute segments. Children read orally for about one minute. First-grade children were engaged in individual reading for about three minutes. Second-graders spent about four minutes in silent reading. When teachers sent students to their seats to do independent seatwork, *none* of them assigned children to read; they did workbooks instead. Fortunately, most teachers now understand that silent reading is legitimate seatwork.

Partner Reading

Many children in all patterns of development enjoy and benefit from reading with a partner. They may read together to simply share books with a friend for the pleasure of it. Teachers might also be partners of children so they can provide support while working out a new story. A form of partner reading that has worked well in schools is a "Buddy Reading" program, where students in a primary-grade class are partners with students in an intermediate-grade class. Both the younger and older children select something to read to each other when they get together once a week to be reading buddies.

Whole-Class Share Times

At the end of the formal block of reading time, a short amount of time, around ten minutes, can be given to sharing books with the whole class. Several children can share daily. Children sign up to share when they are ready and everyone shares before children get another turn. The basic format is the same as that followed in the small group share times, where the child tells a bit about the story, reads a part, and invites the class to make comments and ask questions.

It is important to build in flexibility so that spontaneous sharing of breakthrough events can be celebrated during this time as well. An example of a breakthrough event would be a child who finishes his or her first chapter book. That is cause for recognition and a brief group celebration. The teacher could say, "Jolene, tell us what you accomplished today." Jolene says, "I finished my first chapter book, [title.]" The teacher says, "Let's give a hand and a cheer for Jolene." These

Partner reading, where children share the story, is a motivating opportunity to practice reading strategies.

whole-class share times bring books to the entire classroom community where all can participate successfully without regard to ability.

Readers' Response

Obviously individual and small group conferences, whole-class share times, and most of the other literacy events have readers' response built into them. However, it is often the case that when teachers are looking for places to gain more classroom time for other activities, they tend to minimize readers' response. We do not recommend this. When storybook reading is the central organizing point for literacy lessons and learning, readers' response is an integral component. It allows children to connect with the story in deep and meaningful ways. Children need to have many opportunities to respond to text. They can talk about their personal reactions, how text is making sense to them, and how they are constructing meaning. They should also have opportunities to talk about how they are able to use their problem-solving strategies. With special books they can respond through the language arts: choral reading, readers' theater, story writing, creative dramatizations, puppetry, art, music, pantomime, poetry, and plays.

Although oral language is the major vehicle for responding, through conversations, discussions, and dialogues, writing is another way to encourage children to respond and think more deeply about their reading. Many classroom teachers have their children keep response journals, where they record the title and author of the book they read and then write a reaction. Figure 5-6 is an example of a first-grade reader's response journal.

Home Literacy Links

In kindergarten and the primary grades it is critical that links be made with the home to obtain balance in a learner-centered program. Parents are children's first teachers and continue to be important influences in their children's lives, so they should be included as partners in facilitating their children's learning.

We have known for some time that parents who read regularly to their children have children who do better in school settings. Important attitudes toward books are established as well as some very basic abilities that support the learning-to-read process. An excellent way to keep this important learning link in place is to institute a nightly home reading program. Parents could be invited to participate in an orientation

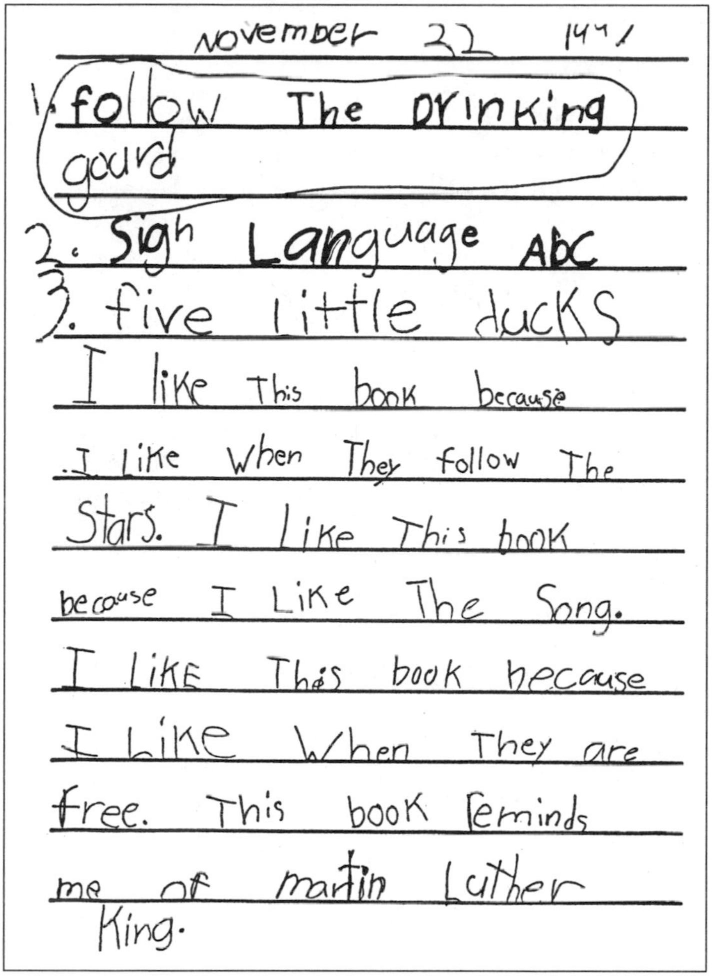

November 22 1997

1. follow The Drinking gourd

2. Sigh Language ABC

3. five little ducks

I like This book because I Like when They follow The Stars. I like This book because I Like The Song. I Like This book because I Like When They are free. This book reminds me of martin Luther King.

Figure 5-6
A Page from Larryjo's Reading Response Journal

during the first parent gathering at school, where teachers could discuss and demonstrate how to do lap reading (see Figure 5-7).

Teachers should also model how to listen to children read. Young readers need lots of patience and positive support from their parents while they are engaging in this new learning. Children can select books to read to the family and books for some family member to read to them and place them in plastic bags on a "Bedtime Book" peg board by the classroom door in readiness for the trip home. Teachers can enclose a note in the bag like the one in Figure 5-8 for the book the child will be reading to the family. These notes can be kept as a record of parent involvement.

Figure 5-7

Checklist for Lap
Reading (Jett-
Simpson, 1986)

Getting Ready

- [ ] comfortable chair or couch for you and your children so they can sit on your lap or cuddle close
- [ ] 20 minutes of uninterrupted time (at least)
- [ ] a good book or several good books (be sure to let your children choose books, too)
- [ ] a book your children will like (return the ones they don't like to the library)

Reading Aloud

I always . . .

- [ ] get the children involved in the story
- [ ] let my voice and reactions show that I am enjoying the story, too
- [ ] make sure that the children can see the book I read
- [ ] let children hold the book or part of the book and turn the pages while I read

Sometimes when the book is right, I . . .

- [ ] invite my children to chime in on
     rhymes
     repeated phrases and sentences
     refrains
- [ ] invite the children to guess what will happen next
- [ ] invite the children to talk about the story
- [ ] invite the children to talk about the pictures
- [ ] invite the children to talk about the words that interest them
- [ ] invite the children to talk about repeated sounds

Conclusion

- [ ] Give them a hug
- [ ] Tuck them into bed
- [ ] Or send them off to play

Organizing Key Literacy Events into Daily Schedules

There is a great deal of variability in the way teachers choose to organize literacy events into workable classroom schedules. In whatever ways teachers decide to organize, it is important to develop a schedule where literacy events occur in a consistent order. By establishing a routine, teachers help students gradually learn to manage their learning more and more independently. Established routines also make classroom management easier for teachers.

FIGURE 5-8

Parent Note

Dear Parents,

Enjoy reading this book with your child. Please help us with the following information.

___ This book was read alone.
___ This book was read with _____
___ This book was read to my child.
___ This book was not read.

Your comments on the book and/or reading.

_____
Parent/Guardian Signature

Kindergarten

The sample schedule for a half-day kindergarten program in Table 5-9 illustrates how some teachers have organized literacy events. These teachers think of literacy as integrated into the entire morning or afternoon rather than as an isolated period. Literacy activities—reading, writing, talking, and listening—are ongoing and integrated with thematic units and topical study units such as science and social studies topics. Math, art, and music are also integrated. The shared book experience can easily feature a book on a science, social studies, or math concept. Of course, teachers also take advantage of snack time and outdoor play.

Table 5-9

Sample Kindergarten Schedule

Sign-in	
8:30–8:45	Journal writing
8:45–8:55	Sustained noisy reading
8:55–9:00	Planning the day's schedule
9:00–9:30	Shared book experience integrated with a thematic unit
9:30–10:30	Center choice time/outdoor play
10:30–10:45	Whole-class share time and snacks
10:45–11:10	Thematic unit focus/specials
11:10–11:30	Teacher read-aloud/Getting ready to go home

Table 5-10

Sample Schedule for a First-Grade Class That Is Mostly
Transitional and Beginning Readers

30 min.	Shared book experience integrated with a thematic unit
5 min.	Planning
45 min.	Learning centers
	Wordplay
	Big book
	Big book babies
	Listening center
	Reading corner
	Language arts response center
	Guided reading
	Individual or small group conferences
	Thematic study center
10 min.	Whole-class share

Primary Grades

Strong primary-grade programs also integrate literacy across the curriculum and support children's developing independence. The schedules presented in Tables 5-10 and 5-11 are modifications of the readers workshop as described by Hansen (1989) and Atwell (1987). They have the following basic structure: a ten-minute mini-lesson, ten minutes of SSR, thirty minutes of workshop time where children read independently and respond in readers' response logs and teachers conference with small groups, and ten minutes of whole-class sharing.

Table 5-10 could be used with children who are entering first grade to facilitate a smooth transition by continuing the shared book experience until such time as most of the children are strong beginning readers and advanced beginners. When the year begins with some of the chil-

Table 5-11

Sample Schedule for a Primary-Grade Class That Is Mostly
Beginners and Advanced Beginners

10 min.	Warm up: reread familiar books
10 min.	Whole-class mini-lesson
30 min.	Workshop time, which can occasionally be integrated with a thematic unit
	Independent reading and responding
	Partner reading
	Small group conferences
	Individual conferences
	Guided reading
10 min.	Portfolio record keeping and reader's response journals
15 min.	Whole-class share

dren's favorite big books from kindergarten, first grade will be a welcoming place as children revisit old friends.

As the children become more able readers, who can use their strategies to figure out new books independently, the plan presented in Table 5-11 could be used. The final step is to move the children into the standard readers' workshop format.

Summary

Learner-centered literacy classrooms are grounded in the principles of developmentally appropriate practice for early childhood; the patterns of reading development; the conditions of learning identified by Cambourne (1988): immersion, demonstration, expectation, engagement, responsibility, use, approximation, and response; and a solid understanding of the reading process. Based on these ideas, teachers can design classroom space and develop schedules that allow for maximum student involvement in learning.

Key literacy events can be organized to best meet student needs and the constraints of the classroom setting. Those events include teacher-guided activities: the shared book experience, creating texts with children, guided reading, individual and/or small group conferences, mini-lessons, and teacher read-alouds. Student-managed literacy events include sustained silent reading, partner reading, whole-class sharing, and responding to literature.

Establishing a home link is also important to a learner-centered program. The home can be a source of positive support for emerging readers.

The teacher's role is to become an excellent observer so that he or she can constantly adjust the learning environment, both physical and social, to best meet the needs of the children in assisting them to become independent strategic readers who love to read.

Suggestions for Further Study

1. Locate a basal reader and select a story from it that is also a children's book. Locate the original children's book and compare the two. How are they alike and different in both words and pictures? Which format will be more appealing to children? Why? Which will best support the child's reading process? Present them both to several children and ask them to make their own comparisons and evaluations. Be sure to ask the children which version they would prefer to read and why.

2. Locate a basal reader teachers' manual and study the directed reading activity. Then compare it with the guided reading activity presented in this chapter. How are they alike? Different? Which one best supports a reader's developing independence? Why?

3. Using the guidelines in this chapter, do a shared book experience with a group of kindergarten and first-grade children. Keep detailed notes on children's responses and interpret them in relationship to the patterns of reading development.

4. Using the descriptions of patterns of reading development, select several children to observe and interview. As part of the interview, have the children select two books to talk about with you: an easy book and a just-right book. Ask the children how they went about selecting the books. Have them tell about the stories and read aloud a section of each book. Keep detailed notes on your observations and children's responses and miscues. What reading behaviors do they have well under control? Which ones are they working on? What are their confusions? What strategies are they using? Where would you say they are developmentally?

5. Using the guidelines in this chapter, do a guided reading lesson with a small group of children.

6. Develop, and teach if possible, a unit for a week of experiences and activities with alphabet books. To do this, read and select alphabet books appropriate for the children's patterns of development. Then, using the ideas in this book and your own creativity, develop lessons that will allow children to have successful literacy experiences with the books and also engage them at the cutting edge of their learning.

7. Read Bredekamp's (1987) monograph and Gullo's (1992) book as starting points for researching the topic of developmentally appro-

priate practice in early childhood literacy. Compare and contrast their positions in a paper on developmentally appropriate practice.

8. Select a topic or theme of interest to a group of children, and develop a unit in which you organize literacy events such as those described in this and other chapters to provide a rich experience with the topic. Also be sure to give attention to the kind of content learning you expect to occur along with the literacy learning.

9. Conduct a small group conference where the children have all read different books or the more formal literature circle. See Hansen (1989) and Atwell (1987) for descriptions of conferences where children are reading different books, and read Peterson and Eeds (1990) and Keegan and Shrake (1991) for the literature circle. Keep notes on the children's responses and interactions in order to describe how the activities worked with the children.

Suggestions for Further Reading

Butler, A., & Turbill, J. (1984). *Towards a reading-writing classroom*. Rozelle, New South Wales, Australia: Primary English Teaching Association.

This thin, very approachable book is for teachers who are beginning child-centered literacy classrooms. There are plans for creating a literacy environment and establishing a workable schedule. The basic components of a literature-based reading program are also discussed.

Fisher, B. (1991). *Joyful learning: A whole language kindergarten*. Portsmouth, NH: Heinemann Educational Books.

This is another very practical book written by teachers. Classroom teachers find it meets their needs for getting child-centered literacy programs started.

Hart-Hewins, L., & Wells, J. (1990). *Real books for reading*. Portsmouth, NH: Heinemann Educational Books.

Written by a primary-grade teacher, this book will be especially useful in starting a literature-based reading program.

McLane, J., & McNamee, G. (1990). *Early literacy*. Cambridge, MA: Harvard University Press.

This book will provide additional theoretical background for the nature of early literacy.

Mills, H., O'Keefe, T., & Stephens, D. (1992). *Looking closely: Exploring the role of phonics in one whole language classroom*. Urbana, IL: National Council of Teachers of English.

This book meets an important need—to illustrate concretely how phonics work in whole language classrooms and dispel the myth that it doesn't exist in these settings.

Morrow, L. (1993). *Literacy development in the early years*. Boston: Allyn & Bacon.

Morrow summarizes the major early literacy research in this volume and relates it to classroom practice.

Schickedanz, J. (1986). *More than the ABCs: The early stages of reading and writing.* Washington, DC: National Association for the Education of Young Children.

Schickedanz directs a day care center at Boston University, where she collected many examples of emerging literacy to explain concretely how children evolve into readers and writers.

Teale, W., & Sulzby, E. (1986). *Emergent literacy: Writing and reading.* Norwood, NJ: Ablex Publishing Company.

A collection of papers that summarizes research in the field provides theoretical foundations for early literacy programs.

Suggested Predictable Books

Bennett, Jill. (1986). *Teeny tiny.* New York: Putnam.
Brown, Ruth. (1991). *A dark dark tale.* New York: Dial Press.
Campbell, Rod. (1983). *Dear zoo.* New York: Four Winds Press.
Carle, Eric. (1969). *The very hungry caterpillar.* New York: Philomel.
Charlip, Remy. (1980). *Fortunately.* New York: Four Winds Press.
Galdone, Paul. (1985). *The three bears.* New York: Clarion.
Ginsburg, Mirra. (1972). *The chick and the duckling.* New York: Greenwillow.
Kraus, Robert. (1970). *Whose mouse are you?* New York: Macmillan.
Lillegard, Dee. (1989). *Sitting in my box.* New York: Dutton.
Martin, Bill, Jr. (1991). *Polar bear, polar bear, what do you hear?* New York: Henry Holt.
———. (1992). *Brown bear, brown bear, what do you see?* New York: Henry Holt.
Williams, Sue. (1990). *I went walking.* New York: Harcourt.
Zolotow, Charlotte. (1983). *Some things go together.* New York: Harper & Row.

Suggested Books About Reading

Cohen, Miriam. (1977). *When will I read?* New York: Greenwillow Books.

Jim is afraid he won't be able to read. In this reassuring story for first-graders, reading signs, remembering stories, and telling stories are part of Jim's journey to learning to read by himself.

Elliot, Dan. (1985). *Grover learns to read.* New York: Random House/Children's Television Workshop.

Lovable Grover is learning to read at school but keeps it a secret from his mother because he is afraid she will not read him stories anymore. But when he babysits Betty Lou, he tries everything to stop her crying. Finally he reads her a story and she stops. When he excitedly tells his mother what he did and his fear, his mother reassures him and they share the reading.

Huff, Barbara. (1990). *Once inside the library.* Boston: Little, Brown.

The poem and illustrations invite the reader to browse through the adventures that await the reader who steps into the library.

Reading Is Fundamental. (1986). *Once upon a time. . . .* New York: Putnam.

In this read-aloud book, children's authors and illustrators share memories, stories, and poems about reading in their lives. Favorite authors included are Dr. Seuss, Stan and Jan Berenstain, Tomie dePaola, Maurice Sendak, and Shel Silverstein.

Stanek, Muriel. (1986). *My mom can't read.* Niles, IL: Albert Whitman & Co.

Tina, a first-grader, suspects that her mom can't read. Her mother refuses to read a new book to her, and she asks the teacher to read a school note to her because she says she doesn't have her glasses, but she doesn't wear glasses. Tina's suspicions are confirmed during a problematic bus trip across town because Mom can't read the signs and directions. The gently written story reaches a satisfying conclusion for all.

References

Adams, M. (1990). *Beginning to read.* Cambridge, MA: MIT Press.

Allington, R. (1983). The reading instruction provided readers of different reading abilities. *Elementary School Journal, 83,* 95–107.

Atwell, N. (1987). *In the middle.* Upper Montclair, NJ: Boynton/Cook.

Bredekamp, S. (1987). *Developmentally appropriate practice in early childhood programs servicing children from birth through age eight.* Washington, DC: National Association for the Education of Young Children.

Cambourne, B. (1987). *Coping with chaos.* Portsmouth, NH: Heinemann.

———. (1988). *The whole story.* New South Wales, Australia: Ashton Scholastic Pty Ltd.

Chall, J. (1983). *Stages of reading development.* New York: McGraw-Hill.

Clay, M. (1991a). *Becoming literate: The construction of inner control.* Portsmouth, NH: Heinemann.

———. (1991b). Introducing a new storybook to young readers. *The Reading Teacher, 45*(4), 264–273.

———. (1993a). *An observational survey.* Portsmouth, NH: Heinemann.

———. (1993b). *Reading recovery: A guidebook for teachers in training.* Portsmouth, NH: Heinemann.

Cummins, J. (1981). The role of primary language development in promoting educational success for language minority students. In California State Department of Education Office of Bilingual Bicultural Education, *Schooling and language minority students: A theoretical framework* (pp. 3–49). Los Angeles: California Evaluation Dissemination and Assessment Center.

Department of Education Wellington. (1985). *Reading in junior classes.* New York: Richard Owen Publishers.

Edelsky, C., Altwerger, B., & Flores, B. (1991). *Whole language: What's the difference?* Portsmouth, NH: Heinemann.

Fisher, B. (1991). *Joyful learning.* Portsmouth, NH: Heinemann.

Gambrell, L. (1984). How much time do children spend reading during teacher-directed reading instruction? In J. A. Jiles (Ed.), *Changing perspectives on research in reading/language processing and instruction* (pp. 193–198). Rochester, NY: National Reading Conference.

Goodman, K. (1969). Analysis of oral reading miscues: Applied psycholinguistics. *Reading Research Quarterly, 1,* 9–30.

———. (1985). Unity in reading. In H. Singer & R. Ruddell (Eds.), *Theoretical models and processes of reading* (2nd ed., pp. 813–840). Newark, DE: International Reading Association.

Goodman, Y. (undated). First encounters with written language. In D. Strickler (Ed.), *Reading comprehension*, Videotape series. Portsmouth, NH: Heinemann.

———. (1984). The development of initial literacy. In H. Goelman, A. Oberg & F. Smith (Eds.), *Awakening to literacy* (pp. 102–109). Exeter, NH: Heinemann Educational Books.

Gough, P. (1972). One second of reading. In J. R. Kavanagh & I. G. Mattingly (Eds.), *Language by ear and eye*. Cambridge, MA: MIT Press.

Gullo, D. (1992). *Developmentally appropriate teaching in early childhood*. Washington, DC: National Education Association.

Hall, M. (1981). *Teaching reading as a language experience*. Columbus, OH: Merrill.

Hansen, J. (1987). *When writers read*. Portsmouth, NH: Heinemann Educational Books.

Holdaway, D. (1979). *The foundations of literacy*. Sydney: Ashton Scholastic.

Jett-Simpson, M. (1986). *Reading resource book: Parents and beginning reading*. Atlanta, GA: Humanics.

Jett-Simpson, M., & Leslie, L. (Eds.). (1994). *Ecological assessment: Under construction*. Schofield, WI: Wisconsin State Reading Association.

Keegan, S., & Shrake, K. (1991). Literature study groups: An alternative to ability grouping. *The Reading Teacher, 44*(8), 542–547.

LeBerge, D., & Samuels, S. J. (1974). Toward a theory of automatic information processing in reading. *Cognitive Psychology, 6*, 293–323.

Newkirk, T., & McClure, P. (1992). *Listening in: Children talk about books (and other things)*. Portsmouth, NH: Heinemann Educational Books.

O'Donnel, M., & Wood, M. (1992). *Becoming a reader: A developmental approach to reading instruction*. Boston: Allyn & Bacon.

Paris, C., Lipson, M., & Wixson, K. (1983). Becoming strategic readers. *Contemporary Educational Psychology, 8*, 293–316.

Peterson, R., & Eeds, M. (1990). *Grand conversations: Literature groups in action*. New York: Scholastic.

Rosenblatt, L. (1978). *The reader, the text, and the poem*. Carbondale, IL: Southern Illinois University.

Routman, R. (1991). *Invitations*. Portsmouth, NH: Heinemann.

Rummelhart, D. (1985). Toward an interactive model of reading. In H. Singer & R. B. Rudell (Eds.), *Models and processes of reading* (3rd ed., pp. 722–750). Newark, DE: International Reading Association.

Smith, F. (1988). *Joining the literacy club*. Portsmouth, NH: Heinemann Educational Books.

Stanovich, K. (1986). The Matthew effects in reading: Some consequences of individual differences in the acquisition of literacy. *Reading Research Quarterly, 21*, 304–406.

Stewig, J. W., & Buege, C. (1994). *Dramatizing literature in whole language classrooms*. New York: Teachers College Press.

Sulzby, E. (1985). Children's emergent reading of favorite storybooks. *Reading Research Quarterly, 20*, 458–481.

Taylor, D., & Strickland, D. (1986). *Family storybook reading*. Exeter, NH: Heinemann Educational Books.

Teale, W. (1981). Parents reading to their children: What we know and need to know. *Language Arts, 59,* 555–570.

Teale, W., & Sulzby, E. (1986). *Emergent literacy: Writing and reading.* Norwood, NJ: Ablex Publishing Corporation.

Verhoeven, L. (1987). Literacy in a second language context: Teaching immigrant children to read. *Educational Review, 39*(3), 245–261.

Wisconsin Department of Public Instruction. (1986). *A guide to curriculum planning in reading.* Madison, WI: Wisconsin Department of Public Instruction.

Children's Books

Brown, Margaret Wise. (1947). *Goodnight moon.* New York: Harper & Row.

Crowly, Joy. (1980). *The hungry giant.* Bothell, WA: Wright Group.

———. (1986). *Mrs. Wishy Washy.* Bothell, WA: Wright Group.

———. (1986). *Yuck soup!* Bothell, WA: Wright Group.

Ehlert, Lois. (1989). *Eating the alphabet.* New York: Harcourt.

Garten, Jan. (1994). *The alphabet tale.* New York: Greenwillow.

Hoberman, Mary Ann. (1986). *A house is a house for me.* Ontario: Scholastic—TAB.

Larche, Douglas W. (1985). *Father Gander nursery rhymes.* Santa Barbara, CA: Advocacy Press.

Lobel, Arnold. (1970). *Frog and Toad are friends.* New York: Harper & Row.

———. (1972). *Frog and Toad together.* New York: Harper & Row.

Martin, Bill, Jr. (1991). *Polar bear, polar bear, what do you hear?* New York: Holt, Rinehart & Winston.

———. (1992). *Brown bear, brown bear, what do you see?* New York: Henry Holt.

Martin, Bill, Jr., & Archambault, John. (1989). *Chicka chicka boom boom.* New York: Simon & Schuster. (Also available in big book format)

Seuss, Dr. (Theodore Geisel). (1940). *Horton hatches the egg.* New York: Random House.

———. (1978). *I can read with my eyes shut.* New York: Random House.

Shelby, Anne. (1991). *Potluck.* New York: Orchard.

Thaler, Mike. (1990). *What could a hippopotamus be?* New York: Simon & Schuster.

Ward, Cindy. (1988). *Cookie's week.* New York: Putnam. (Big book version by Scholastic)

Professional Growth

The Work of the International Reading Association

Contact:

Alan Farstrup, Executive Director
800 Barksdale Road
P.O. Box 8193
Newark, DE 19714-8139

This association with 93,000 members includes teachers, reading specialists, administrators, researchers, librarians, and parents interested in promoting reading and literacy. It seeks to improve the quality of reading instruction at all levels, stimulating and promoting lifetime reading habits. It disseminates research information on early childhood reading, presents citations and awards, and has more than sixty committees. There is a strong system of state and regional affiliates, many of which sponsor conferences on a regular basis. In addition, there is an annual convention and a biennial world congress. The group publishes *The Reading Teacher, The Reading Research Quarterly, The Journal of Reading,* and *Lectura y Vida.*

Six

Understanding Writing As Part of an Integrated Program

Reading aloud, choral readings, reader's theater, and storytelling combine to give all of us—teachers and children alike—layer after layer of experience with language. And this gives us wells to draw on when we write. When poems and riddles and chants and stories dance in our minds; when a gust of wind leads a teacher to recite, "Who has seen the wind, **neither** you nor I"; when a spider's web is examined for words; when secret lands are named Narnia and Terebithia, then our writing will be filled with the sounds of literature.

Calkins & Harwayne (1991, p. 292)

"Writing—you can't be serious. Not in preschool and kindergarten. The children don't even know how!" Many teachers reacted this way when the idea of providing opportunities for children to write in these settings was introduced. The traditional writing curriculum was sequential: learn how to form letters, copy words and sentences, learn to spell words, fill in sentence blanks by selecting provided words, form sentences based on a pattern, write stories that conform to a pattern, and finally write some original pieces. The underlying assumptions were that children can't write until an adult provides direct instruction in how to make letters, mechanics must be learned first, and correct forms must be produced right away. Current research and classroom practice have shown these to be unfounded assumptions. Young children can and do write when they are in environments where they are allowed to do so and where the conditions of learning are met (see Figure 1-3).

In this chapter we will explore what writing is, its developmental characteristics, how to support its development, key writing events in a balanced writing program, and how to observe growth and development.

What Is Writing?

Writing, like reading, is constructing meaning. Authors compose texts to communicate their ideas to audiences. Also like reading, the knowledge, maturity, and experiences of the children, the texts they are creating, and the context for writing all influence composition. Authors use many strategies to relate their knowledge and experience to the text and context. Children, like adults, write to express some kind of meaning relative to the writing context and engage in a variety of problem-solving strategies to do so. A letter to Grandma done in scribble writing has as much meaning to an emerging writer as a letter in standard spelling and paragraph form written by a more advanced writer. In the process of constructing meaning, writers of both letters apply strategies to represent their ideas. They also use strategies to handle text features such as directionality, letter formation, spacing, punctuation, spelling, sentence, paragraph, and other formatting conventions.

Writing is developmental. Just as oral language and reading evolve in gradual approximations toward standard forms with the intent of making meaning, so does writing. Some broad developmental patterns have been identified, but within these patterns there is considerable individual variability. Given the wide range of experiences children have with writing, the patterns are not age specific.

Like reading, writing instruction should be built on careful observation of students' learning. Knowledge of the writing process and the

The teacher takes dictation for the child's scribble-writing story.

characteristics of its development provides the foundations for careful observations, which in turn result in appropriate instruction. By making observation a daily activity, assessment is integrated with instruction. Important areas to observe and accommodate for instructionally are children's knowledge, maturity, and experiences; the contexts for writing; the text modes; and children's production of print.

Children's Knowledge, Maturity, and Experiences

Background Knowledge About the Topic

Success in composing is influenced by the topic. How much background knowledge and experience writers have related to their topics determines how much they have to write about. If writers don't know much, there is little they can say. Whether or not the topic is self-selected or assigned also makes a difference. Children who care deeply about their topics and have strong background knowledge are more likely to write a strong piece (Dyson & Freedman, 1991). A first-grader who knows nothing about snakes and doesn't want to write about them will not write as successful a piece as will the child who is fascinated and knowledgeable about snakes. We conclude that children should be able to choose their own topics most of the time.

Children's Individuality

Children's wide and varied experiences outside school are rich sources of ideas for writing and result in varied topic and story choices. Children are "experts" on the things they know best—what they have experienced. Playing with friends, camping with family, or taking trips, all contain potential stories. Experiences like lack of sleep, hunger, and divorce can also influence writing. One first-grade student was making good progress in both reading and writing but then "shut down." Soon afterward, the teacher found that the family was experiencing a difficult divorce. Other children might tell these painful stories in their writing.

When children honestly write about what *they* want to write about, they typically write about their families, pets, and friends. Some topics, however, may be outside some teachers' experiences—such as drive-by shootings, family members in jail, or drugs. See the first-grader's story in Figure 6-1. All topics children choose are not safe topics, so teachers need to respond with understanding to these as well. Teachers who react negatively may inhibit the child's writing. In some instances, writing may be a cry for help that teachers need to investigate with the assistance of the school counselor.

As discussed earlier, writing requires children to orchestrate their experiences into ideas for composing while trying to figure out how to produce print and relate to the writing context. Each writing event is a new challenge to be met, with all of its complexity to be negotiated. The result is variability in an individual child's writing from piece to piece. Each piece isn't necessarily progressively better than the preceding one. When Jett-Simpson and Smith (1992) collected writing samples from third-graders, they found that every child's writing performance varied from time to time. It was normal for there to be a mix of strong and weak pieces.

Children's Perceptions of the Writing Task

Teachers establish contexts for composing, but what teachers intend isn't necessarily how children understand what they are to do. Recently, a kindergarten teacher was demonstrating to her students different ways kindergartners write: scribbles, scribbles plus pictures, random letters, and temporary spellings. Her goal was for all children to be comfortable with their levels of writing development. One of her students, a

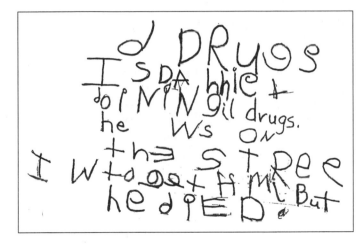

FIGURE 6-1

A First-Grader's Story. "I saw Daniel doing drugs. He was on the street. I went to get him but he died."

strong beginning reader, was using knowledge of letter sound relationships to read but using scribbles and random letters when he wrote. In a conference where he "read" a scribble and random letter story, the teacher asked him if he could write any of the story in book spelling. He said yes and proceeded to write. When she asked him why he had been writing in scribbles, he said, "I thought you wanted me to make it up." It is important to establish communication so that both students and teachers understand the writing task.

Children's Control over Production Aspects of Writing

Not only do children construct ideas, but they also have to produce the print to represent those ideas. Spelling, handwriting, punctuation, and writing conventions must be worked on simultaneously with idea generation. How much control children have over these aspects of writing can impede or facilitate production. The child who knows all the conventions and can produce print automatically has more mental energy for constructing ideas. However, many young readers have minimal fluency simply forming letters, so their hands quickly become physically too tired to do more. Computers may facilitate production for many children, but they still have to learn how to use them with ease. How much and what children write are influenced by the degree of automaticity children bring to producing print. Teachers need to recognize where children are developmentally so they can respond to children's efforts in positive, supportive ways. Children make many approximations on the way toward standard forms of production.

These are only a few examples of how the knowledge, maturity, and experiences of children influence their writing. It is also necessary for teachers to observe and manage both the physical and social contexts in the classroom.

Physical Contexts for Writing

The physical environment should invite children to write as a natural part of learning and exploration. It should also be well organized and predictable so it is a supportive background for writing rather than interfering with it. Critical aspects are the availability and kinds of materials and the room arrangement.

Availability and Kinds of Materials

Something as simple as line placement on the paper can affect children's writing. Typically, first-grade paper in the United States has a wide space for a picture at the top and two sets of solid lines spaced one inch apart with dotted lines between each set as pictured in Figure 6-2. Ollila (1982) wondered about the results of a study that showed that first-grade children in England and Canada wrote longer pieces than American children. He gave first-grade children regular paper to write on instead of first-grade paper. The result was longer pieces. Notice in Figure 6-2 how Drew copes with the limited amount of space for saying what he wants to say. He simply turns the page over and writes on the back. In doing so, the size of his writing shifts to what is natural for

Figure 6-2

Drew Copes with First-Grade Paper. "On a rainy day I like to play at Grandma's restaurant and I like to play Nintendo."

FIGURE 6-3

Ben said, " Stop, ducks ! You can't eat this. No, you can't ! No, ducks ! No ! You can't eat this. "	*Awoman bot some tomatoes* *Hsea is happy* *Hsea is old* *Hsea is at the macit*

him. There is more writing on the back than in the limited space provided by the structured first-grade paper.

Writing materials should be easily accessible at all times. A simple *writing center* could be located on a bookshelf. Different kinds of paper, both lined and unlined, can be organized in stacking files surrounded with cans of markers, pencils, and crayons. Add some envelopes, scissors, and a scrap box of construction paper, and the simple materials for writing letters and making cards and invitations are ready for use. Primary-grade dictionaries will be useful, too. By locating a table close to the bookshelf, a place is identified where a small group of writers can join each other in their writing projects.

The materials used during reading instruction also influence writing. By immersing children in excellent and diverse literature, teachers provide them with opportunities to form personal connections with stories, to hear and read rich written language, and to hear and read a variety of genres. These experiences provide foundations for making connections with writing. Students begin to borrow language and story patterns from these literature models to experiment with in their own stories. Children should have access to these reading materials during writing time for use as references.

The importance of good literature models was underscored in a study of second-graders who were reading highly controlled text (Eckhoff, 1983). The text was organized so there was one simple sentence per line. When exposed to this model of writing over time, students modeled their writing after this structure, as can be seen in Figure 6-3. In addition, their writing was less elaborate and complex than that of children who read more linguistically complex texts.

ROOM ARRANGEMENT

Rooms can be arranged so the organization of space and materials supports not only writing but other writing activities as well. Preschools or kindergartens often feature play areas against the walls with a large open space in the middle of the room. Neuman and Roskos (1990)

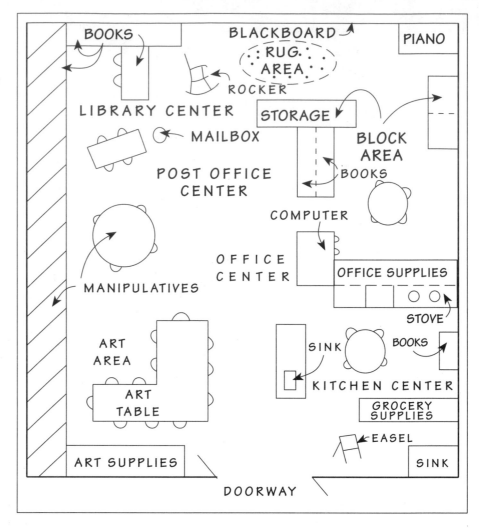

rearranged a kindergarten classroom to create cozy networks of centers, as illustrated in Figure 6-4. In addition to the usual materials, they placed literacy props in the centers that would be natural for them. For example, the kitchen center contained telephone books, a telephone, emergency number decals, cookbooks, food coupons, and grocery store ads. Calendars, an appointment book, signs, magazines for the waiting room, and assorted forms were placed in the office center. In the post office center were stationery and envelopes, a mailbox, computer address labels, posters and signs about zip codes, and a tote bag for mail. The library center contained book return cards, children's books, check-out book stamps, book marks, and a sign-in/sign-out sheet.

After the room was rearranged and literacy props were added, play in the centers changed. Children spontaneously used almost twice as much print for play purposes as they did before the reorganization. Their periods of involvement were much longer, increasing from around two minutes to over five minutes on the average over a two-month period. Scribbling, coloring, pretending to read, making signs, and doing other demonstrations of literacy were embedded functionally within the children's play.

Children in the study also linked literacy behaviors. One of these chains lasted approximately thirty minutes; many lasted fifteen minutes. The following example shows how children interacted across centers:

> Kent and Ricky have been trying to get Dana's attention for some time during the play period, but she has not responded. They retreat to the post office and decide to write to her. Huddling together, Kent dictates "Dear Dana"; Ricky writes [in scribble writing]. Finally, the note is finished and inserted in an envelope. The boys approach Dana. They hand over the envelope, giggling. She smiles, opens the envelope, and pretends to read the note. Kent leans toward her and says, "You wanna come over to our house?" Then they both run back to the post office and repeat the entire writing routine.

Primary classrooms should also be organized to engage children in writing and other literacy activities. A large group area is needed where the teachers can assemble the whole class to participate in shared book experiences, group writing, and creative drama. A student study/work area would include tables and chairs so all students can work in small cooperative groups or independently. At least three centers should be established in classroom corners for writing, reading, and inquiry. The inquiry center features various hands-on activities typically related to science, social studies, or math themes currently under study. A classroom journal could be placed in the inquiry center where students could write about the results of their explorations.

Social Contexts for Writing

The social context, which includes interactions with adults and peers, can also inhibit or encourage writing. Dyson's (1989) research shows the power of social interactions on children's compositions in kindergarten through second grade.

During writing time in the classrooms where she observed, talking, drawing, writing, and imagination were interwoven. Children asked questions seeking information or assistance: "What are you doing?" How do you spell . . . ?" "How do you make . . . ?" Sometimes talk was simply friendly chats unconnected to the writing. Other conversations (Dyson, 1989, p. 119) included critiques on one's own and others' work:

Regina (*talking to herself*):   These are her [the Brownie's] legs.
Maggie: Let me see your picture. You better make some knees on here—on her.

There were assertions about their writing abilities, the real and imaginary nature of the worlds created in the drawings, text, and oral stories. "I can spell. . . ." "I can draw. . . ." "Look what I'm doing." Some children accompanied their work with intricate oral stories in which they dramatized the characters, often inserting (or removing) one of their friends as a character and provided sound effects (p. 126).

Jake: After I finish my bubble car story, I'm gonna do the evil forces of Pedro.
Manuel (*laughs*):   The evil forces.
Jake: The evil forces of Pedroville—Pedro and Ruben. Then I'm going to make the evil forces of Reginaship. Of Regina. (*Dances at her with a teasing, triumphant look.*)
Regina (*very deadpan*):   So what's hard about that?

Other writers were attending to others' talk, asking a question or commenting on the other child's work. "What are you doing?" "What's that?" Audiences for each other, they read their texts to individuals and the group. "This says. . . ." The teacher moved around the room listening to stories, asking questions about the content and meaning children were creating, assisting them with problem solving when they were "stuck," providing opportunities for them to share their work with the class, and generally being another appreciative audience.

In these classrooms, the conditions of learning (see Figure 1-3) were met. Surrounded by demonstrations of composing, children received feedback from peers and teachers. Talk was part of learning. The tone of the classrooms supported risk taking, where children were expected to learn and take responsibility for their writing. Writing approximations were accepted and the meanings of texts were central.

Modes of Writing

The modes of text children use are determined by the amount of experience they have had with those modes as well as the purpose or context for writing. Children can't write in a particular mode if they have no background experience with it; consequently, writers are not equally adept at all modes of writing. If they never hear or read the mode, how can they produce it?

Children who experience print-rich environments both at home and at school will have experienced many modes of writing that they draw upon as models. Not only do they write stories about things that have happened to them in everyday life (the personal narrative), but Newkirk (1989) found that many other forms of writing were also used, such as signs, rules, lists, letters, jokes, riddles, invitations, labels and captions, directions, reports, persuasive pieces, poems, and fictional stories. This leads to the rejection of "the notion that there is a fixed order to the kinds of discourse that children attempt" (Newkirk, 1989, p. 30).

Examining children's modes of writing shows that they move "from basic embryonic forms to writing that increasingly approximates mature [forms]" (Newkirk, 1989, p. 32). We don't know a lot about this evolution, although we understand some of this development for some modes.

Narrative Texts

Young children's first stories are oral, often interwoven with some scribbles, random letters, and drawings. As children gain more control over print, combinations of oral stories and drawings accented by a single word begin to appear. A single word will evolve into several words in a *chain* where children fill in the text between words orally. As phrases and words begin to aggregate around a single topic, children seem to be *centering* the writing, which results in strings of sentences. Centering evolves into *semistructured stories* with some sense of time, beginnings, middles, and ends. Gradually, *structured stories* emerge, which contain setting, characters, and a resolution to the goal or problem for the main character. Each of these story characteristics becomes more refined: characters' motives and intentions are included and episodes appear, which are gradually developed more fully (Temple et al., 1993). Children's experiences with storytelling as part of daily life and listening to others read stories provide models for writing narrative texts.

Drawing

Although there is a tendency to ignore pictures in favor of words in defining writing, Newkirk (1989) argued that "writing language and drawing are both sources of information . . . interweaving of various symbol systems" (pp. 59–60). When children write, they have the following options for combining or not combining text and drawings to represent their meanings (p. 59):

1. Text only.
2. Picture only.
3. Picture and text—redundant. Picture and text duplicate each other.
4. Imbalance—pictorial. The picture carries most of the information.
5. Complementary. Both picture and text contribute information.

6. Imbalance—text. Most of the information is provided by the text.
7. General-specific relationship. Specific examples of a category are identified in the picture, while the general category is presented in the text. General—"Halloween is scary." Specific—The picture portrays a ghost saying "Booo!"

Some kinds of picture/text combinations continue well into second and third grade when, in our culture, text predominates. Teachers must recognize the relationships between drawing and print in children's writing in order to support writing growth.

EXPOSITORY TEXTS

Expository texts describe, explain, give directions, or convince someone of something. Britton (1970) believed that these kinds of texts emerged from personal narratives where children wrote to express personal feelings, accounts, and thoughts. However, Newkirk's (1989) work revealed that children see models of various kinds of expository text in their environments and attempt to produce versions like the models. These versions have some features of adult exposition and so are approximations of it.

The *label* is the first rudimentary form. Labels explain who or what is in a drawing or the action. The first label is the child's name, which indicates "this is me" or "this is mine." Labels evolve into picture *captions*.

Labels and captions are soon followed by another common early form, the *list*. Most children will have had many experiences with lists as a model for presenting information. It is hard to look at print in any environment and not see some kind of list. Sara, Newkirk's daughter, had written fifty-five lists by the age of 6 years, 3 months, including categories like name lists, number lists, Christmas lists, accomplishments lists, shapes lists, money lists, and food-order lists (imaginary restaurant). Each was organized around a single stated or implied category (Newkirk, 1989, pp. 68–69).

An expository form that evolves from the list is the *attribute series*, in which the young author writes about the attributes of a topic, which could appear in any order, and sets up several categories. In the following piece, you can see that the author is writing about two attributes of whales: color and size.

> Whales are black and some are gray.
> Whales are big. They can eat you in one bite.
> There are brown whales and there are black whales too.
> There are white wales.
> There are killer whales (Sowers, 1985, p. 73).

The next form, identified by Newkirk (1989), is the *initial paragraph*. This is "any cluster of three clauses that were coherently related in a nonchronological fashion" (p. 79). Usually the writing includes some attributions and elaborations, such as this example by a second-grader (p. 60):

> The oranutang gang is three boys. Their names are Jamie and Mike and Taylor. We work at recess. If we see a fight we break it up. But if they fight back we tell the teacher.

A longer composition might consist of several initial paragraphs where there is no particular reason one paragraph should precede or follow the other. This evolves into a more advanced form where the writer is able not only to relate sentences within a paragraph but to establish relationships among the paragraphs as well. Both structures are variations on *ordered initial paragraphs*.

In young children's writing, several forms are bridges to *persuasive writing*. DO NAT DSTURB GNYS AT WRK, a now-famous sign written by Glenda Bissex's son, Paul, to keep visitors out of his room (1980, p. 23), is an example of regulatory language shifting to persuasive writing. Paul *regulates*—"Do not disturb"—and *offers a reason* to persuade visitors to comply—"Genius at work." *Requests, apologies, excuses,* and *advertisements* are also bridges. The common strategy children use to develop the initial forms of persuasion into longer arguments is the list. Writers assert and support their positions with lists of evidence.

With everything else that is occurring during writing development, children are also learning how to produce print so their meanings can eventually be read and understood by a variety of audiences. Production of print involves learning to form letters, learning to spell, and learning the conventions of English print such as directionality. A number of researchers have helped us describe the evaluation of this development (Clarke, 1988; Gentry, 1982, 1993; Mass, 1982; Reed, 1974; Sulzby, Barnhart & Hieshima, 1989; and Wood, 1989).

Production of Print

Before Letters

When children no longer eat the crayons, their explorations lead to the discovery of the "power of the pen." A pencil, a crayon, a marking pen, and a piece of chalk are all intriguing to young children who are making their first marks on the world. First marks often decorate furniture and walls as children try to determine what it is about the writing instrument that produces such interesting results. After they discover that the writing implement can record their arm movements, children are soon chatting while they apply marks and pictures to paper. To know the "story" represented, careful attention must be given to the oral language because first compositions are mostly oral with some written accompaniment. The first print efforts look like uncontrolled scribbles. Gradually, among these blobs, repeated lines, some of which look like wobbly tallies, appear. The appearance of repeated marks shows that children are taking more deliberate control (Clay, 1975).

Children begin to attach meaning to their marks before they produce letters. Bryce was almost 4 years old when he produced the story-drawing in Figure 6-5. Lifting the pencil from the page only once, he told this story while the pencil journeyed over the paper, ending with the flourish of a curlycue marked with an arrow.

Noticing that print seems to be organized in lines, children begin to try out their strategies for producing scribbles that resemble adult cursive writing. The scribbles may be produced from bottom to top of the paper in one long connected line, in alternative right-to-left and left-to-right lines, or in any combination as they gradually identify the conventional directionality of print for English. Many of these scribble masterpieces are mailed to interested grandparents as letters that find their way onto refrigerator doors. Whatever the language community, scribbles take on the characteristics of its printed language. Scribbles in Arabic and Hebrew, for example, look quite different from those in English (Harste, Woodward & Burke, 1984). Continuous lines become broken lines resembling word breaks, and letterlike shapes appear with

FIGURE 6-5

Bryce's Story. "He went to a store. He was going away but he didn't want to go so he went back home. And he went and then he went to the grocery store and that's all." Notice that Bryce's story is like a map of the movements of the person he is talking about.

various kinds of drawings. These discoveries are made when children intend to construct meaning: letters, lists, recipes, retellings of television programs, and personal accounts of experiences. Of course you will need a translator to know what meanings are represented. Most children can "read" their own masterpieces with confidence.

The appearance of letters indicates that children are moving into the prephonemic phase of development. However, scribbling behaviors will persist in children's writing long after letters appear. When one new writing behavior appears, the old ones don't automatically disappear. Instead, writing reflects a mix of forms, and the nonstandard forms drop out gradually. To identify advancement, teachers watch for the appearance of new forms that illustrate the discovery of new strategies—the "cutting edges" of learning.

Prephonemic

While writing stories, labeling pictures, and writing notes, children begin to make letters among the scribbles and drawings. Typically, these are important to children for some reason, such as the letters in their names. During the prephonemic phase, children experiment with a number of coping strategies while trying to determine how letters work, what constitutes a word, and how these represent meaning. Children will try different combinations of random letter writing, copying, patterning strategies, and strategies for making meaning, along with continued use of scribble forms and drawings.

Copying can appear in interesting ways. In one kindergarten class, a child filled the page with letters randomly tumbling in a variety of positions. In the middle of the page the word *nontoxic* was written. While writing, the child noticed the word on his crayon and copied it. When the child "read" the piece to the teacher, neither the letters nor *nontoxic* had any relationship to his story. Many children also enjoy copying the alphabet and making lists of words seen in their environment—a kind of "taking inventory" activity.

A common strategy children use during this time is to relate the writing in some way to what they know about the object or objects in the real world. An Argentine boy, Javier, wrote OIA for the word *cat*. On the same page he had written OAIOAIOAI. When asked, he said that it said "kittens" because there were so many of them. Ferreiro and Teberosky (1982) concluded that one of his coping strategies was to use a similar letter pattern when writing about things that were related. A second strategy was to repeat the letter pattern for kitten (OAI) when it represented more than one thing. In the same study, a 5-year-old said, "Write my name. But you have to make it longer because yesterday was my birthday" (Ferreiro & Teberosky, 1982, p. 180).

Children also generate made-up "words" using rules like (1) words must contain multiple marks; (2) words cannot contain too few or too many marks; (3) marks within a word must vary, with no more than two of the same kind appearing in succession; and (4) the same marks can be used to make different words as long as their order is varied across the words (Schickedanz, 1990). The letters (and/or numbers) children use to generate words are limited to the ones they know. Frequently these will be letters in their names. Knowledge of some letters allows them to use the letters' flexibility to produce wordlike strings for different objects, such as in Valaeria's writing (Ferreiro & Teberosky, 1982, p. 189):

A r o n = toad

A o r n = duck

I A o n = house

r A o l = Mom leaves the house

Children also experiment with the formation and placement of letters on the page to determine what is acceptable. There will be numerous reversals, such as the "backward" S (Ƨ), and the orientation of *p, d, q,* and *b* will vary. This doesn't mean that the child who does these things is suffering from dyslexia because of a "reversal problem." It is normal behavior to write letters in different ways as approximations of standard forms during this time. Uncertainty about the formation of some letters typically continues into the subsequent phases of writing—particularly for lowercase *p, d, q,* and *b*.

Discovering the alphabetic principle is the main indicator that children are moving into the semiphonemic phase.

Semiphonemic

"Aha! Letters represent sounds!" Realizing the alphabetic principle leads children to try new strategies for representing their ideas. Alphabet names are children's main referents in determining how the principle works. There are two strategies they use with the names. The first is to use the name as a whole. Application of this strategy results in spellings like the following: the word *you* would be spelled "U" and the word *are* as "R." A second strategy of letter name spelling is to use the phonemes (the sounds) in the name of the letter. When we say the name for "W" the phonemes are /dublu/, for "Y" /wi/, for "X" /eks/, for "C" /se/, for "S" /es/, and for "M" /em/. The opening word for many fairy tales, *once,* becomes /yc/ or /ync/. This kind of spelling is called semiphonemic.

The semiphonemic speller can relate some of the letters to sounds in words but not all of them. Beginning consonants are easiest, so often a single consonant may represent an entire word. The knowledge of the beat or syllables of the languages also is used. Children will write one letter for each syllable in a word. Judith Schickedanz's (1990) son,

FIGURE 6-6

Adam's Syllable
Strategy

Adam, tried making a letter for each beat (or syllable) in his name.
When she asked him about the picture in Figure 6-6, Adam pointed to
the picture and said it was a boy. He then pointed, right to left, to each
letter at a time and said "A-dam."

In typical development, children spell by initial consonants, then initial plus final consonants, and later interior consonants. Soon they
notice, from their visual knowledge of print obtained through reading,
that some letters appear in lots of words, the vowels. They begin using
vowels, not usually the "correct" ones, as place holders. Sometimes, children will use a vowel of the day as a place holder in all of their writing
that day.

Adults can read some of the semiphonemic writing puzzles, particularly if they know the context for the writing. Reading children's writing
during the semiphonemic and phonemic phases presents the same challenges as reading invented spellings on vanity license plates.

Semiphonemic spellers, of course, can write some words from memory in standard form, such as their names, *Mom,* and *Dad.* The amount
of semiphonemic spelling far exceeds standard spelling during this
stage. While children are writing semiphonemically, they are also learning to read, and they have been observed to use the same coping strategies in attempting to decode unfamiliar words. For example, when
Steven met the word *you* in print, his attempt at decoding was /w-w-o/.
For *y* he tried the first phoneme in its name, and for *o* he tried the letter
name. This illustrates how spelling and reading connect. When children

Translations for license plates, in case you were stumped: Furs for you. Aviator. Anyone
can. Two in a BMW.

begin to write a letter for each phoneme (sound) in a word, they are shifting to the next phase of development.

Phonemic

Children's main work during this phase is to segment words into phonemes, to establish a stable concept of "word," and to learn ways to represent the forty-four English phonemes in print. Children do a great deal of "sounding out" and seeking advice from others about "how to spell." Their written texts begin to reveal spaces between "words," indicating an increasing understanding of the concept of word.

An aspect of print children struggle with is that the correspondence between speech sounds and written letters is not a one-to-one match. They develop the following coping strategies to deal with the characteristics of English:

1. The same sound is spelled with different letters.
   /k/ = c as in cat
   ck as in luck
   k as in kind
   ch as in character

2. Different sounds can be spelled with the same letter.
   /a/ = cat, gate, car, care,

3. Two letters can represent one sound.
   /ch/ /sh/ /ng/
   /ai/ /ea/ /oa/

4. Some letters represent no sounds.
   gh in night
   tt, the second t in letter
   e in have and hate

The dominant coping strategy children use is one letter for one sound, so patterns such as /ch/ will be spelled with a single letter. /Ch/ is typically spelled h because "aitch" is the only alphabet name that contains the /ch/ sound.

As children read more and develop a stronger visual memory for words and spelling patterns, they gradually begin to incorporate the characteristics of English spelling into their writing. As children begin to accommodate the variability described above, they shift to the transitional phase of spelling development, which is a combination of phonemic and standard spelling.

Transitional

When children reach this point, they realize that spelling is not simply a game of matching sound and letter, but that what English looks like is also important. Their spelling starts to look more like English as they incorporate their knowledge of visual patterns. Vowels will begin to appear in every syllable (e.g., TIGUR instead of the phonemic TIGR for *tiger*). The discovery of silent "e" will often result in experimentation where children try it out on lots of words. (After all, it is silent, so why should it matter?) When they understand that two letters can represent one sound and that different sounds can be spelled differently, their spelling will change to accommodate their new understandings. Vowel patterns such as /ou/ and /ea/ will appear, as will /ch/ and /sh/. Standard spelling does not necessarily result. Children who are using a visual strategy will often remember all of the letters but may reverse the order, such as HUOSE for *house* (Temple et al., 1993). Reading and spelling instruction facilitates the move to standard spelling, so this is a developmentally appropriate time to begin a spelling program (Gentry & Gillet, 1993). Although children will have acquired many more standard spellings by this time, temporary or invented spellings will still dominate.

Standard

Standard writers are gaining control of many of the variable patterns in English. Relying heavily on their visual coding mechanisms, children develop more advanced understandings of prefixes, suffixes, compounds, contractions, homonyms, and complex spelling patterns. This is a lifelong task. Standard forms dominate their writing, and the percent of correct forms increases as children develop more competence.

The foundational knowledge about writing discussed to this point is necessary for making careful observations and consequently developing appropriate instruction. Twice-monthly observation notes could be collected for children in a format like the one shown in Figure 6-7.

Developing the Writing Program

Writing programs should be designed to meet the learning conditions described in Chapter 1 (Figure 1-3). We create environments where children immerse themselves in meaningful writing each day and where they are surrounded by writing demonstrations. Knowledgeable teachers are essential, who expect children to take responsibility for their writing and use it in a variety of contexts. Teachers provide feedback appropriate to children's writing development, recognizing approximations for what they are—natural steps in learning. Teachers collaborate with children in working through new learnings.

FIGURE 6-7

Writing Observations

Names	The Child: Knowledge, Maturity, Experience	Physical Context	Social Context	Modes of Writing	Production of Print

As discussed earlier, the physical and social contexts of classrooms are important backgrounds for writing activity. A room arrangement where writing materials are made available as part of center activity is optimal. When writing materials are in the block corner, signs such as "DT TH" (*Don't touch*) will begin to appear as part of block construction. In the housekeeping center, grocery lists and telephone messages will be attached to the refrigerator. In the science center, a parakeet chirps in its cage as several children write their observations in a science journal. Sign-in sheets for each center and classroom activity are designed to regulate participation while providing opportunities for children to practice writing their names. This kind of integration invites children to use writing in ways they have seen it used in everyday life. Examples of this, at first and third grade, will be given in Chapter 7.

In this section we will discuss some key components of writing process classrooms (see Figure 6-8). A common way to organize a writing program, the writer's workshop, will also be discussed. We'll describe what each component contributes to a well-rounded program and how it could be included in an early childhood program.

Journals

Journal writing is one of the easiest procedures to integrate into the school day. In the simplest form, teachers provide children with journals (paper stapled together or spiral notebooks) and set aside time daily for them to write about topics of their choice and to share their writing.

When kindergarten children enter the room, they sign in, go to their tables, and begin writing in their journals. This won't necessarily be a quiet time because part of their writing process is oral composition. Many entries will be produced in print the teacher can't read, such as scribbles. Therefore, the teacher walks around the room and asks children to dictate or "read" their pieces individually so they can be written in standard form. It is important to ask the children where they want the dictation written because some children are very particular about where adult writing is placed in relationship to their own writing. Dictation can be treated like language experience, discussed in Chapter 5, in which case the teacher would read back what was said while pointing to the text and invite the children to read along. Teachers can make a few notes about strategies and the writing context during these individual conferences to be added to student observation records. After journal writing, the class comes together for opening activities; as part of this, several children can share what they have written and classmates are invited to comment and ask questions.

"Bear in a suitcase" (Rich, 1985) is another way to incorporate journals in the kindergarten program. A journal and several books that fea-

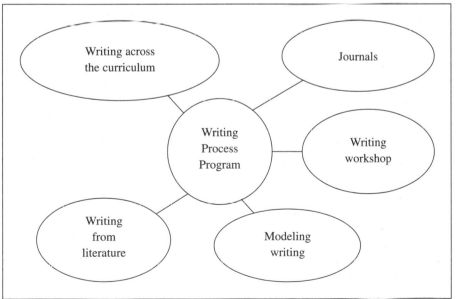

FIGURE 6-8

Components of Writing Process Programs

Writing across the curriculum

Journals

Writing Process Program

Writing workshop

Writing from literature

Modeling writing

ture bears are placed in a small suitcase or backpack, and children take turns taking the bear home over the weekend. The child and/or child and parent write about the bear's weekend adventures. Those adventures are shared with the class on Monday morning. If a bear is not available, any stuffed animal will do.

In the primary grades, *dialogue journals* and *reader's response journals* are commonly used. *Dialogue journals* are written conversations between teachers and students, so students must have reached a point developmentally where they are creating readable texts. Sometimes they are conversations among students. Students write daily for a short time, ten or fifteen minutes, and teachers respond to a fifth of the class each day, so students receive a journal letter from the teacher once a week. Dialogue journals are more interesting to the children if the teacher also writes a journal and allows the children to take turns responding to it. For children who are typically denied access to adults' private writing, the experience is like exploring the "forbidden." Children can also exchange journals with others in the same classroom or across classrooms (Bromley, 1989).

Teachers respond to the contents of children's journal entries, the message of the writing, *not* the mechanics. This is not a time for the red pencil. Honest comments and questions are asked out of interest and a desire to know. In the written response, however, the teacher can model standard spellings of children's temporary spellings if the words fit easily into the response (Gambrell, 1985). For example, a child wrote the following in the journal:

MI DOG SND DID YSTRDY

The teacher response was:

I'm sorry your dog Sandy died yesterday. I felt very sad when my dog Ziggy died. What did you love to do with your dog?

Reader's response journals can be integrated into the reading program when the children are able to produce readable print and compose responses. Children keep spiral notebooks and write reactions to the books they are reading, which are shared with the teacher during conferences (Hansen, 1987). Reader's response journals can also be set up like dialogue journals, in which case the children write letters to their teacher with reactions to their reading and the teacher writes back once a week. Figure 6-9 is an entry from a first-grader's reader's response journal.

Writing Workshop

Once children can write readable text (usually in first grade), it is time to organize a writer's workshop so children have the opportunity to engage in the writing processes most authors experience.

FIGURE 6-9

Sample Reader's
Response Journal
Entry by a First-
Grader to *When the
TV Broke*

Basic Workshop Organization   A well-established organizational
structure supports the writing process. Graves's book, *Writing: Teachers
and Children at Work* (1983), based on research in a first-grade classroom, provides detailed guidance for implementing a writers' workshop. Forty-five minutes to an hour are established for the daily
workshop in primary grades, including these segments:

5–10 min.	Mini-lesson
5 min.	Planning
5 min.	Sustained writing (Everyone writes, including the teacher.)
20 min.	Workshop time Children are writing, reading, conferencing with peers or teacher, rewriting, editing, or publishing. Teachers are conferencing one on one or in small groups, observing and taking notes, or doing embedded teaching.
10 min.	Whole-class share—"Author's Chair"

Short, single-focus mini-lessons are a necessary component of any
writing program. Mini-lessons are based on teachers' observations of
children's writing needs during conferences and from careful observation of children's writing and composing processes. If only a few children need instruction on a specific point, a small group is formed for
that purpose only and then disbanded. If most of the class could benefit,
the lesson is done with the whole group. Broad topics for mini-lessons

include the writer's craft, mechanics, and how to manage the writing process (Graves, 1983).

For example, teachers may observe that most of the class is writing formula beginning sentences for their stories, such as "Once upon a time. . . ." Children could bring their favorite children's books to a whole-class mini-lesson and take turns reading first sentences and discussing how authors capture readers' interest. Consider the power of the following opening sentences from children's books for generating lively discussion:

"There was once a baby koala so soft and round that all who saw her loved her." (*Koala Lou* by Mem Fox)

"Nobody liked to go to the end of Vinegar Lane." (*Captain Snap and the Children of Vinegar Lane* by Roni Schotter)

"On Monday, Cookie fell in the toilet." (*Cookie's Week* by Cindy Ward)

A small group mini-lesson about how to use quotation marks might grow from an observation that some children were starting to put conversation in their stories. The language arts textbook could be used as a reference for how to use this kind of punctuation. Later, when others in class are trying the same thing, these children could teach them how to use quotation marks. If they can teach others, they have truly demonstrated that they have learned the concept.

Process lessons could focus on how to find a topic or what to do when you get stuck, when you don't know how to spell some words, or when you don't know enough about the topic. Teachers who are good observers will identify many other topics for mini-lessons.

Planning   Nancie Atwell called this part of the workshop "status of the class" (1987). During this time the teacher asks the children to quickly tell what they are working on today. After the first day of writing workshop, many of the children will be in different places. Some will spend several days writing a piece but choose not to publish it. Others may finish a piece in a day and be ready to publish. Atwell suggests keeping a class list with five columns for days of the week where teachers can quickly note where the children are in their work. The process focuses the children on their work for the day and gives teachers an overview of student progress.

Sustained Writing   Whether this is sustained noisy writing time or quiet writing time, everyone—including the teacher—writes. Sustained writing settles everyone into writing before the other parts of the workshop begin.

Workshop Time   During workshop time children engage in the writing processes many authors use. Authors move flexibly, in individual ways,

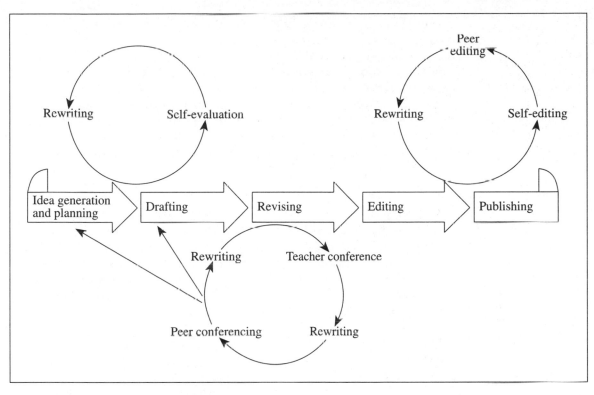

FIGURE 6-10   Writing Process Relationships

among the writing processes depicted in Figure 6-10: idea generation, drafting, revising, editing, and publishing. These processes are part of all modes of writing (Dyson & Freedman, 1991). While students are independently engaged in these processes or working with a peer, the teacher holds conferences with individuals or small groups.

1. *Idea generation.* Teachers may need to help children find topics by periodically including a brainstorming session where children talk about and develop lists of topics they know a lot about. Young children enjoy writing about events in their lives: a trip to Grandma's (see Figure 6-2 on page 236), staying overnight with a friend, playing with a pet, and retelling stories from television, among others. For children who have a burning interest in topics they know little about, teachers can demonstrate how reading helps with writing. Even beginning readers can be shown how to "research" their topics by collecting information through reading text and studying pictures.

2. *Drafting and revising.* Few writers simply sit down and write a piece straight through. Writing is recursive. Most authors rewrite, revise, self-evaluate, and perhaps do some more research—in no particular order except as the need arises. As part of the process, the author may seek feedback from peers or the teacher through short conferences, which may result in more recursive activity. It is effective to call the first draft the "sloppy copy" to develop the mind set that rewriting is a natural and expected part of writing.

Recall that children who are writing single words, chaining, or centering compose most of their stories orally. They are likely to revise orally through social interaction, but they aren't at a point in their development where they can do print revision. Young writers do little content revision because, from their point of view, the writing is the way they want it. As they develop more understanding of audience and story, they will begin to revise content.

Many children worry about spelling during writing. Teachers reassure them that it is the story and ideas that come first. During drafting, their main job is to get the words down the best way they know how and to keep on writing. A system that encourages children to develop independent spelling strategies so they will continue writing is necessary. Table 6-1 lists some workable strategies for helping children develop spelling independence.

3. *Editing. Editing* means changing, altering, adapting, adding to, or taking away from what was originally there. Children can revise, reshape, relocate, and redo in order to say more exactly what they wanted to say originally. Whatever children have written can probably stand some editing. Note that the previous sentence does not read "should be edited." There is a vast difference between pieces that *can* be edited (all writing, at all times) and those pieces that *should* be edited (some writing, sometimes). Graves (1983) suggested that young children select one out of every five pieces to edit for publishing. When children start writing longer pieces, one in two or three can be edited.

After children select pieces to edit for publication, they can *self-edit*. However, the degree to which they can do this depends on their writing development. What we ask children to do is to step back from their work, take a hard look at it, and then impartially make some value judgments about its quality. Doing this is, as anyone knows who has ever attempted it, exceedingly difficult. It is, however, well worth the time it takes. The ability to edit develops slowly. If you are teaching a group that has never done this, it may well take an entire year to bring children to the point where they are demonstrating objectivity. With young children, have them reread their piece and ask themselves simple questions like: Does it make sense? Should I add something? Should I take out something? Should I move anything?

Peer conferences are also very helpful. After children read their pieces to a peer or a small group of peers, other children respond by telling what they liked best and asking questions. Questions guide the writer in thinking about changes that could make the piece stronger.

Table 6-1

Strategies for Spelling During Writing

1. Have children circle their temporary spellings, which will be fixed later during editing.

2. Suggest that children write as many letters in the words as they can and draw a line for the ones they don't know.

3. Allow them to ask a friend for suggestions.

4. Encourage the children to think about where they have seen the word and then go directly to the remembered sources to copy the word. Some of these sources may be library books, big books, basals, wall charts, and other print material in the room. When they are able to use it, a dictionary will be useful, too.

5. "Have a go" is a very useful strategy we inherited from Australia. Children are provided with pieces of scrap paper or teacher-made note pads and encouraged to write the word in as many ways as they can think of and then choose the one that looks right.

6. Construct topical word charts with the children by brainstorming words they think they might need. For example, around holidays, many children elect to write about the holiday, so related words can be written on a topical chart.

7. Have children start personal word dictionaries when they become phonemic spellers. Children develop booklets with at least a page for each letter of the alphabet. Adding words to the dictionary is probably best done during individual conferences. When children ask for words, teachers encourage them to think about where they could find the standard spelling on their own. For a word the children wouldn't be able to find, the teacher writes the word on a slip of paper and the children enter it in their dictionaries.

4. *Conferencing.* A great deal has been written about *conferences with the teacher* (Calkins, 1986; Calkins & Harwayne, 1991). Graves (1983) recommended starting simply: "The teacher attends to what children know and helps them speak about their topics" (p. 104). In the first conference, teachers look for potential in the words, the content, and the way the child goes about the craft of writing, and puts aside concerns about missing information, revising, and mechanics. The focus is on helping children get ideas on paper. The teacher should attend to only one or two features of the text. Subsequent conferences focus on different aspects of writing, depending on the children's developmental needs. Conferences can be held when the first draft is completed, once a week, when the teacher roves around the classroom, and/or just before publishing. A conference structure with predictable starter questions helps the writer stay settled and confident (Graves, 1983):

What is this about?

Where are you in the draft?

What will you do next with the piece?

What part do you like best?

How did you happen to get into this subject?

After conferring with teachers, children should be able to reenact the basic parts of the conference with peers. The children should do most of the talking and feel free to ask questions and talk about possible solutions to problems. It is important to keep the sense of discovery alive.

The last part of editing is to determine whether the mechanics (spelling, grammar, and punctuation) are in order. The teacher may take charge of these with very young writers and have the children assume more responsibility as their writing develops.

5. *Publishing*. Publishing is the final step. Children should do as much of this as possible independently. They can take their edited rough drafts, plan their books, copy the text, and illustrate. If computer publishing is available, children eventually learn to do this as well. This is an excellent point in the process to involve parents, who can be responsible for bookmaking and printing when they are beyond the capabilities of the children. Having extra publishers helps speed up the publishing process.

6. *Whole-class sharing* is also important. Children need feedback from their audiences to better understand their power and impact as authors. Supportive peer responses keep the writing candle lit. Opportunities to share finished pieces and those in progress are provided at the end of each writing class. Several children volunteer to sit in the "author's chair" (Graves & Hansen, 1983) and read their works. The audience tells what they liked or what interested them and asks a few questions.

Some teachers establish an author's day once a week when children share their pieces. Child-authored books can be made available for others to read during reading class. Children also enjoy sharing their work with a former teacher or with a child from another class. Some schools are organized so that children can place their publications in the library. These books should have a response card taped inside so readers can comment to the author.

The writing workshop provides a predictable structure for daily writing. Children need regularly scheduled writing time, which allows them to carry over their work to another day or several days if needed. This system meshes better with the natural writing process than fixed time assignments. Many of you probably remember being assigned a topic and then told to turn in the completed work in thirty minutes. This leaves little or no time to write a first draft, let alone engage in the natu-

The children are getting ready to publish. They are preparing final copies of their stories for their classmates' enjoyment.

ral activities of the writing process: idea production, writing, rewriting, conferencing, editing, and publishing.

In addition to journals and writing workshops, teachers' modeling of the writing process, writing from literature, and writing across the curriculum round out a balanced writing program.

Modeling Writing

In traditional classrooms, giving assignments was a major teachers' role and the children never saw teachers write. Researchers (Graves, 1983; Hansen, 1987) reported that children seem more willing to participate when they know teachers are writers too, and they understand what it means to be an author. Two common ways to model writing are through language experience and personal writing.

Modeling Through Language Experience   Teachers can model writing through a language experience group story, where they record what children say. Imagine that a class participated in a collective experience like a visit to a pumpkin farm. (Often these class compositions are responses to social studies or science experiences.) This is a perfect context for creating a group account of the visit. After preliminary discussion to develop meaning, the teacher invites children to contribute sentences. As each child dictates a sentence, the teacher prints it on a chart and invites the class to work out some of the spellings. The teacher focuses on features of print that are within the range of children's levels of development, so someone in the class can provide some of the information. Small strategies and skills lessons can be embedded in this activity; for example:

Teacher: What do you want to say?
Joe: We rode the bus.
Teacher (*Writes and says "We," then says "rode" slowly*):   Say "rode" slowly with me. What would you expect to see at the beginning of "rode"?
Marleen: I know—"r."
Teacher: OK, Marleen, you can write the "r."

Teacher writes the remainder of the word. Teacher points to what has been written so far and invites the children to read it aloud.

Teacher: Carl, I saw you writing "the" in your journal yesterday. Come up and write "the."

Teacher points to what has been written so far and invites the children to read it aloud.

Teacher: Say "bus" slowly with me. What would you expect to see at the beginning of "bus?"
Shamira: b. (*Shamira writes "b."*) There's an "s" too.
Teacher: Yes. (*Teacher writes the "u" and has Shamira write the "s."*) Now let's read Joe's sentence together. Clayton, you can point to it while we all read.

It isn't wise to do this with the entire story because it would take too long and children would lose interest. The teacher shifts to writing the sentences without the lesson interaction when it seems appropriate. When the piece is finished, the teacher and students reread it together and return to it on subsequent days. The teacher might also type a copy for the children to illustrate and read with each other.

Modeling Through Personal Writing   Teachers also model by composing some of their personal writing publicly, on a large sheet of paper or on a transparency, and by demonstrating writing decisions, talking through their thinking. "Think-alouds" are excellent ways to give children insight into the writing process and for teachers to share who they are as writers. Teachers could talk about how they get topics for writing, how they decide to start and develop their pieces, and how they reread and change parts by replacing words, altering sentences, revising sequences, and adding and deleting parts. They could also "think aloud" about what to do when they don't know how to spell a word, and what they do when they get stuck and the piece doesn't seem to be going anywhere. Teachers do this modeling as mini-lessons during writing workshop. The writing program can be structured so there are regular opportunities for children to model and think aloud about their writing for each other as well.

Writing from Literature

Writing from literature happens because the rich language and structures in children's books provide strong models for writing. Teachers frequently notice that children have independently incorporated bits and pieces into their writing from stories that they have read in class or that teachers have been reading with them. It might be a word that caught a child's attention, a phrase, a character, or even the structure of the story itself. First-grader Krista independently borrowed from the structure and plot line of *Sam's Sandwich* by David Pelham (1990) to create her own version in Figure 6-11.

Children can be guided to experiment directly with an author's techniques, to add writing possibilities to their repertoire. Extension activities from literature can be developed to explore story structures, authors' styles, development of character, development of plot, and interesting use of language, genre, and tone and mood (Stewig, 1990).

Having children write their own words for wordless picture books supports children's work with story and plot structure. You might use the delightfully funny little books by Mercer Mayer (*Frog Goes to Dinner*, 1974; *A Boy a Dog and a Frog*, 1967; *Frog Where are You?*, 1969; and *One Frog Too Many*, 1975). Nancy Tafuri's *Junglewalk* (1988) invites the child into the world of a jungle dream adventure, and her *Follow Me!* (1990) takes the story builder into the depths of the ocean with a baby sea lion and crab. There's an appealing, almost human Rottweiler dog in Alexandra Day's *Good Dog, Carl* (1985), *Carl Goes Shopping* (1989), and *Carl's Christmas* (1990). Wordless picture books are about such a variety of topics that there will be one to please almost every child.

Chris Van Allsburg's *Jumanji* (1981) ends with the suggestion that the story continues and invites writers to create *Jumanji, Part II*. In the story, two children find a jungle adventure game that depends on a very careful reading of the directions, which clearly state that the game is not over until the winner says, "Jumanji." This is a very important direction: every time a player lands on a space, what is written there becomes real. For example, "Lion escapes. Go back two spaces" results in a lion charging around the house. Only when the winner says, "Jumanji" do all of the animals disappear. The children put the game back where they found it and shortly thereafter observe two children, who never read directions, pick up the game and walk off—the end of one story and beginning of another, yet untold story. Most of Van Allsburg's books have some mysterious element in them that is an invitation to writing, particularly *The Mysteries of Harris Burdick* (1984).

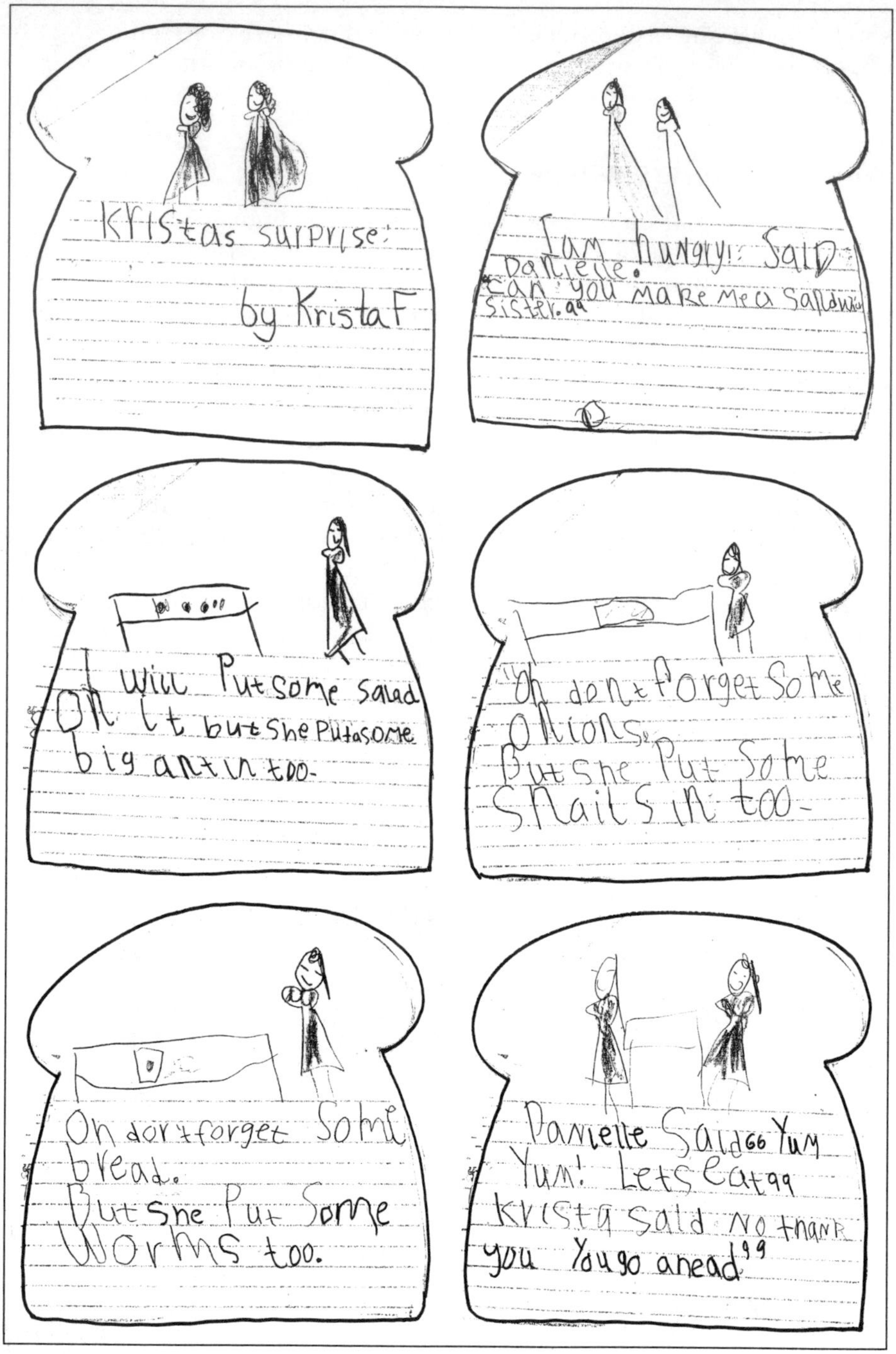

Figure 6-11 Krista's Surprise

Writing a story from a different point of view can be an exciting challenge. *The True Story of the Three Little Pigs As Told by A. Wolf* by John Scieszka (1989) is a hilarious account of the story from the wolf's point of view. *Deep in the Forest* by Brinton Turkle (1976), a wordless picture book, reverses the story of the three bears by having the bear be the intruder. Children might enjoy rewriting *Jack and the Beanstalk* (Ross, 1984) from the giant's point of view, or "Little Miss Muffet" (Sharon, Lois & Bram, 1985) from the spider's point of view.

We recommend that this directed writing be done as extension activities during reading, not during writers' workshop. Children's choice of topic is a key component of writers' workshop and should not be changed. However, teachers can insert examples of literature into discussions and conferences to model how connections with literature can help writers.

From *Frog Goes to Dinner* by Mercer Mayer, with illustrations by the author (Dial, 1974).

WRITING ACROSS THE CURRICULUM

Teachers can demonstrate the functional use of writing by making charts for songs, finger plays, and directions and by making explanatory labels, writing messages of the day, and writing chalkboard letters to the children. In a science center, where many teachers keep a classroom animal, children could keep track of the animal's eating and sleeping habits on a chart, and they could write in a journal their observations of the animal. The idea is to have paper and pencil handy to use functionally throughout the classroom.

Letter writing and report/research writing are two kinds of expository writing that can grow from science, social studies, and the language arts. Letter writing can be interesting and meaningful when real letters are written and mailed to real people who also write back. Developing a pen pal program with another school is a natural context for learning the conventions of letter writing and addressing envelopes. Children can learn about the other geographic area, which is an additional impetus for communicating and sharing information. Writing to favorite authors and writing social action letters and letters of inquiry could also be easily integrated into units of study. Language arts texts can be used as meaningful "how to do it" references.

The *Jolly Postman* books by Janet and Allan Ahlberg (1986, 1991) can motivate the development of an interesting fairy/folk tale unit. In these

From *The Jolly Postman* by Janet and Allan Ahlberg (Little, Brown, 1986).

books, the postman delivers letters to different fairy and folk tale characters. Children could each choose a character to role play from the many brief scenes in these books that can be dramatized. Books about each of the characters could be collected for reading and sharing. Add a postal station with individual mail boxes and the scene is set to engage in a number of valuable language arts activities.

Teachers can model letter writing by including letters as a regular form of communicating with parents. These motivate children, but in addition establish better rapport with parents in general and often result in increased parental attendance at conferences.

Even young children can do simple report/research writing. In one inner-city classroom, the children had just returned from a visit to the zoo and wanted to know more about the animals. The teacher brought in many books from the library, including reference books with a multitude of pictures. These young researchers collected information about their animals by reading, talking, and examining pictures. Among the books children in this classroom particularly enjoyed were Seymour Simon's *Animal Fact/Animal Fiction* (1987), Bianca Lavies's *Lily Pad Pond* (1989), David M. Schwartz's *The Hidden Life of the Meadow* (1988), and Bert Kitchen's *And So They Build* (1993). Children learned as much from the full-color photographs in Lavies and Schwartz and from the elegantly detailed paintings in the Kitchen book, as from the texts themselves.

A semantic map is helpful in organizing reports that have some sequence. Let's use animals as an example because they are of interest to most young children. After each child chooses an animal to research, the class brainstorms to determine what they want to know about their animals. The name of the animal goes in the center of the map. The children then select three or four kinds of information to search for, and the teacher writes them in the boxes of the map. They can write notes on the lines provided under the idea boxes (see Figure 6-12).

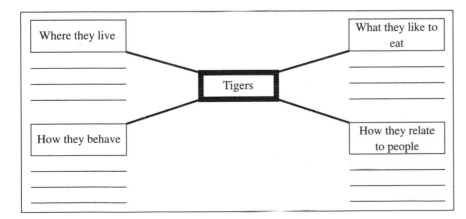

FIGURE 6-12

Idea Mapping

When finished, children work with partners to plan the sequence of their pieces by discussing which arm they should write about first, second, and third. After writing the reports, the children should share them orally or by reading each other's work.

From these writing experiences, teachers can take notes about children's writing behaviors, attitudes, and interests and collect examples of their writing. These examples can be accumulated in individual portfolios to document children's writing development.

Assessing Writing Growth

To understand children's writing growth, all of the factors discussed in this chapter must be taken into consideration. Growth can't be measured by focusing on only one aspect of writing, such as spelling, or by examining one composition: An effective way to keep track of writing growth is to institute a portfolio system in the classroom and across the school system (Jett-Simpson & Leslie, 1994). A portfolio is a file folder where children keep rough drafts and finished pieces of writing. The portfolio and teacher observation notes become an excellent data bank for writing report cards and having conferences with parents. By displaying a child's writing samples, teachers can easily discuss how the child is developing.

Students can self-evaluate the writing in their portfolios by reading the contents periodically, such as a week before each grading period. They identify their best piece and least liked piece, and explain why they made the choices. Teachers follow up this experience by having conferences with students about the self-evaluations. From self-evaluations combined with teacher observations, students can set goals for the reporting period.

At the end of the year, children and teacher can work collaboratively to decide which samples of writing best demonstrate how the children have grown as writers that year. A few samples can be kept in the children's portfolios to be passed to next year's teacher. The remainder of the materials are sent home. When children leave elementary school, some districts select one piece of writing from each school year and bind them into a booklet to be presented to the children as a record of their learning.

Nothing so clearly demonstrates a child's evolution as a writer as concrete evidence. To show how a portfolio can tell the story of a child as a developing writer, we will describe Anna's classrooms and her writing portfolio, which contains writing from 4-year-old kindergarten through second grade.

ANNA'S STORY

Anna's 4- and 5-year-old kindergarten naturally integrated literacy into the physical space and social activity. The teacher had created a classroom that exemplified all of Cambourne's conditions of learning from Figure 1-3. Print was everywhere: on the walls, on charts, in centers, on cards labeling materials and student possessions. A book center with comfortable furniture set the scene for many experiences with fine children's literature. Big books were displayed on a stand by the piano, and charts of songs and finger plays were on the walls. Many children took turns gathering in front of the big book stand, where they played school by reenacting the shared book experience during choice time. Others took turns pointing to the words for the songs and finger plays as they sang or said these together. There was a well-stocked writing center, art center, housekeeping center, science center, building center, and other small areas that invited the children to learn together. In addition, there was a flexible center that the teacher changed to match children's interests and to go with topics of study. A grocery store, filled with empty boxes and cans of products used at home, was a favorite focus of the flexible center. Children made grocery lists, shopped, counted money, wrote receipts, and carried on many shopping conversations. Upon entering the classroom, you immediately knew this was a room that respected children's work because their writing, art work, and other creations decorated the walls and centers, instead of neatly made teacher bulletin boards that said "hands off."

The teacher often demonstrated literacy. She read aloud, did the shared book experience (described in Chapter 5), and demonstrated story and functional writing regularly. For example, if they were going to make gingerbread men after reading *The Gingerbread Boy* by Eric Kimmel (1993), the teacher would write the recipe on a chart, talking about what she was writing. She also made a chart to develop the cooking plans with the children. The teacher always recognized children's developmental levels and responded with comments that let them know what they were doing well and encouraged problem solving. This was a classroom where everyone was recognized as a learner and met with success daily.

The children wrote regularly in journals. Anna's mother kept Anna's journal in a writing portfolio for her at home. Anna's mother continued to collect samples of her writing from her first- and second-grade classrooms in another school as well. Let's look inside Anna's portfolio, which was begun in 4-year-old kindergarten and has followed her to today when she is in second grade. By careful observations, we can see the evolution of her composition and the progression of her spelling development.

Anna's journals in 4- and 5-year-old kindergarten are a typical mixed collection of writing and drawing. The cover of her first journal (Figure 6-13) in August of 4-year-old kindergarten was a mix of experimentation with blue and black marking pens, pink, red, and turquoise crayons, and a red ballpoint pen, resulting in random and controlled scribbles and some controlled boxlike forms superimposed twice with her name. We can see her confusion with "n" in "Аnna." This production was accompanied by ongoing talk with her friends. Turning the pages in the nine-page journal (see Figure 6-13), we see more scribbles, some flower pictures, a sun, drawings of friends with a heart at belly button level, drawings of faces, a few words used as picture labels, and several pages of tic-tac-toe games played with friends. Her most advanced spelling is at the transition stage: *HRTE*. She has included a letter for every sound in the word and an "e" that indicates she knows there is an "e" in the word somewhere but isn't quite sure where.

Anna's September journal from 5-year-old kindergarten (Figure 6-14, page 270) contains random scribbles, some cursivelike scribbles, several pictures of the sun and a rainbow, self-portraits, one of which is accompanied by a speech bubble that says "hi," "I love Mom and Dad" hearts, one page of tic-tac-tac, and several pages of colorful flowers. Drawings dominate the journal, and some print accompanies them on about one-third of the pages. Print completely covers one page, where we can see that she is writing an initial paragraph in an expository piece about a flower. She has included a few standard spellings along with phonemic and standard spellings, which means she is using both phonemes and visual patterns to spell words. We can also see her confusion about how to make "s."

A variety of forms appear in Anna's journal from 5-year-old kindergarten that illustrate her growing control of composition and spelling as well as variability in her writing. She also shows how different modes of composition and phases of spelling can overlap. Some days she does no writing, only drawing, and some days she writes only in linear scribbles. She is moving from a few words on the page (labeling and changing) to several sentences, which are centered around her life experiences, and semistructured stories.

It is important for the observer to collect a number of samples to obtain a clear picture of writing patterns and the most advanced writing characteristics the child is demonstrating. If, for example, we included only the scribble writing journal (Figure 6-17, page 271) in Anna's port-folio, we would have a highly inaccurate picture of her performance, which is represented by Figures 6-15 through 6-24 (pages 271–274).

Toward the end of kindergarten, Anna wrote her first semistructured story, which was followed by a "chapter" book. The rough draft in Figure 6-25 (page 275) shows that Anna's ideas are linked together in sentences and the story structure includes a beginning, middle, and end,

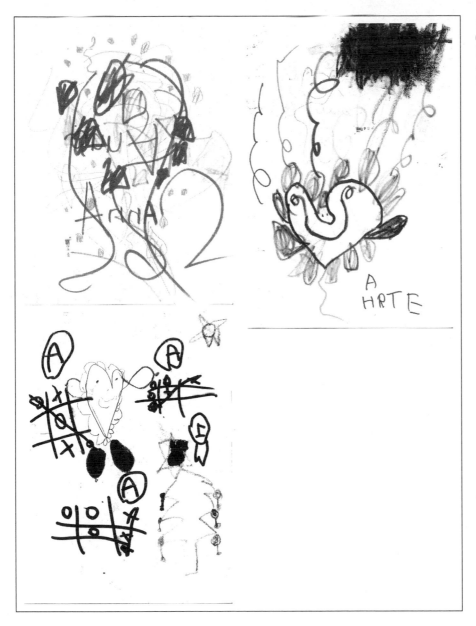

FIGURE 6-13

Pages from Anna's
4-Year-Old
Kindergarten Journal

like the breakfast-to-bed stories found in many children's early writing.
Notice how she has written the story as a personal narrative with Anna
as a main character along with the dinosaur.

Her teacher published the story by computer after a conference with
Anna. During the conference, the teacher responded to the content and

FIGURE 6-14

Pages from Anna's
September 5-Year-
Old Kindergarten
Journal. "A flower
begins as a seed and
then it will get bigger
and bigger until it is
a flower."

helped Anna decide whether she had said all she wanted to say. Then the teacher edited part of it for her and talked with Anna about how she wanted to page the story. Figure 6-26 (page 276) is the published story.

Anna's kindergarten letter to her teacher clearly grew out of a need to express her feelings. She understood and used a form of expression that would work for her—the letter in Figure 6-27 (page 277).

Anna's journal writing in first grade was more structured. The journals were set up to be penmanship exercises where the children usually wrote an answer to the questions of the day such as: "What did you do

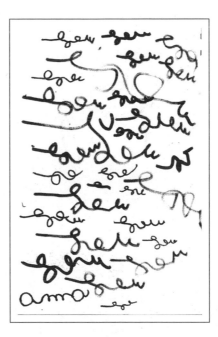

FIGURE 6-15

October—Copied Halloween Words from a Wall Chart

FIGURE 6-16

December—Caption. "This is me in California with my dad."

FIGURE 6-17

January—Linear Cursive Scribbles

FIGURE 6-18

Undated—Anna discovered how to write her brother's name (*Lev*) in cursive

Figure 6-19

February—Personal Narrative. "My Dad is throwing me in. Kersplash!"

this weekend?" "Where would you like to be?" Notice in Figure 6-28 (page 278) that Anna answers the questions easily in standard spelling and provides an accompanying drawing. Also notice the contrast between the natural size of her writing at the top of the page, where she adds a place for name and date in accordance with standard school structure, and the size demanded by the first-grade paper. It is easy to see that she has a writing comfort level for smaller print than the

FIGURE 6-20

March—Cartoonlike Characters in Conversation. "Hey. I see a beehive up above you. I love you." "Yes, I do like it." "Very much."

FIGURE 6-21

March—A Common Theme. "I love. . . ."

FIGURE 6-22

March—Practicing the ABCs

FIGURE 6-23

April—First Appearance of a Book Language Writing Convention. "*Once upon a time* there was a little girl named Anna and one day Anna went outside and when Anna realized. . . ." (Anna said, "I didn't finish that story.") Also notice how she writes in columns.

FIGURE 6-24 May—Influence of Television. "I am an alien from outer space. Take me to your leader."

Panel 1:

WON (One) Dax I 20Ae (saw) A
DANAZORPZ (dinosaur).
it WAZe A
ZAGZORPZ.
He (Stegosaurus) LAt (let) Mi (me)
RID ON HiMe
AND T HAD He (then)
LAt (let) Mi (me) HAVE LHOOe (lunch)
WITH HIM.
AND THANO
He LAte (Ate) Mi WiHe (him)
ZLTP (sleep) WiTH

Panel 2:

#tHe NA✷t (next)
MOMON (morning)
I WOKe AP (up)
ABT (but) THe
ZAGZORPZ
WAZ ZALIPA (still) (was)
AZLIMP (asleep). 20re

Panel 3:

I WOK HiM uP.
AFTR I WOK
HiM uP
We AND ZeM
AMTHR ZAGZORPZ (another)
PLAD
AND TAGe THAD
We PLAD
DRANAZOR DRANOOR
WIRS YOUR
BABe?

Panel 4:

AFTRe THe
ZAGeZORPZeZ FRiend
WINT AWAe.
We WITe BAKe
TOO WIZ KAFe
AND THAN We
ATe DiNRe

FIGURE 6-25   Anna's Rough Draft of "I Saw a Dinosaur"

FIGURE 6-26

Anna's Published
Story: "I Saw a
Dinosaur"

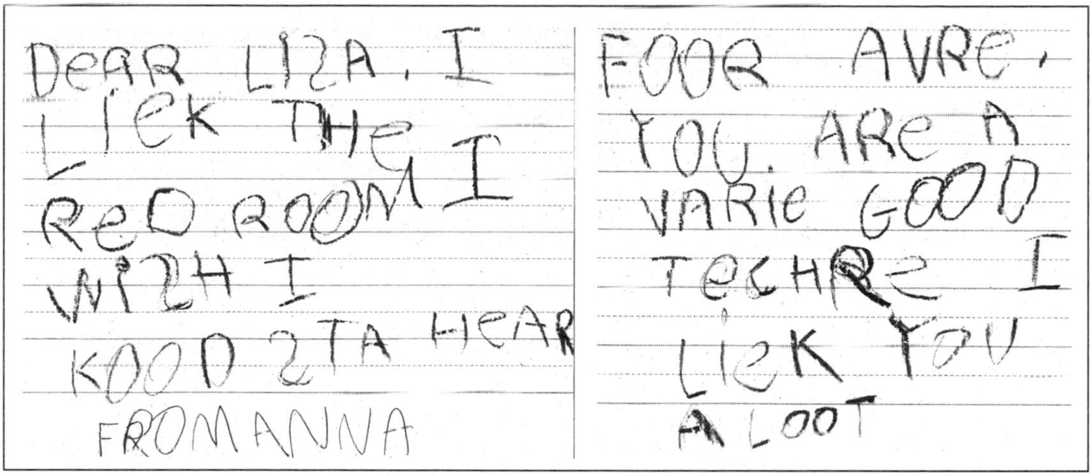

> Dear Liza, I liek the red room I wizh I kood 2 ta hear from Anna foor avre, you are a varie good techre I liek you a loot

FIGURE 6-27 Anna's Letter to Her Teacher

demands of the paper. The influence of first-grade models of writing can be seen in Figure 6-29 (page 278), where Anna is making up her own worksheet. As she wrote this page, she gave herself directions: "Now do them in lowercase."

In spite of a more directed journal-writing experience in first grade, Anna continued her writing advancement, much of which was done at home. Figure 6-30 (page 279) shows her first expression of understanding the humor in the multiple meanings in figurative language. Anna handed the picture to her mom and said, "Mom, this is using your noodle."

Anna, now in second grade, is writing freely in all modes. Her portfolio shows she is gradually developing more complex story structure. In "The Stallion," Anna wrote about a problem, a lost horse, that was resolved when he found a way to get to safety. Her portfolio also includes a research report, a sentence listing of interesting facts she learned about the excavation of dinosaur bones. Her piece titled "Dark Nights" (Figure 6-31, page 279) seems to mix modes of writing: writing to inform and writing to express a personal experience.

In three and a half years, Anna has grown as a writer, gaining control over the spelling system and many other mechanics. Most important, her compositions demonstrate an evolving ability to express herself effectively and creatively in many modes. She has been nurtured at home, and her kindergarten experiences supported her exploration of print by celebrating what she could do and recognizing her unfolding abilities.

Anna is one child. Because not all children experience strong physical and social environments for learning, they will come to school with

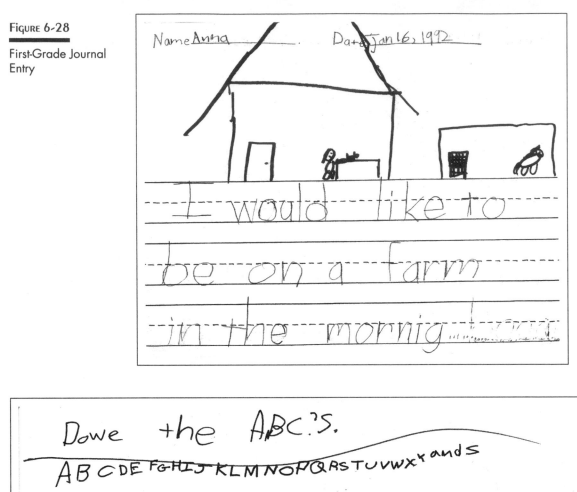

FIGURE 6-28

First-Grade Journal
Entry

Name Anna   Date Jan 16, 1992

I would like to
be on a farm
in the mornig

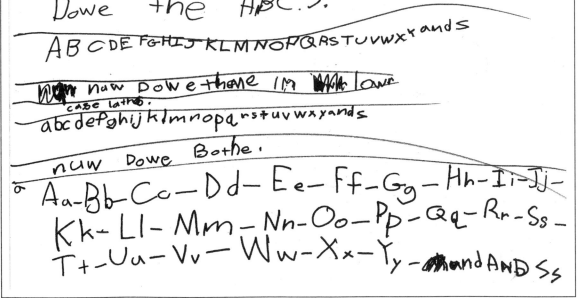

Dowe   the ABC.'S.

AB C DE FG HI J KLM NOP QRS TUVWXY and S

now nuw Dowe the are im low
case latrs.

abc def ghij klmnopq rstuvwx y and s

nuw Dowe Bothe.

Aa-Bb-Cc—Dd—Ee—Ff—Gg—Hh—Ii—Jj—
Kk—Ll—Mm—Nn—Oo—Pp—Qq—Rr—Ss—
Tt—Uu—Vv—Ww—Xx—Yy—and AND Ss

FIGURE 6-29   First-Grade Homemade Worksheet

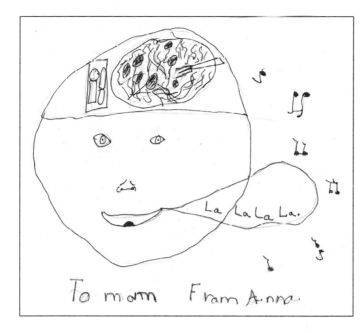

FIGURE 6-30

First-Grade
Demonstration of
Understanding an
Idiom: "using your
noodle"

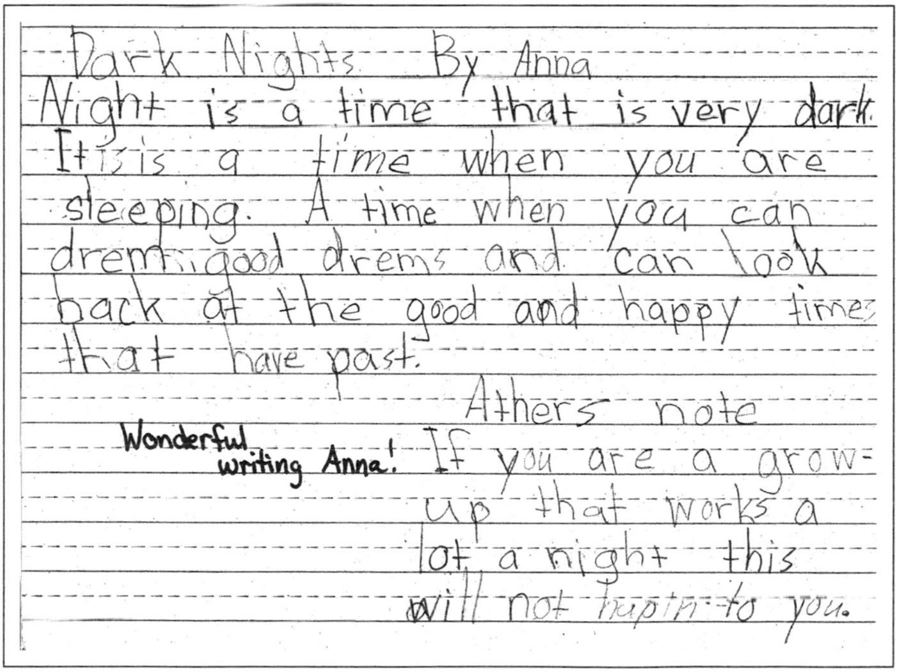

To mom   Fram Anna

Dark Nights By Anna
Night is a time that is very dark.
It is is a time when you are
sleeping. A time when you can
drem good drems and can look
back at the good and happy times
that have past.
                    Athers note
Wonderful
writing Anna! If you are a grow-
up that works a
lot a night this
will not hupin to you.

FIGURE 6-31

Second-Grade
Writing in Mixed
Modes

wide-ranging abilities. Every child, however, is capable of doing something. The teacher's role is to recognize what each child can do and provide a positive, supportive environment that nourishes and sustains growth.

Summary

To develop a strong writing program, teachers need to understand that writing is the construction of meaning through print and is developmental. Writing performances vary greatly from child to child, and a single child's writing will vary as well because of a variety of complex factors that influence the work. Based on these understandings, teachers can make informed observations of children's processes and products that will guide their instruction.

The writing program should reflect the conditions of learning depicted in Figure 1-3. Both physical and social contexts should accommodate the children developmentally. Within this setting, a program can be organized to include journals, writing workshop, modeling writing, writing from literature, and writing across the curriculum.

Writing development can best be evaluated by collecting writing samples over time. A single composition cannot tell a child's writing story. By examining works closely for advancing patterns of development that reflect the "cutting edges" of learning, a teacher can describe the breadth of a child's writing ability.

Suggestions for Further Study

1. Tape record and take notes on a small group conversation during writing time in a kindergarten or first-grade class. Transcribe the tape and analyze the interactions in the conversation, writing, and/or drawing.

2. Collect writing samples from several children's journals for at least a month. Make notes about the writing context for each sample you collect. Then record your observations about the children's patterns of growth and development in writing. Be sure to attend to spelling development as well as modes of writing.

3. Select one of the activities described in the section "Writing from Literature" and teach it. Write up your plan and the results of your instruction. What did you notice about how well the students could carry out the idea, their reactions to the assignments, and the characteristics of their writing?

4. Have the children select a topic and guide them in developing a

semantic map for planning the writing and collecting information about the topic. Have them write and share their pieces. Then write about the results of your work.

5. Read the case study about young children's writing development in Bissex (1980) and develop a paper that is a descriptive overview of the author's findings about the growth and development of young writers. Discuss how this knowledge will influence your teaching.

6. Work through the writing process with two children for one piece, taking their work to publication. Take detailed notes of your observations of the children's strategies and processes during this time. Compare the children in terms of their developmental characteristics. Frame your work in terms of what the children can do and are trying to do. Avoid "can't" statements.

Suggestions for Further Reading

Benjamin, C. (1985). *Writing for kids*. New York: Thomas Y. Crowell.

Though written for children, this simple book can be used by teachers as a source of ideas for helping children during writers' workshop. Some topics include knowing what to do if you can't think of anything to write, keeping a writer's notebook, choosing wonderful words, and developing interesting beginning sentences.

Bissex, G. (1980). *Gnys at wrk: A child learns to read and write*. Cambridge: MA: Harvard University Press.

This developmental case study describes the development of reading and writing through the preschool years to the early school years.

Butler, A., & Turbill, J. (1984). *Towards a reading-writing classroom*. Portsmouth, NH: Heinemann.

This appealing book for teachers who are just starting process writing provides practical examples of classroom organization and activities.

Calkins, L. (1986). *The art of teaching writing*. Portsmouth, NH: Heinemann.

This is an excellent book for teachers who are serious about starting process writing programs. The chapters on conferences are especially useful.

Calkins, L., & Harwayne, S. (1991). *Living between the lines*. Portsmouth, NH: Heinemann.

A follow-up to *The Art of Teaching Writing*, this book expresses Calkins's view of the writing process.

Cambourne, B., & Turbill, J. (1987). *Coping with chaos*. New South Wales, Australia: Primary English Teaching Association.

A change in the nature of classrooms accompanied the change to process writing. To many observers these classrooms looked almost chaotic. Children were discussing and arguing with each other, walking around the room, drawing pictures, writing, reading, thinking aloud, reading their own texts to anyone who would listen, and working with the teacher. The author discusses the underlying structure in these classrooms, describes children's coping strategies, and presents two kindergarten case studies.

Clay, M. (1975). *What did I write? Beginning writing behavior.* Portsmouth, NH: Heinemann.

One of the first books to trace the development of writing in young children, this is still useful in understanding the first principles children use to guide their writing.

Dyson, A. H. (1989). *Multiple worlds of child writers: Friends learning to write.* New York: Teachers College Press.

Dyson observed children over several years in their writing environments to describe how writing and the social context interact.

Gentry, J. R. (1987). *Spel is a four letter word.* Portsmouth, NH: Heinemann.

Written by a poor speller who obtained his Ph.D. in language arts with an emphasis in spelling, this down-to-earth book clarifies myths about spelling and summarizes the best way to study spelling words. His *Teaching Kids to Spell* (Portsmouth, NH: Heinemann, 1993) is based on a developmental perspective of spelling. The program suggestions Gentry makes will be useful to teachers who are establishing spelling programs in child-centered literacy classrooms.

Graves, D. (1983). *Writing, teachers and children at work.* Portsmouth, NH: Heinemann.

This is the classic book for teachers who are beginning writing programs. Graves "takes you by the hand," describing the process of setting up a successful writing program, and answers teachers' most common questions.

Greenfield, H. (1989). *Books from writer to reader.* New York: Crown Publishers.

This book is a comprehensive explanation of how a book is published, starting with the writer's idea and detailing all of the steps until the book is in the bookstore. Teachers can relate information from this book to the processes children are experiencing in writers' workshop.

Harste, J. C., Woodward, V. A., & Burke, C. L. (1984). *Language stories and literacy lessons.* Portsmouth, NH: Heinemann.

Teachers will find the developmental stories of emerging writers and readers fascinating and will gain insights into children's development of coping strategies.

Johnson, P. (1990). *A book of one's own: Developing literacy through making books.* Portsmouth, NH: Heinemann.

This book provides detailed illustrations and directions about a multitude of ways to make interesting books. It also includes a discussion of the book as art and how to unlock the rusty door of the imagination to create stories.

Schickedanz, J. (1990). *Adam's righting revolutions: One child's literacy development from infancy through grade one.* Portsmouth, NH: Heinemann

This case study documents Adam's emerging understanding of the alphabetic principle as he figured out how a word is made. Numerous examples illustrate the developing and changing hypotheses Adam made about words. The book also includes a highly readable discussion of the research connections of this case study with others.

Smith, F. (1981). *Writing and the writer.* New York: Holt, Rinehart & Winston.

Smith explores the writing process as well as the evolving role of the writer and develops a theory for process writing.

Stewig, J. W. (1990). *Read to write* (3rd ed.). New York: Richard C. Owen.

This resource provides teachers with many excellent ways to use literature as a stimulus for writing, including many writing samples from kindergarten through third grade.

Teale, W., & Sulzby, E. (1986). *Emergent literacy: Writing and reading.* Norwood, NJ: Albex Publishing Corp.

This collection of multidisciplinary papers and reacher reports on children's reading and writing from birth to school age seeks to understand how children learn to read and write.

Suggested Periodicals

Childhood Education, 11501 George Ave., Suite 315, Wheaton, MD 20902 (1-800-423-3563).

A publication of the Association for Childhood Education International, this journal is concerned with developmentally appropriate practice across the curriculum, including the language arts.

Language Arts, 1111 Kenyon Rd., Urbana, IL 61801 (217-328-3870).

Published by the National Council of Teachers of English, this journal contains articles about the language arts for elementary and middle school teachers.

The New Advocate, 480 Washington St., Norwood, MA 01062 (617-762-5577).

Integrating the language arts with literature is the major theme of this journal. Articles by authors and illustrators of children's books can be shared with students.

The Reading Teacher, 800 Barksdale Rd., P.O. Box 8139, Newark, DE 19714-8139.

Published by the International Reading Association, this journal includes articles about reading and about the language arts in elementary and middle grades as well.

The Writing Notebook: Creative Word Processing in the Classroom, P.O. Box 1268, Eugene, OR 97440-1268 (503-344-7125).

Young Children, 1834 Connecticut Ave. NW, Washington, DC 20009-5768 (202-232-8777).

Published by the National Association for the Education of Young Children, this journal keeps readers current in recent developments in early childhood education through a combination of research, practice, and therapy.

Suggested Books for Children

Aliki. (1986). *How a book is made.* New York: Thomas Y. Crowell.

Illustrated with eye-catching cartoons, this book shows how the author thinks and writes, the role of the illustrator, and the technical side of publishing. Teachers can share the book with primary-grade children.

Caseley, Judith. (1991). *Dear Annie.* New York: Greenwillow.

This book motivates letter writing between relatives.

Delton, Judy. (1982). *The goose who wrote a book*. Minneapolis, MN: Carol-rhoda.

When Goose shares her book with friends and asks their opinion of her writing, everyone has a different piece of advice. Grief, frustration, and humorous results follow.

Drescher, Henrick. (1983). *Simon's book*. New York: Lothrop, Lee & Shepard.

Simon falls asleep while writing a book, and while he sleeps the characters finish the book for him.

DuPasquier, Philippe. (1985). *Dear Daddy*. . . . New York: Bradbury Press.

This book motivates letter writing.

Goffstein, M. B. (1984). *The writer*. New York: Harper & Row.

Goffstein tells how a writer is a collector of images through observation of the everyday world.

Irvine, Joan. (1992). *How to make super pop-ups*. New York: Morrow Junior Books.

Young book publishers and teachers will enjoy using this book for ideas of interesting ways to illustrate books by using pop-ups.

Joyce, William. (1985). *George shrinks*. New York: Harper.

This book motivates letter writing.

Leedy, Loreen. (1991). *Messages in the mailbox: How to write a letter*. New York: Holiday House.

The children in Mrs. Gator's classroom have a problem: no one ever sends them any mail. That's when they decide to write letters so that they can receive some. Types of letters such as friendly letters, business letters, postcards, and letters of sympathy, apology, and love are illustrated, and their purposes are communicated in cartoonlike illustrations and conversation bubbles.

Stevenson, James. (1986). *When I was nine*. New York: Greenwillow.

Reading aloud this picture book autobiography and discussing how the author told his story might give some children ideas about writing their own life stories: "When I was . . . ."

Williams, Vera B., & Williams, Jennifer. (1988). *Stringbean's trip to the shining sea*. New York: Scholastic.

The postcards and snapshots Stringbean and his brother sent home to their family one summer are collected in this book to tell the story of their journey—a format that may be intriguing for young writers.

Ziefert, Harriet. (1985). *Birthday card, where are you?* New York: Puffin Books.

Kindergartners enjoy this lift-the-flap book that traces the journey of a birthday card to a friend's house via the mailbox, the postman's jeep, the post office, airport transport truck, airplane, mail truck, and mail carrier.

References

Atwell, N. (1987). *In the middle*. Portsmouth, NH: Heinemann.

Bissex, G. (1980). *Gyns at wrk: A child learns to read and write*. Cambridge, MA: Harvard University Press.

Britton, J. (1970). *Language and learning*. Harmondsworth, England: Penguin Books.

Bromley, K. (1989). Buddy journals make the reading-writing connection. *The Reading Teacher, 43*(2), 122–129.

Calkins, L. (1986). *The art of teaching writing*. Portsmouth, NH: Heinemann.

Calkins, L., & Harwayne, S. (1991). *Living between the lines*. Portsmouth, NH: Heinemann.

Clarke, L. (1988). Invented versus traditional spelling first graders' writings: Effects on learning to spell and read. *Research in Teaching of English, 11*(3), 281–308.

Clay, M. (1975). *What did I write?* Portsmouth, NH: Heinemann.

Dyson, A. H. (1989). Reading, writing and language: Young children's solving the written language puzzle. *Language Arts, 59*(8), 829–839.

Dyson, A., & Freedman, S. (1991). Writing. In J. Flood, J. Jensen, D. Lapp & J. Squire (Eds.), *Handbook of research on teaching the English language arts* (pp. 754–774). New York: Macmillan.

Eckhoff, B. (1983). How reading affects children's writing. *Language Arts, 60*(5), 607–616.

Ferreiro, E., & Teberosky, A. (1982). *Literacy before schooling* (trans. K. G. Castro). Portsmouth, NH: Heinemann.

Gambrell, L. (1985). Dialogue journals: Reading-writing interaction. *The Reading Teacher, 38*(6), 512–515.

Gentry, J. R. (1982). An analysis of developmental spelling GNYS AT WRK. *The Reading Teacher, 36*(1), 192–200.

———. (1993). *Teaching kids to spell*. Portsmouth, NH: Heinemann.

Gentry, J. R., & Gillet, J. (1993). Learning to spell developmentally. *The Reading Teacher, 35*(2), 378–381.

Graves, D. (1983). *Writing: Teachers and children at work*. Portsmouth, NH: Heinemann.

Graves, D., & Hansen, J. (1983). The author's chair. *Language Arts, 60*(2), 176–183.

Hansen, J. (1987). *When writers read*. Portsmouth, NH: Heinemann.

Harste, J., Woodward, V., & Burke, C. (1984). *Language stories and literacy lessons*. Portsmouth, NH: Heinemann.

Jett-Simpson, M., & Leslie, L. (Eds.). (1994). *Ecological assessment: Under construction*. Schofield, WI: Wisconsin State Reading Association.

Jett-Simpson, M., & Smith, P. (1992). *Children's patterns of writing performance*. Paper presented at the University of Wisconsin—Milwaukee School of Education Research Conference, Milwaukee, WI.

Mass, L. (1982). Developing concepts of literacy in young children. *The Reading Teacher, 35*(6), 670–675.

Neuman, S., & Roskos, K. (1990). The influence of literacy-enriched play settings on preschooler's engagement with written language. In J. Zuttell & S. McCormick (Eds.), *Literacy theory and research: Analyses from multiple paradigms* (pp. 179–189). Chicago: National Reading Conference.

Newkirk, T. (1989). *More than stories*. Portsmouth, NH: Heinemann.

Ollila, L. (1982). *Observations of 100 first graders' writing*. Paper presented at the National Council of Teachers of English Conference, Minneapolis, MN.

Reed, C. (1974). Pre-school children's knowledge of English phonology. *Harvard Educational Review, 41*(1), 1–34.

Rich, S. (1985). The writing suitcase. *Young Children, 40*(3), 42–44.

Sowers, S. (1985). The story and the all-about book. In J. Hansen, T. Newkirk & D. Graves (Eds.), *Breaking ground: Teachers relate reading and writing in the elementary school* (pp. 73–82). Portsmouth, NH: Heinemann.

Stewig, J. W. (1990). *Read to write*. New York: Richard C. Owen.

Schickedanz, J. (1990). *Adam's righting revolutions: One child's literacy development from infancy through grade one*. Portsmouth, NH: Heinemann.

Sulzby, E., Barnhart, J., & Hieshima, J. A. (1989). Forms of writing and pre-reading from writing, a preliminary report. In J. Mason (Ed.), *Reading and writing connections* (pp. 31–64). Boston: Allyn & Bacon.

Temple, C., Nathan, R., Temple, F., & Burris, N. (1993). *The beginnings of writing*. Boston: Allyn & Bacon.

Wood, M. (1989). Invented spelling revisited. *Reading Today, 6*(6), 22.

Children's Books

Ahlberg, Janet & Allan. (1986). *The jolly postman or other people's letters*. Boston: Little, Brown.

———. (1991). *The jolly Christmas postman*. Boston: Little, Brown.

Day, Alexandra. (1985). *Good dog, Carl*. New York: Green Tiger Press.

———. (1989). *Carl goes shopping*. New York: Farrar, Straus & Giroux.

———. (1990). *Carl's Christmas*. New York: Farrar, Straus & Giroux.

Fox, Mem. (1988). *Koala Lou*. New York: Harcourt, Brace, Jovanovich.

Kimmel, Eric. (1993). *The gingerbread boy*. New York: Holiday House.

Kitchen, Bert. (1993). *And so they build*. Cambridge, MA: Candlewick Press.

Lavies, Bianca. (1989). *Lily pad pond*. New York: Dutton.

Mayer, Mercer. (1967). *A boy, a dog, and a frog*. New York: Dial Press.

———. (1969). *Frog where are you?* New York: Dial Press.

———. (1974). *Frog goes to dinner*. New York: Dial Press.

———. (1975). *One frog too many*. New York: Dial Press.

Pelham, David. (1990). *Sam's sandwich*. New York: Dutton Children's Books.

Ross, Tony. (1984). *Jack and the beanstalk*. London: Methuen.

Schotter, Roni. (1989). *Captain Snap and the children of Vinegar Lane*. New York: Orchard Books.

Schwartz, David M. (1988). *The hidden life of the meadow*. New York: Crown Publishers.

Scieszka, Jon. (1989). *The true story of the 3 little pigs as told by A. Wolf*. New York: Viking Press.

Sharon, Lois and Bram's Mother Goose. (1985). Boston: Atlantic Monthly Press.

Simon, Seymour. (1987). *Animal fact/animal fiction*. New York: Crown Publishers.

Tafuri, Nancy. (1988). *Junglewalk*. New York: Greenwillow.

———. (1990). *Follow me!* New York: Greenwillow.

Turkle, Brinton. (1976). *Deep in the forest*. New York: Dutton.

Van Allsburg, Chris. (1981). *Jumanji*. Boston: Houghton Mifflin.

———. (1984). *The mysteries of Harris Burdick*. Boston: Houghton Mifflin.

Ward, Cindy. (1988). *Cookie's week*. New York: Putnam.

Professional Growth

The National Writing Project Network

The National Writing Project began as the Bay Area Writing Project at the University of California at Berkeley in 1974. There are now over 170 affiliate groups located across the United States. Based on the premise that the best teachers of teachers are other teachers, their training sessions are designed to train experienced teachers with a special expertise in writing in how-to-do workshops and in-service for other teachers. For the location of the National Writing Project group nearest you, write to The National Writing Project, School of Education, University of California, Berkeley, CA 94720.

SEVEN

❀

INTEGRATING THE SEPARATE STRANDS OF A PROGRAM

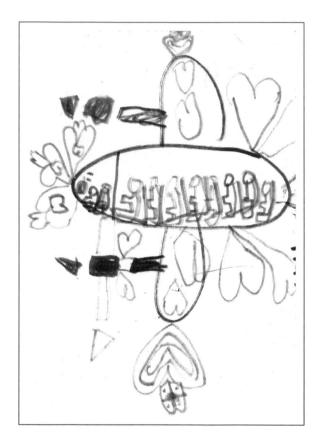

An enduring argument for integration is that it represents a way to avoid the fragmented and irrelevant acquisition of isolated facts, transforming knowledge into personally useful tools for learning new information.

Lipson et al. (1993, p. 252)

In the previous chapters, we have separated and examined at length the various components of an integrated program. The purpose of separating strands that in teaching practice should be integrated is to gain more space to describe at greater length the possibilities that exist. Here, we will put the parts back together by describing two exemplary units. The descriptions of the individual pieces of the experience will be more brief, with an emphasis on how the various components grow from one another.

The term *integrating* can be used in a wide variety of ways. Two of the most common are examined in this chapter. First, we will describe an approach that integrates within the language arts. An effective unit of study ties together listening, speaking, reading, and writing, as well as other less-often-included components such as drama. Second, we will describe an approach that integrates across the curriculum, incorporating activities in science, social studies, and math, among other content areas. Busching and Schwartz (1983) provided a more extensive discussion of these two and other ways of integrating curriculum.

Why are teachers interested in integrating the curriculum? Research evidence suggests a variety of positive outcomes. For example, Schmidt (1985) pointed out that in integrating within the language arts, students learned a "great deal of content" (p. 310), and the teachers didn't have to teach skills isolated from other language content being taught. Furthermore, talking about integrating across the curriculum, Diamond (1982) pointed out that this allows teachers to "achieve multiple goals within one lesson" and thus gain "free time for other curricular pursuits" (p. 2).

An Integrated Language Arts Unit

A major underlying principle in planning language arts activities is that we want students to sense the wholeness of language, since one use of language grows naturally from another and leads to yet another. Too frequently, in contrast, children leave elementary school perceiving, albeit unconsciously, that the language arts are a random collection of isolated, unrelated activities. Frequently, these activities are skill-based hierarchies, although as Walp and Walmsley (1989) pointed out, these have never been empirically demonstrated to have validity as discrete activities.

In contrast to such skill sequences, which prepare children to use language "later" for real purposes, throughout this book we have stressed an alternative holistic approach. We advocate building clusters of experiences based on children's books. Using a book as a seed, we can grow an array of related activities, emphasizing the connectedness of the various language arts, as parts of a plant are connected to each other. The following description of a teaching unit on *The Three Little Pigs* is provided to show a process that teachers could use with many other books.

We begin this unit with an observing and describing activity to help develop children's abilities to use language for these two thinking purposes. A significant way we learn is by seeing how an unfamiliar person, place, object, or experience is like or unlike those we've encountered before. To foster such comparing and contrasting in this literature-based unit, bring a bunch of turnips, tops and all, to class. Encourage children to use their eyes to note color, shape, and size; their fingers to note contrasting texture and resistance; their noses to note the varying smells of roots and greens. With the class, make lists of all the words they can generate for each of the types of sensory experiences you're including in the unit. Left posted in the room, these word lists become idea banks, to which children can return as they are writing later in the unit.

Then cut into the turnip so that the children can taste what is probably an unfamiliar vegetable. All the descriptive words students suggest may be listed on the chalkboard in categories according to the sense involved. Help children see that some descriptive words fit into more than one category—for example, some textures can be seen as well as felt. In the process, we are moving from sensory impressions to words, which will later be shaped into factual accounts of the activity.

Maintain the turnip theme by reading aloud *The Three Little Pigs*, a story in which turnips are integral. The purpose of reading aloud in this case is to provide a variety of stories that children can discuss. Walmsley and Walp (1990) described at length the wider variety of purposes reading aloud serves. Since a major purpose of this particular unit is to encourage children to compare and contrast different versions of the same tale, you could get copies of the following books to use:

Bishop, Gavin. (1990). *The three little pigs.* New York: Scholastic.

> This large-sized version features pleasantly casual watercolor and pen line drawings in a contemporary setting (Mrs. Pig is shown beside her swimming pool). In this version, the first two pigs do get eaten, and the episode of going to the fair is included. The scratchy crosshatching gives a nervous energy to these pictures that could effectively be contrasted with the crosshatching in illustrations by Blegvad.

Blegvad, Erik. (1980). *The three little pigs.* New York: Atheneum.

> This small-sized version features dapper, clothed pigs, who must leave their mother because "she was poor and had not enough to keep them." The countryside is distinctly English in appearance. Some of the pictures reflect the reality of the text: the picture of the second pig in the roasting pan with an apple in his mouth, while the wolf wields a pepper mill, is particularly vivid! It's a very elegantly furnished house the third pigs inhabits; when he sits down to dine on wolf, he enjoys candlelight and a bot-

tle of wine. (A video of this is available from Weston Woods Studios, 389 Newton Turnpike, Weston, CT 06883.)

Cauley, Lorinda Bryan. (1980). *The story of the three little pigs.* New York: Putnam.

Children enjoy the brightly bordered, trim illustrations by Cauley, which show the many details, including pieced quilts on the bed and ruffled curtains at the window of the third pig's house. There is some interesting vocabulary; the second pig buys a "bundle of furze." The double-page spread of the fair is crammed with interesting activity and can serve as a lead-off into dramatization.

Hooks, William H. (1989). *The three little pigs and the fox,* with illustrations by S. D. Schindler. New York: Macmillan.

Read this version particularly for the richness of language, which grows from the lively art of storytelling in Appalachia. An author's note introduces this to teachers, and we follow the adventures of Rooter ("a fair-sized shoat"), Oinky ("a real mama's boy"), and Hamlet ("a tiny little girl runt"), who in the end proves clever enough to save them all.

Marshall, James. (1989). *The three little pigs.* New York: Dial Books for Young Readers.

Use this for the clearly tongue-in-cheek approach that contrasts so effectively with the more serious outlook in such other versions as the one by Blegvad. We get a sense of the personalities of the pigs; for example, the first one, responding to the advice from the man selling the straw, tells him, "Mind you own business, thank you." The house built by the third pig is remarkable architecture, full of eccentric details. This includes all the episodes of getting turnips, getting apples, and going to the fair.

Reinl, Edda. (1983). *The 3 little pigs.* Natick, MA: Picture Book Studio USA.

This version allows you to initiate a discussion of artists' media. The book is done in batik, a wax-resist process that in this case results in brilliantly colored, semi-abstract, and highly patterned illustrations. Each of the pigs is distinguished from the others in the text. The first, for example, "read some picture books until he got sleepy" and then took a nap. The way the wolf meets his end is unique. Talk with children about whether they like this way or the more traditional way better.

Ross, Tony. (1983). *The three pigs.* New York: Pantheon Books.

Focus children's attention on the endpapers. Compare these pigs with distinctly different expressions, despite the similarity of their size and color, with the endpapers in Reinl, which show the entire body of each pig, repeated rhythmically to make a pattern. There is some interesting vocabulary to explore; the wolf calls out his repeated refrain "in a treacly voice." The book is full of the idiosyncratic details readers expect from Ross. At the end, the pig gobbles the wolf up "with some asparagus tips and potato puffs."

Rounds, Glen. (1992). *Three little pigs and the big bad wolf.* New York: Holiday House.

In this version, the pigs don't build their houses in the same overt way we see them physically constructing houses in other versions. The first pig, for example, says he can build a house inside a pile of straw he finds. The third pig actually comes upon an abandoned brick house. The wolf in this version is a decidedly emaciated, mangy-

From *The Three Pigs* by Tony Ross, with illustrations by the author (Pantheon, 1983).

looking creature; it is easy to see visually why he is hungry. The typesetting reinforces the drama of the text. When the line reads "And then he ate the little pig!" the size of the type is twice as large as it usually is. There's much use made of capital letters for emphasis as well.

Scieszka, Jon. (1989). *The true story of the three little pigs! by A. Wolf,* illustrated by Lane Smith. New York: Viking Kestrel.

You might choose to start a unit with this version because it is the one most children know; it has become very popular. The idea of narration by one of the other characters is appealing, and the innocent, misunderstood wolf gets children's sympathy. Try having children write the story from the point of view of one of the pigs, after they talk about the first person narration in this book. The illustrations are less realistic than in other books described here, and children delight in some of the details, like the rabbit ears in the mixing bowl!

Trivizas, Eugene. (1993). *The three little wolves and the big bad pig,* illustrated by Helen Oxenbury. New York: McElderry Books.

The stars of this retelling are "three cuddly little wolves with soft fur and fluffy tails" who, despite living in the brick house they've built together, still have trouble eluding the big bad pig. He does indeed have a shifty-eyed expression, and though his trotters

From *The Three Little Wolves and the Big Bad Pig* by Eugene Trivizas, with illustrations by Helen Oxenbury (McElderry, 1993).

are tiny, he's robust in body—clearly a menace to the wolves, amiably playing croquet on the lawn. Oxenbury shows us the clever system the wolves devise for building the concrete house they must construct after the pig destroys the brick one. In the end, rather improbably, they find that kindness overcomes.

Zemach, Margot. (1988). *The three little pigs*. New York: Farrar, Straus & Giroux.

This medium-scaled watercolor and ink line version by a Caldecott medalist features a wolf arrayed in coat and top hat trying to beguile the first two pigs, which he subsequently eats before trying to go for turnips and apples and to the fair with the third one. In the end, the third pig has wolf soup for supper, and the illustration is replete with the wolf's tail hanging out of the pot.

If you want to do some detective work, you might see if you can locate, or if your librarian can help you find, a copy of Virginia Haviland's *Favorite Fairy Tales Told in Italy* (1965). Perhaps you could locate a copy through the interlibrary loan service available to you. Included in this collection is "The Three Goslings" (pp. 67–77), a variation of this story that would interest children.

Listening Experiences

To begin, read one version of the story each day, using as many versions as seems appropriate with the children in your class. Encourage the children to contribute their observations about the story line, the vocabulary used, and the nature of the illustrations. As students listen to each other and observe the teacher recording their comments in a list on the board, they have an opportunity to see the interrelatedness of the language arts. Again, we are moving from sensory impressions through oral language into written language, as children may later follow up this step with compositions describing which of the versions they prefer and why.

Recently, we used the Cauley, Hooks, and Zemach versions with a third-grade class in an urban school.[1] The children were used to being read to and having a sustained silent reading period each day, but they had not done an integrated unit like this one before. We shared these versions because they offer some readily observable differences in language and visuals. We read the books aloud to the entire class, although it is possible for third-grade students to meet in small groups to read a version aloud, analyze it, and report back to the entire class.

Dramatizing

As with most integrated language arts/reading units, teachers should plan ways to include drama activities. Many of the actions in this story can be mimed: the pigs building their houses, pulling turnips and picking apples, examining the churn maker's booth at the fair, and selecting a churn. There are also plenty of scenes for student-generated paired dialogues: the distraught mother pig bidding her sons farewell, the devious wolf beguiling the pig into going apple picking, the clever pig explaining his use of the churn to elude the wolf. To introduce this idea, choose one of your highly verbal children and demonstrate the process of making up words for the characters to say. Then pair all the students, and let each pair create dialogue at the same time. Having everyone work at the same time eliminates self-consciousness (Stewig & Buege, 1994). Follow up the mimes and dialogues by inviting the children to write a narrative to link the scenes together in their own words. Then put the various scenes in sequence and share the improvised presentations with other children to encourage their observing and listening skills.

Another possibility is to follow a suggestion offered by James Moffet and Betty J. Wagner (1983). In classes of older students, the student observers can take notes during the drama presentations and then write up their observations as factual accounts, describing what they saw. This points out effectively for students that several observers who see

---

[1] Thanks to Mrs. Judith Cole, third-grade teacher at Hartford Avenue School, Milwaukee, Wisconsin, and her children for providing a space, a group, and their many ideas.

the same series of events (a dramatization) will notice different aspects of it.

Oral Language

Other oral activities grow naturally. Storytelling can follow watching a filmed version of *The Three Little Pigs*. [You might show the animated version available from Troll Associates (100 Corporate Dr., Mahwah, NJ 07430) or another from SVS (16th Floor, 1700 Broadway, New York, NY 10009).] Let children view the film with the sound turned off and tape record their descriptions of the events. Students can illustrate some of the events in the story, working either in groups or individually. Then the illustrations can be shared with younger students while they listen to the taped versions of the tale. Such cross-grade grouping is always a convenient way to provide an authentic audience for language activities, which Wagner (1985) points out is critical.

Writing

Writing experiences evolve easily from this story. Read the book to the point at which the wolf is threatening to jump down the chimney. Even if the children already know the usual ending, invite them to brainstorm as many other possible endings as they can think of. Generating ideas can serve as a prewriting experience, and the children can select from these ideas in later compositions. You might have each child choose one of the characters and rewrite the story from the point of view of that character. A group discussion can prepare students for writing these narratives. Some sample questions follow:

What were the mother pig's misgivings as she sent her children into the world?

How could the first two pigs have been so gullible while their sibling was more aware of what might happen?

Why didn't the wolf anticipate a trap in the chimney?

For young children, whose inscribing skills are still limited, make arrangements with a teacher of intermediate grades to "borrow" some of her students. These older boys and girls, paired with your youngsters, can provide help in getting the ideas down on paper. In the process, the older students serving as scribes consolidate their own mastery of encoding skills.

Recasting a third person narration into a first person account helps mature children become aware of their own ethnocentrism and how they can move beyond it. They can begin to explore, orally or in writing, the reasons characters do certain things, how they feel about what they do, and what happens to them.

Try a story extension with your class. Invite students to write about what the third pig did the day after dining on boiled wolf. Introduce them to the assignment by asking such questions as: Where did the third pig go the following day? Who did he meet? What did they do? Arrange for students to read their stories to children in a younger class. Such cross-grade sharing provides a tangible audience for any writing task. This activity gives older students the opportunity to respond to and write about classic tales a second time, and students in the intermediate grades enjoy tales that they or the teacher might initially consider too juvenile. Children's writings in response to these activities show the imaginative story creation that can result (Stewig, 1987).

Speaking and Writing

In the third-grade class mentioned earlier, we decided to do a comparison chart to identify differences in the stories and pictures. Rather than structuring the responses ahead of time, it is most helpful to begin with a blank grid and allow children to decide what aspects *they* want to compare. We started with large sheets of brown wrapping paper; the lines were drawn, but the only thing written in was the authors' names. Then we asked children what they wanted to compare. Table 7-1 is a composite of the several sheets of paper on which children identified and then compared these three versions.

Table 7-1

Children's Observations About Differences in Text and Pictures in Versions of the Same Folk Tale

	Title Page	Leaving	Cane	Pig's Response	Apple Tree	Straw House	Butter Churn	Names of Pigs
Zemach	Pigs are outside.	Only mother is crying.	Wolf has a cane.	"Not by the hair on my chinny, chin, chin."	Pig sits above apples, has a basket of apples.	Bound bundles of straw.	No butter churn; a barrel is used.	No names.
Cauley	Pigs are inside.	Pigs and mother are crying.	Wolf does not have a cane.	"Not by the hair of my chinny, chin, chin."	Pig sits below apples; has a sack of apples.	Mound of straw.	Used to frighten wolf.	No names; "the three little pigs."
Hooks	One pig is peeking from behind the house.	There is no crying.	Fox does not have a cane.	"Not on the fuzz of your bushy tail. . . ."	There is no apple tree.	There is no straw house.	Trick fox into hiding in butter churn and throw it in the river.	Rooter, Oinky, Hamlet.

	Fox's/Wolf's Tail	Spots on the Pigs	The Three Little Pigs Have Hairs All Over Their Bodies	Reason They Leave	Eaten Pigs	Wolf Blows	Clothes	Sticks	Rules
Zemach	The *wolf's* tail hangs out of the pot.	One pig has spots.	They have hair all over their bodies.	The mother can't afford to feed them.	Two pigs are eaten.	At the air.	Mom's hat.	Thick.	No rules.
Cauley	Nothing about the *wolf's* tail.	Two pigs have spots.	They have hair on their bodies.	They are too old.	Two pigs are eaten.	At the house.	Mom's scarf.	Thin.	No rules.
Hooks	The *fox's* tail is smashed in the door.	Two pigs have spots.	The pigs have hair.	They are too fat.	None of the pigs is eaten.	Doesn't blow on a house.	Mom's bonnet.	No sticks.	Three rules.

	Meeting Times			What Time the Third Pig got There			Who Builds the House?	Type of Pig	Pot of . . .	Color of Bricks	Title	The Straw House
	Turnips	Apples	Fair	Turnips	Apples	Fair						
Zemach	10	9	8	9	8	7	All three pigs.	All males.	Soup.	Light red bricks.	*The Three Little Pigs*	Shows pig building a straw house.
Cauley	6	5	3	5	4		All three pigs.	All males.	Water.	Dark red bricks.	*Joseph Jacobs' The Story of the Three Little Pigs*	Does not show pig building straw house.
Hooks	Not included.			Not included.			Only one pig.	Two males, one female.	Pot of nothing.	The house is made of gray stones.	*The Three Little Pigs and the Fox*	Stone house; no straw house.

	Second Pig Uses	Turnips	At Fair	Turnip Field	Transporting Sticks/Furze	Color of Wolf	Back of Book	Name for Mother
Zemach	Sticks.	Basket.	Barrel knocked down.	No scarecrow.	In wheelbarrow.	Grey.	Nothing.	Momma pig.
Cauley	Furze.	Potfull.	Butter churn frightened away.	Has a scarecrow.	In arms.	Brown.	Picture of pigs.	Old sow.
Hooks	Doesn't get a chance to build house.	No turnips.	No fair.	No turnip field.	No sticks.	Brown fox.	Wood.	Mama pig.

The advantage of starting with a blank grid is clearly apparent here. This group of children came up with several aspects to compare that didn't occur to us as teachers. A more extensive reporting on the art in the books used in this unit and on children's talking and writing about it is available in Stewig (1992).

Reading

Though in this case the teacher initially read the versions to the class, children themselves chose to go back to the texts while doing the comparison charts to verify the accuracy of details they wanted to put on the charts. In addition to this, other versions of the tale, like those by Lang (1965), Laird (1981), or Haviland (1965), could be made available for individuals to use at the reading table in independent work time. All three of these are engagingly different. Because they are older, or in the case of Laird from a small publisher, they may be more difficult to obtain than the ones on which we built our unit activities.

Art for Talking and Writing

On a succeeding day, we introduced the idea of doing vegetable prints. The bunch of turnips with tops provided many experiences in touching, tasting, smelling, and talking about sensory input, as children described their reactions to a vegetable that was largely unfamiliar to them. We arranged the turnips from largest to smallest, located and measured the largest and smallest leaves, and weighed the turnips. All of this resulted in a lot of talk and could have been recorded on data observation charts. These were teacher-initiated activities. But once again, in an effort to see how children themselves were thinking, we asked how else, in addition to size, the turnips could be arranged or grouped. Among other responses, one child came up and arranged them on a continuum from the turnip that had the most purple to the one that had the least. Another child grouped them into two categories: the bumpy turnips and the smooth ones.

The children were encouraged to "write something" about what we had been doing. That sounds like a very unfocused question, and it was done that way on purpose. We were interested in finding out which aspects of the set of experiences the children would choose to write about. We pointed out that they could either do a retelling of their own or describe for someone who had not been there what went on in the class sessions. Following are some of the pieces of writing that resulted.

THE PRINT OF A LEAF

We got some greens and a tray and paint and a roller and we put the paint in the tray. Then we put the leaf in the tray full of paint and used the roller to paint the leaf and flatten it. Next we turned the leaf over and rolled it on the other side. Then we took the leaf and put it on a piece of paper and put another piece of paper on top of the leaf. Then we took the leaf out of the paper and took the pieces of paper apart and we looked at the prints. I liked my prints!

Fred

The turnips tasted a little strong but they tasted good. The greens smelled like rotten pumpkins. When we cut the turnips open they smelled like dirty potatoes. They smelled like cabbage when they weren't cut open. The turnips felt like wax. The stem of the turnips felt like slime. The greens felt like a leaf from a bush.

James

My favorite thing to do was to paint the leaves by dipping the leaves in the paint. The color of my leaf was a greenish blue. I am glad that it came out that color. Then we made a stamp out of a turnip. The color of my stamp was yellow and now it is green. We tasted the leaves and turnips. The leaves smell like the inside of a pumpkin. The leaves tasted like lettuce. The turnips tasted sweet in the inside and hot on the outside.

Claire

Our classroom learned about turnips and greens. We learned about that by reading *The Three Little Pigs*. If you never seen a turnip, I could tell you. The turnip is shaped into a ball. The color of a turnip is purple and white. A turnip smells like a potato. They taste like cabbage and onions. Here is a recipe!

Turnip Noodle Soup

3 cups of water

2 turnips

1 bag of noodles/pasta

2 tsps garlic

2 tsps of hot sauce

Cut tomato in little bits. Cut the turnips the same way as you did the tomato. Put the 3 cups of water in a pot. Then put the noodles in the pot. Put the oven on 375°. Then put the tomato and the turnips in the pot. Then add the garlic and hot sauce in the pot too. When you get done putting in all of the ingredients, stir the soup up. Then when the soup is done you can eat it and say, "I am a very good cook and I did not know that." The End!!!

Patrice

The Leaf

The leaf is blue. It tastes like cabbage and it's a little spicy. Would you want to taste the blue leaf or the green leaf? I would want to taste both of the leaves. The reason is that I never tasted the blue before. I've tasted the green leaf before. The reason why I tasted the green leaf and not the blue leaf is because the green leaf is a vegetable and the blue leaf is like paint on a wall. I had fun painting the leaf. Would you want to paint a leaf?

Amy

How to Make a Leaf Print

1. Pick a leaf out.
2. Put washable paint in a pan.
3. Get a paint roller.
4. Smooth out the leaf.
5. Get a piece of paper and a paper towel.
6. Put the leaf in the pan.
7. Put paint on the roller and roll the leaf out.
8. Take out the leaf, put it on the paper, and cover it with the paper towel.
9. Let it dry out, and you have a leaf print!

Rollin

We learned about the three little pigs and how the stories were different. One reason is that the wolf said he will come for you so we both can go and pick turnips. But the little pig got up an hour earlier. So when the wolf got there he asked the little pig "Are you ready?" And the little pig said that he already had picked turnips and got a pot of them ready for dinner. The next day the wolf said he will come for you and we both can go to the fair. But the little pig got up an hour earlier and went to the fair when the little pig was coming out of the fair he saw the wolf and hid in a butter churn and he turned the butter churn over and it started rolling down. The wolf saw that and he ran. And the wolf never got to go to the fair. I only told you one story.

Austin

Fortunately, the conclusion of the unit coincided with parent-teacher conferences at the end of the reporting period. Thus, the host classroom teacher had the writing and the vegetable prints on display so parents would know what the children had been doing. Seeing their own child's work in the context of the work by the entire class gives parents a much clearer idea of the child's work than would a letter grade.

This unit extended over several days, providing children opportunities to listen, speak, read, and write. The dramatizations disappeared as soon as they were finished, although we could indeed have videotaped them to have the tapes available during the parent-teacher meetings as well. The pieces of writing became, after they served their purpose at the conferences, something the children proudly took home. This particular school does not as yet have a portfolio system in place. If it had, copies of the stories could have been included there as a record for the teacher next year.

Such are the ways a piece of traditional literature can provide a springboard into an integrated language arts unit. But such an integrated unit need not be based on only traditional tales. If you're hungry, try growing a unit; lots of books contain seeds. For example, plant *Avocado Baby* by John Burningham (1993) in your classroom and see how it grows. It's a thoroughly charming, though somewhat improbable, contemporary tale of a puny baby who gathers extraordinary strength from eating an avocado. Many other children's books provide such organic opportunities as described here. Your language arts program will gather strength as you grow into wholeness from such books as these and others that you can locate and nurture into a flourishing unit.

A Unit Integrating Across the Curriculum

In addition to integrating within the language arts, another possibility is to develop units that reach across the curriculum, incorporating other areas like science, math, social studies, health, and the arts. This section reports on the work of a first-grade teacher who has been developing this sort of program for several years, planning experiences that help her inner-city, mostly minority children sense the interrelatedness of subject matter.

A Flexible Schedule

What does an integrated day look like? Since this may be quite different from the approach used when you were in elementary school yourself, we'll begin by describing how the day unfolds in this first grade. This is a general description of structure, although Ms. Sylvester allows the time demarcations to be fluid, depending on the children's involvement.[2] After this structural description, we'll turn our attention to the content of a sample unit.

8:30 to 9:15 A.M.—Writing Workshop Children come into the room, take their writing folders from the place they are stored, and begin to

[2] Thanks to Ms. Christine Sylvester, first-grade teacher at LaFollette School, Milwaukee, Wisconsin, and her children for providing a space, a group, and their many ideas.

write. Every day opens this way, thus presenting a pleasant, anticipatable beginning to the day. Some children write about their own personal experiences, others continue writing about some aspect of the general organizing theme currently being used in the room, and still others may be working on imaginative stories unrelated to either of these two possibilities. At some time during the forty-five-minute period, the teacher does a directed mini-lesson on an aspect of writing that she has observed will benefit the children.

These writing folders are in essence rough draft notebooks, and it is from them that the children themselves decide which of their many pieces they will choose to bring to final, public form. During this time block, the teacher confers with individual children, helping them edit their work, asking questions, and giving suggestions. Also during this time, as children are ready, they may take a "storyboard," a duplicated premade sheet with eight blank panels. Into this they fit their computer-generated texts, which they cut and paste to fit, and then add drawings for each of the panels. Following this, the panels are folded, cut, and stapled, and a small book results.

Ms. Sylvester begins this routine early in the fall, demonstrating it by doing a group-created class book. Later, children choose a partner and replicate the experience the teacher has modeled. Then they move into the stage where they work with a partner or work alone. As children's attention span increases, the time devoted to this part of the program grows longer. During the conferences and as she is observing the children at work, the teacher keeps a record of the stages various children

The teacher is conferring individually with students as they prepare their reports after individual study of a group topic.

are at. Different working tempos mean that at any given time some children are beginning a new piece of writing while others are finishing correcting mechanics on their final draft.

9:15 to 10:00 A.M.—Reading Workshop   During workshop time, the teacher leads small group work, independent reading, large group share, and a regularly scheduled phonics mini-lesson. In this block of time, children are involved in different ways, but the general focus is on activities related to literature.

In heterogeneous work groups of nine or ten, children choose to be involved in independent reading, in shared or guided reading, or in creative drama activities that grow from the books they are reading. Some of the children are reading independently. On Mondays, children pick out three books in categories the teacher has helped them understand to be *easy, just right,* and *challenging*. This terminology was described in Chapter 5. Children may also choose from magazines the teacher has provided that relate to the organizing theme. This is what is called sustained noisy reading (described in Chapter 5). This is not a silent reading time because Ms. Sylvester realizes that at this age children may need to be able to vocalize as they are reading. Children know that by Friday they are to have chosen which of the three books or magazines they'd like to share in the total group. During this time, as they find it appropriate, individual children write in their record books a reaction to what they are reading, telling about a favorite part, giving a reason why they are choosing what they'll share, or writing anything else they want.

While independent reading is going on, the teacher is leading shared reading or guided reading experiences. These two types of reading experiences were described more completely in Chapter 5, so they won't be reexplained here. Or the teacher may be helping a small group of children decide which scene they'll dramatize for the class from a story one of them has read. These activities take place four days a week.

On Fridays, this time block is used for "The Reading Club," which is whole-group book sharing. This activity began with just ten minutes a day in September, but the teacher told children she was going to increase it a minute each day. A kitchen timer keeps track of the minutes; the teacher began using one so she wouldn't be the one to bring this pleasant period to a close. She reports that the children really enjoy having the timer going. Once, when it broke, the children were very concerned until another was available.

10:00 to 10:15 A.M.—Phonics Block   Ms. Sylvester feels it is important to do something with the information she gathers about children as she is monitoring their individual writing and reading. So in this time period she brings the entire group together and teaches a brief phonics lesson, the content of which is drawn from their own needs.

Sometimes she makes up the content of these lessons herself. At other times she uses commercially produced phonics materials, picking those activities that will benefit the largest number of children and creating her own sequence, which varies from year to year.

10:15 to 11:00 A.M.—Special Subjects   In a sequence through the week, children go to teachers in music, science, art, library, and ethnic heritage. (This last is a program designed to help children understand and appreciate their African American heritage.)

11:15 to 11:45 A.M.—Lunch

11:45 to 12:10 P.M.—Quiet Time and Teacher Read-Aloud   Ms. Sylvester reads aloud to the class, picking a book that reinforces the theme, one by a favorite author or illustrator, or perhaps one that will lead into an understanding of relationships between books. For example, if the theme involved a fictional story about pets (like *My New Boy* by Joan Phillips, 1986), the reading might be an informational book about pets (like *Koko's Kitten* by Francine Patterson, 1985). This would allow for discussion of the differences in form apparent between fiction and nonfiction. Often these theme books are made available for children to enjoy individually later as they review the pictures and remember the story, while perhaps recognizing some or many of the words used. Or the teacher may read a book to children that she thinks they will enjoy but that would be too difficult for them to read by themselves, thus stretching their awareness of literary qualities in books to come. For example, you might read parts of Desmond Morris's *The World of Animals* (1993), a book more difficult than children this age could read themselves, but one enriched with helpful illustrations students will return to on their own.

12:30 to 1:00 P.M.—Math Time   Children work in two large groups doing activities that in some way relate to the theme. For example, one of the theme-related math activities was keeping a running graph showing how many minutes they were reading.

1:00 to 1:30 P.M.—Theme-Related Whole-Class Activity   During this time, the teacher engages children in viewing a film or tape, in listening to and asking questions of a guest speaker, or in doing another teacher-led activity that extends their understanding of the theme. This is the time in the program where the veterinarian spoke (described later in the content section).

1:30 to 2:30 P.M.—Center Time   This block is based on the High Scope approach to early childhood education of involving children in three steps of their own learning (Hohmann, Banet & Weikart, 1978). In brief summary, children are to (1) plan it, (2) do it, and (3) review it. Children select which center they will go to. These include a house center (with creative dramatics possibilities), an art center, a block center, a quiet center (incorporating tapes and headphones for listening, books, and puzzles), a writing center, and a math center. The content of these changes when the theme changes, so that much—though not all—of the choices within the center are theme-related. At the close of center time, children return to the large group to take part in the third stage—reviewing it, or sharing what they did.

CONTENT OF THE THEMES

Sometimes the teacher chooses the theme, at other times it evolves between the teacher and the children, and at yet other times some outside influence affects the theme choice. For example, Ms. Sylvester and her group were given a pair of parakeets. This led into a more general unit on pets, which will be described here.

In the writing workshop, children are encouraged to make a free choice of topic. Since the parakeets arrived in early September, however, when the children were still learning how the writing workshop process worked, Ms. Sylvester suggested to children that they write about their pets. In their small group time, she made available many books about them, including several big books that they used together. During writing, she noticed that a lot of children wrote about cats, so she and the children did a word family activity, going through the alphabet systematically to see how many other -at words could be made. As a follow-up to that, she tied into art, using *Looking at Paintings. Cats* by Peggy Roalf (1992) from a superb new series of art books organized about many topics children explore in the elementary curriculum, like horses, families, and circuses. What distinguishes this series is the lucid writing and the full-page, full-color illustrations of the paintings, representing many different time periods and cultures.

The theme tied into their math because they graphed how many kids wrote about cats. Math series today generally give much more attention to stories and poems about aspects of math by recognized authors than they did previously. *Curriculum and Evaluation Standards for School Mathematics* (1989) published by the National Council of Teachers of Mathematics emphasized the role of language arts in learning math, and this publication resulted in major changes in the way this subject is taught. For instance, in the *Math Anthology* from the program entitled "I Can" (Macmillan/McGraw-Hill, 1993), many well-known authors are included. The anthology includes such works as "Annie's Pet" by Barbara Brenner and "Square As a House" by Karla Kuskin.

As another math activity, the teacher provided cut-out photographs of animals with prices attached. She then gave kids paper money. The children's task was to write a problem describing what they did and

From *Who Says a Dog Goes Bow-Wow?* by Hank De Zutter, with illustrations by Suse MacDonald (Doubleday, 1993).

what the results were. For example, a picture of a parakeet was marked $4. Each child had been given $5. How could they write the story problem describing what they did?

To tie into a pet theme, teachers might make available in a math center *Pigs Will Be Pigs* by Amy Axelrod (1994), a book that provides fun and practice in a basic look at money. As the pigs' adventures unfold, children can practice addition, subtraction, multiplication, and division, and in the process think about how these pigs would be as pets.

Talking about their pets revealed that several children had dogs. Children can enjoy the pictures of dogs in *Breathtaking Noses* by Hana Machotka (1992), an information book that focuses on just this specialized part of many different animals. Talking about sounds their dogs make could lead children into enjoying *Who Says a Dog Goes Bow-wow?* by Hank De Zutter (1993), a fascinating exploration of the various ways animal sounds are represented in different languages.

Choice time involved many theme-related activities. In art, children could draw their own pet or a pet they would like to own. They made three-dimensional representations of pets out of playdough. Children had seen how Barbara Reid used plasticene in making the many animals she depicts in *Two by Two* (1992), a book in their classroom library, and they were interested in trying to make their own animals out of a similar material.

Pet puppets were included in the house center, and this led to much oral language as children developed dialogue for these puppets.

The math center included a large quantity of plastic links. Children decided to put them together to make a leash, and then they could walk their pet. Creative drama was embedded in the math center, as one child was the pet and another the walker. Then children made a record of how many links they needed to make a leash for a pet of a particular size. The writing center included rubber stamps, and children chose the ones about pets to illustrate stories they wrote. In the block area children made a cage for a pet and practiced writing directions for the steps in the process.

In the quiet area, the teacher had placed tapes of animal sounds and tapes of stories about pets. This center also includes books of two types. One type is books the teacher has used in group time, which children revisit on their own. For instance, youngsters enjoyed looking again at the watercolor illustrations in Jim Arnosky's *A Kettle of Hawks* (1990) even though they couldn't read the words themselves. The teacher had used this, an information book about terms for groups of animals, like a *cloud* of tadpoles and a *colony* of ants. The second type of books are simple books children can use on their own, which the teacher didn't introduce to the entire group. For instance, *Baby Animals* by Angela Royston (1992), which features fine full-color photographs, is easy enough for children to enjoy by themselves. This center also includes tape or record sets, so children can both see and hear the words, developing the meaning of the story. Such sets, available from many publishers, usually include a tape and a paperback copy of the book. In this classroom, children especially enjoyed *Arthur Goes to Camp* by Marc Brown, *Curious George* by H. A. Rey, and an information set, *Panther Dream* by Bob and Wendy Weir.

Expanding Themes

Often themes develop in ways not originally envisioned by the teacher or the class. For example, in the pet unit, one child was concerned that it not be limited only to pets because she wanted to learn about wild animals. To facilitate this, the teacher located and brought to class several of the fine new information books on wild animals. Children enjoyed looking at pictures and reading as much as they could of such books as *Never Kiss an Alligator!* by Colleen Stanley Bare (1989) and *Jane Goodall's Animal World. Gorillas* (1990). In addition, she showed the entire group the video "Pets and Their Wild Relatives" available from National Geographic (17th and M Streets NW, Washington, DC 20036). This is characteristic of themes; they can and should be preplanned because they are not simply haphazard. On the other hand, they often take on a life of their own, which necessitates the teacher finding new materials or people resources while the unit is underway. Ms. Sylvester hadn't planned before beginning to make this connection between tame and

Children are consulting a wide variety of materials during their integrated unit on dinosaurs. This theme of extinct animals grew from an earlier unit on common domestic animals.

wild animals. When she had taught the unit in previous years, this connection hadn't been brought up by a child. Because it did this year, the unit turned out to be different, even though the title of it was the same as in previous years.

A theme like pets can tie into social studies concerns, as a teacher reaches into the community. For example, if your city has a Humane Society, a field trip there to find out what its goals are and how it operates could be included in your unit. Or if there is a veterinarian nearby, perhaps that person would come to be a classroom resource, talking with children about pet care, costs involved, and anything else children might be interested in. A trip to a zoo might be introduced using Tana Hoban's *A Children's Zoo* (1985) or Hana Machotka's *What Do You Do at a Petting Zoo?* (1990). *Dear Bronx Zoo* by Joyce Altman and Sue Goldberg (1990) is a collection of answers to questions children ask about zoos.

Always before we do an experience like this, either a field trip or a classroom visitor, we involve children in generating questions to which they want answers. As a follow-up to the experiences, we spend time developing a group chart story about the event and involve children in writing thank-you notes to the people involved. An actual letter really mailed to a live person provides a much more meaningful context in which to teach letter-writing skills than does the usual lesson in a textbook series.

Partnerships with Parents

To encourage parent involvement, this teacher regularly sends home a class newsletter to report on what the current theme is and to involve parents and guardians in their children's learning. One issue included an invitation telling parents they were welcome to bring the child's pet to school. Even this encouraged children in generating language. One of the children reported that his pet couldn't come "because he drags his leg." Another child asked, "Do you mean he's handicapped?" and the discussion went from there about the meaning of that word.

As another way of fostering home and school relationships, Ms. Sylvester videotapes classroom learning experiences, recording various aspects of several different days during the unit. She then makes these available for children to check out and take home. Although this is an inner-city school that serves many poor children, the teacher became aware that many of the homes had video playback equipment. The response from the parents to this opportunity to see the classroom in action has been, in Ms. Sylvester's words, "unbelievable." In this school, attendance at parent-teacher events is often low because of the difficulty single, working parents have in getting to school at a prescribed time. This way of communicating the life in the classroom with parents was well worth the effort it takes to do the videotaping.

Summary

Putting the pieces of a program together is the greatest challenge and the most satisfying aspect of developing an integrated curriculum. More and more teachers are discarding preestablished sequences of learning and tailoring the learning experiences to the needs of the particular group of children they are working with in any given year. To do this, many early childhood teachers turn to literature as the base for the curriculum, not only in language arts but also across the curriculum. Rather than thinking about unvarying time blocks that segment the day, teachers are organizing in larger units to emphasize how one subject leads into another and how all the components relate to each other. Earlier in this book we devoted our attention separately to the various strands of an integrated program to build your knowledge base. Here, we have described how two excellent teachers, committed to helping children see the interrelationships among topics, have organized learning in their classrooms. We have done this so you could see how all the pieces of a program fit together. Now, we hope you are well equipped to go out to teach, ready to meet the challenge of creating your own integrated program that is responsive to the needs of children.

Suggestions for Further Reading

Busching, B. A., & Schwartz, J. I. (Eds.). (1983). *Integrating the language arts in the elementary school.* Urbana, IL: National Council of Teachers of English.

In an important early book on this topic, the editors drew together nearly two dozen writers, including college professors, elementary classroom teachers, and administrators, to provide a wide-ranging look at the process and product of integrating. The articles are short and grouped into helpful categories—for example, integrating "within one language mode," "within different language modes," and "with other subject matter." A concluding section focuses on such issues as home-school relationships, teaching monolingual and multilingual children, and planning in-service education. Each chapter includes its own bibliography, augmented at the end with an annotated bibliography. The book would be useful for students entering education or teachers making changes in their curricula. The writing is direct and pragmatic. In addition, it represents the values of the editors (the chapter on Native American studies) and the enthusiasm of the writers (the chapter on how drama leads to writing).

Crawford, L. W. (1993). *Language and literacy learning in multicultural classrooms.* Boston: Allyn & Bacon.

This practical book is designed to assist teachers in developing language arts through multicultural themes and topics. The activities, embedded in literature, focus on race, ethnicity, and culture. Eight chapters thoroughly cover teaching in a multicultural classroom. The final section, The Teacher Resource Kit of over 100 pages, provides detailed model lessons, an exhaustive list of recommended books, and a wide variety of evaluation formats.

Cullinan, Bernice. (1992). *Invitation to read: More children's literature in the reading program.* Newark, DE: International Reading Association.

This book, which contains fourteen chapters by different writers, may well become one of the best resources for the "teacher of the nineties." The prologue discusses whole language programs while encouraging reading aloud and providing activities that support the use of literature in reading and writing.

Every chapter contains research-backed ideas with immediate classroom application. The applications are highlighted in an easy-to-use boxed format, captioned as *Teaching Ideas.* This resource connects each chapter, providing a continuous and connected approach to activities without in the process becoming a "cookbook." The chapters are grouped under broad topics: Genre Studies (including a chapter on books for the emergent reader), Thematic Units (including an author study on Tomie de Paola), and Putting It All Together (organizing the program).

As the reader peruses each selection, there is much to enjoy. Concrete examples are used by Dianne L. Monson in her section on "Realistic Fiction and the Real World." M. Jean Greenlaw discusses informational books in Chapter 4, which deals with both current and historical events, including the impact of Columbus. "Enriching the Arts and Humanities" by Sam Leaton Sebesta connects literature with the visual arts, drama, and music.

The popular alphabet book, *Chicka Chicka Boom Boom,* by Bill Martin, Jr., and J. Archambault is the topic of a chapter that provides activities for both pre-K and fourth-grade students.

A particularly interesting, timely chapter is Rudine Sims Bishop's titled "Extending Multicultural Understanding." The chapter is divided into the following topics: Start with Information, Folklore, Realistic Fiction, Poetry, and A Vehicle for Change (a book list that alone makes this chapter valuable).

The book contains a chapter on award-winning books from five English-speaking countries (with an excellent book list), a comprehensive chapter on "Responding to Literature: Activities for Exploring Books," a chapter on readers at risk, and even a chapter on censorship. This is an outstanding resource book, with something for everyone.

Feitstritzer, Patricia. (1979, May). Entering the world of children. *Momentum*, pp. 11–23.

Drama as it could be — integral, not peripheral, to education—is described in this report of the work of the Austrian philosopher Rudolph Steiner. In the Waldorf schools based on his ideas, then numbering 165 around the world, storytelling and creative dramatics are basic in language arts, history, science, and math. A class may spend as much as eight weeks (daily classes) on a single story as the teacher uses the material to challenge curiosity and aid concentration.

Harris, V. J. (Ed.). (1992). *Teaching multicultural literature in grades K–8.* Norwood, MA: Christopher-Gordon.

A comprehensive resource for teachers, this book's beginning chapters examine the politics of children's literature and the importance of choosing culturally authentic portrayals of ethnic and racial groups. Literature has been selected by experts in all major cultures and arranged in separate chapters. Materials have been listed, annotated, and analyzed, with suggestions for instructional activities. The final chapter is replete with information on other resources.

Hollingsworth, S. H., Teel, K., & Minarik, L. (1992). Learning to teach Aaron: A beginning teacher's story of literacy instruction in an urban classroom. *Journal of Teacher Education, 43,* 116–127.

This is the story of how a teacher, in the third year of her career, learned to teach Aaron, an African American second-grader. Although Aaron had many problems, this beginning instructor struggled to modify her curriculum, and Aaron did eventually learn to read and write. For anyone new to a classroom of culturally diverse students, this article offers help from a peer.

Johnson, T. D., & Louis, D. R. (1990). *Bringing it all together.* Portsmouth, NH: Heinemann.

The authors discuss the distinction between integration and correlation of different subjects. In an integrated program, certain important aspects of two or more subjects are deployed to achieve goals centered around a substantial theme; correlation occurs when a trivial topic is used as a justification to tie together unrelated activities.

The authors' philosophy is that correlation doesn't help children perceive their world as a dynamic set of interconnections. Successful integration, they maintain, is founded on a substantial conceptual base. They recommend using literature as a springboard for formulating units around topic, form, structure, or theme.

The book includes numerous sample lessons and units. These activities are based on a theme or within a structure. For example, the book contains a week-long project for second grade on a plot structure called "Home Is Best," in which a small defenseless character leaves home, enters a dangerous world, and is threatened. The character escapes and returns to home, which is warm, loving, and safe. Numerous charts, daily lesson plans, and book lists are provided.

This is an excellent resource guide for the (K–5) teacher who already believes in integrating the curriculum. It contains more concrete and connected activities than most resource books.

Lehr, Susan. (1991). *The child's developing sense of theme.* New York: Teachers College.

This resource book deals with research on how children construct meanings from their readings and practical application in the classroom of these findings. These meanings are often different from adults' expectations (Piaget and Applebee). Lehr stresses that children *can* and *do* understand the concept of theme in books:

> *Given time to think, time to speak, and open-ended questions about the text, many children will offer their views of meaning in narrative. Listening is a key factor in this process. Children need time to formulate their thoughts, and they need the freedom to speak openly without fear of being labeled wrong.*

This philosophy has implications in all subject areas. Children need encouraging contexts in which to query and offer insights. Lehr feels that educators must take part of the blame for teaching children not to think on their own and for teaching children that there is always a right answer.

Thinking in terms of theme encourages thinking abstractly. Research indicates that children interactively construct meaning with others, so oral discussion is critical in developing a sense of theme. Much exposure to children's literature correlates highly with the child's level of thematic awareness. This suggests we must provide students with a rich literature background in a variety of genres.

Thinking in terms of theme also encourages critical thinking. The book contains suggestions for the classroom teacher to involve different levels of thought and questioning across the curriculum. The author describes the uses of book discussions, comparison charts, informal drama, and response journals, helpful for teachers in K–8.

Thompson, G. (1991). *Teaching through themes.* New York: Scholastic Professional Books.

Theme teaching, which presents topics that have meaning to children and ideas that they can use in their everyday life, offers opportunities to set up an environment that fosters and encourages process learning. Teaching through themes allows the teacher to integrate learning and allows children to explore a particular topic in depth.

It is paramount that the unit connects learning to the children's individual world, that the children understand the purpose of the lesson (Why am I learning this?), the meaning of the lesson (What am I learning?), and the function of the theme (How does the theme or activity work?).

Theme teaching's real purpose is to give the children opportunities to spend time researching, thinking, writing, reading, and observing a specific topic. It can cover many areas of the curriculum.

The book includes several thematic units for both younger children and older children. The units for younger children (K–3) are People, Friendship, and Habitats. Each unit has an introduction, selected readings with a lesson plan that includes activities, a culminating activity, a bibliography (which includes suggested poetry sources as well as video and fine arts), and a list of related themes.

Each theme moves across the curriculum, providing activities in writing, social studies/language arts, physical education, science, and creative arts.

According to the author, this type of teaching is a full circle of learning and sharing. The teacher starts with what the child knows, builds to what he or she wants to know, and then finishes with what has been learned.

Virginia Department of Education. (1990). *Taking a close look at oral language.* Richmond: Commonwealth of Virginia.

This is a useful brief pamphlet, only ten pages long, that summarizes simply the justification for planning an oral language strand in a language arts curriculum, the ways teachers can ensure student improvement, and a concluding evaluation checklist that curriculum committees can use in evaluating current programs. The emphasis is on succinct language, based on research, but specific references are not given.

Weaver, C. (1990). *Understanding whole language. From principles to practice.* Portsmouth, NH: Heinemann.

Whole language is a term widely used, yet often not completely understood. In practice, most teachers on both sides of this artificial fence combine elements of traditional and whole language models in their classrooms. Weaver's book clearly defines what whole language is and is not in a classroom environment in which "language is kept whole, not fragmented into 'skills'" (p. 6). Yet, as Weaver demonstrates, skills are part of the whole, and teachers still teach.

References

Busching, B. A., & Schwartz, J. I. (Eds.). (1983). *Integrating the language arts in the elementary school.* Urbana, IL: National Council of Teachers of English.

Diamond, B. (1982). Making more time for teaching. *Communication Quarterly, 5*(1), 2.

Hohmann, M., Banet, B., & Weikart, D. (1978). *Young children in action: A manual for preschool educators.* Ypsilanti, MI: High/Scope Press.

Lipson, M., Valencia, S. W., Wixson, K. W., & Peters, C. W. (1993, April). Integration and thematic teaching: Integration to improve teaching and learning. *Language Arts, 70*(4), 252–263.

Math Anthology. (1994). New York: Macmillan/McGraw Hill.

Moffett, J., & Wagner, B. J. (1983). *Student-centered language arts and reading, K–13* (3rd ed.). Boston: Houghton Mifflin.

National Council of Teachers of Mathematics. (1989). *Curriculum and evaluation standards for school mathematics.* Reston, VA: NCTM.

Schmidt, W. H. (1985). The uses of curriculum integration in language arts instruction: A study of six classrooms. *Journal of Curriculum Studies, 17*(3), 305–320.

Stewig, J. W. (1987). Joseph Jacobs' English fairy tales: A legacy for today. In P. Nodelman (Ed.), *Touchstones: Reflections on the best in children's literature* (pp. 128–139). West Lafayette, IN: Children's Literature Association.

———. (1992). The interlinking of text and pictures. A study of "The Three Pigs." In G. D. Schmidt & D. R. Hettinga (Eds.), *Sitting at the feet of the past. Retelling the North American folktale for children* (pp. 155–170). Westport, CN: Greenwood Press.

Stewig, J. W., & Buege, C. (1994). *Dramatizing literature in whole language classrooms*. New York: Teachers College Press.

Wagner, B. J. (1985). ERIC/RCS report: Integrating the language arts. *Language Arts, 62*(5), 558–561.

Walmsley, S. A., & Walp, T. P. (1990). Integrating literature and composing into the language arts curriculum: Philosophy and practice. *The Elementary School Journal, 90*(3), 252–274.

Walp, T. P., & Walmsley, S. A. (1989). Instructional and philosophical congruence: Neglected aspects of coordination. *Reading Teacher, 42*(6), 364–368.

Children's Books

Altman, Joyce, and Goldberg, Sue. (1990). *Dear Bronx Zoo*. New York: Macmillan.

Arnosky, Jim. (1990). *A kettle of hawks*. New York: Lothrop, Lee & Shepard.

Axelrod, Amy. (1994). *Pigs will be pigs*. New York: Four Winds Press.

Bare, Colleen Stanley. (1989). *Never kiss an alligator!* New York: Cobblehill Books.

Brown, Marc. (n.d.). *Arthur goes to camp*. Boston: Little, Brown, cassette and paperback book.

Burningham, John. (1993). *Avocado baby*. New York: HarperCollins.

De Zutter, Hank. (1993). *Who says a dog goes bow-wow?* New York: Doubleday.

Goodall, Jane. (1990). *Gorillas*. New York: Atheneum.

Haviland, Virginia (Reteller). (1965). "The Three Goslings." In *Favorite Fairy Tales Told in Italy* (pp. 67–77). Boston: Little, Brown.

Hoban, Tana. (1985). *A children's zoo*. New York: Greenwillow Books.

Laird, Donivee Martin. (1981). *The three little Hawaiian pigs and the magic shark*. Honolulu: Barnaby Books.

Lang, Andrew (Ed.). (1965). "The Three Little Pigs." In *The Green Fairy Book* (pp. 100–105). New York: Dover Publications.

Machotka, Hana (1990). *What do you do at a petting zoo?* New York: Morrow Junior Books.

———. (1992). *Breathtaking noses*. New York: Morrow Junior Books.

Morris, Desmond. (1993). *The world of animals*. New York: Viking Press.

Patterson, Francine. (1985). *Koko's kitten*. New York: Scholastic.

Phillips, Joan. (1986). *My new boy*. New York: Random House.

Reid, Barbara. (1992). *Two by two*. New York: Scholastic.

Rey, H. A. (n.d.). *Curious George*. Boston: Houghton Mifflin, cassette and paperback book.

Roalf, Peggy. (1992). *Cats*. New York: Hyperion Books for Children.

Royston, Angela. (1992). *Baby animals*. New York: Aladdin Books.

Weir, Bob and Wendy. (n.d.). *Panther dream*. New York: Hyperion, cassette and paperback book.

Index

T

Tafuri, Nancy, 261
Tales from the Enchanted World, 151
Talking Eggs, The, 144–145
Talk throughs, 210–212
Tape recording, 105, 117, 141, 143, 157, 166, 205, 280, 307
Taylor, Barbara, 123
Taylor, D., 40, 178
Teacher modeling, 76, 96–97, 201, 204, 207, 213–214
Teacher read-alouds, 215–216, 304
Teacher think-alouds, 207
Teale, W., 30, 42, 178–179, 226, 283
Teeny Tiny, 226
Television, and listening, 92
Temple, C., R. Nathan, F. Temple, and N. Burris, 241, 249
Text, 177–178, 190–191
Thaler, Mike, 212
Thematic units, 221–223
Themes, 35, 208, 216, 225, 303–308, 312
Theodore and the Talking Mushroom, 110
There's a Train Going by My Window, 155
Think alouds, 207, 213, 260–261
This Old Man, 61
Three Bears, The, 226
Three Blind Mice, 138–141
Three Jovial Huntsmen, 70
Three Little Pigs, The, 290–293
Three Little Pigs and the Big Bad Wolf, The, 35
Three Little Pigs and the Fox, The, 291
Through the Looking Glass, 20–21
Thy Friend, Obadiah, 57
Timbre, 106
Time to . . . , 59
Time to Get Out of the Bath, Shirley, 149
Tomie dePaola's Mother Goose, 36, 43
Too Much Noise, 122
Trade books, 51, 58, 79
Transitional writers, 245–246, 268
Travers, Pamela, 81
Tresselt, Alvin, 123
Trivizas, Eugene, 292–293
True Story of the Three Little Pigs as Told by A. Wolf, The, 263, 292
Turkle, Brinton, 57, 263
Turn taking, 25–26
26 Letters and 99 Cents, 43
Two by Two, 306
Two Greedy Bears, 147–148

U

Units of action, 144–145, 151, 164

V

Van Allsburg, Chris, 261
Van Rynbach, Iris, 154
Verbal obbligatos, 156–157
Verb forms, 13, 19, 46–48
Verhoeven, L., 185
Very Hungry Caterpillar, The, 43, 226
Very Quiet Cricket, The, 43
Video tape, 117, 167, 301, 309
Visiting the Art Museum, 61
Visual patterns, memory, 248–249
Vocabulary, 8–9, 20–23, 63, 136, 176, 190, 191, 196, 213, 290, 294
  comparative relationships, 21–22
  developing through listening, 145
  individual word meanings, 21
  multiple meanings, 12, 24–25, 110
  opposites, 22
  relational vocabulary, 21–22
  socially shared word meanings, 21
Voice/print match, 182, 184, 205–206
Voices, listening to, 104–105
  describing, 140–141
Vowel patterns, 188, 247, 249

W

Wagner, B. J., 295
Wait time, 135
Wake Up, Farm!, 123
Waldorf schools, 311
Wall murals, 208
Ward, Cindy, 39, 43, 203, 207, 254
Wasps at Home, 60
Weeks, T., 6, 43
Weil, Zaro, 52
Weir, Bob, and Wendy Weir, 307
Wellesley College Center for Research on Women, 26, 42
Wells, G., 112
Wells, Rosemary, 43
We're Going on a Bear Hunt, 158
Werker, P., and R. Tess, 10, 42
Wescott, Nadine Bernard, 160–161
What Can Rabbit Hear? 98
What Could a Hippopotamus Be? 212
What Do You Do at a Petting Zoo? 308
What Happens When You Listen? 123
What Happens When You Talk? 168–169
"What If" questions, 152–153, 161
What Instrument Is This? 61
What Is That Sound? 79
What's That Noise? 122
Wheel on the School, The, 58
When I Was Nine, 284
When Will I Read? 226
Where Did That Naughty Little Hamster Go? 57
Where's Spot? 43
Where the Wild Things Are, 65, 71, 77
White, B., 26, 43
Whole class share, 217, 222, 253, 258, 303
Whole language, 130, 313
Who Says a Dog Goes Bow-Wow? 306
Who Says That? 123
Whose Mouse Are You? 226
Widman, Christine, 71
Wildsmith, Brian, 71
Williams, Sue, 32, 39, 43, 226
Williams, Vera B., and Jennifer Williams, 284
Williams-Ellis, Amabel, 151
Will You Take Me to Town on Strawberry Day? 61
Wilson, April, 71
Wilt, M., 91
Witch's Hat, The, 70
Wolcott, Patty, 56
Word, concept of, 248
Word analysis, *see* Crosschecking system

CREDITS

This page constitutes an extension of the copyright page.

p. 3. Figure 1–1 reprinted with the permission of Macmillan College Publishing Company from *Language Development* 3/e by Robert Owens. Copyright © 1993 by Macmillan College Publishing Company, Inc.

p. 14. Figure 1–2 reprinted with the permission of Macmillan College Publishing Company from *The Development of Language* by Jean Berko Gleason. Copyright © 1993 by Macmillan College Publishing Company, Inc.

p. 23. Illustration from *Is It Larger? Is It Smaller?* by Tana Hoban, with photographs by the author. Copyright © 1985 by Tana Hoban. Reprinted by permission of Greenwillow Books, a division of William Morrow & Company, Inc.

p. 31. Illustration excerpt from *I Went Walking* by Sue Williams, illustrations copyright © 1989 by Julie Vivas, reproduced by permission of Harcourt Brace & Company.

p. 60. From *Sea Squares* by Joy N. Hulme, illustrated by Carol Schwartz. Copyright © 1991 by Hyperion Books for Children. Reprinted by permission.

p. 68. From *The Ornery Morning* by Patricia Brennan Demuth, illustrated by Craig McFarland Brown. Copyright © 1991 by Craig McFarland Brown, illustrations. Used by permission of Dutton Children's Books, a division of Penguin Books USA Inc.

p. 88. From *Even That Moose Won't Listen to Me* by Martha Alexander. Copyright © 1988 by Martha Alexander. Used by permission of Dial Books for Young Readers, a division of Penguin Books USA Inc.

p. 98. From *The Quiet Noisy Book* by Margaret Wise Brown. Copyright 1950 by Margaret Wise Brown. Copyright renewed 1978 by Roberta Brown Rauch and Leonard Weisgard. Selection reprinted by permission of HarperCollins Publishers.

p. 107. "Cat" by Mary Britton Miller. Copyright estate of Mary Britton Miller.

p. 109. "The Mysterious Cat" by Vachel Lindsay. Reprinted with permission of Simon & Schuster from *Collected Poems of Vachel Lindsay* (New York: Macmillan, 1925).

p. 140. Illustration from *Three Blind Mice* by John W. Ivimey, with illustrations by Victoria Chess (Little, Brown, 1990). Reprinted with permission of Victoria Chess.

p. 141. Illustration from *Three Blind Mice* by John W. Ivimey, with illustrations by Paul Galdone. Illustration copyright © 1987 by the Estate of Paul Galdone. Reprinted by permission of Clarion Books/Houghton Mifflin Company. All rights reserved.

p. 146. Illustration from *The Moon's Choice* by John Warren Stewig, with illustrations by Jan Palmer. © 1993. Used by permission of the publisher, Simon & Schuster Books for Young Readers, New York.

p. 156. From "A Goblin Lives in Our House" adapted from *Sugar and Spice*, edited by Rose Fyleman. © 1935 Western Publishing Company, Inc. Used by permission.

p. 177. Figure 5–1 reprinted from *A Guide to Curriculum Planning in Reading* with permission from the Wisconsin Department of Public Instruction, 125 South Webster Street, Madison, WI 53702.

pp. 181 & 183. THE FAMILY CIRCUS reprinted with special permission of King Features Syndicate.

p. 195. Illustration from *Polar Bear, Polar Bear, What Do You Hear?* by Bill Martin, Jr., with illustrations by Eric Carle. Illustrations copyright © 1991 by Eric Carle. Reprinted by permission of Henry Holt and Company, Inc.

pp. 197 & 198. Illustrations from *The Alphabet Tale* by Jan Garten, illustrated by Muriel Batherman. Copyright © 1964, renewed 1992, 1994 by Muriel Batherman. Reprinted by permission of Greenwillow Books, a division of William Morrow & Company, Inc.

p. 263. Illustration from *Frog Goes to Dinner* by Mercer Mayer. Copyright © 1974 by Mercer Mayer. Used by permission of Dial Books for Young Readers, a division of Penguin Books USA Inc.

p. 264. Illustration from *The Jolly Postman* by Janet and Allan Ahlberg. Copyright © 1986 by Janet and Allan Ahlberg. By permission of Little, Brown and Company.

p. 292. Illustration from *The Three Pigs* by Tony Ross. Copyright © 1983 by Tony Ross. Reprinted by permission of Alfred A. Knopf, Inc.

p. 293. Illustration reprinted with the permission of Margaret K. McElderry Books, an imprint of Macmillan Publishing, from *The Three Little Wolves and the Big Bad Pig* by Eugene Trivizas, illustrated by Helen Oxenbury. Illustrations copyright © 1993 Helen Oxenbury. Also by permission of Reed Consumer Books Ltd.

p. 306. Illustration, copyright © 1993 by Suse MacDonald, from *Who Says a Dog Goes Bow-Wow?* by Hank De Zutter, illustrated by Suse MacDonald. Used by permission of Bantam Doubleday Dell Books for Young Readers.